ISA & EISA

By Edward Solari

Theory and Operation

Including PC, XT, AT, ISA, and EISA I/O Bus Operation

Annabooks
San Diego

ISA & EISA THEORY AND OPERATION
by
Edward Solari

PUBLISHED BY

Annabooks
11848 Bernardo Plaza Ct., Suite 110
San Diego, CA. 92128
USA

619-673-0870

Printed in the United States of America

ISBN 0-929392-15-9

Second Printing October 1993

Library of Congress Cataloging-in-Publication Data

Solari, Edward.
    ISA & EISA : PC, XT, AT, and EISA PC I/O BUS timing / by Edward
Solari.
        p.   cm.
    Includes bibliographical references and index.
    ISBN 0-929392-15-9
    1. Microcomputers--Buses. 2. EISA (Computer bus)   I. Title.
II. Title: ISA and EISA.
TK7895.B87S66 1992
621.39'81--dc20   92-39819
                                                        CIP

The publisher and author would like to acknowledge the co-operation of the IEEE P996 Working Group. Scott Hopkinson of Dernier Corporation and Mike Fung of S3 Corporation were particularly helpful in obtaining permission of the IEEE to quote portions of the P996 proposed standard.

The A.C. timing tables and signal waveform drawings in this book represent a composite of information from several sources in addition to the information that is original to this book. The following sources have provided portions of the A.C. timing and signal waveforms:

"ISA BUS SPECIFICATIONS and APPLICATION NOTES, January 30, 1990", Copyright 1989, Intel Corporation
"TECHNICAL REFERENCE GUIDE, EXTENDED INDUSTRY STANDARD ARCHITECTURE EXPANSION BUS", Copyright Compaq Computer Corp., 1989
"EXTENDED INDUSTRY STANDARD ARCHITECTURE SPECIFICATION Rev. 3.12", Copyright 1989-1992 BCPR Services, Inc.
"PERSONAL COMPUTER BUS STANDARD P996" DRAFT D2.02, January 18, 1990, Copyright IEEE Inc., 1990.

Dedication

To my mother and father for my education, and to my wife for her patience.

ISA & EISA THEORY AND OPERATION

Contents

List of Figures

List of Figures (Continued)

List of Figures (Continued)

Page

List of Figures (Continued)

List of Figures (Continued)

List of Figures (Continued)

List of Figures (Continued)

List of Tables

List of Tables (Continued)

List of Tables (Continued)

List of Tables (Continued)

List of Tables (Continued)

List of Tables (Continued)

Foreword

When we published Ed Solari's first book "AT Bus Design" in early 1990, the PC revolution had been under way for over eight years. And for all of those years, clones and add-on cards had been designed by hundreds of designers working without a formal and uniform specification. Millions of PCs and tens of millions of add-in cards were produced, sold to the masses, installed usually by amateurs, and, in spite of the nearly limitless number of possible combinations, the resulting systems almost always worked. Truly a tribute to the conservative original designers at IBM, and to the idea of an open architecture. Unfortunately, however, not quite so open as to provide engineers with everything they needed to know. So let's also have a round of applause for all the nervous designers betting their company on their reverse engineering talents!

As the performance demands on the PC grew, designs became less and less conservative. The need for publicly available specifications grew as the bus speed increased and the timing tolerances became tighter. One result was the formation of the IEEE 996 committee, which reverse engineered the newly-named Industry Standard Architecture (ISA) bus so that a uniform standard could be published. And since Solari and Annabooks came out with "AT Bus Design" we have shipped thousands of copies to over 60 countries.

The Extended Industry Standard Architecture (EISA) bus is being formally specified from the start, as is necessary for a higher-performance bus. And an important consideration is backwards compatibility to the ISA bus. So while the pure 32 bit portion of the EISA bus (or 64 bits for Fast EISA) holds promise for a fresh, pristine architecture, the important requirement for ISA compatibility adds a great deal of complication. Which brings us to this book.

There are now, and probably always will be, more ISA designs in progress than EISA designs. Just the growth in popularity of ISA compatibility for embedded systems practically guarantees this. So we don't want to force the ISA designer to extract from the EISA specification the information he needs to produce his design. On the other hand, we didn't want to keep "AT Bus Design" in print. The reason is that Ed wants to present ISA in an improved way, more consistent with the way in which EISA is presented. So aside from correcting a few errors in the original book, the most important consideration is a slightly different, more consistent, and better organized presentation.

The first part of each chapter covers ISA, so the ISA designer shouldn't have too much concern with the rest of the material until it is needed. The remainder of each chapter concerns E-ISA (8 and 16 bit systems that use some of the EISA features) and EISA. Much of the remaining detail involves the mixture of 8, 16, 24, and 32 bit platforms and resources. We've tried to bring order to the bewildering array of possibilities.

As Ed points out in the Preface, there are actually two sets of numbers presented in this book. It should always be clear which direction the conservative designer should go. When adequate time has not been allowed for bus settling times, Ed says so, and suggests an appropriate number. And if the designer uses a different pull-up value or has a different capacitive load, the effect should be evident. The important thing is to build stuff that works.

It's been a pleasure to work with Ed on such a challenging subject. His productivity and attention to detail are amazing. And we've also been impressed, along with the students, by his classes at Annabooks University. The direct feedback we get from you, the designer, is valuable in organizing material for presentation in person or in a book. So we all benefit from your comments. Please let us hear from you.

John P. Choisser
Annabooks
San Diego, California

Preface

The ISA bus, based on the IBM AT, continues to dominate the personal computer platform architecture. As more power is needed for network servers and workstations, some platforms are implementing the Enhanced ISA (EISA) bus as an extension of the ISA bus. The widening use of these two busses requires solid bus specifications. The lack thereof is the key motivation for writing this book.

The ISA bus at first evolved without any generally-available written specifications, in spite of the highly desirable open nature of the architecture. The IEEE 996 committee and my previous book "AT Bus Design" attempted to document the architecture, timing, and mechanical specifications to promote the compatible design of ISA platforms and add-on cards. The early versions of the EISA bus specification from COMPAQ also attempted to document the ISA bus, as well as the enhancements added to form the EISA bus. This book represents the next step in documenting both the ISA and EISA busses. It corrects errors in the IEEE 996 specification that "AT Bus Design" was based upon and clarifies the bus operation as outlined in both my previous book and the COMPAQ EISA specification. In addition, this book provides missing information in the EISA specification to insure proper operation of EISA or ISA add-on cards installed in EISA compatible platforms.

You will notice that this book contains two sets of A.C. bus timings. One set is from the EISA Rev. 3.12 bus specification. This specification does not always indicate if the timings were based on an 8.00 or 8.33 MHz bus clock, does not always include sufficient bus settling time, and, in some cases, is overly restrictive in its A.C. timing requirements. Consequently, the other set of numbers represents a recalculation that includes bus settling, and includes entries for both 8.00 and 8.33 MHz bus clocks. Also, where the EISA bus specification was unclear, too restrictive, or incomplete, the recalculations have used the Intel 350DT chip set timings as the defacto standard. (After all, in some ways the EISA standard has been guided by the implementation of the bus by the Intel chip set.)

Both Annabooks and I are interested in the continuing evolution, clarification, and corrections to this book. Please direct any related inputs to Annabooks.

Finally, special thanks to John Choisser of Annabooks for the editing and data transcription. Also special thanks to Phil Vargas of Designline Creative Services for the graphics and jacket design.

Ed Solari
Monmouth, Oregon

CHAPTER ONE

ARCHITECTURAL OVERVIEW

INTRODUCTION

There are now three basic iterations of the IBM Personal Computer: the original PC, the XT, and the AT. The platform CPU for the PC and XT is the 8 bit Intel 8088, and for the AT it is the 16 bit Intel 80286. The platforms vary in other ways besides the processor, such as memory capacity, existence of an audio cassette interface, and the number of slots for the add-on cards. There are two versions of the add-on card slots: the 8 bit slots on the PC and XT, and the 8 and 8/16 bit slots on the AT.

The PC and XT both use the Intel 8284A chip for clock generation, the Intel 8288 chip for bus control, a 4.77 MHz platform CPU and bus clock, and the Intel 8237A-5 DMA controller. The operation of the 8 bit slots on the two platforms is identical, and establishes the standard 8 bit compatibility for processor access cycles and DMA transfer cycles. Both platforms use one of the DMA channels to execute refresh cycles on the bus.

The AT differs from the PC and XT in other ways besides processor type and the data width of the bus slots. First, the AT uses the Intel 82284 chip for clock generation and the Intel 82288 chip for bus control. Second, the AT comes in two versions with two different system and platform CPU clocks: 6 and 8 MHz. Third, additional DMA channels and interrupt signal lines are present on the bus. Fourth, add-on cards can replace the platform CPU as the bus owner. Fifth, an additional signal line is available to support faster no-wait-state cycles. Finally, the refresh cycle execution by the DMA controller on the PC and XT is replaced by discrete circuitry.

The differences in the AT relative to the PC and XT are further complicated because companies other than IBM have replaced the platform CPU with the Intel 80386 or 80486 CPUs. The use of these CPUs eliminates the use of the Intel bus controller and clock generation chips, and permits the use of other platform CPU clock frequencies.

Compaq has introduced a further extension of the IBM Personal Computer. This extension supports all PC, XT, and AT hardware (add-on cards) and software. Additionally, it supports an enhancement for a bus width of 32 data bits in a 32 bit address space.

In order to permit the development of add-on cards in some reasonable fashion, the IEEE, Intel, and a consortium of companies (lead by Compaq) have developed three sets of bus specifications. The IEEE and Intel have focused on the 8 and 8/16 bit slots of the AT as the standard. The COMPAQ-led consortium also focused on the 8 and 8/16 bit slots of the AT as part of its expanded 32 bit standard.

> *This book is focused on the PC, XT, and AT bus requirements established by IBM and the expanded 32 bit bus established by the COMPAQ-led consortium. The generic name for the 8 bit and 8/16 bit PC, XT, and AT compatible bus is INDUSTRY STANDARD ARCHITECTURE (ISA). This book will also focus on the 32 bit extension to the ISA standard developed by the COMPAQ-led consortium known as the EXTENDED INDUSTRY STANDARD ARCHITECTURE (EISA).*

In developing the EISA bus specification, the COMPAQ-led consortium added features beyond the increase of the data and address width. Some of these features can be used by ISA platforms that only support 8 and 8/16 bit slots. Thus, for the purposes of this book, the following definitions will be used:

ISA refers to the PC, XT (8 slot), and AT compatible (8 or 8/16 slot) bus specification. It does not use any of the enhancements of the EISA bus specification, and does not have the extra connector pins to support the enhanced 32 data bit EISA bus.

An E-ISA platform is the same as an ISA platform, except it includes those EISA enhancements that do not require EISA cycles or the additional pins of the 8/16/32 bit EISA slots. An E-ISA platform can be viewed as the 8 and 8/16 bit slots of an EISA platform that uses only ISA compatible signal lines.

An EISA platform conforms to the full EISA bus specification, which includes all of the ISA and E-ISA features. It also contains extra circuitry and connector pins to support EISA cycles and 8, 8/16, and 8/16/32 bit EISA slots. In that the additional signal lines needed to support EISA are not included in the 8 and 8/16 bit slots, by definition these slots are E-ISA compatible.

Finally, by definition, the references to ISA compatible signal lines also apply to E-ISA.

ISA COMPATIBLE PLATFORM

The ISA platform is the basic model for all PC, XT, and AT platforms. (See Figure 1-1.) The basic platform consists of the following:

HOST BUS

This is the generic bus for all platform resources (i.e. the resources not attached via the connectors on the ISA bus). On most systems, the Host bus consists of several busses; usually the platform CPU and cache are one bus, the platform memory another, and the balance of the resources are on a third bus.

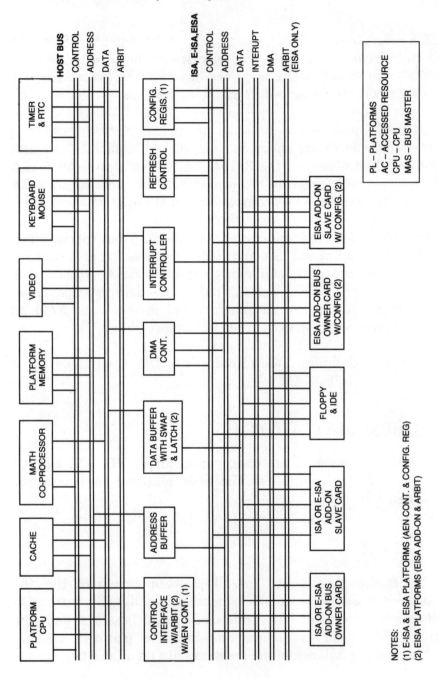

FIGURE 1-1:   ISA, E-ISA, & EISA PLATFORM

ISA BUS

This is a set of connectors interconnected by the ISA bus signal lines. Each connector site is called a slot. Two types of connectors can reside at each slot: 8 bit and 8/16 bit. The 8 bit slot is a single 62 pin connector, and only supports 8 bit add-on slave cards. The 8/16 bit slot contains both the 8 bit slot 62 pin connector and an additional 36 pin connector. This expanded connector supports a larger address space, additional DMA channels, additional interrupt request lines, and additional data lines. The expanded connector also allows add-on bus owner cards to be used. PC and XT compatible platforms only support the 8 bit slot (62 pin connector).

PLATFORM CPU

This is the primary CPU of the platform. It is the first bus owner after power up and after every reset. All other bus owners must obtain bus ownership by halting code execution by the platform CPU. It is directly tied to the clock circuitry which drives the bus clock; consequently, it is the only resource that can use the no-wait-state access cycles. For software compatibility, it must be compatible to the Intel 8088, 80286, 80386, 80486, X86 family of processors.

MATH CO-PROCESSOR

This resource is a companion to the platform CPU. It is an option that computes math-related functions faster than the platform CPU. It is invisible to the slot in terms of bus cycles. In some of the more advanced Intel processors, it is integrated into the platform CPU.

CACHE

This is a high speed memory resource accessible only by the platform CPU.

MEMORY

Memory resources can exist either on the platform or on the bus as an add-on slave card. Platform memory can be of any byte width compatible to the platform CPU. The data width of the add-on memory slave card does not have to match the platform CPU. Circuitry exists to compensate for data size mismatches. Conversely, the data size for bus owner add-on cards accessing the platform memory does not have to match the data size of the platform memory. Platform memory is commonly implemented with DRAM.

DMA CONTROLLER

This is one of the platform resources that can become system owner. Its purpose is to transfer data between I/O and memory resources with minimum circuitry needed by either resource. It is the only resource on the bus that monitors the DMA signal lines on the bus. An active DMA request signal line will cause the DMA controller to obtain bus ownership and execute transfer cycles.

On an ISA or E-ISA platform, the DMA controller also operates as the arbiter for the system ownership by the platform CPU, DMA controller, refresh controller, and add-on bus owner cards.

REFRESH CONTROLLER

This is one of the other platform resources that can become system owner. Its purpose is to execute refresh cycles for platform and bus memory components. On the PC and XT it is actually a

DMA channel 0 cycle. On the AT, E-ISA and EISA compatible platforms it is composed of separate dedicated circuitry.

INTERRUPT CONTROLLER

This platform resource supports all of the bus interrupt request signal lines. The software can enable or disable individual interrupt channels. An active interrupt signal line on an enabled channel generates an interrupt to the platform CPU, and provides information to identify which interrupt signal lines are active.

KEYBOARD and MOUSE

On the PC and XT platforms, the keyboard interface is handled by discrete circuitry. On the AT, E-ISA, and EISA compatible platforms, this function is provided by the Intel 8042 microcontroller with a built-in BIOS. Recent platforms have implemented the mouse interface using the Intel 8042.

VIDEO

There is a wide variety of video controllers that are software compatible. The reading and writing of registers and video memory creates a display on the user's CRT.

TIMER and REAL TIME CLOCK (RTC)

These platform resources are needed for software compatibility and have no direct relationship with the ISA bus. The timer generates a pulse every 15.6 microseconds to the refresh circuitry to request a refresh cycle. The real time clock provides time and date information.

INTERFACE CIRCUITRY

This circuitry consists of three parts: Control Interface, Address Buffer, and Data Buffer with Swap. The purpose of these platform resources are to interface the resources on the host bus with the resources on the ISA bus.

- Control Interface: Translates the Host Bus control lines protocol to the ISA bus control lines protocol and vice versa.

- Address Buffer: Buffers the address signal lines between the two buses.

- Data Buffer With Swap: Buffers the data signal lines between the two buses. It also contains the circuitry to swap data between the low and high byte lanes for data size mismatches.

ADD-ON CARDS

The bus allows for the insertion of add-on cards. Add-on cards that only respond to access, transfer, or refresh cycles are defined as add-on slave cards. Add-on cards that can become bus owners are defined as add-on bus owner cards. An add-on card may be of both types; but, for a given bus cycle, it can only be either a bus owner or a slave.

ISA add-on slave cards will work on AT compatible platforms. The ISA 8 bit version of these cards will also work on PC and XT platforms.

Add-on bus owner cards can only be installed in AT compatible platforms of the ISA family.

E-ISA COMPATIBLE PLATFORM

The lack of a generally available industrial standard for the AT bus, prior to the efforts of Intel, the IEEE P996 committee, and the EISA consortium, has resulted in the defacto ISA standard. Unfortunately, this defacto standard has had to reflect design errors in early platforms, misinterpretation of bus cycles, and other types of errors and inconsistencies. The operation of the 8 and 8/16 bit slots in a platform compatible with the EISA bus specification must maintain compatibility with the ISA standard, at the same time allowing the use of the enhancements outlined in the EISA bus specification. In order to differentiate between 8 and 8/16 bit slots on platforms that adhere to the ISA standard versus platforms and add-on cards that adhere to the full EISA bus specification, the concept of E-ISA compatible platforms and add-on cards has been adopted.

THE E-ISA COMPATIBLE PLATFORM SHOULD BE VIEWED SIMPLY AS A CONCEPT. IT IS USED TO DISTINGUISH BETWEEN "HISTORICAL" ISA BUS PLATFORMS (PC, XT, and AT) AND THE "ENHANCED" ISA BUS (8 AND 8/16 BIT SLOTS CONFORMING TO THE EISA BUS SPECIFICATION).

An E-ISA compatible platform is conceptually the same as the ISA compatible platform. It only supports 8 and 8/16 bit slots, and is compatible with ISA add-on cards. However, it provides enhancements provided by the EISA bus specification that can be exploited by E-ISA compatible add-on cards.

An E-ISA add-on card is conceptually the same as an ISA add-on card. It can function in ISA and E-ISA 8 and 8/16 bit slots, and can also be used in a platform that adheres to the full EISA bus specification.

The significance of an E-ISA compatible platform is that it is an enhanced ISA platform that only adopts the 8 and 8/16 "asynchronous" slots of the EISA bus specification. It does not adopt the additional overhead of the full 8/16/32 "synchronous" slots of the EISA bus specification.

The enhancements of an E-ISA compatible platform or add-on card versus an ISA compatible platform or add-on card are as follows:

- Configuration space is supported.

- I/O space addressing is slot specific.

- Maximum frequency of the BCLK signal line is 8.33 MHZ.

- The INTERRUPT signal lines can be programmed for edge or level trigger. The level trigger provides the "ORING" of several interrupts on a single INTERRUPT signal line.

- The IOCHRDY and DRQx signal lines are referenced to the BCLK signal line.

- The SRDY* signal line (permitting no-wait-state access cycles) can be supported by add-on bus owner cards.

- 8 data bit memory and I/O resources support an expanded definition of no-wait-state access cycles.

- Any DMA channel may be programmed for 8 or 16 bit transfers.

- Add-on I/O slave cards can support faster DMA transfer rates (TYPE A and TYPE B).

- The TC signal line is bi-directional.

CONFIGURATION SPACE

Except for the Configuration Space, the above enhancements do not change the architecture of the platform or add-on cards. The Configuration Space consists of input and output registers within the I/O address space which are reserved for platform and add-on card configuration. These input and output registers allow software configuration and monitoring of hardware. (See Figure 1-1.)

E-ISA add-on slave cards will work on AT platforms. The 8 bit version of these cards will also work on PC and XT platforms. Any software written for these add-on cards must be adjusted for the loss of the configuration space when these cards are installed in an ISA compatible platform.

E-ISA add-on bus owner cards can execute cycles commensurate with an 8.33 MHz BCLK signal line frequency. On an AT platform, the E-ISA add-on bus owner card must execute cycles commensurate with an 8 MHz BCLK signal line frequency. E-ISA add-on bus owner cards cannot be installed into PC or XT compatible platforms.

CONTROL INTERFACE WITH ARBITER & AENx CONTROL

This functional block is enhanced over the version used for an ISA compatible platform. The Arbiter actually only applies to the EISA compatible platform. The AENx CONTROL function is used by both E-ISA and EISA compatible platforms. The AENx CONTROL circuitry decodes a portion of the I/O address space, and drives individual AENx signal lines to the slots to support specific slot I/O addressing.

EISA COMPATIBLE PLATFORM

The EISA platform is conceptually identical to an ISA compatible platform with enhancements outlined for the E-ISA compatible platform. Its support of 8 and 8/16 bit slots is the same as the slots on an E-ISA compatible platform. The major distinction for EISA is that some slots have a special connector. The design of the connector allows add-on cards compatible to ISA or E-ISA compatible platforms to use the slot without contacting the EISA specific signal lines. The special connector supplies additional ADDRESS and DATA signal lines, additional add-on bus owner card support functions, and synchronous control signal lines to support EISA compatible add-on cards. The extra ADDRESS and DATA signal lines provide a full 32 data bits over a four gigabyte address space. The additional add-on bus owner card functions provide a more sophisticated arbitration structure for the card to become bus master.

The synchronous control signal lines provide a new set of capabilities. The ISA and E-ISA buses are essentially asynchronous; that is, most of the signal lines on the 8 and 8/16 bit slots become active and inactive independent of the BCLK signal line. The EISA compatible platform bus still operates the signal lines on the 8 and 8/16 bit slots asynchronously, but some additional cycle types unique to EISA are executed using only the synchronous control signal lines on the special connector. The support of both asynchronous and additional synchronous cycles allows EISA compatible platforms to be compatible with ISA and E-ISA compatible add-on cards, and also provides a method for improved bus performance with the synchronous cycles.

Even though the SRDY* signal line on the ISA platform is synchronized to the BCLK signal line, the ISA platform is still defined as an asynchronous bus. Similarly, an E-ISA platform is essentially an asynchronous bus, even though it does synchronize some other bus signal lines.

The EISA specific functions shown in Figure 1-1 are as follows:

CONTROL INTERFACE WITH ARBITRATION & AENx CONTROL

The existence of slots on an EISA compatible platform that support 8 and 8/16 bit slots with asynchronous cycles and 8/16/32 bit slots with synchronous cycles presents some problems. First, the EISA bus must be able to execute both asynchronous and synchronous access cycles using two sets of control lines. Thus, an EISA compatible platform adds some functions to the ISA or E-ISA compatible CONTROL INTERFACE. It functions in the same fashion on the ISA and E-ISA platforms; that is, it translates the CONTROL signal lines between HOST and ISA, E-ISA, or EISA bus. It also translates the control signals when an add-on bus owner card accesses platform resources. In addition, it provides an interface between EISA and ISA or E-ISA compatible add-on bus owner cards and ISA or E-ISA and EISA compatible add-on slave cards, respectively.

Another functional difference between EISA and ISA or E-ISA compatible platforms is arbitration. On an ISA or E-ISA platform, the arbitration for system ownership is through the DMA controller. This is also true on an EISA platform for ISA and E-ISA compatible add-on bus owner cards. For EISA compatible add-on bus owner cards, the arbitration is not through the DMA controller. Separate circuitry is added to arbitrate for system ownership between platform CPU, DMA controller, refresh controller, and EISA compatible add-on bus owner card.

SUMMARY OF BUS STANDARD DIFFERENCES

Tables 1-1 to 1-5 are summaries of the differences between platforms relative to the platform CPU, add-on cards, and DMA controllers. The other chapters in this book will explain these differences in detail.

Table 1-1 provides an overview of the different attributes of the platforms, aside from the EISA compatible platform supporting EISA specific cycles. Of particular note is the DATA SIZE column, which indicates the "rated" data size of the bus master or resource. The actual data size of access or transfer cycle is a "subset" of the rated size. That is, a 16 data bit resource supports the access or transfers of 8 and 16 data bits. A 32 data bit resource supports the access or transfer of 8, 16, 24, and 32 data bits.

PLATFORM	IOCHRDY REF. TO BCLK	MAX BCLK (MHZ)	INTERRUPT TRIGGER	CONFIG SPACE	I/O SLOT ADDRESS	MEMORY ADDRESS SPACE	I/O ADDRESS SPACE	DATA SIZE	DATA SIZE MISMATCH
PC/XT (3)	NO	4.77	EDGE	NO	NO	1 M	768 + 256 FOR PLAT.	8	NA
AT (3)	NO	8.00	EDGE	NO	NO	16 M	768 + 256 FOR PLAT.	8 16	DOUBLE MASTER CYCLES
E-ISA	YES	8.33	EDGE/LEV	YES	YES	16 M	768 + + 1K / SLOT(1)	8 16	DOUBLE MASTER CYCLES
EISA	YES	8.33	EDGE/LEV	YES	YES	4 G	768 + 1K / SLOT(1)	8 16 32	SINGLE MASTER CYCLE(2)

TABLE 1-1: GENERAL PLATFORM FEATURES

NOTES:
(1) The platform has reserved 1 K bytes.
(2) ISA and E-ISA bus masters as platform and add-on bus owner cards must do double master cycle.
(3) Collectively called ISA.

PLAT.	DMA CHANNEL SIZE PROGRAM.	DMA TYPES SUPPORTED	ISA OR E-ISA ADD-ON BUS OWNER CARD EXECUTES READY & NO WAIT STATE CYCLE LIKE PLAT. CPU	PLATFORM CPU EXECUTES 8 BIT MEM & I/O RESOURCE (4) NO WAIT STATE CYCLE	16 BIT I/O RSRCE (4) NO WAIT STATE CYCLE	16 BIT MEMORY RSRCE (4) NO WAIT STATE CYCLE	BCLK IS STAR- BURST
PC/XT	NO	COMPAT.	NA	NA	NA	NA	NO
AT	NO	COMPAT.	NO (2)	YES (1)	NO	YES	NO
E-ISA	YES	COMPAT., "A" & "B" WITH NO CONVER.	YES	YES	NO	YES	YES
EISA	YES	COMPAT., "A", "B", & "C" WITH CONVER.	YES	YES (3)	NO	YES	YES

TABLE 1-1: GENERAL PLATFORM FEATURES (CONTINUED)

NOTES:
(1) The IBM AT platform supported 8 data bit no-wait-state cycles. It is unclear if all clone platforms do.
(2) IBM AT platform did not support this access. It is unclear how many clone platforms do.
(3) "NO" for I/O resources.
(4) ISA or E-ISA resource.

Tables 1-2 to 1-4 summarize the various access cycles that are supported for the different platforms and bus masters. Of particular importance is the following definition of data size:

- Data size of an ISA or E-ISA bus master is defined by the SA0 and SBHE* signal lines at the time of access. Data size requested is either 8 or 16 bits.

- Data size of an EISA bus master is defined by the MASTER16* signal line. When the MASTER16* signal line = 0, the data size is 16 bits. When the MASTER16* signal line = 1, the data size is 32 bits. (MASTER16* is also called MASTER* on ISA and E-ISA platforms.)

- Data size of an ISA or E-ISA compatible accessed resource is defined by MEMCS16* and IOCS16* signal lines.

- Data size of an EISA compatible accessed resource is defined by the EX16* and EX32* signal lines.

The data size listed in Tables 1-2-A, B and 1-3-A, B for platform CPU and add-on bus owner card equals the data size requested.

The data size listed in Tables 1-4-A to D for platform CPU or add-on bus owner card is defined by the MASTER16 signal line.*

The data size listed in Tables 1-2-A, B; 1-3-A, B; and 1-4-A to D for accessed resource are defined by the MEMCS16, IOCS16*, EX16*, and EX32* signal lines.*

The data size requested is not always equal to the data size of the bus master or accessed resource. For an ISA or E-ISA compatible access, the data size requested is defined by the SBHE* and SA0 signal lines. The data size of an ISA or E-ISA bus master (platform CPU or add-on bus owner card) equals the data size requested. For an EISA compatible access, the data size requested is defined by the BE* signal lines; consequently, the data size requested does not always equal the data size of the bus master.

PLATFORM TYPE/ ACCESSED RESOURCE	CYCLES TO PLATFORM RESOURCES OR ADD-ON SLAVE CARD PLATFORM CPU VIEWPOINT					
	NO WAIT		STANDARD		READY	
	8 BIT	16 BIT	8 BIT	16 BIT	8 BIT	16 BIT
PC or XT/ PC or XT	NA	NA	MEM I/O	NA	MEM I/O	NA
AT/ PC or XT CARD	NA	NA	MEM I/O	(1)	MEM I/O	(1)
AT/ AT or E-ISA CARD	(3)	MEM	MEM I/O	MEM I/O	MEM I/O	MEM I/O
E-ISA/ PC or XT CARD	NA	NA	MEM I/O	(1)	MEM I/O	(1)
E-ISA/ AT CARD	MEM,I/O (3)	MEM	MEM I/O	MEM I/O	MEM I/O	MEM I/O
E-ISA/ E-ISA CARD	MEM I/O	MEM	MEM I/O	MEM I/O	MEM I/O	MEM I/O

TABLE 1-2-A: ADD-ON CARD SUPPORT ON PC, XT, AT, OR E-ISA PLATFORMS.   PLATFORM CPU DATA SIZE LESS THAN OR EQUAL TO ACCESSED RESOURCE DATA SIZE

PLATFORM TYPE/ ACCESSED RESOURCE	CYCLES TO PLATFORM RESOURCES OR ADD-ON SLAVE CARD PLATFORM CPU VIEWPOINT					
	NO WAIT		STANDARD		READY	
	8 BIT	16 BIT (4)	8 BIT	16 BIT (4)	8 BIT	16 BIT (4)
PC or XT/ 8 BIT PC or XT CARD	NA	NA	(2)	NA	(2)	NA
AT/ 8 BIT PC or XT CARD	NA	NA	(2)	MEM I/O	(2)	MEM I/O
AT/ 8 BIT AT or E-ISA CARD	(2)	NA	(2)	MEM I/O	(2)	MEM I/O
E-ISA/ 8 BIT PC or XT CARD	NA	NA	(2)	MEM I/O	(2)	MEM I/O
E-ISA/ 8 BIT AT CARD	(2)	MEM	(2)	MEM I/O	(2)	MEM I/O
E-ISA/ 8 BIT E-ISA CARD	(2)	MEM	(2)	MEM I/O	(2)	MEM I/O

TABLE 1-2-B: ADD-ON CARD SUPPORT ON PC, XT, AT, AND E-ISA PLATFORMS. PLATFORM CPU DATA SIZE GREATER THAN ACCESSED RESOURCE DATA SIZE

NOTES for TABLE 1-2:
(1) See Table 1-2-B.
(2) See Table 1-2-A.
(3) Historically, it is unclear if all AT compatible clone platforms support no-wait-state cycles for 8 data bit memory or I/O. The IBM AT platform CPU sampled the SRDY* signal line in the fourth period of the BCLK signal line to support this cycle for 8 data bits.
(4) Executed as two 8 data bit access cycles.

PLATFORM TYPE/ ACCESSED RESOURCE	CYCLES TO PLATFORM RESOURCES OR ADD-ON SLAVE CARD ISA BUS OWNER ADD-ON CARD VIEWPOINT					
	NO WAIT		STANDARD		READY	
	8 BIT (5,6)	16 BIT (6)	8 BIT (5,6)	16 BIT (6)	8 BIT (3,5,6)	16 BIT (3,6)
AT/ PC or XT CARD	NA	NA	MEM I/O	(1)	MEM I/O	(1)
E-ISA or EISA/ PC or XT CARD	NA	NA	MEM I/O	(1)	MEM I/O	(1)
AT/ AT or E-ISA CARD OR PLTFRM	(2)	(2)	MEM I/O	MEM I/O	MEM I/O	MEM I/O
E-ISA or EISA/ AT, or E-ISA CARD or PLATFORM	MEM I/O	MEM	MEM I/O	MEM I/O	MEM I/O	MEM I/O
EISA/ EISA CARD	MEM	NA	MEM	NA	MEM,I/O (4)	MEM,I/O (4)

TABLE 1-3-A: ADD-ON CARD SUPPORT. ADD-ON BUS OWNER CARD DATA SIZE LESS THAN OR EQUAL TO ACCESSED RESOURCE DATA SIZE

PLATFORM TYPE/ ACCESSED RESOURCE	CYCLES TO PLATFORM RESOURCES OR ADD-ON SLAVE CARD ISA ADD-ON BUS OWNER CARD VIEWPOINT					
	NO WAIT		STANDARD		READY	
	8 BIT (5,6)	16 BIT (6,7)	8 BIT (5,6)	16 BIT (6,7)	8 BIT (3,5,6)	16 BIT (3,6,7)
AT/ 8 BIT PC or XT CARD	NA	NA	(8)	MEM I/O	(8)	MEM I/O
E-ISA or EISA/ 8 BIT PC or XT CARD	NA	NA	(8)	MEM I/O	(8)	MEM I/O
AT/ 8 BIT AT, E-ISA CARD, or PLATFORM	(8)	(2)	(8)	MEM I/O	(8)	MEM I/O
E-ISA or EISA/ 8 BIT AT or E-ISA CARD or PLATFORM	(8)	MEM I/O	(8)	MEM I/O	(8)	MEM I/O
EISA/ 8 BIT EISA CARD	(8)	MEM	(8)	MEM	(8)	MEM,I/O (4)

TABLE 1-3-B: ADD-ON CARD SUPPORT. ADD-ON BUS OWNER CARD DATA SIZE GREATER THAN ACCESSED RESOURCE DATA SIZE

PLATFORM TYPE/ ACCESSED RESOURCE	CYCLES TO PLATFORM RESOURCES OR ADD-ON SLAVE CARD E-ISA ADD-ON BUS OWNER CARD VIEWPOINT					
	NO WAIT		STANDARD		READY	
	8 BIT	16 BIT	8 BIT	16 BIT	8 BIT	16 BIT
AT / PC or XT CARD	NA	NA	MEM I/O	(1)	MEM I/O	(1)
E-ISA or EISA/ PC or XT CARD	NA	NA	MEM I/O	(1)	MEM I/O	(1)
AT/ AT or E-ISA CARD or PLATFORM	(2)	(2)	MEM I/O (6)	MEM I/O (6)	MEM I/O (6)	MEM I/O (6)
E-ISA or EISA/ AT, or E-ISA CARD or PLATFORM	MEM I/O	MEM	MEM I/O	MEM I/O	MEM I/O	MEM I/O
EISA/ EISA CARD	MEM	NA	MEM	NA	MEM I/O (4)	MEM I/O (4)

TABLE 1-3-C: ADD-ON BUS OWNER CARD CYCLE SUPPORT. ADD-ON BUS OWNER CARD DATA SIZE LESS THAN OR EQUAL TO ACCESSED RESOURCE DATA SIZE

PLATFORM TYPE/ ACCESSED RESOURCE	CYCLES TO PLATFORM RESOURCES OR ADD-ON SLAVE CARD E-ISA ADD-ON BUS OWNER CARD VIEWPOINT					
	NO WAIT		STANDARD		READY	
	8 BIT	16 BIT(7)	8 BIT	16 BIT(7)	8 BIT	16 BIT(7)
AT / 8 BIT PC or XT CARD	NA	NA	(8)	MEM I/O	(8)	MEM I/O
E-ISA or EISA/ 8 BIT PC or XT CARD	NA	NA	(8)	MEM I/O	(8)	MEM I/O
AT / 8 BIT AT or E-ISA CARD or PLATFORM	(8)	(2)	(8)	MEM I/O (6)	(8)	MEM I/O (6)
E-ISA or EISA/ 8 BIT AT or E-ISA CARD or PLATFORM	(8)	MEM I/O	(8)	MEM I/O	(8)	MEM I/O
EISA/ 8 BIT EISA CARD	(8)	MEM	(8)	MEM	(8)	MEM I/O (4)

TABLE 1-3-D: ADD-ON BUS OWNER CARD CYCLE SUPPORT. ADD-ON BUS OWNER CARD DATA SIZE GREATER THAN ACCESSED RESOURCE DATA SIZE

NOTES FOR TABLE 1-3:

(1) See Tables 1-3-B or 1-3-D.

(2) Add-on bus owner cards on AT compatible platforms cannot support no-wait-state cycles because of BCLK skew. No-wait-state access cycles are not defined for PC/XT cards.

(3) Not all ISA add-on bus owner cards support ready cycles because the IBM AT platform did not drive the IOCHRDY signal line when platform resources were accessed.

(4) As an I-MIX cycle if the accessed resource is an 8 data bit EISA I/O resource or 16 data bit EISA memory or I/O resource. If the accessed resource is an 8 data bit ISA, E-ISA, or EISA resource, an ISA access cycle is executed.

(5) Not all AT add-on bus owner cards support 8 bit accesses because the IBM AT platforms did not support 8 bit accesses to platform resources.

(6) Not all add-on bus owner cards support accesses to I/O resources because the IBM AT platforms did not support I/O access cycles to platform resources.

(7) Executed as two 8 bit access cycles.

(8) See Tables 1-3-A or 1-3-C.

PLATFORM TYPE/ ACCESSED RESOURCE	CYCLES TO PLATFORM RESOURCES OR ADD-ON SLAVE CARD					
	EISA PLATFORM CPU & EISA ADD-ON BUS OWNER CARD VIEWPNT					
	E-MIX VERSION OF EISA STANDARD		EISA STANDARD		EISA READY	
	16 BIT	32 BIT	16 BIT	32 BIT	16 BIT	32 BIT
EISA/ PC or XT CARD	(1)	(1)	NA	NA	NA	NA
EISA/ AT CARD	MEM I/O	(1)	NA	NA	NA	NA
EISA/ PLATFORM or EISA CARD	(1)	(1)	MEM I/O	MEM I/O	MEM I/O	MEM I/O

TABLE 1-4-A: EISA BUS MASTER CYCLE SUPPORT. DATA SIZE REQUESTED (BE*) LESS THAN OR EQUAL TO ACCESSED RESOURCE DATA SIZE (MEMCS16*, IOCS16*, EX16*, AND EX32*)

NOTES:

(1) See Table 1-4-C.

PLATFORM TYPE/ ACCESSED RESOURCE	CYCLES TO PLATFORM RESOURCES OR ADD-ON SLAVE CARD EISA PLATFORM CPU OR EISA ADD-ON BUS OWNER CARD VIEWPOINT			
	EISA COMPRESSED(1)		EISA BURST	
	16 BIT	32 BIT	16 BIT	32 BIT
EISA/ PC or XT CARD	NA	NA	NA	NA
EISA/ AT CARD	NA	NA	NA	NA
EISA/ PLATFORM or EISA CARD	MEM I/O	MEM I/O	MEM	MEM

TABLE 1-4-B: EISA BUS MASTER CYCLE SUPPORT. BUS MASTER DATA SIZE REQUESTED (BE*) LESS THAN OR EQUAL TO ACCESSED RESOURCE DATA SIZE (MEMCS16*, IOCS16*, EX16*, AND EX32*)

NOTE:
(1) EISA add-on bus owner cards do not support COMPRESSED cycles. Only platform CPUs can execute compressed cycles.

PLATFORM TYPE/ ACCESSED RESOURCE		CYCLES TO PLATFORM RESOURCES OR ADD-ON SLAVE CARD EISA PLATFORM CPU OR EISA ADD-ON BUS OWNER CARD VIEWPOINT					
		E-MIX VRSN OF EISA STD OR DATA-MATCHING		EISA STANDARD W/ DATA-MATCHING		EISA READY	
		16 BIT	32 BIT	16 BIT	32 BIT	16 BIT	32 BIT
EISA/ PC or XT CARD	8 BIT	MEM I/O (3)	MEM I/O (3)	NA	NA	NA	NA
EISA/ AT CARD	8 BIT	MEM I/O (3)	MEM I/O (3)	NA	NA	NA	NA
	16 BIT	(1)	MEM I/O	NA	NA	NA	NA
EISA/ PLATFORM or EISA CARD	8 BIT	MEM I/O (2,3)	MEM I/O (2,3)	NA	NA	NA	NA
	16 BIT	NA	NA	(1)	MEM I/O (4)	(1)	NA
	32 BIT	NA	NA	(1)	(1)	(1)	(1)

TABLE 1-4-C: EISA BUS MASTER CYCLE SUPPORT. BUS MASTER DATA SIZE REQUESTED (BE*) GREATER THAN ACCESSED RESOURCE DATA SIZE (MEMCS16*, IOCS16*, EX16*, AND EX32*).

NOTES:

(1) See Table 1-4-A.

(2) Platform circuitry cannot tell the difference between an ISA, E-ISA, or EISA compatible 8 data bit memory resource and must execute as if it were an ISA or E-ISA compatible 8 data bit memory resource. The resource only uses ISA or E-ISA compatible signal lines. For an EISA compatible 8 data bit I/O resource, the above statement is also true, except the I/O resource uses the EISA compatible signal lines.

(3) If the BE* signal lines indicate an 8 data bit access for memory an E-MIX access cycle is executed.

(4) If the BE* signal lines indicate a 16 data bit access, the EISA standard access cycle is executed.

PLATFORM TYPE/ ACCESSED RESOURCE	CYCLES TO PLATFORM RESOURCES OR ADD-ON SLAVE CARD EISA PLATFORM CPU & ADD-ON BUS OWNER CARD VIEWPOINT			
	EISA COMPRESSED(3)		EISA BURST	
	16 BIT	32 BIT	16 BIT	32 BIT
EISA/ 8 BIT PC or XT CARD	NA	NA	NA	NA
EISA/ AT 8 BIT or E-ISA	NA	NA	NA	NA
CARD 16 BIT	NA	NA	NA	NA
EISA/ 8 BIT PLATFORM	NA	NA	NA	NA
or EISA 16 BIT CARD	(1)	NA	(1)	MEM (2)
32 BIT	(1)	(1)	(1)	(1)

TABLE 1-4-D: EISA BUS MASTER CYCLE SUPPORT. BUS MASTER DATA SIZE REQUESTED (BE*) GREATER THAN ACCESSED RESOURCE DATA SIZE (MEMCS16*, IOCS16*, EX16*, AND EX32*)

NOTES:

(1) See Table 1-4-B.

(2) Only if EISA bus master supports downshift.

(3) Only platform CPU can execute.

Tables 1-5-A and B outline the DMA transfer cycles types that can be executed for a given pair of resources on a given platform. See Chapters 3 and 7 for more information.

PLATFORM	PARTICIPANTS MEMORY : I/O	TRANSFER TYPES				TC (1)	PROGRAM CHANNEL SIZE	CONVER. SUPPORT	DEMAND & BLOCK TRANSFER INTERRUPTIBLE
		COMP	"A"	"B"	"C"				
PC/XT	PC/XT : PC/XT	YES	NO	NO	NO	UNI	NO	NO	NO
AT	PC/XT : PC/XT	YES	NO	NO	NO	UNI	NO	NO	NO
	PC/XT : AT	YES	NO	NO	NO	UNI	NO	NO	NO
	AT : PC/XT	YES	NO	NO	NO	UNI	NO	NO	NO
	AT : AT	YES	NO	NO	NO	UNI	NO	NO	NO
							NO	NO	NO
E-ISA	PC/XT : AT	YES	NO	NO	NO	UNI	YES	NO	NO
	AT : AT	YES	NO	NO	NO	UNI	YES	NO	NO
	PC/XT : E-ISA	YES	NO	NO	NO	BI	YES	NO	NO
	AT : E-ISA	YES	NO	NO	NO	BI	YES	NO	NO
	E-ISA : PC/XT (2)	YES	NO	NO	NO	UNI	YES	NO	NO
	E-ISA : AT (2)	YES	NO	NO	NO	UNI	YES	NO	NO
	E-ISA : E-ISA (2)	YES	NO	NO	NO	BI	YES	NO	NO
	E-ISA : PC/XT (3) (4)	YES	YES	YES	NO	UNI	YES	NO	YES (5)
	E-ISA : AT (3) (4)	YES	YES	YES	NO	UNI	YES	NO	YES (5)
	E-ISA : E-ISA (3) (4)	YES	YES	YES	NO	BI	YES	NO	YES (5)

TABLE 1-5-A: PC, XT, AT, AND E-ISA PLATFORM DMA TRANSFER CYCLES

PLATFORM	PARTICIPANTS MEMORY : I/O	TRANSFER TYPES				TC (1)	PROGRAM CHANNEL SIZE	CONVER. SUPPORT	DEMAND & BLOCK TRANSFER INTERRUPTIBLE (5)
		COMP	"A"	"B"	"C"				
EISA	PC/XT : PC/XT (4)	YES	YES	YES	NO	UNI	YES	YES	YES
	PC/XT : AT (4)	YES	YES	YES	NO	UNI	YES	YES	YES
	AT : PC/XT (4)	YES	YES	YES	NO	UNI	YES	YES	YES
	AT : AT (4)	YES	YES	YES	NO	UNI	YES	YES	YES
	PC/XT : EISA	YES	YES	YES	YES	BI	YES	YES	YES
	EISA : PC/XT (4)	YES	YES	YES	NO	UNI	YES	YES	YES
	AT/ISA : EISA	YES	YES	YES	YES	BI	YES	YES	YES
	EISA : AT (4)	YES	YES	YES	NO	UNI	YES	YES	YES
	EISA : EISA	YES	YES	YES	YES	BI	YES	YES	YES
	PLATFORM EISA MEMORY : EISA	YES	YES	YES	YES	BI	YES	YES	YES
	PLATFORM EISA MEMORY: PC/XT (4)	YES	YES	YES	NO	UNI	YES	YES	YES
	PLATFORM EISA MEMORY:AT (4)	YES	YES	YES	NO	UNI	YES	YES	YES

TABLE 1-5-B: EISA PLATFORM DMA TRANSFER CYCLES

NOTES:
(1) UNI = UNIdirectional ... DMA controller to I/O resource, BI = BIdirectional.
(2) E-ISA memory is an add-on card ONLY.
(3) E-ISA memory is the platform memory ONLY.
(4) Most DMA add-on slave cards support TYPE A DMA transfer cycles, and some DMA add-on slave cards support TYPE B DMA transfer cycles.
(5) "NO" if a DMA COMPATIBLE transfer cycle is executed.

Notes

CHAPTER TWO

MEMORY AND I/O ADDRESS SPACE

INTRODUCTION

ISA, E-ISA, and EISA platforms contain two address spaces: memory and I/O. To maintain compatibility for software written for earlier platforms, there are certain requirements placed on the memory and I/O address spaces. This chapter will briefly outline the requirements relative to add-on card design. For software development, more detailed information is required from the platform developer.

MEMORY ADDRESS SPACE

The memory address space is divided into three sections: platform memory, EPROM, and slot memory resources. The first 640K bytes (00 0000H to 09 FFFFH) are reserved for platform and bus memory resources. (See Figure 2-1.) The next 256K bytes (0A 0000H to 0D FFFFH) are assigned for bus memory resources such as video and hard disk. (Some of these resources may be built on the platform, so not all of the accesses to these address locations will result in bus cycles.) The next 128K bytes (0E 0000H to 0F FFFFH) are assigned to the ROM sockets, which include space for the BIOS.

For a PC or XT compatible platform, 20 ADDRESS signal lines are supported; consequently, the total address space of one megabyte is defined from 00 0000H to 0F FFFFH. AT and E-ISA

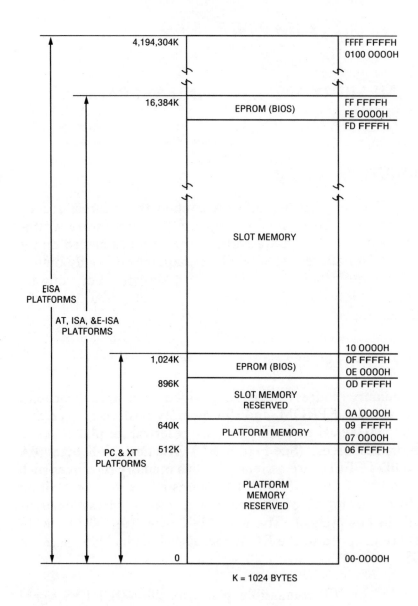

FIGURE 2-1:   MEMORY ADDRESS SPACE

compatible platforms support 24 ADDRESS signal lines; consequently, a total address space of 16 megabytes is defined from 00 0000H to FF FFFFH. The EISA compatible platform supports 32 ADDRESS signal lines; consequently, a total address space of 4 gigabytes is defined from 0000 0000H to FFFF FFFFH.

The first one megabyte on the AT, E-ISA, and EISA compatible platforms is defined in the same fashion as for the PC and XT compatible platforms. The 128K at the top of the 16 megabyte address space (FE 0000H to FF FFFFH) is a copy of the ROM (BIOS) space (0E 0000H to 0F FFFFH) in the first megabyte. The remaining memory address space is assigned to bus (slot) memory resources.

> *Some platforms are designed with part of the bus memory address space above 10 0000H allocated for platform memory resources. The address point that is the "top" of the platform memory is dependent simply on its total size. On ISA and E-ISA compatible platforms, it is very easy for platform memory to exceed the bus memory address of 16 megabytes with platform memory. Some chip sets allow "holes" to be programmed in the platform memory address space to allow access to the bus memory address space.*

> *The first 512K of the address space (00 0000H to 07 FFFFH) is designated for interrupt vectors, BIOS data, DOS, and user applications.*

I/O ADDRESS SPACE

The size of the I/O address space of the platform CPUs used on the ISA, E-ISA, EISA compatible platforms is 64K. However, the size of the available I/O address space varies from platform to platform.

On ISA compatible platforms, it historically has been assumed that only 1K of the total 64K I/O address space is used. The first 256 bytes are reserved for I/O platform resources, such as the interrupt and DMA controllers (addresses 0000H to 00FFH). (See Figure 2-2.) The remaining 768 bytes are available to "general" add-on I/O slave card resources (addresses 0100H to 03FFH). In that only 1K of the address space was supported, ISA add-on I/O slave cards only decode the first 10 ADDRESS signal lines; consequently, the SA <10-15> signal lines can be any value. The result of not decoding all of the ADDRESS signal lines results in the 256 platform address locations and the 768 bus address locations being repeated 64 times in the address space. (See Figure 2-2.) This repetition occurs on 1K address boundaries. Software running on the platform needs only one of the 64 repetitions of the 256 address locations to access platform resources. The E-ISA and EISA compatible platforms exploit these facts by assigning 63 of the 64 repetitions of the 256 address locations to specific add-on card slots. The partitioning is such that four groups of 256 address locations is assigned to each slot for a total of 1024 specific address locations per slot. (See Figure 2-3.)

Slot 0 is defined as the platform; thus, a total of 1K I/O addresses are assigned to the platform. The first 256 address locations are the same platform resources as defined across all platforms. The remaining three groups of 256 address locations are defined for E-ISA and EISA compatible platforms according to the EISA bus specification.

Since existing ISA add-on I/O slave cards only decode the first ten ADDRESS signal lines, they will respond to the "general" 768 bytes that are repeated 64 times. To maintain compatibility with these boards, this repetition is maintained on all platforms including E-ISA and EISA compatible platforms. (See Figure 2-3.)

In order for the 1K I/O addresses to be uniquely accessed for each slot, individual AEN (AENx) signal lines are routed to each

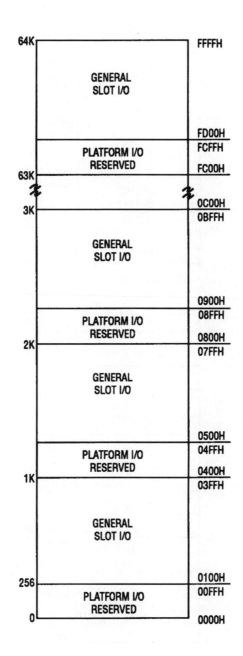

FIGURE 2-2: *ISA I/O ADDRESS SPACE*

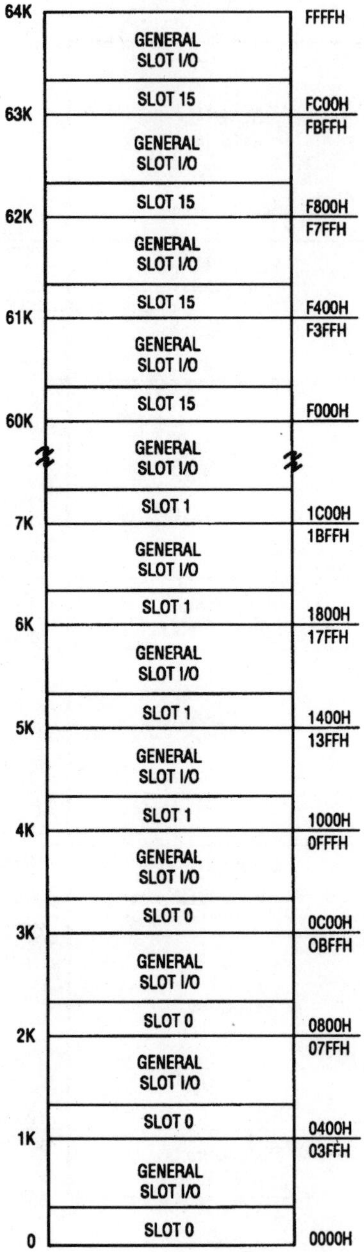

64K	FFFFH
GENERAL SLOT I/O	
SLOT 15	FC00H
63K	FBFFH
GENERAL SLOT I/O	
SLOT 15	F800H
62K	F7FFH
GENERAL SLOT I/O	
SLOT 15	F400H
61K	F3FFH
GENERAL SLOT I/O	
SLOT 15	F000H
60K	
GENERAL SLOT I/O	
SLOT 1	1C00H
7K	1BFFH
GENERAL SLOT I/O	
SLOT 1	1800H
6K	17FFH
GENERAL SLOT I/O	
SLOT 1	1400H
5K	13FFH
GENERAL SLOT I/O	
SLOT 1	1000H
4K	0FFFH
GENERAL SLOT I/O	
SLOT 0	0C00H
3K	0BFFH
GENERAL SLOT I/O	
SLOT 0	0800H
2K	07FFH
GENERAL SLOT I/O	
SLOT 0	0400H
1K	03FFH
GENERAL SLOT I/O	
SLOT 0	0000H
0	

FIGURE 2-3:   E-ISA AND EISA I/O ADDRESS SPACE

slot. During an access to a slot specific address, the associated
AENx signal line is driven inactive.

The AENx signal lines of the other slots are driven active. Of
course, when the access is to the "general" 768 address locations, all
AENx signal lines of all of the slots are driven inactive. During a
DMA transfer cycle, all the AENx signal lines are driven active.

*Even though an E-ISA and EISA compatible add-on I/O slave
card has access to the SA<0-15> (LA<2-15> for EISA) signal
lines, only the SA<0-11> (LA<2-11> for EISA) signal lines are
decoded. The control of the individual AENx signal lines of
each slot eliminates the need to decode the SA <12-15> and
LA<12-15> signal lines.*

*The E-ISA and EISA platform method of assigning four groups
of 256 address locations allows 16 "logical slots" to be defined.
Traditionally, only 8 to 10 slots have been available on a
platform. The AC timings specified by the IEEE P996, the EISA
bus specifications, and this book are only for 8 slots.*

*The EISA Rev. 3.12 bus specification defines that I/O
resources that are memory mapped should decode the full 32
address signal lines and reside above the two gigabyte
address level.*

Notes

CHAPTER THREE

GENERIC BUS CYCLES

This Chapter consists of the following Subchapters:

INTRODUCTION

This chapter is an introduction to the basic bus cycles. It is important to understand the basic bus cycle concepts in order to understand the information in Chapter 4. A more detailed explanation of the signal lines and bus cycles are in Chapters 5 through 9.

The basic bus cycles on an ISA platform are asynchronous. With one exception, signal lines are not referenced to the system clock. Some signal lines change logic state at any time, while others change within a specific time relative to a logic state change of other signals. The basic bus cycles on an E-ISA platform are also essentially asynchronous, although a few signal lines are referenced to the system clock.

On ISA, E-ISA, and EISA compatible platforms, there are four different bus cycles: bus master (platform CPU and add-on bus owner cards) access cycles, DMA transfer cycles, memory refresh cycles, and bus arbitration cycles. The bus master access cycle (access cycle) is executed by the platform CPU or an add-on bus owner card to read or write data from or to a memory or I/O resource. The DMA transfer cycle (transfer cycle) is executed by the DMA controller to transfer data between memory and I/O resources. The memory refresh cycle (refresh cycle), is executed by the refresh controller to refresh any volatile memory. The add-on bus owner card arbitration cycle (arbitration cycle), is executed by the add-on bus owner card to obtain bus ownership.

There are three types of access cycles executed on ISA or E-ISA compatible platforms: standard, ready, and no-wait-state. There are seven types of access cycles executed on EISA compatible platforms: EISA standard, EISA ready, EISA data-matching, EISA compressed, EISA burst, E-MIX, and I-MIX. The first five are EISA specific; that is, both resources involved in the cycle must be EISA compatible. The other two access cycles involve a mixture of EISA and ISA or E-ISA compatible resources.

DMA transfer and refresh cycles on an EISA platform operate in a similar fashion as on ISA or E-ISA platforms. The major differences relate to the EISA specific signal line supported, and the finer details of transfer cycle execution.

The arbitration cycles on an EISA compatible platform are a superset of the arbitration cycles on an ISA or E-ISA compatible platform.

The EISA Rev. 3.12 bus specification only defines three types of EISA bus cycles and uses slightly different names. The additional cycle types and the names used in this document were chosen to provide a clearer explanation and better differentiation between the cycles.

3.0 ISA SPECIFIC ACCESS CYCLES ON ISA and E-ISA PLATFORMS

The ISA specific access cycle is executed by the platform CPU or the add-on bus owner card to read and write data with memory and I/O resources. There are three types of access cycles: standard, ready, and no-wait-state.

NOTE: THE TERMS "STANDARD", "READY", AND "NO-WAIT-STATE" BY CONVENTION REFERS TO THE ISA COMPATIBLE ACCESS CYCLES. SIMILARLY NAMED EISA COMPATIBLE CYCLES WILL HAVE AN "EISA" PREFIX.

NOTE: THE ISA SPECIFIC ACCESS CYCLES ALSO REPRESENT E-ISA SPECIFIC ACCESS CYCLES. ANY DIFFERENCES WILL BE SO NOTED.

The standard access cycle executed when the platform CPU is bus owner is shown in Figure 3-1. The bus address latch enable line, BALE, is pulsed active at the beginning of a valid bus cycle, and indicates that the ADDRESS and associated signal lines on the bus are valid.

The accessed resource on the bus responds to the address with an indication of its size. Either the MEMCS16* or IOCS16* signal line is activated if the resource is 16 data bits in size; otherwise, the resource is assumed to be 8 data bits. The COMMAND signal lines, which include MEMR*, MEMW*, IOR*, and IOW*, are activated by the bus owner. The COMMAND signal lines also include the SMEMR* and SMEMW* signal lines, which are driven by platform circuitry. The length of the active COMMAND signal line is predetermined, and depends on the resource data width and whether the cycle is memory or I/O. For a write cycle, the active COMMAND signal line indicates to the accessed resource valid data on the bus. For a read cycle, the active COMMAND signal line provides a reference point to the accessed resource as to when data on the bus must be valid.

The standard access cycle executed by an ISA or E-ISA add-on bus owner card is the same as for the platform CPU, except that the BALE signal line is held active.   Consequently, the COMMAND signal lines becoming active are the only indication of the beginning of the cycle. (See Figure 3-2.) The lack of a pulsed BALE signal line also requires that both the LA<17-23> and SA<0-19> signal lines are held valid for the entire active period of the COMMAND signal lines. See Chapter 6 for more detailed information.

The second type of access cycle is the ready access cycle. (See Figures 3-1 and 3-2.) It can be executed by either the platform CPU or by an ISA or E-ISA add-on bus owner card. The standard access cycle becomes a ready access cycle when the accessed resource deactivates the IOCHRDY signal line. The COMMAND signal line will remain active until the IOCHRDY signal line becomes active. The result is a longer active COMMAND pulse than the standard access cycle, which allows access cycles to be lengthened for slower resources.

The increase in the length of a ready cycle is a multiple of one BCLK signal line period.   The ISA compatible platform implementation of the IOCHRDY signal line does not reference it to the BCLK line; however, the E-ISA compatible platform implementation   does.   See   Chapter   5   for   more   detailed information.

If the IOCHRDY signal line is inactive at the same time that the SRDY* signal is active, the cycle is executed as a ready cycle.

The third type of access cycle is the no-wait-state access cycle, which can only be executed by the platform CPU in an ISA compatible platform, or by the platform CPU and E-ISA add-on bus master card in an E-ISA compatible platform. (See Figure 3-3.)   The no-wait-state access cycle allows access cycles to be

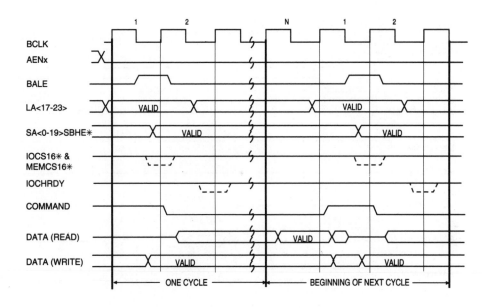

BCLK
AENx
BALE
LA<17-23>
SA<0-19>SBHE*
IOCS16* &
MEMCS16*
IOCHRDY
COMMAND
DATA (READ)
DATA (WRITE)

VALID

ONE CYCLE
BEGINNING OF NEXT CYCLE

FIGURE 3-1: **GENERIC ISA AND E-ISA STANDARD AND READY ACCESS CYCLE (PLATFORM CPU)**

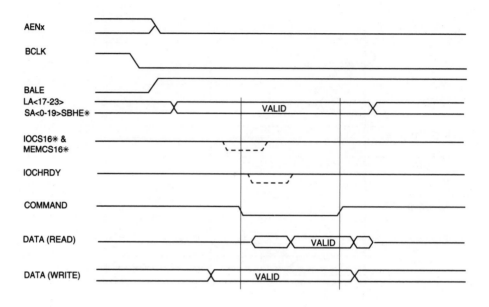

AENx

BCLK

BALE
LA<17-23>
SA<0-19>SBHE✶   VALID

IOCS16✶ &
MEMCS16✶

IOCHRDY

COMMAND

DATA (READ)   VALID

DATA (WRITE)   VALID

FIGURE 3-2: *GENERIC ISA AND E-ISA STANDARD AND READY ACCESS*
CYCLE (ADD-ON BUS OWNER CARD)

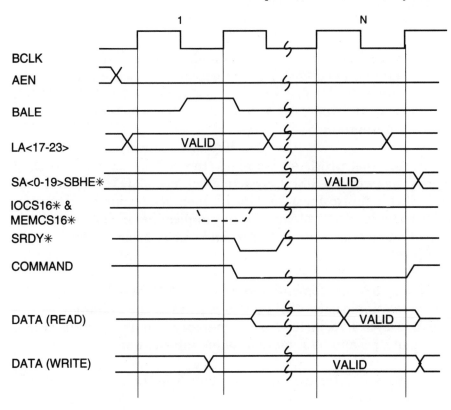

BCLK

AEN

BALE

LA<17-23>

SA<0-19>SBHE∗

IOCS16∗ &
MEMCS16∗

SRDY∗

COMMAND

DATA (READ)

DATA (WRITE)

FIGURE 3-3: *GENERIC ISA AND E-ISA NO WAIT STATE CYCLE (PLATFORM CPU AND E-ISA ADD-ON BUS OWNER CARD) (BALE IS HIGH)*

shortened for faster resources. A standard access cycle becomes a no-wait-state access cycle when the accessed resource activates the SRDY* signal line. The result is a shorter active COMMAND pulse than in the standard access cycle. See Chapter 6 for more detailed information.

The original IBM AT samples the SRDY* line in such a manner that with an 8 MHz system clock the SRDY* signal line is very difficult to use for a 16 data bit memory resource. However, the ISA and E-ISA implementation samples the SRDY* signal line so that it works with an 8.0 and 8.33 MHz system clock, respectively.

The E-ISA implementation of the ISA bus has made the implementation easier. It has also expanded the definition of no-wait-state cycles to include 8 bit memory and I/O access cycles. See Chapters 5 and 6 for more detailed information.

The access cycles can support either 8 or 16 data bit cycles in both the memory and I/O address spaces. However, not all platforms and bus owners can support all types of access cycles to all resources. The platform CPU does not require the add-on slave cards to support all access cycles for all data widths. Table 3-1-A summarizes the different support levels.

BUS MASTER	BUS MASTER VIEWPOINT	ACCESSED RESOURCE	ACCESSED RESOURCE VIEWPOINT	CYCLE CATEGORY
AT, E-ISA PC/XT (3)	ISA STANDARD	AT, E-ISA PC/XT	ISA STANDARD	STANDARD
AT, E-ISA PC/XT (1,3)	ISA READY	AT, E-ISA PC/XT	ISA READY	READY
AT, E-ISA (2)	ISA NO WAIT STATE	AT, E-ISA	ISA NO WAIT STATE	NO WAIT STATE

TABLE 3-1-A: PC, XT, ISA, AND E-ISA PLATFORM ACCESS CYCLES ... ALL DATA SIZES

NOTES:

(1) Not all ISA add-on bus owner cards support ready access cycles because the IBM AT platform did not drive the IOCHRDY signal line when platform resources were accessed.

(2) ISA or E-ISA add-on bus owner cards CANNOT execute no-wait-state access cycles on ISA compatible platforms because the SRDY* signal line requires the BCLK signal line to be distributed in a starburst fashion. Also, the IBM AT platform did not drive the SRDY* signal line when platform resources were accessed. E-ISA add-on bus owner cards CAN execute no-wait-state access cycles on E-ISA compatible platforms because E-ISA compatible platforms "starburst" the BCLK signal line.

(3) On PC and XT platforms, only the platform CPU can be bus master.

3.1 EISA BUS MASTER ACCESS CYCLES TO EISA RESOURCES ON EISA PLATFORMS

As previously discussed, there are five types of access cycles that execute between EISA bus masters (platform CPU or EISA add-on bus owner card) and EISA compatible accessed resources: EISA standard, EISA ready, EISA data-matching, EISA compressed, and EISA burst. Additionally, an EISA bus master can access an ISA or E-ISA add-on slave card with E-MIX access cycles. An ISA or E-ISA add-on bus owner card can access an EISA compatible resource (platform or add-on card) with an I-MIX access cycle. See subsequent subchapters concerning E-MIX and I-MIX access cycles.

Table 3-1-B outlines all the ACCESS CYCLES on an EISA PLATFORM, including those not executed by an EISA bus master. The interpretation of the table is as follows:

- The data size requested by an EISA bus master is defined by the number of BE* signal lines driven at the beginning of the cycle. The data size requested by an ISA or E-ISA bus master is defined by the SA0 and SBHE* signal lines.

- The data size of the ACCESSED RESOURCE is defined by the EX16* and EX32* signal lines for EISA resources, and MEMCS16* and IOCS16* for ISA or E-ISA resources.

BUS MASTER/ SIZE REQ.	BUS MASTER VIEWPOINT	ACCESSED RESOURCE	ACCESSED RESOURCE VIEWPOINT	CYCLE CATEGORY
EISA/ 16 BIT	EISA STANDARD	EISA 16 BIT	EISA STANDARD	EISA STANDARD
EISA/ 32 BIT	EISA STANDARD	EISA 32 BIT	EISA STANDARD	EISA STANDARD
EISA/ 8-16-24 BIT	EISA STANDARD	EISA 32 BIT	EISA STANDARD	EISA STANDARD
EISA/ 8 BIT	EISA STANDARD	EISA 16 BIT	EISA STANDARD	EISA STANDARD
EISA/ 16 BIT	EISA READY	EISA 16 BIT	EISA READY	EISA READY
EISA/ 32 BIT	EISA READY	EISA 32 BIT	EISA READY	EISA READY
EISA/ 8-16-24 BIT	EISA READY	EISA 32 BIT	EISA READY	EISA READY
EISA/ 8 BIT	EISA READY	EISA 16 BIT	EISA READY	EISA READY
EISA/(1) 16 BIT	EISA COMPRESSED	EISA 16 BIT	EISA COMPRESSED	EISA COMPRESSED
EISA/(1) 32 BIT	EISA COMPRESSED	EISA 32 BIT	EISA COMPRESSED	EISA COMPRESSED
EISA/(1) 8 BIT	EISA COMPRESSED	EISA 16 BIT	EISA COMPRESSED	EISA COMPRESSED
EISA/(1) 8-16-24 BIT	EISA COMPRESSED	EISA 32 BIT	EISA COMPRESSED	EISA COMPRESSED
EISA/ 16 BIT	EISA BURST	EISA 16 BIT	EISA BURST	EISA BURST
EISA/ 32 BIT	EISA BURST	EISA 32 BIT	EISA BURST	EISA BURST
EISA/ 8 BIT	EISA BURST	EISA 16 BIT	EISA BURST	EISA BURST
EISA/ 8-16-24 BIT	EISA BURST	EISA 32 BIT	EISA BURST	EISA BURST
EISA/ 8 BIT	E-MIX VERSION EISA STANDARD	AT,E-ISA 8 BIT XT, EISA 8 BIT(4)	ISA STANDARD OR READY	E-MIX VERSION OF STANDARD
EISA/ 16 BIT	E-MIX VERSION EISA STANDARD	AT,E-ISA 16 BIT	ISA STANDARD OR READY	E-MIX VERSION OF STANDARD
EISA/ 8 BIT	E-MIX VERSION EISA STANDARD	AT,E-ISA 8 BIT & EISA 8 BIT (4)	ISA NO-WAIT-STATE	E-MIX VERSION OF STANDARD
EISA/ 16 BIT	E-MIX VERSION EISA STANDARD	AT,E-ISA 16 BIT	ISA NO-WAIT-STATE	E-MIX VERSION OF STANDARD

TABLE 3-1-B: ALL EISA PLATFORM ACCESS CYCLES ... BUS MASTER REQUESTED DATA SIZE IS EQUAL TO OR LESS THAN ACCESSED RESOURCE DATA SIZE

BUS MASTER/ SIZE REQ.	BUS MASTER VIEWPOINT	ACCESSED RESOURCE	ACCESSED RESOURCE VIEWPOINT	CYCLE CATEGORY
ISA,E-ISA/ 8-16 BIT (6)	ISA READY	EISA 16 BIT	EISA STANDARD OR READY	I-MIX
ISA,E-ISA/ 8-16 BIT (6)	ISA READY	EISA 32 BIT	EISA STANDARD OR READY	I-MIX
ISA,E-ISA/ 8 BIT (6)	ISA STD, RDY, OR NO WAIT ST	EISA MEMORY 8 BIT (7)	ISA STD, RDY, OR NO-WAIT-STATE	ISA STD, RDY, OR NO WAIT ST
ISA,E-ISA/ 8 BIT (6)	ISA READY	EISA I/O 8 BIT (5)	ISA STANDARD OR READY SPEC. 8 BIT VER.	I-MIX
ISA,E-ISA/ 8 BIT (6)	ISA STANDARD OR READY	AT, XT, E-ISA PC 8 BIT	ISA STANDARD OR READY	ISA STANDARD OR READY
ISA,E-ISA/ 8 BIT (6)	ISA NO WAIT STATE	AT, E-ISA, 8 BIT	ISA NO-WAIT-STATE	ISA NO WAIT STATE (3)
ISA,E-ISA/ 8-16 BIT (6)	ISA STANDARD OR READY	AT, E-ISA 16 BIT	ISA STANDARD OR READY	ISA STANDARD OR READY (2)
ISA,E-ISA/ 8-16 BIT (6)	ISA NO WAIT STATE	AT, E-ISA 16 BIT	ISA NO WAIT STATE	ISA NO WAIT STATE (3)

TABLE 3-1-B: ALL EISA PLATFORM ACCESS CYCLES ... BUS MASTER REQUESTED DATA SIZE IS EQUAL TO OR LESS THAN ACCESSED RESOURCE DATA SIZE (CONTINUED)

NOTES:

(1) Platform CPU only.

(2) Traditional ISA add-on bus owner cards do not execute ready access cycles because the IBM AT platform did not drive the IOCHRDY signal line when platform resources were accessed. E-ISA add-on bus owner cards do support the ready access cycle.

(3) Traditional ISA add-on bus owner cards did not execute no-wait-state access cycles because the IBM AT platform resources did not drive the SRDY* (NOWS*) signal line, and BCLK signal line skew was a problem. E-ISA add-on bus owner cards do support the no-wait-state access cycle when installed in an E-ISA or EISA platform.

(4) Platform circuitry cannot tell the difference between an ISA, E-ISA, or EISA 8 bit resource.   The EISA 8 data bit memory resource uses only ISA or E-ISA compatible signal lines.   The EISA 8 data bit I/O resource uses the EISA compatible signal lines with an E-MIX access cycle.

(5) Platform circuitry cannot tell the difference between an ISA or EISA 8 bit resource.

(6) By definition an ISA or E-ISA bus master on an EISA platform is an add-on bus owner card.

(7) An 8 data bit EISA memory resource is "actually" only an 8 data bit ISA or E-ISA resource.

BUS MASTER/ SIZE REQ.	BUS MASTER VIEWPOINT	ACCESSED RESOURCE	ACCESSED RESOURCE VIEWPOINT	CYCLE CATEGORY
EISA/ 24-32 BIT	EISA DATA-MATCHING	EISA 16 BIT	EISA STANDARD OR READY	EISA DATA MATCHING
EISA/ 24-32 BIT	EISA DATA-MATCHING	AT & E-ISA 16 BIT	ISA STANDARD, READY, OR NO WAIT	E-MIX VERSION OF EISA DATA-MATCHING
EISA/ 16-24-32 BIT	EISA DATA-MATCHING	ISA,E-ISA,EISA 8 BIT (5)	ISA STANDARD, READY, OR NO WAIT	E-MIX VERSION OF EISA DATA-MATCHING
EISA/ 16-24-32 BIT	EISA DATA-MATCHING	PC,XT 8 BIT	ISA STANDARD OR READY	E-MIX VERSION OF EISA DATA-MATCHING
EISA/(2) 24-32 BIT	EISA BURST	EISA 16 BIT	EISA BURST	EISA BURST
ISA,E-ISA/ 16 BIT (6)	ISA STANDARD OR READY	PC,XT,AT,E-ISA, 8 BIT	ISA STANDARD OR READY	ISA STANDARD OR READY (3)
ISA,E-ISA 16 BIT (6)	ISA NO WAIT STATE	AT,E-ISA, 8 BIT	ISA NO-WAIT-STATE	ISA NO WAIT STATE (4)
ISA,E-ISA/ 16 BIT (6)	ISA STD, RDY, OR NO WAIT ST	EISA MEMORY 8 BIT (7)	ISA STD, READY, OR NO-WAIT-STATE	ISA STD, RDY OR NO WAIT ST
ISA, E-ISA 16 BIT (6)	ISA READY	EISA I/O 8 BIT (5)	EISA STD. READY, OR NO-WAIT-STATE SPEC. 8 BIT VER.	I-MIX

TABLE 3-1-C: ALL EISA PLATFORM ACCESS CYCLES ... BUS MASTER REQUESTED DATA SIZE IS GREATER THAN ACCESSED RESOURCE DATA SIZE

NOTES:

(1) Platform CPU only.

(2) Only if EISA master supports downshifting.

(3) Traditional ISA add-on bus owner cards do not execute ready access cycles because the IBM AT platform did not drive the IOCHRDY signal line when platform resources were accessed. E-ISA add-on bus owner cards do support the ready access cycle.

(4) Traditional ISA add-on bus owner cards did not execute no-wait-state access cycles because the IBM AT platform resources did not drive the SRDY* (NOWS*) signal line, and BCLK signal line skew was a problem.

(5) Platform circuitry cannot tell the difference between an ISA, E-ISA, or EISA 8 bit resource.

(6) By definition, an ISA or E-ISA bus master on an EISA platform is an add-on bus owner card. If the no-wait-state access cycle is going to be used, the "starburst" implementation of the BCLK signal line is required.

(7) An 8 data bit EISA memory resource is "actually" only an 8 data bit ISA or E-ISA resource.

The EISA standard access cycle is executed by the platform CPU or the EISA compatible add-on bus owner card (collectively called EISA bus masters) to access platform and EISA compatible resources (collectively called EISA accessed resources). (See Figure 3-4). The START* signal line is driven active by the EISA bus master to indicate to other bus resources that a cycle is beginning and that it has driven ADDRESS (LA<2-31>) and M-IO signal lines valid. The accessed resource responds by driving the EX16* or EX32* signal lines active. Driving either EX16* or EX32* active indicates an EISA resource, as well as indicating the data size of the resource.

Subsequent to an active START* signal line, the EISA bus master drives the BE*<0-3> and W-R signal lines valid. The BE* signal lines complete byte level addressing and indicate the data size requested. The W-R signal line indicates data direction. For the cycle to execute as an EISA standard access cycle, the data size requested must be equal to or less than the data size of the EISA accessed resource, the EXRDY signal line must remain active, and the accessed resource must be EISA compatible. If these conditions are not met, the cycle is completed as one of the other EISA access cycles.

In response to an active START* signal line, the CMD* signal line is driven active by platform circuitry (not the EISA bus master) and establishes the length of the cycle. The START* signal line is driven active only for one BCLK period and the LA, M-IO, BE*, and W-R signal lines remain valid until the START* signal line is driven inactive.

The active length of the CMD* signal line for an EISA standard cycle is one BCLK period. Thus, the total length of an EISA standard cycle is two BCLK periods. For a write cycle, the active CMD* signal line indicates to the EISA accessed resource valid data on the bus. For a read cycle, the active CMD* signal line provides a reference point to the EISA accessed resource as to when data on the bus must be valid.

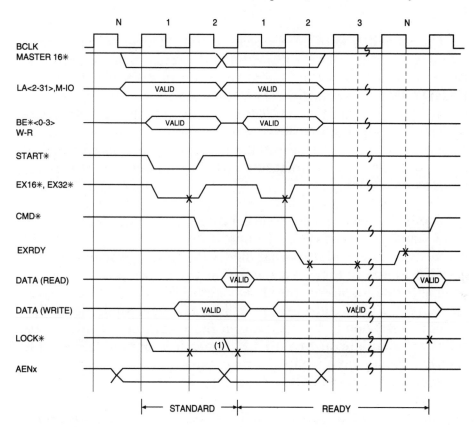

X = SAMPLE POINT
(1) PLATFORM CPU

FIGURE 3-4: GENERIC EISA STANDARD AND READY ACCESS CYCLE

The second type of access cycle is the EISA ready access cycle (see Figure 3-4). The EISA standard access cycle becomes an EISA ready access cycle when the accessed resource drives the EXRDY signal line inactive. The other conditions for a cycle to be executed as an EISA ready access cycle are that the data size requested is equal to or less than the data size of the accessed resource, and the accessed resource must be EISA compatible. If these conditions are not met, the cycle is completed as one of the other access cycles.

The EISA ready access cycle executes in the same fashion as an EISA standard access cycle, the only difference being the length of the cycle. The CMD* signal line will remain active until the EXRDY signal line becomes active which allows access cycles to be lengthened for slower resources. The EXRDY* line is sampled by the platform circuitry in the middle of each BCLK signal line period; consequently the increase in the length of a ready access cycle is a multiple of one BCLK signal line period. When the EXRDY signal line is sampled active, the access cycle is completed at the end of the same BCLK signal line period.

The third type of access cycle is the EISA data-matching access cycle (see Figure 3-5). The EISA standard access cycle becomes an EISA data-matching access cycle when the EISA bus master requests a 24 or 32 data bit (indicated by the BE* signal lines) access cycle and the EISA accessed resource drives the EX16* signal line active. The active EX16* signal line indicates that the accessed resource can only support an 8 or 16 data bit access. In response to this condition, the EISA bus master holds the LA and the W-R signal lines valid for the entire cycle.

For explanation purposes, observe a 32 data bit access to a 16 data bit accessed resource in Figure 3-5. The initial BE* signal lines indicate a 32 data bit access, and the accessed resource simply honors the value of the BE* <0-1> signal lines; that is, only the lower word. For a read access cycle, the word is latched into a holding register by the platform circuitry. For a write access cycle, the accessed resource only accepts the lower word in the first part

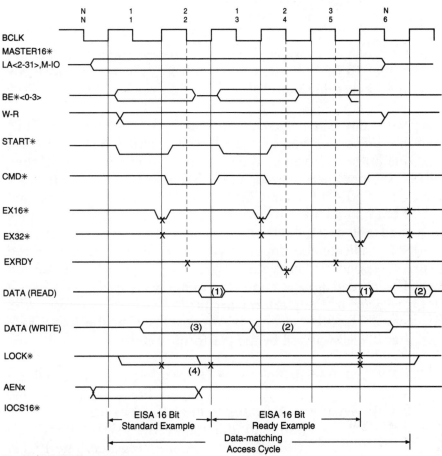

X = SAMPLE POINT
(1) = Driven By Accessed Resource
(2) = Driven By Platform Circuitry
(3) = Driven By Bus Master and Platform Circuitry
(4) = Platform CPU

FIGURE 3-5:   GENERIC EISA DATA-MATCHING ACCESS CYCLE (32 DATA BIT
BUS MASTER TO 16 DATA BIT ACCESSED RESOURCE EXAMPLE)

of the cycle. As an example, Figure 3-5 demonstrates that the first part of the EISA data-matching cycles appears as an EISA standard access cycle to the EISA accessed resource.

As with the EISA standard access cycle, the first START* signal line pulse is driven by the EISA bus master and the CMD* signal line pulse is driven by the platform control circuitry. Unlike an EISA standard access cycle, the EISA data-matching cycle has a second set of START* and CMD* signal line pulses. The second pulse of both signal lines are driven by the platform circuitry. Also, the second set of BE* signal lines are driven by the platform circuitry to indicate the upper word of the access. The accessed resource responds by activating the EX16* signal line a second time. For a read access cycle, the upper word is latched into a holding register by the platform circuitry. For a write access cycle, the accessed resource accepts the upper word on the lower byte lanes after it was swapped by the platform circuitry.

The EISA data-matching cycle is completed by the platform circuitry activating the EX32* signal line. For a read cycle, the active EX32* signal line indicates to the EISA bus master that the bytes requested (according to the initial BE* signal lines) are available from the platform circuitry holding registers one BCLK signal line period later. For a write cycle, the active EX32* signal line indicates to the EISA bus master that all of the bytes available according to the initial BE* signal lines have been accepted by the accessed resource. Note: the EISA Rev. 3.12 bus specification indicates that only EX32* is driven active at the end of the cycle. The Intel 358DT chip set indicates that both EX16* and EX32* signal lines are driven active at the end of the cycle.

The data-matching cycle can be executed with or without the EXRDY signal line becoming active. The portion of the cycle that samples the EXRDY signal line always active resembles an EISA standard access cycle. The portion of the cycle that samples the EXRDY signal line inactive resembles an EISA ready access cycle, as shown in Figure 3-5.

The description and the example in Figure 3-5 is for a 32 data bit access (requested) to a 16 data bit resource. The EISA data-matching access cycle is also used to access three bytes. These bytes are either 1, 2, and 3 OR 0, 1, and 2 byte lanes (BE*<3:0> = 0001 or BE*<3:0> = 1000). In this case, one of the access cycles executed within the EISA data-matching access cycle is only for one byte. See Chapter 6 for more information.

The EISA data-matching access cycle discussed above is applicable when the accessed resource is EISA compatible (as indicated by the EX16* signal line being driven active). If the accessed resource is an 8 data bit EISA compatible or an ISA compatible resource (i.e. EX16* and EX32* are not driven active at the beginning of the cycle), an E-MIX version of the data-matching access cycle is executed. See the E-MIX ACCESS CYCLE sections in Chapters 3 and 6 for more information.

The EISA data-matching access cycle described above is for an EISA add-on bus owner card. If the platform CPU is the EISA bus master, the operation is the same except during read access cycles there is no need to "redrive" the data onto the bus and during read or write access cycles there is no need to drive the EX16* and EX32* signal lines active at the end of the cycle.

The fourth type of access cycle is the EISA compressed access cycle. The EISA compressed access cycle can only be executed by the platform CPU and is shown in Figure 3-6. This access cycle allows for a longer memory address decode time than the EISA burst access cycle and higher data rates than the EISA standard access cycle. The EISA compressed access cycle begins as an EISA standard access cycle. The START* signal line is driven active by the platform CPU to indicate to other bus resources that a cycle is beginning and the ADDRESS and M-IO signal lines are valid. The accessed resource responds by driving the EX16* or EX32* signal lines active. Driving either EX16* or EX32* active indicates an

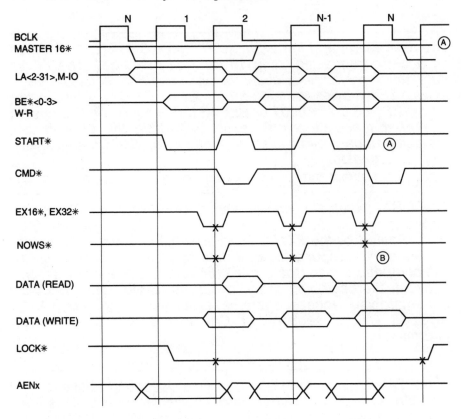

X = SAMPLE POINT

FIGURE   3-6:   GENERIC EISA COMPRESSED ACCESS CYCLE

EISA resource, as well as the data size of the resource. Subsequent to an active START* signal line, the platform CPU drives the BE* < 0-3 > and W-R signal lines valid.

The EISA standard access cycle becomes an EISA compressed access cycle when three events happen. First, the EISA compatible accessed resource drives the SRDY* (NOWS*) signal line active. Second, the platform circuitry responds to the active NOWS* signal line with a "shorter" active pulse for the CMD* signal line. Third, also in response to an active NOWS* signal line, the platform circuitry drives longer "low" portions of the BCLK signal line.

The platform control circuitry continues sampling the NOWS* signal line and maintaining longer low portions of the BCLK signal line and shorter active pulses for the CMD* signal line. The sequence of compressed cycles terminates at Point "A" when the BCLK signal is high earlier than previous cycles and the START* signal line remains inactive. This "termination" of the EISA compressed access cycle results from the accessed resource not driving the NOWS* signal line active at Point "B". The EISA compressed access cycle can also be terminated by the platform circuitry unilaterally driving the BCLK and the START* signal lines as previously described at Point "A".

For a write cycle, the active CMD* signal line indicates to the accessed resource valid data on the bus. For a read cycle, the active CMD* signal line provides a reference point to the accessed resource as to when data on the bus must be valid.

The fifth type of access cycle is the EISA burst access cycle. The EISA burst access cycle can only be executed by the platform CPU or EISA add-on bus owner (collectively called EISA bus masters) when accessing EISA compatible memory resources. The generic cycle is shown in Figure 3-7.

The EISA burst access cycle begins as an EISA standard access cycle. The START* signal line is driven active by the EISA bus

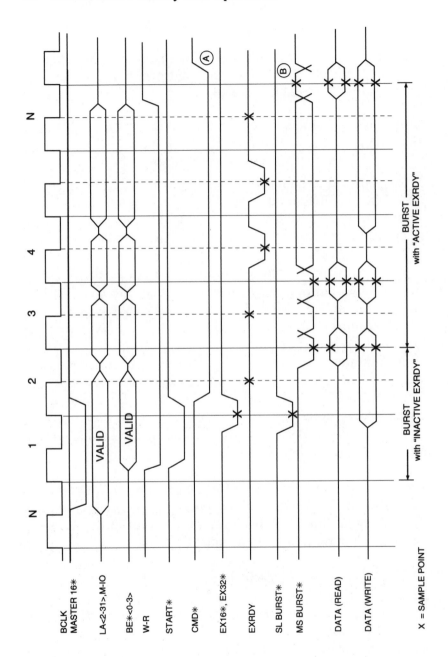

FIGURE 3-7: GENERIC EISA BURST ACCESS CYCLE

master to indicate to other bus resources that a cycle is beginning and the LA and M-IO signal lines are valid. The accessed resource responds by driving the EX16* or EX32* signal lines active, which indicates an EISA resource, as well as the data size. Subsequent to an active START* signal line, the EISA bus master drives the BE* and W-R signal lines valid. The EISA standard access cycle becomes an EISA burst access cycle when two events happen: first, the accessed resource drives the SLBURST* signal line active to indicate support of EISA burst access cycles; secondly, in response to the active SLBURST* signal line, the EISA bus master drives the MSBURST* signal line active.

In response to an active START* signal line, the CMD* signal line is driven active by platform circuitry. The platform control circuitry samples the active SLBURST* and MSBURST* signal lines active and maintains a constant active CMD* signal line until the cycle is completed. The sequence of burst cycles terminates at Point "A" when the MSBURST* signal line has been sampled inactive at Point "B". Notice that the SLBURST*, EX16*, and EX32* signal lines are sampled only once. Also notice that the MSBURST* signal line is only sampled when data is valid as dictated by an active EXRDY signal line a half BCLK signal line period earlier.

The entire burst access cycle is unidirectional; that is, data is either all read or all written. The read data must be valid relative to the rising edge of the BCLK signal if the EXRDY* signal line was sampled valid at the previous falling edge of the BCLK signal line. The write data is always valid prior to the rising edge of the very next BCLK signal line under the assumption that the EXRDY* signal line may be inactive.

3.2 EISA BUS MASTER ACCESS CYCLES TO ISA AND E-ISA RESOURCES ON EISA PLATFORMS

The sixth type of access cycle supported on an EISA platform is the E-MIX access cycle. (See Table 3-1-B for a summary of when an E-MIX access cycle is executed.) The E-MIX access cycle can be executed by the platform CPU or an EISA compatible add-on bus owner card (collectively called EISA bus masters) when the access is to an ISA or E-ISA compatible resource. The E-MIX access cycle relies on the intermixing of the different EISA and ISA access cycles. From the EISA bus master viewpoint, the E-MIX access cycles implement the EISA standard or data-matching access cycles. From the ISA compatible accessed resource viewpoint, the E-MIX access cycles implement the ISA or E-ISA compatible standard, ready, and no-wait state access cycles (see Figures 3-8-A to 3-8-D). There are two versions of the E-MIX access cycle. One, called the E-MIX version of the EISA standard access cycle, does no data byte assembly or disassembly. The other, called the E-MIX version of the EISA data-matching access cycle, does data-byte assembly and disassembly.

When the E-MIX version of the EISA standard access cycle is being executed by an EISA add-on bus owner card, it appears slightly different than a "regular" EISA standard access cycle. First, the LA and M-IO signal lines are held until 1/2 BCLK signal line period after the CMD* signal line is driven inactive. The W-R signal line is driven valid until one BCLK signal line period after the CMD* signal line is driven inactive. Second, the EISA bus master must tri-state the START* and BE* signal lines (Point D in Figures 3-8-A to D) as is done for the EISA data-matching access cycle. Third, the platform circuitry supports the appropriate ISA compatible signal lines. Fourth, the EX16* and EX32* signal lines are not driven active until the end of the cycle to indicate cycle completion (Point C in Figures 3-8-A to D). If the EX16* or EX32* signal lines were driven active at Point B, by definition it would not be an E-MIX access cycle. Fifth, for a write access cycle, the DATA signal lines are also tri-stated by the EISA bus master

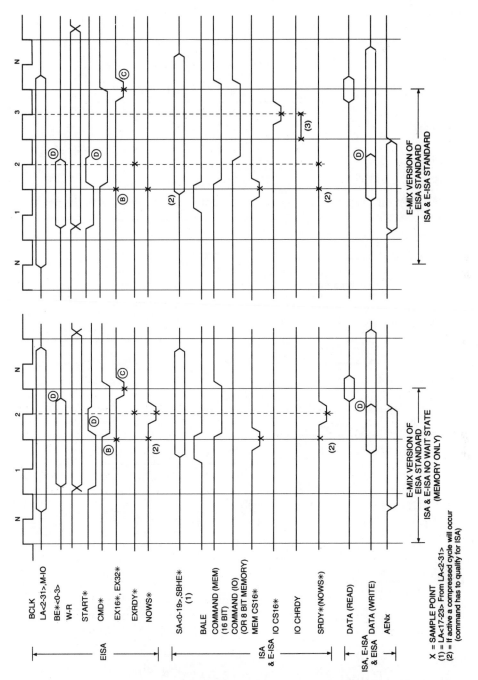

FIGURE   3-8-A: *E-MIX VERSION OF EISA STANDARD ACCESS CYCLE (16 DATA BIT ACCESS CYCLE TO ISA OR E-ISA 16 DATA BIT ADD-ON SLAVE CARD) (MASTER16* = 0)*

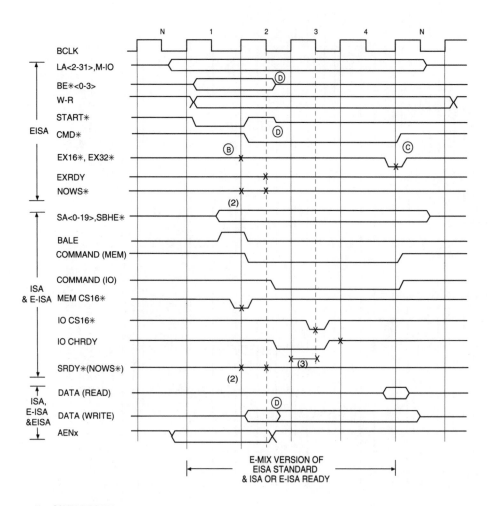

X = SAMPLE POINT
(1) = LA<17-23> From
      LA<2-31>
(2) = If active a compressed cycle will occur
      (command has to qualify for ISA)

FIGURE 3-8-B: E-MIX VERSION OF EISA STANDARD ACCESS CYCLE
                (16 DATA BIT ACCESS CYCLE TO ISA OR E-ISA 16
                DATA BIT ADD-ON SLAVE CARD) (MASTER16* = 0)

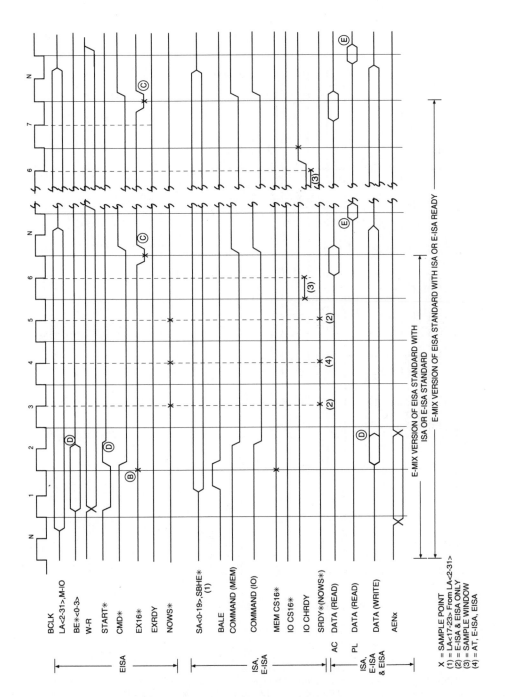

FIGURE 3-8-C: E-MIX VERSION OF EISA STANDARD ACCESS CYYCLT
                 (8 DATA BIT ACCESS TO ISA OR E-ISA 8 DATA BIT
                 ADD-ON CARD) (MASTER16* = 0 OR 1)

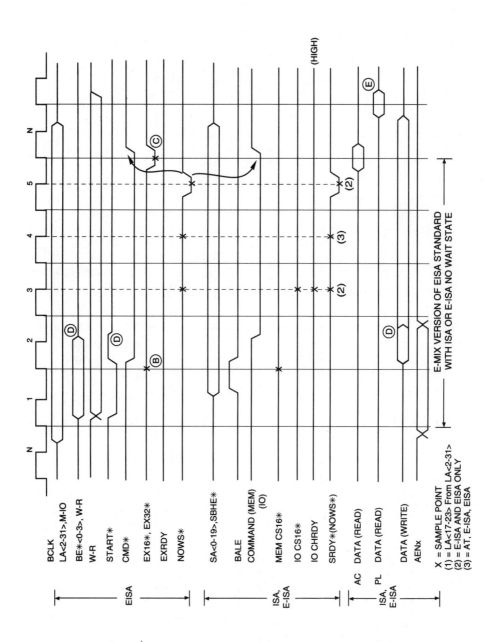

FIGURE 3-8-D: *E-MIX VERSION OF EISA STANDARD ACCESS CYCLE (8 DATA BIT ACCESS CYCLE TO ISA OR E-ISA 8 DATA BIT ADD-ON CARD) (MASTER16* = 0 OR 1)*

(Point D in Figures 3-8-A to D) and then driven by platform circuitry. Sixth, for a read access cycle, the platform circuitry "re-drives" the DATA signal lines one BCLK signal line period after the CMD* signal line is driven inactive (Point E in Figures 3-8-C and D) when the EISA bus master data size (indicated by the MASTER16* signal line) is greater than the ISA or E-ISA compatible accessed resource data size (indicated by the MEMCS16* and IOCS16* signal lines). (See Table 6-25 in Chapter 6.) Otherwise data is read directly from the accessed resource and not redriven by platform circuitry (see Figure 3-8-A and B).

The timing for the EISA bus master tri-stating certain signal lines and then driving them for the next cycle mimics the timings outlined for the EISA data-matching access cycle.

The E-MIX version of the standard access cycle takes place when an EISA bus master accesses an ISA or E-ISA compatible resource, and under the following conditions:

- The initial BE* signal lines indicated an 8 data bit access.
        OR
- The initial BE* signal lines indicated a 16 data bit access when the MEMCS16* (when M-IO = 1) or IOCS16* (when M-IO = 0) signal line is active.

When the The E-MIX version of the EISA standard access cycle is being executed by the platform CPU, it executes the access cycle in the same fashion as an EISA add-on bus owner card. However, there are three differences: first, the START* and CMD* signal lines are not tri-stated because the platform CPU and platform circuitry are essentially one and the same. Second, the EX16* and EX32* signal lines are not driven active at the end of the cycle. Third, for a read access, the DATA signal lines are not "re-driven" one BCLK signal line period after the CMD* signal line is driven inactive.

When the E-MIX version of the EISA data-matching access cycle is being executed, it appears as a "regular" EISA data-matching access cycle to the EISA add-on bus owner card (see Figure 3-5). The differences are: first, the ISA compatible signal lines operate as outlined in Figure 3-8-A to D; secondly, both the EX16* and EX32* signal lines are only driven active at the end of the cycle.

The E-MIX version of the EISA data-matching cycle is different than the E-MIX version of the EISA standard access cycle in two ways: first, the data read is always redriven one BCLK signal line period after the CMD* signal line is driven inactive; secondly, the platform circuitry executes multiple ISA access cycles in conjunction with multiple active START* and CMD* signal line pulses.

The E-MIX version of the EISA data-matching access cycle occurs when an EISA bus master is accessing an ISA or E-ISA resource under the following conditions:

- The data size requested by the initial BE* signal lines is larger than the data size of the accessed resource as defined by MEMCS16* and IOCS16* signal lines being inactive (8 data bit resource).

   - The initial BE* signal lines indicated a 24 or 32 data bits access when the MEMCS16* (when M-IO = 1) or IOCS16* (when M-IO = 0) signal line is active.

   - The initial BE* signal lines indicate a word access to an odd address (BE*3 = 1, BE*2 = 0, BE*1 = 0, and BE*0 = 1).

> *When the E-MIX version of the data-matching access cycle is being executed by the platform CPU, it appears as a "regular" data-matching access cycle, except for the following differences: first, the LA, M-IO, W-R, START*, CMD*, and DATA signal lines (for writes) are driven by the platform CPU. Second, the platform circuitry supports the appropriate ISA or E-ISA compatible signal lines. Third, for read access cycles, the DATA signal lines do not have to be redriven (see Point E of Figure 3-5). Fourth, the cycle is completed with the last CMD* signal line active pulse, and the EX16* and EX32* signal lines do not have to be driven active at the end of the cycle (see Point C of Figure 3-5).*

> *For the remainder of the E-MIX access cycle discussion, the viewpoint will be that of an EISA add-on bus owner card. The execution of the E-MIX access cycle by the platform CPU is clearly a subset.*

The E-MIX (either the EISA standard or EISA data-matching access cycle version) access cycle begins as an EISA standard access cycle. The START* signal line is driven active by the EISA bus master to indicate to other bus resources that a cycle is beginning and the LA and M-IO signal lines are valid. Subsequent to an active START* signal line, the EISA bus master drives the BE* and W-R signal lines valid. The EISA standard access cycle becomes an E-MIX access cycle when neither the EX16* nor the EX32* signal lines are sampled active when the START* signal line is active. The EISA bus master will then execute an E-MIX version of the EISA standard or data-matching access cycle. The platform circuitry drives the ISA compatible COMMAND signal lines (MEMR*, MEMW*, SMEMR*, SMEMW*, IOR*, or IOW*) active. Simultaneously, the platform circuitry drives the EISA compatible CMD* signal line active.

In order to meet any of the possible cycle requirements, the platform circuitry (prior to determining if an ISA or E-ISA compatible resource is involved) has driven the SA and SBHE* signal lines active (from the LA and BE* signal lines) and has pulsed the BALE signal line. From the ISA or E-ISA compatible accessed resource viewpoint, it executes ISA compatible standard, ready, and no-wait-state access cycles. If data-matching is required, the platform circuitry will execute multiple ISA compatible access cycles.

The EISA bus master (except a platform CPU) waits until the EX16* and EX32* signal line is sampled active when the CMD* signal line is active to complete the total access cycle.

Figures 3-8-A to D provide examples of the E-MIX version of the EISA standard access cycle. The E-MIX version of the EISA data-matching access cycle is not shown, but is simply a regular EISA data-matching cycle with EX16* and EX32* driven at the end of the cycle, and DATA (read) redriven.

The EISA Rev. 3.12 bus specification indicates that at the end of the E-MIX access cycle the EX16* signal line is driven active if the MASTER16* signal line = 0 to indicate a 16 data bit EISA bus master. Similarly, the EX32* signal line is driven active if the MASTER16* line = 1 to indicate a 32 data bit EISA bus master. The Intel 358DT chip set indicates that both the EX16* and EX32* signal lines are driven active at the end of the cycle. For compatibility reasons, the EISA bus master should use the EISA bus specification definition.

By convention, an 8 data bit EISA memory resource is "identical" to an 8 data bit ISA or E-ISA memory resource. The EISA memory resource only uses ISA and E-ISA compatible signal lines. Consequently, the EISA bus master must use an E-MIX access cycle to access any 8 data bit memory resource. Also by convention, an 8 data bit EISA I/O resource cannot be distinguished from an 8 data bit ISA or E-ISA I/O resource. The EISA I/O resource uses the EISA compatible signal lines and the NOWS* signal line in a "special way". Consequently, the EISA bus master must use an E-MIX access cycle to access any 8 data bit I/O resource. See Chapter 6 for more information.

3.3 ISA AND E-ISA BUS MASTER ACCESS CYCLES TO EISA RESOURCES ON EISA PLATFORMS

The seventh type of access cycle supported on an EISA platform is the I-MIX access cycle. (See Table 3-1-B for a summary of when an I-MIX access cycle is executed.) The I-MIX access cycle is executed by platform circuitry when an ISA or E-ISA add-on bus owner card accesses an EISA compatible resource. The I-MIX access cycle relies on the intermixing of EISA and ISA access cycles. From the ISA or E-ISA bus master's viewpoint, the I-MIX access cycle permits the ISA ready access cycle to access a 16 data bit EISA compatible memory or I/O resource. Also, from the ISA or E-ISA bus master's viewpoint, the I-MIX access cycle implements an ISA ready access cycle for an 8 data bit EISA compatible I/O resource. The EISA compatible 16 data bit accessed resource implements the EISA standard and ready access cycles. The 8 data bit EISA compatible I/O resource implements a "special version" of the EISA standard and ready access cycles. (See Figure 3-9.)

The 8 data bit EISA memory resource operates in an identical fashion to an ISA or E-ISA 8 data bit resource. Consequently, the ISA or E-ISA bus master executes ISA standard, ready, or no-wait-state access cycles without the platform circuitry and therefore without I-MIX.

The I-MIX access cycle begins with the ISA bus master driving the LA<17-23>, SA<0-19>, and SBHE* signal lines valid. These signal lines are translated into the LA<2-16> and BE*<0-3> signal lines by the platform circuitry. Subsequently, the ISA bus master drives one of the COMMAND (MEMR*, MEMW*, IOR*, and IOW*) signal lines active. The platform circuitry translates the active COMMAND signal line and drives the M-IO and W-R signal lines valid, and drives the START* signal line active. The platform circuitry also drives the IOCHRDY signal line inactive because of the time constraints for a valid IOCHRDY signal line to be returned to the ISA or E-ISA bus master.

After a minimum period of time, the START* signal line is driven inactive and the CMD* signal line is driven active. Simultaneously, the EISA accessed resource has driven the EX16*, EX32*, and EXRDY signal lines valid. The platform circuitry translates these signal lines into the MEMCS16* and IOCHRDY signal lines. The EISA slave also drives the IOCS16* signal lines valid if appropriate. (See Chapter 6 for more information as to why an EISA accessed resource is driving an ISA compatible signal line.)

For a write access cycle to a 16 data bit EISA resource, the platform circuitry monitors the EXRDY signal lines and accordingly drives the CMD* and IOCHRDY signal lines active and inactive, respectively. Once the IOCHRDY signal line is driven active, the ISA or E-ISA bus master can terminate the access cycle according to the ISA access cycle protocol.

For a read access cycle, the platform circuitry monitors the EXRDY signal lines and accordingly drives the IOCHRDY signal lines inactive. Once the IOCHRDY signal line is driven active, the ISA bus master can terminate the access cycle according to the ISA access cycle specifications. The platform circuitry holds the CMD* signal line active until the ISA bus master drives the appropriate COMMAND signal line inactive to insure that the data read from the EISA resource is valid for the ISA bus master.

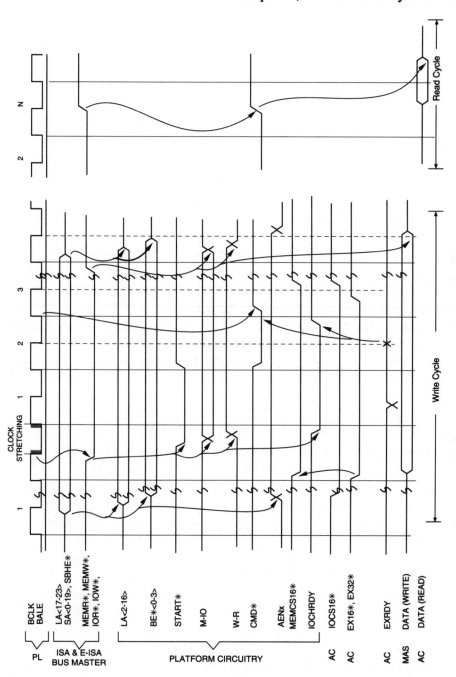

FIGURE   3-9:   *GENERIC I-MIX ACCESS CYCLE (ISA BUS OWNER CARD TO EISA 16 DATA BIT ACCESSED RESOURCE)*

3.4 DMA TRANSFER CYCLES ON ISA AND E-ISA PLATFORMS

Transfer cycles operate differently than access cycles. A transfer cycle is executed only by the platform DMA controller to transfer data between I/O and memory resources.

There are two versions of transfer cycles: standard and ready. The execution of either version of the transfer cycle begins with the activation of both a single DMA acknowledge (DACKx*) signal line and the AENx signal line by the platform. (See Figures 3-10 and 3-11.) The activation of these lines is in response to an I/O resource driving a DMA request (DRQx) signal line active. The activation of the DACKx* signal line defines which I/O resource is part of the transfer, and that a transfer cycle is beginning. The AENx line indicates to all other I/O resources that a transfer cycle specific to an I/O resource is occurring, and that the ADDRESS and COMMAND lines must be ignored. Figure 3-10 illustrates the I/O read and memory write transfer cycle, and Figure 3-11 illustrates the I/O write and memory read transfer cycles.

The LA<17-23> and SA<0-19> signal lines are both driven valid prior to the activation of the memory COMMAND signal lines. They are held constant for the entire cycle. The ADDRESS signal lines are only referenced to the memory COMMAND signal lines, because only the memory resources can be addressed. The I/O resources involved in the cycle are "accessed" solely by enabling their specific DACKx* signal line.

The length of the COMMAND pulses for the standard transfer cycle is predetermined. A standard transfer cycle becomes a ready transfer cycle if the memory resource deactivates the IOCHRDY within a specific time relative to an active memory COMMAND line. The memory COMMAND line will remain active until the IOCHRDY signal line becomes active.

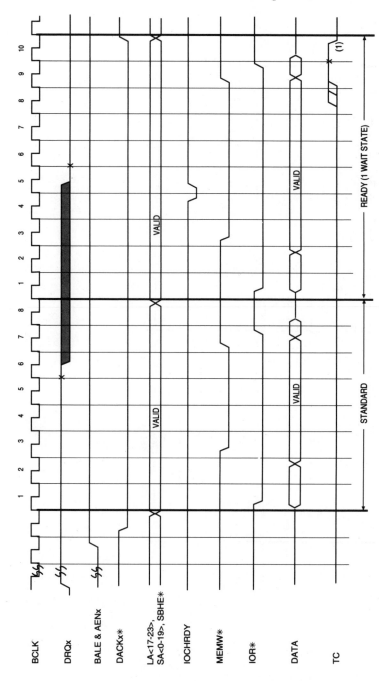

X = SAMPLING POINT
(1) INPUT TO DMA E-ISA AND EISA COMPATIBLE PLATFORMS ONLY

*FIGURE   3-10:   GENERIC COMPATIBLE TRANSFER CYCLE
(I/O READ-MEMORY WRITE)*

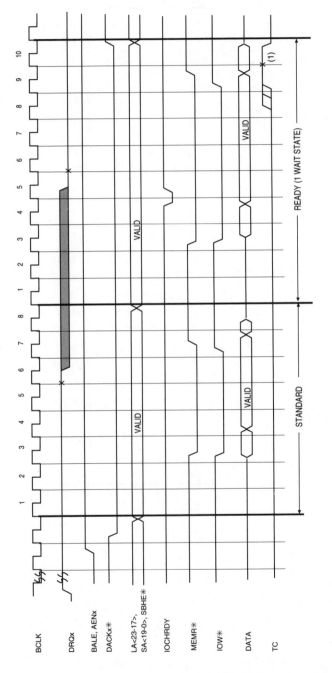

FIGURE 3-11:   GENERIC COMPATIBLE TRANSFER CYCLE (I/O WRITE-MEMORY READ)

The increase in the length of a ready cycle is a multiple of two BCLK periods on an ISA platform. The E-ISA platform extends the ready cycles in multiples of one and two BCLK periods. The ISA platform implementation of the IOCHRDY line does not reference it directly to the BCLK line; however, the E-ISA platform implementation does. See Chapter 5 for more detailed information.

During a transfer cycle, only the memory resource can inactivate the IOCHRDY signal line. The I/O resource must be ready for the transfer within the cycle length of a standard cycle.

On an ISA compatible platform, the bus contains several DMA channels. An add-on slave card can be either the I/O or memory resource in the transfer. Each DMA channel has a pair of DMA request and acknowledge lines. DMA channels numbered 0-3 support only 8 data bit transfers, and channels numbered 5-7 support only 16 data bit transfers. 16 data bit memory resources are designed to allow single bytes to be read and written; consequently, an 8 data bit I/O resource can interact with a 16 data bit memory resource. The 16 data bit I/O resource does not allow single bytes to be read or written. Therefore, transfers between 16 bit I/O and 8 data bit memory resources are not supported. These restrictions allow the data to be transferred in a single transfer cycle. Table 3-2 summarizes DMA transfer cycles in ISA compatible platforms.

PLATFORM	PARTICIPANTS MEMORY : I/O	TRANSFER TYPES COMP	"A"	"B"	"C"	TC (1)	RESOURCE SIZE MEM:I/O		TRANSFER SIZE	DEMAND & BLOCK TRANSFER INTERRUPTIBLE
PC,XT	PC,XT : PC,XT	YES	NO	NO	NO	UNI	8	8	8	NO
AT	PC,XT : PC,XT	YES	NO	NO	NO	UNI	8	8	8	NO
	PC,XT : AT	YES	NO	NO	NO	UNI	8	8	8	NO
	AT : PC,XT	YES	NO	NO	NO	UNI	8/16	8	8	NO
	AT : AT	YES	NO	NO	NO	UNI	8/16	8	8	NO
							16	16	16	NO

TABLE 3-2: ISA COMPATIBLE PLATFORM DMA TRANSFER CYCLES
NOTE:
(1) UNI = UNIdirectional ... DMA controller to I/O resource. BI = BIdirectional.

The EISA bus specification has expanded the definition to support TYPE A, TYPE B, and TYPE C (BURST) transfer cycles in addition to the COMPATIBLE transfer cycles. E-ISA platforms support have adopted TYPE A and TYPE B transfer cycles WITHOUT "CONVERSION" in addition to supporting the COMPATIBLE transfer cycle. The conditions for support of the TYPE A and TYPE B transfer cycles on an E-ISA compatible platform are as follows:

- The memory resource must be the platform memory.

- The I/O resource data size must be less than or equal to the data size of the memory resource.

- The I/O resource is designed for TYPE A and TYPE B transfer cycles, and the associated DMA channels have been programmed for these transfer cycle types.

- The DMA controller on an E-ISA platform allows each DMA channel to be programmed individually for 8 or 16 data bits.

Table 3-3 outlines the broader transfer cycle support on an E-ISA platform.

PLATFORM	PARTICIPANTS MEMORY : I/O	TRANSFER TYPES COMP	"A"	"B"	"C"	TC (1)	RESOURCE SIZE MEM: I/O	TRANSFER SIZE	DEMAND & BLOCK TRANSFER INTERRUPTIBLE
E-ISA	PC,XT :PC,XT,AT	YES	NO	NO	NO	UNI	8 8	8	NO
	AT : PC,XT	YES	NO	NO	NO	UNI	8,16 8	8	NO
	AT : AT	YES	NO	NO	NO	UNI	8,16 8 16 16	8 16	NO
	PC,XT : E-ISA	YES	NO	NO	NO	BI	8 8	8	NO
	AT : E-ISA	YES	NO	NO	NO	BI	8,16 8 16 16	8 16	NO
	E-ISA : PC,XT (2)	YES	NO	NO	NO	UNI	8,16 8	8	NO
	E-ISA : AT (2)	YES	NO	NO	NO	UNI	8,16 8 16 16	8 16	NO
	E-ISA : E-ISA (2)	YES	NO	NO	NO	BI	8,16 8 16 16	8 16	NO
	E-ISA : PC,XT (3) (4)	YES	YES	YES	NO	UNI	8,16 8	8	YES (5)
	E-ISA : AT (3) (4)	YES	YES	YES	NO	UNI	8,16 8 16 16	8 16	YES (5)
	E-ISA : E-ISA (3) (4)	YES	YES	YES	NO	BI	8,16 8 16 16	8 16	YES (5)

TABLE 3-3: E-ISA COMPATIBLE PLATFORM DMA TRANSFER CYCLES

NOTES:
(1) UNI = UNIdirectional ... DMA controller to I/O resource. BI = BIdirectional.
(2) E-ISA memory is an add-on card ONLY.
(3) E-ISA memory is the platform memory ONLY.
(4) MOST AT, PC, and XT DMA add-on slave cards support the TYPE A transfer cycle. SOME AT, PC, and XT DMA add-on slave cards support the TYPE B transfer cycle.
(5) "NO" if DMA COMPATIBLE transfer cycle.

On the E-ISA compatible platform, the basic operation of the COMPATIBLE cycle is the same as on the ISA compatible platform. (See Figures 3-10 and 3-11.) The operation of the TYPE A and TYPE B transfer cycles are similar to the COMPATIBLE transfer cycles except cycle length and associated cycle timings have been shortened. In that only the platform memory is the memory resource, the focal point of these transfer cycles are the I/O resource. Also, the length of the TYPE A and TYPE B transfer cycles can be lengthened in increments of one BCLK signal line periods. The IOCHRDY signal line is not shown in the following figures because only platform memory is used. The comparison of the transfer cycle lengths are outlined in Figure 3-12. Figures 3-13-A and B and 3-14-A and B outline I/O read and I/O write transfer cycles, respectively.

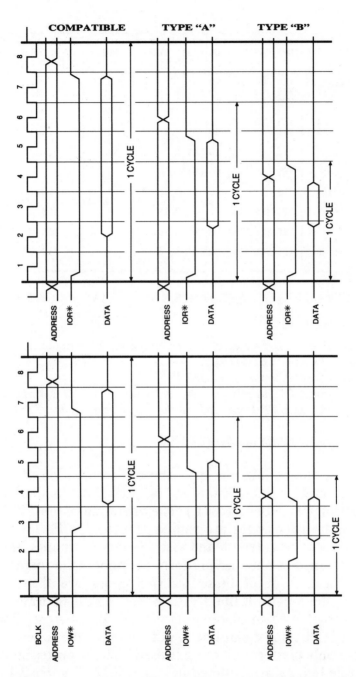

*FIGURE 3-12:   RELATIVE ADDRESS, COMMAND AND DATA SIGNAL DURATIONS
FOR AN E-ISA PLATFORM (STANDARD CYCLE EXAMPLE)*

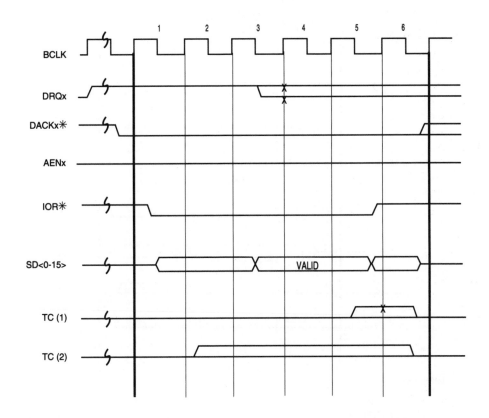

X = SAMPLING POINT
    (E-ISA ONLY)
(1) = INPUT TO PLATFORM
(2) = OUTPUT TO PLATFORM

FIGURE 3-13-A: TYPE A STANDARD E-ISA & EISA ONLY. . . I/O READ
TRANSFER CYCLE

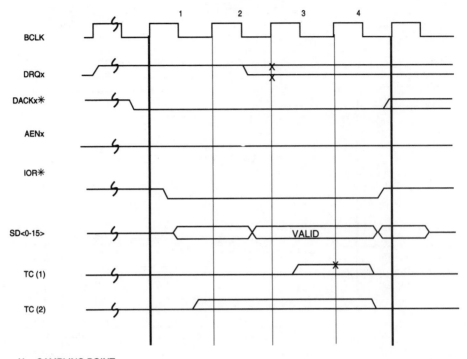

X = SAMPLING POINT
      (E-ISA ONLY)
(1) = INPUT TO PLATFORM
(2) = OUTPUT TO PLATFORM

*FIGURE   3-13-B: TYPE B STANDARD E-ISA AND EISA ONLY. . . I/O READ
                    TRANSFER CYCLE*

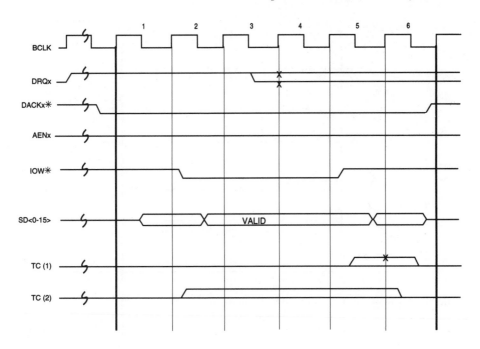

X = SAMPLING POINT
(1) = INPUT TO PLATFORM
(2) = OUTPUT TO PLATFORM

FIGURE 3-14-A: TYPE A STANDARD E-ISA & EISA ONLY... I/O WRITE TRANSFER CYCLE

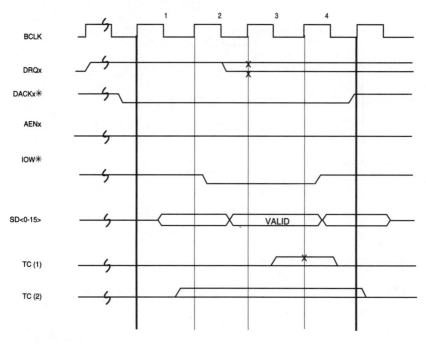

X = SAMPLING POINT
(1) = INPUT TO PLATFORM
(2) = OUTPUT TO PLATFORM

FIGURE   3-14-B: TYPE B STANDARD E-ISA & EISA ONLY. . . I/O WRITE
TRANSFER CYCLE

3.5 DMA TRANSFER CYCLES ON EISA PLATFORMS

As mentioned above, the EISA bus specification has expanded the definition of transfer cycles to support TYPE A, TYPE B, and TYPE C (also called BURST) transfer cycles in addition to the COMPATIBLE transfer cycles. The EISA platform operates these transfer cycles in the same fashion as the ISA and E-ISA platforms with the following enhancements:

- COMPATIBLE transfer cycles include ISA, E-ISA, and EISA compatible memory located on both platform and add-on slave cards.

- TYPE A and TYPE B transfer cycles include ISA, E-ISA, and EISA compatible memory located on both platform and add-on slave cards. CONVERSION allows these transfer cycles to occur with ISA and E-ISA compatible memory add-on slave cards, which were not supported on the E-ISA platform for TYPE A and TYPE B transfer cycles.

- TYPE A and TYPE B transfer cycles are supported between I/O resources with a data size greater than the data size of the memory resource. CONVERSION allows the support of this data size mismatch.

- The EISA platform also supports the TYPE C transfer cycle. The primary purpose of the TYPE C transfer cycle is to do "burst-like" transfer cycles between EISA compatible memory and I/O resources.

- TYPE C transfer cycles include ISA, E-ISA, and EISA compatible memory located on both platform and add-on slave cards. "CONVERSION" allows the TYPE C transfer cycle to interface with ISA and E-ISA add-on memory slave cards.

- TYPE C transfer cycles are supported between I/O resources with a data size greater than the data size of the memory resource. "CONVERSION" allows the support of this data size mismatch.

Table 3-4 outlines the broader transfer cycle support on an EISA platform.

PARTICIPANTS MEMORY: I/O	TRANSFER TYPES							TC (2)	RESOURCE SIZE MEM:I/O		TRANSFER SIZE (5)	DEMAND & BLOCK XFER INTERUP-TIBLE
	COMP	"A"	"A"/W CONV (1)	"B"	"B"/W CONV (1)	"C" (7)(8)	"C"/W CONV (1,7)(6)					
PC,XT:PC,XT (3)	YES	NO	YES	NO	YES	NO	NO	UNI	8	8	8	YES
PC,XT : AT (3)	YES	NO	YES	NO	YES	NO	NO	UNI	8	8	8	
	NO	NO	YES	NO	YES	NO	NO	UNI	8	16	2x8 MULT	
PC,XT:E-ISA	YES	NO	YES	NO	YES	NO	NO	BI	8	8	8	
	NO	NO	YES	NO	YES	NO	NO	BI	8	16	2x8 MULT	
AT, E-ISA :PC,XT (3)	YES	NO	YES	NO	YES	NO	NO	UNI	8,16	8	8	
AT, E-ISA :E-ISA	YES	NO	YES	NO	YES	NO	NO	BI	8,16	8	8	
AT,E-ISA:AT (3)	YES	NO	YES	NO	YES	NO	NO	UNI	8,16	8	8	
	YES	NO	YES	NO	YES	NO	NO	UNI	16	16	16	
	NO	NO	YES	NO	YES	NO	NO	UNI	8	16	2x8 MULT	
AT, E-ISA :E-ISA	YES	NO	YES	NO	YES	NO	NO	BI	8,16	8	8	
	YES	NO	YES	NO	YES	NO	NO	BI	16	16	16	
	NO	NO	YES	NO	YES	NO	NO	BI	8	16	2x8 MULT	
PC,XT : EISA	YES	NO	YES	NO	YES	NO	YES	BI	8	8	8	
	NO	NO	YES	NO	YES	NO	YES	BI	8	16	2x8 MULT	
	NO	NO	YES	NO	YES	NO	YES	BI	8	32	4x8 MULT	
EISA : PC,XT (3)	YES	NO	YES	NO	YES	NO	NO	UNI	8	8	8	
	YES	YES	NO	YES	NO	NO	NO	UNI	16,32	8	8	
AT, E-ISA :EISA	YES	NO	YES	NO	YES	NO	YES	BI	8,16	8	8	
	YES	NO	YES	NO	YES	NO	YES	BI	16	16	16	
	NO	NO	YES	NO	YES	NO	YES	BI	8	16	2x8 MULT	
	NO	NO	YES	NO	YES	NO	YES	BI	8	32	4x8 MULT	
	NO	NO	YES	NO	YES	NO	YES	BI	16	32	2x16MULT	
EISA : AT (3)	YES	NO	YES	NO	YES	NO	NO	UNI	8	8	8	
	YES	YES	NO	YES	NO	NO	NO	UNI	16,32	8	8	
	NO	NO	YES	NO	YES	NO	NO	UNI	8	16	2x8 MULT	
	YES	YES	NO	YES	NO	NO	NO	UNI	16,32	16	16	
EISA:E-ISA	YES	NO	YES	NO	YES	NO	NO	BI	8	8	8	
	YES	YES	NO	YES	NO	NO	NO	BI	16,32	8	8	
	NO	NO	YES	NO	YES	NO	NO	BI	8	16	2x8 MULT	
	YES	YES	NO	YES	NO	NO	NO	BI	16,32	16	16	

PARTICIPANTS MEMORY : I/O	COMP	"A"	"A"/W CONV (1)	"B"	"B"/W CONV (1)	"C" (7)(8)	"C"/W CONV (1,7)(6)	TC (2)	RESOURCE SIZE MEM:I/O	TRANSFER SIZE (5)	DEMAND & BLOCK XFER INTERUP-TIBLE
EISA : EISA	YES	NO	YES	NO	YES	YES	YES	BI	8 8	8	YES
	YES	YES	NO	YES	NO	YES	YES	BI	16,32 8	8	
	YES	YES	NO	YES	NO	YES	YES	BI	16,32 16	16	
	YES	YES	NO	YES	NO	YES	YES	BI	32 32	32	
	NO	NO	YES	NO	YES	NO	YES	BI	8 16	2x8 MULT	
	NO	NO	YES	NO	YES	NO	YES	BI	8 32	4x8 MULT	
	NO	NO	YES	NO	YES	NO	YES	BI	16 32	2x16MULT	
PLAT. EISA MEMORY: EISA	YES	YES	NO	YES	NO	YES	YES	BI	8 8	8	
	YES	YES	NO	YES	NO	YES	YES	BI	16,32 8	8	
	YES	YES	NO	YES	NO	YES	YES	BI	16,32 16	16	
	YES	YES	NO	YES	NO	YES	YES	BI	32 32	32	
	NO	NO	YES	NO	YES	NO	YES	BI	8 16	2x8 MULT	
	NO	NO	YES	NO	YES	NO	YES	BI	8 32	4x8 MULT	
	NO	NO	YES	NO	YES	NO	YES	BI	16 32	2x16MULT	
PLAT. EISA MEMORY:PC,XT (3)	YES	YES	NO	YES	NO	NO	NO	UNI	8 8	8	
	YES	YES	NO	YES	NO	NO	NO	UNI	16,32 8	8	
PLAT. EISA MEMORY:AT (3)	YES	YES	NO	YES	NO	NO	NO	UNI	8 8	8	
	YES	YES	NO	YES	NO	NO	NO	UNI	16,32 16	16	
	YES	NO	YES	NO	YES	NO	NO	UNI	8 16	2x8 MULT	
PLAT. EISA MEMORY :E-ISA	YES	YES	NO	YES	NO	NO	NO	BI	8 8	8	
	YES	YES	NO	YES	NO	NO	NO	BI	16,32 16	16	
	YES	NO	YES	NO	YES	NO	NO	BI	8 16	2x8 MULT	

TABLE 3-4: EISA COMPATIBLE PLATFORM DMA TRANSFER CYCLES

NOTES:

"w/CONV" means "with CONVERSION"

Demand and Block transfers are interruptible EXCEPT when DMA COMPATIBLE transfer cycles are executed.

(1) A "YES" in this column, when the memory data size is greater than or equal to the I/O data size, indicates a "SINGLE CONVERSION" cycle without multiple reads or writes of the memory resource. From the I/O resource viewpoint, the timing is that of a COMPATIBLE TRANSFER CYCLE. Otherwise, a "MULTIPLE CONVERSION" cycle is executed. "W/CONV." means "with conversion".

(2) UNI = UNIdirectional ... DMA controller to I/O resource. BI = BIdirectional.

(3) MOST AT, PC, and XT DMA add-on slave cards can support the TYPE A transfer cycle, and SOME AT, PC, and XT DMA add-on slave cards can support the TYPE B transfer cycle.

(5) MULT = "MULTIPLE CONVERSION" ... when the memory resource data size is smaller than the I/O resource data size, multiple assembly/disassembly will occur.

(6) A "YES" in this column, when an EISA compatible memory resource is involved, indicates that the memory data size is greater than or equal to the I/O data size, and the memory resource did not drive the SLBURST* signal line active.

(7) All transfer cycle types support SINGLE, DEMAND, and BLOCK DMA modes except TYPE C and TYPE C with conversion, which only support DEMAND and BLOCK DMA modes.
(8) A "YES" in this column indicates that the memory resource drove the SLBURST* signal line active.

Transfer cycles operate differently than access cycles. A transfer cycle is executed only by the platform DMA controller to transfer data between I/O and memory resources.

On an EISA platform, the DMA controller drives the ISA, E-ISA, and EISA signal lines. For a DMA COMPATIBLE transfer cycle, ISA and E-ISA compatible MEMR*, MEMW*, BALE, SA, and SBHE* signal lines are driven valid in case the memory resource is ISA or E-ISA compatible. The DMA controller must monitor the IOCHRDY and EXRDY signal lines to properly control the length of the cycle. If the memory resource drives the EXRDY (for EISA) or IOCHRDY (for ISA or E-ISA) signal lines, the transfer cycle length is extended as a ready transfer cycle. Otherwise, the length of the transfer cycle is the standard transfer cycle. (See Figures 3-15-A and 3-15-B.) For a DMA COMPATIBLE transfer cycle, the data size of the memory resource must be greater than or equal to the data size of the I/O resource.

As with the DMA COMPATIBLE transfer cycle, the TYPE A, TYPE B, and TYPE C transfer cycles can be supported on an EISA compatible platform. As for a DMA COMPATIBLE transfer cycle, the ISA and E-ISA compatible MEMR*, MEMW*, SA, and SBHE* signal lines are driven valid in case the memory resource is ISA or E-ISA compatible. The DMA controller must monitor the IOCHRDY and EXRDY signal lines to properly control the length of the cycle. If the memory resource drives the EXRDY (for EISA) or IOCHRDY (for ISA or E-ISA) signal lines, the transfer cycle length is extended as a ready transfer cycle. Otherwise, the length of the transfer cycle is the standard transfer cycle. (See Figures 3-16-A, B, C, and D.)

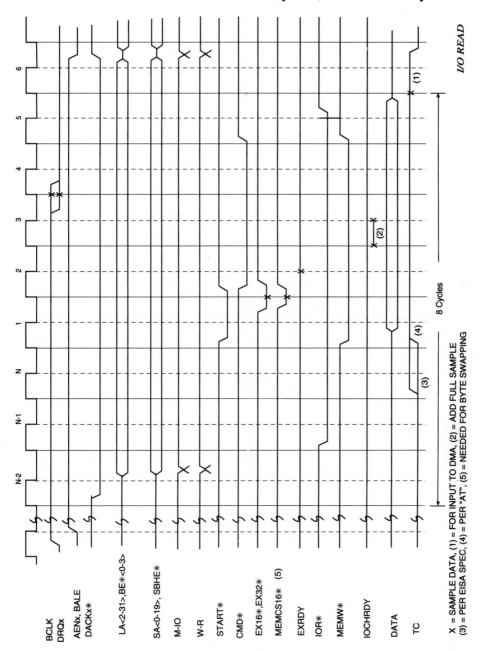

I/O READ

8 Cycles

X = SAMPLE DATA, (1) = FOR INPUT TO DMA, (2) = ADD FULL SAMPLE
(3) = PER EISA SPEC, (4) = PER "AT", (5) = NEEDED FOR BYTE SWAPPING

BCLK
DRQx
AENx, BALE
DACKx*
LA<2-31>,BE*<0-3>
SA<0-19>, SBHE*
M-IO
W-R
START*
CMD*
EX16*,EX32*
MEMCS16* (5)
EXRDY
IOR*
MEMW*
IOCHRDY
DATA
TC

*FIGURE 3-15-A: ISA, E-ISA & EISA STANDARD AND READY COMPATIBLE
TRANSFER CYCLE. . . DMA CONTROLLER & PLATFORM
CIRCUITRY VIEWPOINT*

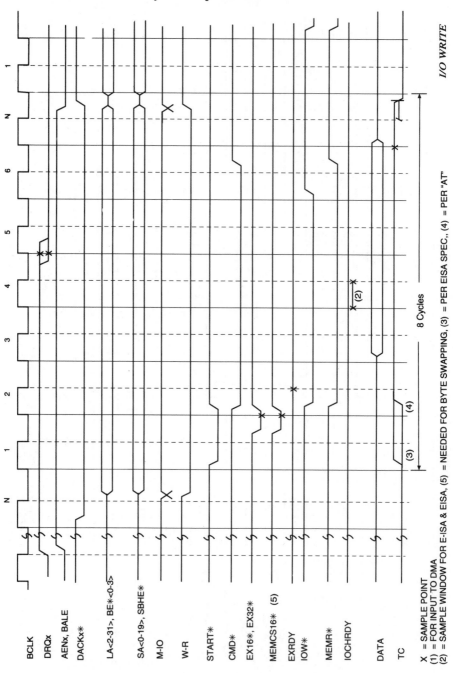

FIGURE   3-15-B: *ISA, E-ISA & EISA STANDARD AND READY COMPATIBLE TRANSFER CYCLE . . . DMA CONTROLLER & PLATFORM CIRCUITRY VIEWPOINT*

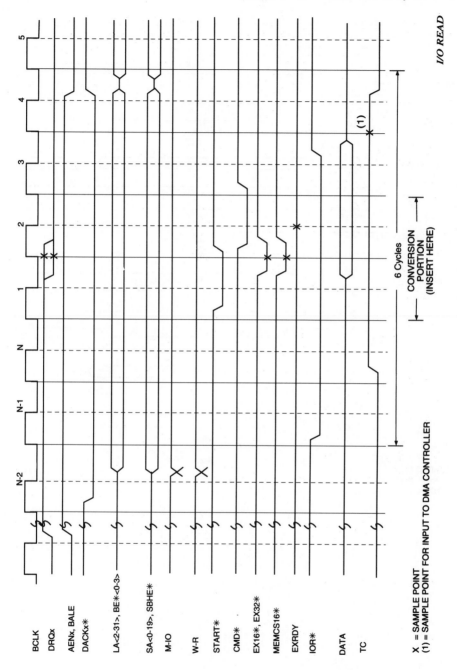

FIGURE 3-16-A: *E-ISA & EISA STANDARD AND READY TYPE A TRANSFER CYCLE... DMA CONTROLLER & PLATFORM CIRCUITRY VIEWPOINT*

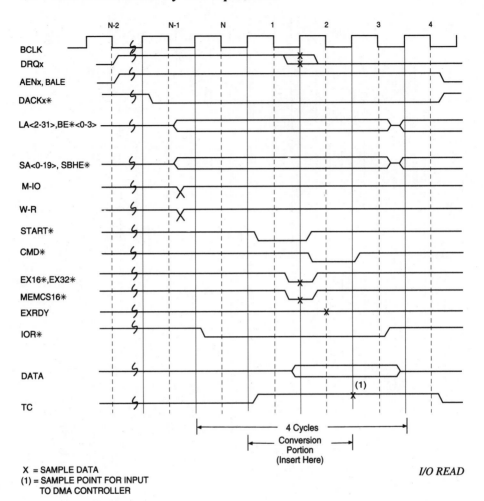

X = SAMPLE DATA
(1) = SAMPLE POINT FOR INPUT
       TO DMA CONTROLLER

I/O READ

*FIGURE   3-16-B: E-ISA & EISA STANDARD AND READY TYPE B TRANSFER
                     CYCLE (NO CONVERSION) . . . DMA CONTROLLER AND
                     PLATFORM CIRCUITRY VIEWPOINT*

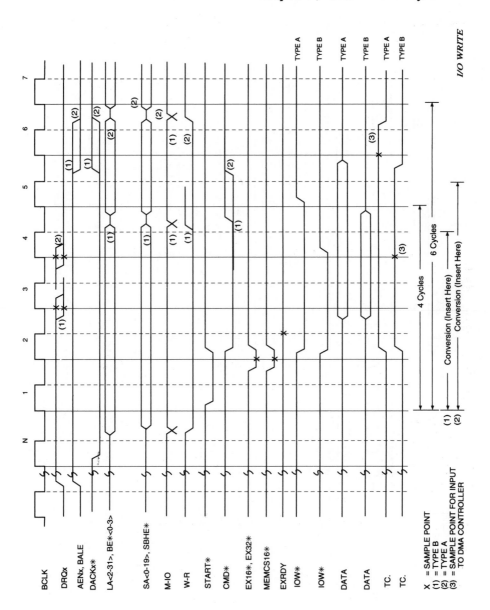

FIGURE 3-16-C: *E-ISA & EISA STANDARD AND READY TYPE A & B TRANSFER CYCLE (NO CONVERSION). . . DMA CONTROLLER & PLATFORM VIEWPOINT*

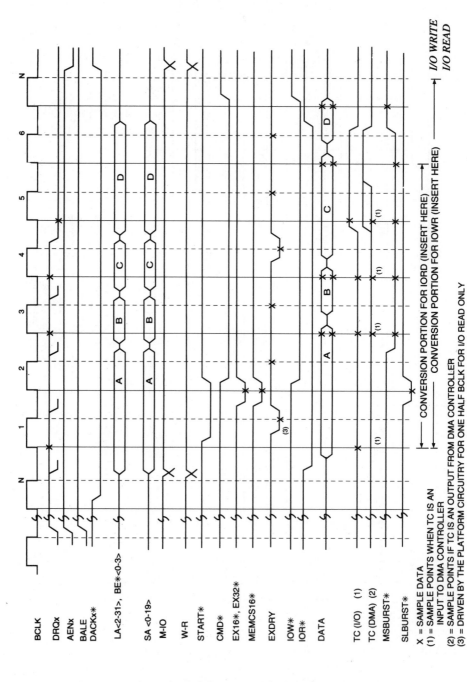

FIGURE   3-16-D: E-ISA AND EISA STANDARD AND READY TYPE C (BURST)
TRANSFER CYCLE (NO CONVERSION) . . . DMA CONTROLLER
& PLATFORM VIEWPOINT

The DMA COMPATIBLE transfer cycle is only supported between ISA, E-ISA (add-on slave card), and EISA (platform or add-on slave card) compatible memory resources. Also, the data size of the I/O resource must be less than or equal to the data size of the memory resource. The DMA TYPE A, TYPE B, and TYPE C transfer cycles on an EISA compatible platform support a broader set of memory resources than on an E-ISA compatible platform due to CONVERSION as follows:

- For a DMA TYPE A, TYPE B, or TYPE C transfer cycle, the memory resource does not have to be a platform resource. The memory resource can be an ISA or E-ISA add-on slave card. If the memory resource is ISA or E-ISA compatible, the DMA controller does a CONVERSION version of the transfer cycle.

- If the data size of the memory resource is less than the I/O resource, the transfer cycle for a DMA TYPE A, TYPE B, or TYPE C is completed as a CONVERSION version of the transfer cycle.

- In order for the DMA controller to properly execute the transfer cycle, it must monitor the MEMCS16*, EX16*, and EX32* signal lines. These signal lines indicate memory resource type and data size.

The CONVERSION version of the transfer cycle is a simple extension of the regular transfer cycle. The DMA controller simply executes access cycles within the CONVERSION PORTION of the transfer cycle. If the memory resource is ISA or E-ISA compatible, the appropriate signal lines are supported. If the data size of the memory resource is less than the I/O resource, the CONVERSION PORTION contains multiple memory accesses with the appropriate signal lines. See Chapter 7 for more detailed information concerning DMA transfer cycles with CONVERSION.

When the DMA transfer cycle is executed without CONVERSION, the increments in ready transfer cycle times are defined as two BCLK signal line periods if a COMPATIBLE transfer cycle is executed. Otherwise, the increment in the ready transfer cycle is one BCLK signal line period.

When the DMA transfer cycle is executed WITH CONVERSION, the memory resource operates as if it is executing an access cycle.

3.6 REFRESH CYCLE

On an ISA or E-ISA compatible platform, the refresh cycle is executed only by the platform refresh controller. There are two versions of the refresh cycle: standard and ready. The execution of either version of the refresh cycle begins with the activation of the REFRESH* signal line. The REFRESH* signal line is driven active by the add-on bus owner card (when it is bus owner) or by the refresh controller. The actual refresh cycle is a simplified memory access cycle. (See Figure 3-17 and 18.) The platform or add-on bus owner card will tri-state the ADDRESS and COMMAND signal lines prior to the refresh controller driving them. The SA<0-7> signal lines contain the valid refresh address. The ADDRESS signal lines are driven valid before the MEMR* and SMEMR* signal lines are driven active. The ADDRESS signal lines are held valid until the COMMAND signal lines are driven inactive.

The length of the standard refresh cycle is predetermined. A standard refresh cycle becomes a ready refresh cycle if the memory resource of the transfer deactivates the IOCHRDY signal line within a specific time relative to active MEMR* signal line. This signal line will remain active until the IOCHRDY signal line becomes active. During a refresh cycle, only the memory resource can inactivate the IOCHRDY signal line.

The increase in the length of a ready cycle is a multiple of one BCLK period.   The ISA platform implementation of the

IOCHRDY signal line does not reference it to the BCLK signal line, but the E-ISA platform implementation does. See Chapters 5 and 8 for more detailed information.

The refresh cycle on an EISA compatible platform is a superset of the refresh cycle on an ISA or E-ISA compatible platform. In addition to the aforementioned signal lines, an EISA compatible platform drives the START*, W-R, CMD*, and LA signal lines. In addition to monitoring the IOCHRDY signal line, the refresh controller also monitors the EXRDY signal line if the cycle needs to be lengthened (in increments of one BCLK signal line periods). The EISA refresh controller places an expanded refresh address on both the LA and SA signal lines.

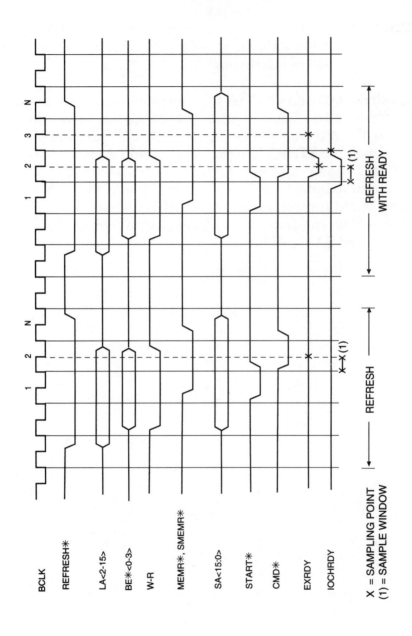

FIGURE   3-17:   REFRESH CYCLE TIMING

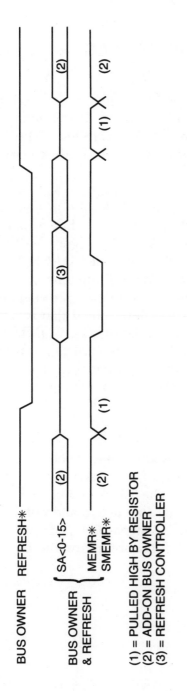

FIGURE 3-18: *ISA OR E-ISA ADD-ON BUS OWNER CARD REFRESH REQUEST*

3.7 ARBITRATION CYCLE

There are two methods for add-on bus owner cards to arbitrate for bus ownership.   ISA and E-ISA add-on bus owner cards "sublease" bus ownership from the DMA controller.   The EISA add-on bus owner cards arbitrate through central arbiter circuitry on the platform.

The arbitration cycle for an ISA or E-ISA add-on bus owner card begins as a DMA transfer cycle. The add-on bus owner card drives one of the DRQx signal lines active. (See Figure 3-19.) The DMA controller responds by driving the associated DACKx* signal line active. The add-on bus owner card has a finite amount of time to drive the MASTER16* signal line active to obtain ownership of the bus. Once the DMA controller has determined that it is not a normal transfer cycle, it tri-states the ADDRESS, COMMAND, and DATA signal lines. The add-on bus owner card can proceed to execute access cycles to memory and I/O resources. The add-on bus owner card relinquishes bus ownership by driving the DRQx and MASTER16* signal lines inactive. See Chapter 9 for more detailed information.

The arbitration cycle for EISA add-on bus owner cards are simpler. Each slot (that can support a bus master) has a pair of signal lines MREQx* and MAKx*. The EISA add-on bus owner card simply drives the MREQx* signal line active and obtains bus ownership when the associated MAKx* signal line is driven active by the central arbiter. See Chapter 9 for more information.

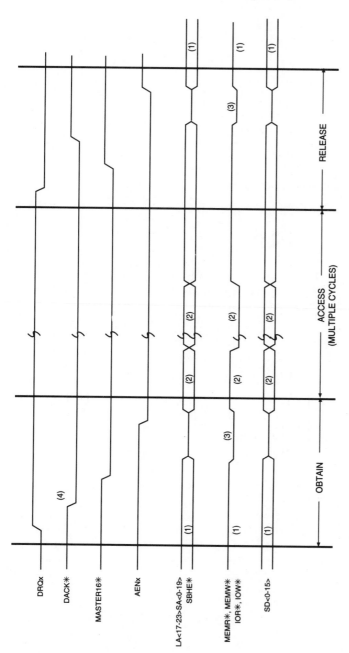

FIGURE` 3-19:   *ARBITRATION CYCLE*

(1) DRIVEN BY DMA CONTROLLER
(2) DRIVEN BY ADD-ON BUS OWNER CARD
(3) PULLED UP BY RESISTOR
(4) INDETERMINATE PERIOD OF TIME

Notes

CHAPTER FOUR

INTERACTION AMONG ISA, E-ISA, and EISA ADD-ON CARDS AND PLATFORM RESOURCES

This Chapter consists of the following Subchapters.

4.0 GENERAL INFORMATION
4.1 ISA COMPATIBLE ADD-ON SLAVE CARDS
4.2 ISA COMPATIBLE ADD-ON BUS OWNER CARDS
4.3 E-ISA COMPATIBLE ADD-ON SLAVE CARDS
4.4 E-ISA COMPATIBLE ADD-ON BUS OWNER CARDS
4.5 EISA COMPATIBLE ADD-ON SLAVE CARDS
4.6 EISA COMPATIBLE ADD-ON BUS OWNER CARDS
4.7 REFRESH
4.8 ARBITRATION

4.0 GENERAL INFORMATION

An add-on card can operate in two basic modes on the bus: either as a slave or as a bus owner. An add-on card can be designed to support either or both modes. The interaction details between add-on cards are sometimes different than the interaction between add-on cards and platform resources.

As outlined in Chapter 1, add-on card resources can also reside on the platform. The exact add-on card resources that reside on the platform vary from platform to platform. Thus, in order to understand the operation of the ISA, E-ISA, and EISA buses the following conventions have been adopted:

- The main focus of this book is the operation of the ISA, E-ISA or EISA bus relative to add-on cards.

- The platform CPU accessing a platform resource, such as platform memory, will not execute a bus cycle. Similarly, the DMA controller executing a transfer cycle between platform resources will not execute a bus cycle.

- A platform CPU accessing an add-on slave card will generate a bus cycle. Similarly, an add-on bus owner card accessing an add-on slave card or a platform resource will also execute a bus cycle. Finally, a DMA controller executing a transfer cycle involving an add-on slave card will execute a bus cycle.

TO PROVIDE THE PROPER FOCUS, THE EMPHASIS OF THIS BOOK IS ON THE PLATFORM CPU ACCESSING AN ADD-ON SLAVE CARD. AN ADD-ON BUS MASTER CARD ACCESSING AN ADD-ON SLAVE CARD OR PLATFORM RESOURCE IS COVERED BY THIS METHOD. IF THERE IS ANY DIFFERENCE BETWEEN AN ACCESS TO A PLATFORM RESOURCE OR AN ADD-ON SLAVE CARD IT WILL BE NOTED. THUS ANY DISCUSSION OF AN ADD-ON SLAVE CARD ACCESS BY AN ADD-ON BUS OWNER CARD IS APPLICABLE TO AN ACCESS TO A PLATFORM RESOURCE.

SIMILARLY, THE FOCUS OF A DMA TRANSFER CYCLE IS BETWEEN ADD-ON MEMORY AND I/O SLAVE CARD RESOURCES. IF THE I/O PARTICIPANT IS A PLATFORM RESOURCE, IT WILL FUNCTION IN THE SAME FASHION AS AN ADD-ON SLAVE CARD AND IS COVERED BY THIS METHOD. IF THE MEMORY PARTICIPANT IS A PLATFORM RESOURCE, IT WILL NOT ALWAYS FUNCTION AS AN ADD-ON SLAVE CARD; THE IOCHRDY, MCS16*, EXRDY, EX16*, AND EX32* SIGNAL LINES MAY NOT BE DRIVEN ONTO THE BUS BECAUSE THE DMA CONTROLLER IS INTEGRAL TO THE PLATFORM.

HOWEVER, THE BASIC OPERATION IS COVERED BY THE AFOREMENTIONED FOCUS. IF THERE IS ANY DIFFERENCE BETWEEN A TRANSFER CYCLE INVOLVING A PLATFORM RESOURCE OR AN ADD-ON SLAVE CARD IT WILL BE NOTED. THUS ANY DISCUSSION OF TRANSFER CYCLE INVOLVING AN ADD-ON SLAVE CARD IS APPLICABLE TO A PLATFORM RESOURCE.

4.1 ISA COMPATIBLE ADD-ON SLAVE CARDS

An add-on slave card can support bus access and transfer cycles as outlined in Table 1-1. Refresh and arbitration cycles are also supported. ISA add-on slave cards collectively refer to PC, XT and AT add-on cards.

MEMORY ACCESS CYCLES TO ISA COMPATIBLE ADD-ON SLAVE CARDS

An ISA add-on slave card can support memory cycles as an 8 or 16 bit resource. As an 8 data bits resource it can reside in either an 8 bit slot of a PC or XT compatible platform, the 8 or 8/16 bit slot of an ISA or E-ISA compatible platform, or the 8 or 8/16 or 8/16/32 bit slot for an EISA compatible platform. As a 16 bit resource, the add-on slave card can only reside in an 8/16 or 8/16/32 bit slot.

8 DATA BIT MEMORY RESOURCE

An 8 data bit add-on slave card installed in an 8 bit slot only has the first 20 ADDRESS, SMEMR*, and SMEMW* signal lines available. Therefore, an 8 data bit add-on slave card memory cycle is restricted to the first one megabyte of the address space. In order to work properly in AT, E-ISA, and EISA compatible platforms, the SMEMR* and SMEMW* signal lines are only driven active by the platform circuitry for the first one megabyte of the address space. An 8 data bit add-on slave card installed in an 8/16 bit slot has access to all 24 ADDRESS signal lines. Consequently, it can reside anywhere within the 16 megabyte address space. If it wants to respond beyond the first one megabyte, it must only use the MEMR* and MEMW* signal lines and properly decode all of the ADDRESS signal lines.

The various types of access cycles that can be used with an 8 data bit add-on slave card are outlined in Chapter 1 as follows:

- Platform CPU access: Tables 1-2-A and B, and 1-4-A to D

- ISA or E-ISA add-on bus owner card access: Tables 1-3-A to D.

- EISA add-on bus owner card access: Tables 1-4-A to D

16 DATA BIT MEMORY RESOURCE

An add-on slave card that is designed as a 16 bit memory resource can only reside in 8/16 or 8/16/32 bit slots of the various platforms. The MEMR* and MEMW* signal lines, in conjunction with the 24 ADDRESS signal lines, are available to support the full 16 megabyte address space.

The various types of access cycles that can be used with a 16 data bit add-on slave card are outlined in Chapter 1 as follows:

- Platform CPU access: Tables 1-2-A and B, and 1-4-A to D

- ISA or E-ISA add-on bus owner card access: Tables 1-3-A to D

- EISA add-on bus owner card access: Tables 1-4-A to D

An add-on slave card that is designed as a 16 data bit memory resource must support the MEMCS16* signal line. The activation of this line indicates to a platform CPU or add-on bus owner card that either 8 or 16 data bits can be accessed or transferred. It also indicates that the add-on card is either ISA or E-ISA compatible.

The MEMCS16* signal line is monitored by platform CPUs, ISA and E-ISA add-on bus owner cards, and byte swapping circuitry during access cycles and transfer cycles.

> *The add-on slave card cannot use the memory COMMAND signal lines to qualify a 16 bit access. It must blindly decode the LA<17-23> signal lines and activate the MEMCS16* signal line if required. Consequently, the entire 128K byte block selected by LA<17-23> must be the same data width. This "blind" decode does not use the memory or I/O COMMAND signal lines as qualifiers; consequently, it may activate the MEMCS16* signal line during I/O cycles. It is the responsibility of the platform CPU or add-on bus owner card to ignore the MEMCS16* signal line during I/O access cycles.*

A 16 bit resource above the first one megabyte must use the MEMR* or MEMW* signal lines, and not the SMEMR* or SMEMW* signal lines. The latter two command lines are only active for the first one megabyte of the address space.

ISA COMPATIBLE ADD-ON MEMORY SLAVE CARD ISSUES

The use of the SRDY* signal line allows a shorter cycle time. Because a platform CPU or add-on bus owner card is not required to support a no-wait-state access cycle, the add-on slave card must be designed to support the longer standard or ready access cycles even if it activates the SRDY* signal line.

The SRDY* signal line is available on an 8 bit slot on an ISA compatible platform. On the PC and XT compatible platform, this signal line was not used as an SRDY* signal line.

On some AT compatible clone platforms, a no-wait-state cycle is restricted to 16 bit memory resources. A no-wait-state memory access cycle was supported on the IBM AT platform for both 8 and 16 data bit accesses.

The use of the IOCHRDY signal line by ISA compatible add-on slave cards allows the cycle to be extended. Some add-on bus owner cards do not recognize the IOCHRDY signal line, and all of the memory access cycles are run as standard access cycles. An add-on slave card that activates the IOCHRDY signal line will expect a ready access cycle; consequently, the data may not be valid at the end of the standard access cycle. Add-on slave cards should support standard access cycles when being accessed by an ISA compatible add-on bus owner card. When an E-ISA or EISA compatible add-on bus owner card is the bus owner, the IOCHRDY signal line is supported; consequently, a ready access cycle can be executed. See the aforementioned tables in Chapter 1 for more information.

Table 4-1 summarizes which signal lines are driven by which resource during a memory access cycle to an add-on slave card. "PLAT. CIRCUIT" in some cases may simply be a pull-up resistor. In this table, "PLAT." is the abbreviation for "platform". "BUS MASTER" may be either a platform CPU or add-on bus owner card.

LINE	DRIVEN BY	LINE	DRIVEN BY
AENx	PLAT. CIRCUIT	MEMR*	BUS MASTER
BALE	PLAT. CIRCUIT	MEMW*	BUS MASTER
DACKx*	PLAT. DMA	OSC	PLAT. CIRCUIT
DRQx	I/O RESOURCE	REFRESH*	PLAT. REF. CONT.
IOCHK*	ANY RESOURCE	RESET	PLAT. CIRCUIT
IOCHRDY	ADD-ON SLAVE	SA	BUS MASTER
IOCS16*	I/O RESOURCE	SBHE*	BUS MASTER
IOR*	BUS MASTER	SD	BUS MASTER (WR)
IOW*	BUS MASTER	SD	ADD-ON SLAVE (RD)
IRQx	ANY RESOURCE	SMR/SMW*	PLAT. CIRCUIT
LA	BUS MASTER	BCLK	PLAT. CIRCUIT
MASTER*	ADD-ON BUS OWN	TC	PLAT. DMA
MEMCS16*	ADD-ON SLAVE	SRDY*	ADD-ON SLAVE

TABLE 4-1: ISA AND E-ISA ADD-ON SLAVE CARD AS MEMORY RESOURCE

I/O ACCESS CYCLES TO ISA COMPATIBLE ADD-ON SLAVE CARDS

An ISA add-on slave card can support I/O cycles as an 8 or 16 bit resource. As an 8 bit resource, it can reside in either an 8 bit slot of a PC or XT compatible platform, the 8 or 8/16 bit slot of an ISA or E-ISA compatible platform, or the 8 or 8/16 or 8/16/32 bit slot of an EISA compatible platform. As a 16 bit resource, the add-on slave card can only reside in an 8/16 or 8/16/32 bit slot.

8 DATA BIT I/O RESOURCE

An 8 data bit resource installed in either an 8 bit or 8/16 bit slot has access to the first 16 ADDRESS lines, plus the IOR* and IOW* lines. The entire 64K address space in theory could be supported (see the ISA COMPATIBLE ADD-ON I/O SLAVE CARD ISSUES section).

The various types of access cycles that can be used with an 8 data bit add-on slave card are outlined in Chapter 1 as follows:

- Platform CPU access: Tables 1-2-A and B, and 1-4-A to D

- ISA or E-ISA add-on bus owner card access: Tables 1-3-A to D

- EISA add-on bus owner card access: Tables 1-4-A to D

16 DATA BIT I/O RESOURCE

A 16 bit I/O resource can only be installed in 8/16 or 8/16/32 bit slots. It interacts with the bus in nearly the same fashion as an 8 bit resource, since the ADDRESS and COMMAND signal lines are the same in the two cases.

The various types of access cycles that can be used with a 16 data bits add-on slave card are outlined in Chapter 1 as follows:

- Platform CPU access: Tables 1-2A and B, and 1-4-A to D

- ISA or E-ISA add-on bus owner card access: Tables 1-3-A
  to D

- EISA add-on bus owner card access: Tables 1-4-A to D

An add-on slave card that is designed as a 16 data bit I/O resource must support the IOCS16* signal line. The activation of this line indicates to platform CPU or add-on bus owner cards that either 8 or 16 data bits can be accessed or transfered. It also indicates that the add-on card is either ISA or E-ISA compatible. The only method that can be used to determine a 16 bit cycle is the decode of the SA<0-15> address lines by the add-on slave card. Because the entire I/O address space can be decoded down to the byte level, there are no restrictions on the grouping together of identical byte widths, as there are for memory resources.

The IOCS16* signal line is monitored by platform CPUs, ISA and E-ISA add-on bus owner cards, and byte swapper circuitry.

> *The add-on slave card must decode the SA<0-9> signal lines, and blindly activate the IOCS16* line when appropriate. It cannot use any of the memory or I/O COMMAND signal lines as qualifiers. Consequently, it will activate the IOCS16* signal line during memory cycles. It is the responsibility of the platform CPU or add-on bus owner card to ignore the IOCS16* signal line during memory cycles.*

ISA COMPATIBLE ADD-ON I/O SLAVE CARD ISSUES

The use of the SRDY* signal line allows a shorter cycle time. Since a platform CPU or add-on bus owner card is not required to support a no wait state access cycle, the add-on slave card must be designed to support the longer standard or ready access cycles even if it activates the SRDY* signal line.

16 bit I/O resources do not support the SRDY* signal line. The I/O command signal line for a 16 data bit access is activated later relative to the memory and 8 data bit I/O commands; consequently, there is insufficient time for the add-on slave card to properly drive the SRDY* signal line.

The SRDY* signal line is available on an 8 bit slot on an ISA compatible platform. On PC and XT compatible platforms, this signal line was not used as an SRDY* signal line. On some AT compatible platforms, a no-wait-state cycle is restricted to 16 data bit I/O resources. A no-wait-state I/O access cycle was supported on the IBM AT platform for 8 data bit accesses.

The use of the IOCHRDY signal line by the add-on slave card allows the cycle to be extended. Some ISA compatible add-on bus owner cards do not recognize the IOCHRDY signal line, and all of the I/O access cycles are run as standard access cycles. An add-on slave card that activates the IOCHRDY signal line will expect a ready access cycle; consequently, the data may not be valid at the end of the standard access cycle. Add-on slave cards should support standard access cycles when being accessed by an ISA compatible add-on bus owner card. When an E-ISA or EISA compatible add-on bus owner card is the bus owner, the IOCHRDY signal line is supported; consequently, a ready access cycle can be supported. See the aforementioned tables in Chapter 1 for more information.

All SA<0-15> signal lines are available to the add-on I/O slave card. However, by convention, only the first 10 ADDRESS signal lines are decoded. Consequently, only 1K bytes are addressable in the I/O address space on an ISA compatible platform. See Chapter 2 and Subchapter 4.2 for further information.

Table 4-2 summarizes which signal lines are driven by which resources during an I/O access cycle to an add-on slave card. "PLAT. CIRCUIT" in some cases may simply be a pull-up resistor.

In this table, "PLAT" is the abbreviation for "platform".   "BUS MASTER" may be either platform CPU or add-on bus owner card

LINE	DRIVEN BY	LINE	DRIVEN BY
AENx	PLAT. CIRCUIT	MEMR*	BUS MASTER
BALE	PLAT. CIRCUIT	MEMW*	BUS MASTER
DACKx*	PLAT. DMA	OSC	PLAT. CIRCUIT
DRQx	I/O RESOURCE	REFRESH*	PLAT. REF. CONT.
IOCHK*	ALL RESOURCES	RESET	PLAT. CIRCUIT
IOCHRDY	ADD-ON SLAVE	SA	BUS MASTER
IOCS16*	ADD-ON SLAVE	SBHE*	BUS MASTER
IOR*	BUS MASTER	SD	BUS MASTER (WR)
IOW*	BUS MASTER	SD	ADD-ON SLAVE
IRQx	ANY RESOURCE	SMR/SMW*	PLAT. CIRCUIT
LA	BUS MASTER	BCLK	PLAT. CIRCUIT
MASTER*	ADD-ON BUS OWN	TC	PLAT. DMA
MEMCS16*	MEM. RESOURCE	SRDY*	PLAT. CIRCUIT

TABLE 4-2: ISA AND E-ISA ADD-ON SLAVE CARD AS I/O RESOURCE

ACCESS CYCLE DATA SIZE MISMATCH WITH ISA COMPATIBLE ADD-ON SLAVE CARDS

An add-on slave card that is a 16 data bit resource (indicated by an active MEMCS* or IOCS16* signal line) cannot force the bus master to execute a 16 data bit access if the bus master only requested an 8 data bit (as indicated by the SA0 and SBHE* signal lines) access cycle.   Conversely, a bus master that intends to execute a single 16 data bit access cycle cannot do so if the accessed resource is only an 8 data bit resource (indicated by an inactive MEMCS16* or IOCS16* signal line).   The proper interpretation of the MEMCS16*, IOCS16*, SA0, and SBHE* signal lines allows data size mismatch to occur on the ISA or E-ISA platforms. For PC and XT, all of these mismatch size issues do not exist because 16 data bit add-on cards cannot be installed.

If the SA0 line is a logic low and the SBHE* signal line is active, the bus master intends to execute a single 16 data bit access. The activation of the MEMCS16* or IOCS16* signal line by the accessed resource indicates to the bus master that the access can be completed in the present cycle, since the SD<0-15> signal lines map directly to an even address new word location.   The non-activation of the MEMCS16* or the IOCS16* signal line by the accessed resource forces the access to be completed in two 8 data bit cycles. The first cycle will be completed as an 8 data bit cycle with the SD<0-7> signal lines mapped directly to an even address byte location. The next cycle the bus master executes will be an 8 data bit access in order to access the upper order byte of the word in the previous cycle. The bus master will drive the SA0 signal line to a logic high and the SBHE* signal line active to indicate an 8 data bit access cycle with the data byte accessed on the SD<8-15> signal lines. For a read access cycle, the platform byte swapping circuitry insures that the data available on the lower byte (SD<0-7>) is also available on the upper byte (SD<8-15>). For a write cycle, the bus master must tri-state the SD<0-7> lines; the data byte has been swapped between the upper order and the lower order data lines by the platform byte swapping circuit.

If the SA0 signal line is a logic low and the SBHE* signal line is inactive, the bus master intends to execute a single 8 data bit access to an even address byte. The data byte will be on the SD<0-7> signal lines, and can be directly mapped to the even address byte. The state of the MEMCS16* or IOCS16* signal line does not always affect the access cycle, because the bus master does not always complete the access as an 8 data bit cycle. See Note (2) for Table 4-3 for more information.

If the SA0 signal line is a logic high and the SBHE* signal line is active, the bus master intends to execute a single 8 data bit access to an odd address byte with the data on the upper data lines. In that the value of the MEMCS16* or IOCS16* signal line is not known until the middle of the cycle, the byte swapping circuitry copies the lower byte (SD<0-7>) to the upper byte (SD<8-15>). For this reason, the bus master must tri-state the lower byte (SD<0-7>) for a write access cycle. For a read access cycle, the bus master obviously has the upper and lower bytes as inputs.

> If the bus master is requesting an 8 data bit read access cycle to a 16 data bit (to an odd address) add-on slave card that can drive the upper order data lines, the upper order data lines must not be driven by the add-on slave card unless xxCS16* will be driven active. This prevents buffer fights on the upper order data lines between the byte swapping circuitry and the add-on slave card. If the bus master is requesting an 8 data bit write access cycle to an odd address, the lower byte (SD<0-7>) must not be driven. This prevents a conflict from the bus master and byte swapping circuitry both driving the lower byte.

Table 4-3 outlines the interpretation by the platform byte swapper circuitry of specific signal lines.

BUS MASTER			ADD-ON SLAVE		BYTE	AT ADD-ON CARD	
VALID DATA	SBHE*	SAO	DATA	XXCS16*	SWAP	VALID DATA	MAPPING ADDRESS
8 BITS							
SD<0-7>	INACT.	0	8	INACT.	NO	SD<0-7>	EVEN BYTE
SD<8-15>	ACTIVE	1	8	INACT.	YES	SD<0-7>	ODD BYTE
SD<0-7>	INACT.	0	16	ACTIVE	NO	SD<0-7>	EVEN BYTE(2)
SD<8-15>	ACTIVE	1	16	ACTIVE	NO (1)	SD<8-15>	ODD BYTE(2)
16 BITS							
SD<0-15>	ACTIVE	0	8	INACT.	NO	SD<0-7>	EVEN BYTE
SD<0-15>	ACTIVE	0	16	ACTIVE	NO	SD<0-15>	EVEN WORD

TABLE 4-3: BYTE SWAPPING FOR ACCESS CYCLES TO ISA AND E-ISA ADD-ON SLAVE CARDS

NOTES:
(1) In that data can be successfully accessed on the upper byte lane (SD<8-15>), the byte swapping is NOT needed. BUT, because the value of the XXCS16 is not known until the "middle" of the cycle, byte swapping must occur in case an 8 data bit resource is being accessed for a write. For a read, the swapping circuit must wait for the xxCS16* signal line to determine if swapping is needed.*
(2) For an odd or even address byte read, the bus master can use 16 bit timing and access cycles if it chooses. For an odd or even address byte write, the add-on card must assume valid write data timing per the 8 bit specification. Even though the add-on card indicated a 16 bit resource, there is no assurance that the bus master had begun the access cycle with 16 bit data set up to write command timing.

The condition of SBHE* inactive and SA0 logical 1 is not allowed for an AT, E-ISA, or EISA platform. For a PC or XT platform this does not apply because 16 bit add-on cards cannot be installed and SBHE* signal line does not exist on the connector.

TRANSFER CYCLES AND ISA COMPATIBLE ADD-ON SLAVE CARDS

An add-on slave card can request the DMA controller on the platform to transfer data between memory and I/O resources. The add-on I/O slave card requests the transfer by activating one of the DRQx signal lines. The DMA controller acknowledges that the ensuing cycles are DMA transfer cycles that involve the add-on I/O slave card by activating the appropriate DACKx* signal line. The memory resource of the transfer may be on the platform or another add-on slave card.

One difference between a platform CPU or add-on bus owner card access cycle and a DMA transfer cycle is that the I/O and memory COMMAND signal lines are active simultaneously for the DMA transfer cycle. The simultaneous activation of the I/O and memory COMMAND signal lines allows the data to be placed onto and retrieved from the bus during the same cycle. During a transfer cycle, the address on the bus is for memory and does not represent a valid I/O address. The AENx signal line is activated by the platform as indication to the add-on I/O slave cards to ignore the ADDRESS and the I/O COMMAND signal lines. Only the add-on I/O slave card that has activated the DRQx and DACKx* signal lines responds to the activation of the I/O COMMAND signal lines. If the transfer includes memory on an add-on memory slave card, only that card responds to the ADDRESS and memory COMMAND signal lines.

Another difference between a platform CPU or add-on bus owner card access cycle and a DMA transfer cycle is the operation of BALE and the LA<17-23> signal lines. BALE is driven to logical "1" by platform circuitry. Consequently, the LA<17-23> signal lines must be driven valid by the DMA controller for the entire transfer cycle.

Table 1-5-A in Chapter 1 outlines the various DMA transfer cycles supported on ISA and E-ISA compatible platforms. Tables 4-4 to 4-7 outline which signal lines are driven by which of the resources under the four transfer structures. "PLAT. CIRCUIT" in some cases may simply be a pull-up resistor. In the following tables, "PLAT." is the abbreviation for "platform circuitry".

LINE	DRIVEN BY	LINE	DRIVEN BY
AENx	PLAT. CIRCUIT	MEMR*	PLAT. DMA
BALE	PLAT. CIRCUIT	MEMW*	PLAT. DMA
DACKx*	PLAT. DMA	OSC	PLAT. CIRCUIT
DRQx	ADD-ON SLAVE	REFRESH*	PLAT. REF. CONT.
IOCHK*	ALL RESOURCES	RESET	PLAT. CIRCUIT
IOCHRDY	MEMORY RESOURCE	SA	PLAT. DMA
IOCS16*	PLAT. CIRCUIT	SBHE*	PLAT. DMA
IOR*	PLAT. DMA	SD	MEM. RES. (RD)
IOW*	PLAT. DMA	SD	ADD-ON SLAVE (WR)
IRQx	ANY RESOURCE	SMR/SMW*	PLAT. CIRCUIT
LA	PLAT. DMA	BCLK	PLAT. CIRCUIT
MASTER*	PLAT. CIRCUIT	TC	PLAT. DMA (1)
MEMCS16*	PLAT. CIRCUIT	SRDY*	PLAT. CIRCUIT

TABLE 4-4: ISA AND E-ISA ADD-ON SLAVE CARD AS I/O RESOURCE (DATA DESTINATION) FOR TRANSFER CYCLES

LINE	DRIVEN BY	LINE	DRIVEN BY
AENx	PLAT. CIRCUIT	MEMR*	PLAT. DMA
BALE	PLAT. CIRCUIT	MEMW*	PLAT. DMA
DACKx*	PLAT. DMA	OSC	PLAT. CIRCUIT
DRQx	ADD-ON SLAVE	REFRESH*	PLAT. REF. CONT.
IOCHK*	ALL RESOURCES	RESET	PLAT. CIRCUIT
IOCHRDY	ADD-ON SLAVE	SA	PLAT. DMA
IOCS16*	PLAT. CIRCUIT	SBHE*	PLAT. DMA
IOR*	PLAT. DMA	SD	MEM. RES. (WR)
IOW*	PLAT. DMA	SD	ADD-ON SLAVE (RD)
IRQx	ANY RESOURCE	SMR/SMW*	PLAT. CIRCUIT
LA	PLAT. DMA	BCLK	PLAT. CIRCUIT
MASTER*	PLAT. CIRCUIT	TC	PLAT. DMA (1)
MEMCS16*	PLAT. CIRCUIT	SRDY*	PLAT. CIRCUIT

TABLE 4-5: ISA AND E-ISA ADD-ON SLAVE CARD AS I/O RESOURCE (DATA SOURCE) FOR TRANSFER CYCLES

LINE	DRIVEN BY	LINE	DRIVEN BY
AENx	PLAT. CIRCUIT	MEMR*	PLAT. DMA
BALE	PLAT. CIRCUIT	MEMW*	PLAT. DMA
DACKx*	PLAT. DMA	OSC	PLAT. CIRCUIT
DRQx	I/O RESOURCE	REFRESH*	PLAT. REF. CONT.
IOCHK*	ALL RESOURCES	RESET	PLAT. CIRCUIT
IOCHRDY	I/O RESOURCE	SA	PLAT. DMA
IOCS16*	PLAT. CIRCUIT	SBHE*	PLAT. DMA
IOR*	PLAT. DMA	SD	MEM. RES. (WR)
IOW*	PLAT. DMA	SD	ADD-ON SLAVE (RD)
IRQx	ANY RESOURCE	SMR/SMW*	PLAT. CIRCUIT
LA	PLAT. DMA	BCLK	PLAT. CIRCUIT
MASTER*	PLAT. CIRCUIT	TC	PLAT. DMA (1)
MEMCS16*	PLAT. CIRCUIT	SRDY*	PLAT. CIRCUIT

TABLE 4-6: ISA AND E-ISA ADD-ON SLAVE CARD AS MEMORY RESOURCE (DATA DESTINATION) FOR TRANSFER CYCLES

LINE	DRIVEN BY	LINE	DRIVEN BY
AENx	PLAT. CIRCUIT	MEMR*	PLAT. DMA
BALE	PLAT. CIRCUIT	MEMW*	PLAT. DMA
DACKx*	PLAT. DMA	OSC	PLAT. CIRCUIT
DRQx	I/O RESOURCE	REFRESH*	PLAT. REF. CONT.
IOCHK*	ALL RESOURCES	RESET	PLAT. CIRCUIT
IOCHRDY	ADD-ON SLAVE	SA	PLAT. DMA
IOCS16*	PLAT. CIRCUIT	SBHE*	PLAT. DMA
IOR*	PLAT. DMA	SD	I/O RES. (WR)
IOW*	PLAT. DMA	SD	ADD-ON SLAVE (RD)
IRQx	ANY RESOURCE	SMR/SMW*	PLAT. CIRCUIT
LA	PLAT. DMA	BCLK	PLAT. CIRCUIT
MASTER*	PLAT. CIRCUIT	TC	PLAT. DMA (1)
MEMCS16*	PLAT. CIRCUIT	SRDY*	PLAT. CIRCUIT

TABLE 4-7: ISA AND E-ISA ADD-ON SLAVE CARD AS MEMORY RESOURCE (DATA SOURCE) FOR TRANSFER CYCLES

NOTE:

(1): On an E-ISA compatible platform, the TC signal line can also be driven by the add-on I/O slave card.

TRANSFER CYCLE DATA SIZE MISMATCH WITH AN ISA COMPATIBLE ADD-ON SLAVE CARD

The I/O resource that uses one of the 8 data bit DMA channels must be an 8 data bit resource. The data will be transferred between the add-on I/O slave card and the memory resource only on the SD<0-7> signal lines. The memory resource, whether on the platform or on an add-on slave card, can be either 8 or 16 data bits in size. The data will be swapped between the SD<0-7> and SD<8-15> signal lines by the platform byte swapping circuitry if the SA0 signal line equals logic 1 to indicate an odd address and in case the memory resource is 16 data bits in size (MEMCS16* = 0).

For this reason, the 16 data bit memory resource must tri-state the lower byte (SD<0-7>) during a read cycle. Otherwise, the data will be only available on the SD<0-7> signal lines. In either case, the memory resource can directly map the byte into odd address locations. A transfer cycle involving an even address memory byte requires both SA0 to be logic 0 and SBHE* to be inactive. The data will only be available on the SD<0-7> signal lines independent of the MEMCS16* or IOCS16* signal line being activated. The data can be directly mapped into the even address location.

The I/O resource that uses one of the 16 data bit DMA channels must be a 16 data bit resource. The data can only be transferred with a memory resource, whether on the platform or on an add-on slave card, that is also a 16 data bit resource, for ISA and E-ISA resources. No transfers are allowed between 16 data bit I/O and 8 data bit memory resources except on EISA compatible platforms. The 16 data bit transfer involving a memory word requires both the SA0 signal line to be logic 0 and the SBHE* signal line to be active. The data is available on the SD<0-15> signal lines, and can be directly mapped to the even memory address location.

The MEMCS16* signal line is used in transfer cycles on EISA compatible platforms. Transfer cycles between 16 data bit I/O resources and 16 bit memory resources do not require the MEMCS16* or IOCS16* signal line to be activated on ISA and E-ISA compatible platforms. By definition, a 16 data bit transfer cycle can only occur between resources of the same size because data assembly and disassembly are not supported as on ISA and E-ISA compatible platforms. The transfer cycles between 8 data bit I/O resources and 16 bit memory resources do not require the MEMCS16* signal line to be activated to properly control the byte swapping circuitry.

If the SA0 signal line is a logical "1" and the SBHE* signal line is active, the platform byte swapping circuitry will drive the low byte to the high byte for a read from the memory resource. A 16 data bit memory resource must not drive the lower byte because the platform byte swapping circuitry will drive the lower byte.

Table 4-8 outlines the interpretation by the platform byte swapping circuitry of specific signal lines during a transfer cycle.

I/O RESOURCE VALID DATA	MEM. RESOURCE			DMA		BYTE SWAP
	VALID DATA	MEMCS16*	MAPPING ADDRESS	SBHE*	SA0	
8 BITS						
SD<0-7>	SD<0-7>	INACT	EVEN BYTE	INACT	0	NO
SD<0-7>	SD<0-7>	INACT	ODD BYTE	ACT	1	NO (1)
SD<0-7>	SD<0-7>	ACT	EVEN BYTE	INACT	0	NO
SD<0-7>	SD<8-15>	ACT	ODD BYTE	ACT	1	YES
16 BITS						
SD<0-15>	SD<0-15>	ACT	EVEN WORD	ACT	0	NO

TABLE 4-8: BYTE SWAPPING FOR ISA AND E-ISA COMPATIBLE MEMORY AND I/O RESOURCES FOR TRANSFER CYCLES

NOTE:
(1) In that data can be successfully transferred on the lower byte lane (SD<0-7>), byte swapping is NOT needed. BUT, because the value of the XXCS16* is not known until the "middle" of the cycle, byte swapping must occur in case a 16 data bit resource is being accessed.

The condition of SBHE* inactive and SA0 logical 1 is not allowed for an AT, E-ISA, or EISA platform. For a PC or XT platform this does not apply because 16 bit add-on cards cannot be installed and SBHE* signal line does not exist on the connector.

4.2 ISA COMPATIBLE ADD-ON BUS OWNER CARDS

An add-on card can be designed as a bus owner. This type of add-on bus owner card is only supported on AT, E-ISA, and EISA compatible platforms. To become bus owner, it must first execute the obtain portion of the arbitration cycle, and after it no longer has an immediate need for bus ownership, it executes the release portion of the arbitration cycle. See Chapter 9 for more detailed information.

The various types of access cycles that can be executed by an add-on bus owner card are outlined in Chapter 1 as follows:

- ISA add-on bus owner card access: Tables 1-3-A and B

An add-on bus owner card has complete access to the entire memory and I/O address space. However, the platform architecture and software executing on the platform CPU assume that only the platform CPU has access to certain specific memory and I/O resources. For example, an add-on bus owner card cannot normally access the math co-processor memory registers. An add-on bus owner card usually does not access the I/O registers of the interrupt, DMA, and keyboard controllers, nor the timer, DMA page, and real time clock. In addition, the add-on bus owner card usually does not access the NMI chip select circuitry and Port B.

Of particular note is the fact that ISA bus ownership is awarded via the platform's DMA controller. Throughout the add-on card's bus ownership, the platform CPU and other platform resources assume that DMA transfer cycles are being executed. The activation of the MASTER16* signal line by the add-on bus owner card immediately deactivates the AENx signal line, so I/O resources will respond to access cycles. Access cycles are the only bus cycles that can be executed by the add-on bus owner.

Add-on bus owner cards can be designed to execute access cycles in the same manner as the platform CPU. Resources on the bus are unable to determine if the platform CPU or an add-on bus owner card is executing the cycle unless the MASTER16* and BALE signal lines are monitored. The single major difference between a platform CPU and an add-on bus owner card access cycle is the operation of BALE and the LA<17-23> lines. Since BALE is driven to logical "1" by platform circuitry, the LA<17-23> signal lines must be driven valid by the add-on bus owner card for the entire access cycle, with the same timing as the SA<0-19> signal lines.

The original IBM AT platform architecture was designed with the MEMCS16*, IOCS16*, SRDY*, and IOCHRDY signal lines as inputs, and all were attached to +5 volts by pull-up resistors. Consequently, when add-on bus owner cards access platform resources, they appear as 8 data bit resources that support a standard access cycle. The aforementioned non-access of platform I/O resources, combined with the 16 data bit size of the IBM AT platform memory, has historically caused add-on bus owner cards to execute only 16 bit memory access standard cycles. These "early" add-on bus owner cards did not monitor the SRDY*, MEMCS16*, IOCS16*, and IOCHRDY signal lines. For the above reasons, ISA compatible add-on bus owner cards are defined as executing 16 data bit standard access cycles to 16 data bit memory resources. These restrictions do not apply to E-ISA and EISA bus owner add-on cards. Please see Subchapters 4.4 and 4.6 for more information.

4.3 E-ISA COMPATIBLE ADD-ON MEMORY AND I/O SLAVE CARDS

E-ISA compatible add-on memory and I/O slave cards operate in the same fashion as ISA compatible add-on slave cards. The various types of access cycles that can be used with an E-ISA compatible add-on slave card are described in Chapter 1 as follows:

- Platform CPU access: Tables 1-2-A and B, and 1-4-A to D

- ISA or E-ISA add-on bus owner card access: Tables 1-3-A to D

- EISA add-on bus owner card access: Tables 1-4-A to D

There are two important differences between ISA and E-ISA compatible add-on card memory or I/O slave cards. First, the E-ISA compatible add-on I/O slave card supports slot specific I/O addressing beyond the non-slot specific 1K I/O address space for ISA compatible add-on I/O slave cards. Second, the E-ISA and EISA compatible add-on cards can optionally support configuration space. The configuration space is contained within the I/O address space of an E-ISA or EISA compatible platform. The support of these two differences is explained in the following paragraphs.

As described in Chapter 2, certain I/O address spaces are reserved. The need to reserve these addresses can be traced back to the history of I/O add-on slave card design. Even though the original PC supplied all 16 address lines to the bus, early add-on slave cards only decoded the first 10 address lines. The decode of only the first 10 address lines caused duplicate data to be read or written at every 1K increment from the base address. The first 256 byte block was reserved for platform I/O resources, and is repeated 63 additional times in the 64K address space at 1K boundaries. E-ISA and EISA compatible platforms exploit this fact by assigning the first four blocks to the platform I/O resources. The next four blocks are assigned to slot 1, the next four blocks are assigned to slot 2, and so forth. This results in 1K bytes of addresses being uniquely assigned to each slot.

For add-on I/O slave cards that decode only the first 10 address lines, any I/O access in the address range of 0100H to 03FFH is valid. The data written and read to this 768 byte block equals those at the same address displaced by 1K multiples. For those add-on slave cards that want to be compatible to ISA-only platforms, the first 10 address signal lines (SA<0-9>) must be decoded, and only the addresses within the 768 byte block will be valid. All other addresses will not constitute valid I/O bus accesses.

The previously described ISA compatible add-on card will also work with E-ISA and EISA compatible platforms. However, it will not support the E-ISA or EISA configuration space and slot specific I/O addressing. To support these special E-ISA or EISA functions, the first twelve signal lines (SA<0-11>) must be decoded by an E-ISA compatible add-on slave card. See Chapters 2 and 12 for more information on the configuration space and slot-specific I/O addresses.

Finally, an 8 data bit E-ISA compatible add-on card supports an expanded definition of no-wait-state access cycles. See Chapter 6 for more information.

TRANSFER CYCLES AND E-ISA COMPATIBLE ADD-ON SLAVE CARDS

The operation of DMA transfer cycles with an E-ISA compatible add-on card resource is nearly the same as with ISA compatible add-on cards. The only difference is that the TC signal line is bi-directional on an E-ISA compatible add-on I/O slave card when installed in an E-ISA or EISA compatible platform.

The ISA compatible platform supports only the DMA COMPATIBLE transfer cycle. The E-ISA compatible platform supports COMPATIBLE, TYPE A, and TYPE B DMA transfer cycles. "All", "most", and "some" ISA compatible add-on I/O slave cards support COMPATIBLE, TYPE A, and TYPE B transfer cycles, respectively. E-ISA compatible add-on I/O slave cards support the same DMA transfer cycle types; the difference is that the configuration space clarifies which DMA cycle type is supported.

Table 1-5-A in Chapter 1 outlines the various DMA transfer cycles supported on ISA and E-ISA compatible platforms.

TRANSFER CYCLE DATA SIZE MISMATCH WITH AN E-ISA COMPATIBLE ADD-ON SLAVE CARD

The data size mismatch is managed in the same fashion as with ISA compatible add-on slave cards. The only difference is that the DMA channels do not have a fixed data size. The data size for each DMA channel is programmable in the DMA controller.

4.4 E-ISA COMPATIBLE ADD-ON BUS OWNER CARDS

An E-ISA compatible add-on bus owner card operates in the same fashion as an ISA compatible card. The types of access cycles are outlined in tables 1-3-C to 1-3-D. The only differences in an E-ISA compatible add-on bus owner card relative to an ISA one are as follows:

- The E-ISA compatible platform by convention distributes the BCLK signal line in a "starburst" pattern; consequently, the slot to slot skew on the bus is minimized. The minimum clock skew allows the add-on bus owner card to support the SRDY* signal line and, consequently, no wait state access cycles. Also, in addition to supporting the ISA compatible asynchronous IOCHRDY signal line, the starburst BCLK signal line distribution allows the add-on bus owner card to support the enhanced version of the IOCHRDY signal line.

- The E-ISA compatible platform supports the MEMCS16*, IOCS16*, SRDY*, and IOCHRDY signal lines when the accessed resource is on the platform. Thus, an E-ISA add-on bus owner card can execute all of the access cycles to platform resources that can be executed by the platform CPU of ISA, E-ISA, and EISA (E-MIX cycles) compatible platforms to add-on slave cards.

> *A jumper or configuration space option is needed to force 16 data bit accesses independent of the MEMCS16* and IOCS16* signal lines to maintain compatibility with the IBM AT platform and other ISA platforms. E-ISA compatible add-on bus owner cards installed in an IBM AT platform will sample the IOCHRDY and MEMCS16* or IOCS16* signal lines inactive, and will implement the cycles accordingly. The IBM AT platform and other "faithful" ISA clones which do not drive the IOCHRDY, MEMCS16*, or IOCS16* signal lines will have no compatibility problem when accessed by an E-ISA bus owner card because all of the cycles will be executed as 8 data bit standard cycles.   The only problem is that performance will suffer.*

If an E-ISA compatible add-on bus owner card is installed in ISA compatible platform, then by convention it operates as an ISA compatible add-on bus owner card.

4.5 EISA COMPATIBLE ADD-ON SLAVE CARDS

EISA add-on slave cards can be divided into two types. One type consists of ISA or E-ISA compatible add-on slave cards which can also be installed in ISA and E-ISA compatible platforms and will operate in their respective "native" modes. These add-on slave cards can also be installed in EISA compatible platforms, and will operate in the ISA and E-ISA "native" modes; consequently, these add-on slave cards are not defined as EISA compatible add-on slave cards. The other type of add-on slave cards do not use the ISA or E-ISA bus protocols to operate and can only be installed in an EISA compatible bus. Their "native mode" implements the EISA specific signal lines; consequently, they are defined as EISA compatible add-on slave cards.

MEMORY ACCESS CYCLES TO EISA COMPATIBLE ADD-ON SLAVE CARDS

An EISA add-on slave card can support memory cycles as a 16 or 32 data bit resource. It can reside in the 32 bit EISA slot on an EISA compatible platform, but cannot reside on an 8 or 8/16 bit ISA or E-ISA slot.

8 DATA BIT MEMORY RESOURCE

The EISA bus specification only supports EX16* and EX32* signal lines; consequently, it is not possible for an 8 data bit add-on slave card to indicate that it is EISA compatible. An 8 data bit EISA memory resource cannot be distinguished from an ISA compatible one; consequently, an E-MIX cycle must be executed which drives the MEMR*, SMEMR*, MEMW*, and SMEMW* signal lines active. The 8 data bit EISA add-on memory card is accessed as if it were an ISA or E-ISA compatible resource. See Subchapter 6.2 for more information.

> *An 8 data bit EISA add-on memory card is simply an ISA add-on memory card; consequently, it can be installed in an ISA or E-ISA compatible platform's 8 or 8/16 bit slots. It can also be installed in an EISA compatible 8/16/32 bit slot.*

The various types of access cycles that can be used with an EISA compatible add-on slave card are outlined in Chapter 1 as follows:

- EISA compatible platform CPU or EISA add-on bus owner card: Tables 1-4-A to D

- ISA or E-ISA add-on bus owner card access: Tables 1-3-A to D

16 & 32 DATA BIT MEMORY RESOURCES

An add-on slave card that is designed as a 16 or 32 data bit memory resource can only reside in an EISA slot. The M-IO and W-R signal lines, in conjunction with the BE* and LA signal lines, are available to support the full four gigabyte address space. The add-on slave card can respond to several different types of access cycles. Unless "special" signal lines are active, the access cycles executed are standard and ready. When the "special" signal lines (NOWS*, MSBURST*, and SLBURST*) are driven active, a compressed or burst access cycle is executed, respectively.

The various types of access cycles that can be used with a 16 or 32 data bit add-on slave card are outlined in Chapter 1 as follows:

- EISA compatible platform CPU or EISA add-on bus owner card access: Tables 1-4-A to D

- ISA or E-ISA compatible add-on bus owner card access: Tables 1-3-A to D

An add-on slave card that is designed as a 16 data bit memory resource must support the EX16* signal line. The activation of this line indicates to a platform CPU or add-on bus owner that either 8 or 16 data bits can be accessed or transferred according to the BE* signal lines. It also indicates that the add-on card is EISA compatible.

An add-on slave card that is designed as a 32 data bit memory resource must support the EX32* signal line. The activation of this line indicates to a platform CPU or add-on bus owner that either 8, 16, 24, or 32 data bits can be accessed or transferred according to the BE* signal lines. It also indicates that the add-on card is EISA compatible.

The add-on slave card cannot use the BE* signal lines to qualify the access. Additionally, the ADDRESS signal lines do not support LA0 or LA1 address signal lines. Consequently, the entire four byte block selected by the LA<2-23> and LA*<24-31> signal lines must be the same data width.

Table 4-9 summarizes which signal lines are driven by which resource during a memory access cycle to an add-on slave card. "PLAT. CIRCUIT" in some cases may simply be a pull-up resistor. In this table, "PLAT." is the abbreviation for "platform". "BUS MASTER" may be either the platform CPU or an add-on bus owner card.

LINE	DRIVEN BY	LINE	DRIVEN BY
AENx	PLAT. CIRCUIT	M-IO	BUS MASTER
START*	BUS MASTER (1)	W-R	BUS MASTER
DACKx*	PLAT. DMA	OSC	PLAT. CIRCUIT
DRQx	I/O RESOURCE	REFRESH*	PLAT. REF. CONT
IOCHK*	ANY RESOURCE	RESET	PLAT. CIRCUIT
EXRDY	ADD-ON SLAVE	LA	BUS MASTER
EX16*	ADD-ON SLAVE (1)	BE*	BUS MASTER (1)
EX32*	ADD-ON SLAVE (1)	SD	BUS MASTER (WR)
CMD*	PLAT. CIRCUIT	SD	ADD-ON SLAVE (RD)
IRQx	ANY RESOURCE	LOCK*	BUS MASTER
LA	BUS MASTER	BCLK	PLAT. CIRCUIT
MASTER16*	BUS MASTER	TC	PLAT. CIRCUIT
MREQx*	ADD-ON BUS OWNER	MAKx*	PLAT. CIRCUIT
NOWS*	ADD-ON SLAVE	SLBURST*	ADD-ON SLAVE
MSBURST*	BUS MASTER		

TABLE 4-9: EISA ADD-ON SLAVE CARD AS MEMORY RESOURCE

NOTE:
(1) During EISA data-matching access cycles, these signal lines are also driven by the platform circuitry.

I/O ACCESS CYCLES TO EISA COMPATIBLE ADD-ON SLAVE CARDS

An EISA add-on slave card can support I/O cycles as an 8, 16, 24, or 32 data bit resource. It can reside on the 8/16/32 data bit EISA slot on an EISA compatible platform.

8 DATA BIT I/O RESOURCE

An 8 data bit resource has access to the first 16 address lines, the EISA compatible signal lines, and the IOR* and IOW* lines.

The entire 64K address space in theory could be supported. The actual address space supported is the same as for an E-ISA add-on I/O slave card.

The various types of access cycles that can be used with an 8 data bit add-on slave card are outlined in Chapter 1 as follows:

- EISA compatible platform CPU or EISA add-on bus owner card access: Tables 1-4-A to D

- ISA or E-ISA add-on bus owner card access: Tables 1-3-A to D

The EISA bus specification only supports EX16* and EX32* signal lines; consequently, it is not possible for an 8 data bit add-on slave card to indicate that it is EISA compatible. An 8 data bit EISA compatible I/O resource cannot be distinguished from an ISA compatible one. Consequently, an E-MIX cycle must be executed, which drives the IOR* and IOW* signal lines. But unlike an 8 data bit EISA memory add-on slave card, an 8 data bit EISA I/O add-on slave card does exist and is different than an 8 data bit ISA or E-ISA add-on slave card.

By definition, an E-MIX access cycle also drives the EISA compatible signal lines. Thus, the 8 data bit EISA compatible add-on I/O slave card can make full use of the EISA compatible signal lines. If the add-on I/O slave card was actually ISA compatible, then by definition the ISA compatible signal lines are also available. See Subchapter 6.2 for more information.

16 & 32 DATA BIT I/O RESOURCE

An add-on slave card that is designed as a 16 or 32 data bit I/O resource can only reside in an EISA slot. The M-IO and W-R signal lines, in conjunction with the BE* and LA signal lines, are available. The entire 64K address space in theory could be supported. The actual address space supported is the same as for an E-ISA add-on I/O slave card. The add-on slave card can respond to several different types of access cycles. Unless "special" signal lines are active, the access cycles executed are EISA standard and EISA ready. When the "special" NOWS* signal line is driven active, a compressed access cycle is executed.

The various types of access cycles that can be used with a 16 or 32 data bit add-on slave card are outlined in Chapter 1 as follows:

- EISA compatible platform CPU or E-ISA add-on bus owner card access: Tables 1-4-A to D

- ISA or E-ISA add-on bus owner card access: Tables 1-3-A to D

An add-on slave card that is designed as a 16 data bit I/O resource must support the EX16* signal line. The activation of this line indicates to a platform CPU or add-on bus owner that either 8 or 16 data bits can be accessed or transfered according to the BE* signal lines. It also indicates that the add-on card is EISA compatible.

An add-on slave card that is designed as a 32 data bit I/O resource must support the EX32* signal line. The activation of this line indicates to a platform CPU or add-on bus owner that either 8, 16, 24, or 32 data bits can be accessed or transfered according to the BE* signal lines. It also indicates that the add-on card is EISA compatible.

The add-on slave card cannot use the BE* signal lines to qualify the access. Additionally, the ADDRESS signal line group do not support the LA0 or LA1 address signal lines. Consequently, the entire four byte block selected by the LA<2-11> signal lines must be the same data width.

Table 4-10 summarizes which signal lines are driven by which resource during a memory access cycle to an add-on slave card. "PLAT. CIRCUIT" in some cases may simply be a pull-up resistor.

In this table, "PLAT." is the abbreviation for "platform". "BUS MASTER" may be either a platform CPU or an add-on bus owner card.

LINE	DRIVEN BY	LINE	DRIVEN BY
AENx	PLAT. CIRCUIT	M-IO	BUS MASTER
START*	BUS MASTER (1)	W-R	BUS MASTER
DACKx*	PLAT. DMA	OSC	PLAT. CIRCUIT
DRQx	I/O RESOURCE	REFRESH*	PLAT. REF. CONT.
IOCHK*	ANY RESOURCE	RESET	PLAT. CIRCUIT
EXRDY	ADD-ON SLAVE	LA	BUS MASTER
EX16*	ADD-ON SLAVE (1)	BE*	BUS MASTER (1)
EX32*	ADD-ON SLAVE (1)	SD	BUS MASTER (WR)
CMD*	PLAT. CIRCUIT	SD	ADD-ON SLAVE (RD)
IRQx	ANY RESOURCE	LOCK*	BUS MASTER
LA	BUS MASTER	BCLK	PLAT. CIRCUIT
MASTER16*	BUS MASTER	TC	PLAT. CIRCUIT
MREQx*	ADD-ON BUS OWNER	MAKx*	PLAT. CIRCUIT
NOWS*	ADD-ON SLAVE	IOCS16*	ADD-ON SLAVE (2)

TABLE 4-10: EISA ADD-ON SLAVE CARD AS I/O RESOURCE

NOTES:
(1) During EISA data-matching access cycles these signal lines are also driven by the platform circuitry.
(2) An EISA compatible 16 data bit I/O resource must drive this signal line if it is to be accessed by an ISA or E-ISA add-on bus owner card. This is required due to timing constraints. See Subchapter 6.3 for more information.

ACCESS CYCLE DATA SIZE MISMATCH WITH EISA COMPATIBLE ADD-ON SLAVE CARDS

An add-on slave card that is a 16 data bit resource (according to the EX16* signal line) cannot force the bus master to execute a 16 data bit access if the bus master only requested an 8 data bit (according to the BE* signal lines) access cycle. A similar statement can be made for a 32 data bit resource and accesses of 8, 16, or 24 data bits.

Data size mismatch with an EISA compatible add-on slave card is very simple. The BE* signal lines specify which byte lanes the data is written to or read from.

A bus master that intends to execute a single 16 data bit access cycle (indicated by the BE* signal lines) cannot do so if the accessed resource is only an 8 data bit (indicated by the EX16* and EX32* signal lines) resource. Similar statements can be made for a 24 or 32 data bit access to an 8 data bit resource or a 24 data bit access to a 16 data bit resource. The platform circuitry does the byte swapping to align the data to the byte lanes that a given accessed resource supports. Additionally, for an EISA bus master, the platform circuitry will execute additional access cycles to assemble and disassemble the data. The EISA bus master only "sees" a single access cycle of the data size it requested.

If the bus master is an ISA or E-ISA add-on bus owner card, the platform circuitry allows the access cycle to execute in the same fashion as on the ISA or E-ISA compatible platforms. The platform circuitry will not assemble or disassemble the data bytes; instead, the bus master must execute multiple access cycles.

The proper interpretation of the MEMCS16*, IOCS16*, SA0, and SBHE* signal lines allows data size mismatch to occur on EISA compatible platforms when the ISA or E-ISA compatible resources are involved in the access cycle. See the previous ISA and E-ISA sections for byte swapping for data size mismatch.

TRANSFER CYCLES AND EISA COMPATIBLE ADD-ON SLAVE CARDS

The operation of the DMA transfer cycles on an EISA compatible platform are a superset of those on an E-ISA compatible platform. Please see the section "TRANSFER CYCLES AND E-ISA COMPATIBLE ADD-ON SLAVE CARDS". The improvements are as follows:

- In addition to the COMPATIBLE, TYPE A, and TYPE B transfer cycles, the EISA compatible resources also support the TYPE C transfer cycle.

- For TYPE A, TYPE B, and TYPE C transfer cycles, the memory resource can be an add-on slave card in addition to the platform memory.

- For TYPE A, TYPE B, and TYPE C transfer cycles, the data size of the I/O resource can be larger than the data size of the memory resource. The ability to support this data size mismatch is due to multiple transfer cycles executed by the platform circuitry by a process called CONVERSION. CONVERSION also allows for DMA transfer cycles between dissimilar technology (i.e., EISA compatible I/O resource with an ISA compatible memory, etc.).

- In that data sizing is supported by the EISA compatible DMA controller (via CONVERSION), the MEMCS16*, EX16*, and EX32* signal lines of the memory resource are monitored. As with the ISA and E-ISA compatible I/O resources, the data size of the I/O resources are programmed in the DMA controller.

The one strong similarity between ISA, E-ISA, and EISA compatible I/O resources that support DMA transfer cycles is the use of the DRQx, DACKx*, AENx, IOW*, and IOR* signal lines. These signal lines are defined as they are on an ISA or E-ISA compatible platform. The IOW* and IOR* signal lines are used on EISA compatible resources because the M-IO and W-R signal lines are used for the memory resource.

Table 1-5-B in Chapter 1 outlines the various DMA transfer cycles supported on EISA compatible platforms. Table 4-11 outlines which signal lines are driven by which resources under generic transfers. "PLAT. CIRCUIT" in some cases may simply be a pull-up resistor. In the following tables, "PLAT." is the abbreviation for "platform circuitry".

LINE	DRIVEN BY	LINE	DRIVEN BY
AENx	PLAT. CIRCUIT	MEMR*	PLAT. DMA
BALE	PLAT. CIRCUIT	MEMW*	PLAT. DMA
DACKx*	PLAT. DMA	OSC	PLAT. CIRCUIT
DRQx	ADD-ON SLAVE	REFRESH*	PLAT. REF. CONT.
IOCHK*	ALL RESOURCES	RESET	PLAT. CIRCUIT
IOCHRDY	MEMORY RESOURCE	SA	PLAT. CIRCUIT
IOCS16*	PLAT. CIRCUIT	SBHE*	PLAT. DMA
M-IO	PLAT. DMA	W-R	PLAT. DMA
START*	PLAT. DMA	CMD*	PLAT. CIRCUIT
EX16*	MEM. RESOURCE	EX32*	MEM RESOURCE
IOR*	PLAT. DMA	SD	MEM., I/O RES.
IOW*	PLAT. DMA	BE*	PLAT. DMA
IRQx	ANY RESOURCE	SMR/SMW*	PLAT. CIRCUIT
LA	PLAT. DMA	BCLK	PLAT. CIRCUIT
MASTER16*	PLAT. CIRCUIT	TC	PLAT. DMA (1)
MEMCS16*	MEM. RESOURCE	SRDY*	PLAT. CIRCUIT

TABLE 4-11: DMA TRANSFER CYCLES ON EISA COMPATIBLE
PLATFORMS

NOTE:
(1) On an EISA compatible platform, the TC signal line can also be driven by the add-on I/O slave card.

TRANSFER CYCLE DATA SIZE MISMATCH WITH AN EISA COMPATIBLE ADD-ON SLAVE CARD

The data size of each DMA channel for each I/O resource is programmed into the DMA controller. The data size of the memory resource is determined by the DMA controller monitoring the MEMCS16*, EX16*, and EX32* signal lines. If the platform memory is the resource in the DMA transfer, the DMA controller knows the data size.

The data assembly and disassembly for CONVERSION cycles and the associated byte swapping is very complex in an EISA platform. See Subchapter 7.2 for more information.

4.6 EISA COMPATIBLE ADD-ON BUS OWNER CARDS

An add-on card can be designed as a bus owner. The EISA compatible platform can support AT, E-ISA, and EISA add-on bus owner cards. However, an EISA add-on bus owner card cannot be supported on PC, XT, ISA, or E-ISA compatible platforms.

For an EISA add-on card to become bus master, it must first execute the obtain portion of the arbitration cycle. After it no longer has immediate need for bus ownership, it can execute the release portion of the arbitration cycle. See Chapter 9 for more detailed information.

The EISA add-on bus owner card can execute all of the access cycles that the EISA platform CPU can, except for EISA compressed access cycles. When an add-on bus owner card accesses an ISA or E-ISA compatible resource, it does it as an E-MIX version of the EISA standard and data-matching access cycles. The platform circuitry does all of the signal line translations between the ISA and EISA bus protocols. The various types of access cycles that can be executed by an add-on bus owner card are outlined in Chapter 1, Tables 1-4-A to 1-4-D.

An add-on bus owner card has complete access to the entire memory and I/O address space. However, the platform architecture and software executing on the platform CPU assume that only the platform CPU has access to certain specific memory and I/O resources. For example, an add-on bus owner card cannot normally access the math co-processor memory registers. An add-on bus owner card usually does not access the I/O registers of the interrupt, DMA, and keyboard controllers, nor the timer, DMA page, and real time clock. In addition, the add-on bus owner card usually does not access the NMI chip select circuitry and Port B.

Of particular note is the fact that EISA bus ownership can be awarded to an add-on bus owner card in two ways. If the add-on bus owner card is ISA or E-ISA compatible, a DMA channel is used, as was previously described. If the add-on bus owner card is EISA compatible, it uses the MREQx* and MAKx* signal lines. An individual pair of these lines are routed to each EISA slot that is designed to support EISA add-on bus owner cards.

Access cycles are the only bus cycles that can be executed by the EISA add-on bus owner cards. Add-on bus owner cards perform access cycles in the same manner as the platform CPU. The accessed resources on the bus are unable to determine if the platform CPU or an EISA compatible add-on bus owner card is executing the cycle. An active MASTER* signal line, when an ISA or E-ISA compatible add-on bus owner card owns the bus, indicates that it is not the platform CPU. This same signal line has been redefined for EISA access cycles as the MASTER16* signal line. Thus, this signal line only indicates the data size of the EISA bus master, not the "source" of the ownership.

4.7 REFRESH

The refresh cycle is executed by the platform refresh controller every 15.6 microseconds. An ISA or E-ISA add-on bus owner card can request a refresh cycle by driving the REFRESH* signal line active. An EISA add-on bus owner card cannot request a refresh cycle because of preemption. The refresh controller on an EISA compatible platform can preempt bus ownership by the EISA add-on bus owner card.

Some chip sets queue up pending refresh cycles, and execute several back to back; consequently, a refresh does not occur exactly every 15.6 microseconds.

4.8 ARBITRATION

Ownership of the bus is established through two mechanisms. For ISA and E-ISA compatible platforms, the add-on bus owner card "subleases" a DMA channel from the DMA controller. ISA and E-ISA add-on bus owner cards installed in EISA compatible platforms can obtain bus ownership in the same fashion as on ISA or E-ISA compatible platforms. EISA add-on bus owner cards obtain bus ownership without subleasing a DMA channel. Each EISA slot (that supports EISA bus masters) has an individual pair of signal lines (MREQx* and MAKx*) which are attached directly to the platform arbiter. An EISA add-on bus owner card requests bus ownership by driving its specific MREQx* signal line active. Bus ownership is granted when the associated MAKx* signal line becomes active. The bus owner is notified that it has been preempted when the arbiter drives the MAKx* signal line inactive.

Notes

CHAPTER FIVE

SIGNAL LINE DEFINITION

INTRODUCTION

This chapter describes in detail all of the signal lines for an ISA, E-ISA, or EISA compatible bus. The signals can be grouped into seven distinct categories: address, data, cycle control, bus control, interrupt, DMA, and power.

The implementation of the various bus signal lines vary for both the type of cycle and for the current bus owner. In some cases, it is platform circuitry that drives a particular bus line and not necessarily the current bus owner. The possible bus masters (owners) are the platform CPU, the DMA and refresh controllers, and add-on bus owner cards.

In an ISA or E-ISA compatible platform, the bus masters, platform resources, and add-on cards use the PC, XT, and AT SPECIFIC signal lines. In an EISA compatible system the bus masters, platform resources, and EISA compatible add-on cards use some of the PC, XT, and AT SPECIFIC and all of the EISA SPECIFIC signal lines. ISA or E-ISA compatible add-on cards in an EISA compatible system only use the PC, XT, and AT SPECIFIC signal lines.

OVERVIEW OF ISA AND E-ISA COMPATIBLE SIGNAL LINES

Tables 5-1-A to 5-1-E provide summaries of the ISA and E-ISA compatible signal lines that will be discussed in this chapter. For comparison, the PC and XT signal lines have been included. The PC and XT signal lines are a subset of the ISA and E-ISA signal lines reflecting the smaller data width, address space, fewer DMA and interrupt channels, lack of support of add-on bus owner cards, and the non-support of the no-wait-state access cycle.

ADDRESS SIGNALS	ISA & E-ISA		FUNCTION
	PC & XT SPECIFIC	AT SPECIFIC	
BALE	X	X	LATCH THE ADDRESS, AENx, SBHE*
SA<0-19>	X	X	FIRST MEGABYTE OF MEMORY ... ALL I/O
LA<17-23>		X	16 MEGABYTE MEMORY
SBHE*		X	VALID DATA ON SD<8-15>
AENx	X	X	INACTIVE=ACCESS CYCLE ACTIVE=TRANSFER CYCLE

TABLE 5-1-A: ISA AND E-ISA SIGNAL LINE OVERVIEW

DATA SIGNALS	ISA & E-ISA		FUNCTION
	PC & AT SPECIFIC	AT SPECIFIC	
SD<0-7>	X	X	1ST ORDER DATA BYTE
SD<8-15>		X	2ND ORDER DATA BYTE

TABLE 5-1-B: ISA & E-ISA SIGNAL LINE OVERVIEW

CYCLE CONTROL SIGNALS	ISA & E-ISA		FUNCTION
	PC & AT SPECIFIC	AT SPECIFIC	
SMEMR*, SMEMW*	X	X	FIRST MEGABYTE MEMORY RD/WR
MEMR*, MEMW*		X	16 MEGABYTE MEMORY RD/WR
IOR*, IOW*	X	X	I/O RD/WR
MEMCS16*, IOCS16*		X	ACCESSED RESOURCE IS 16 BITS
IOCHRDY	X	X	WAIT STATES NEEDED
SRDY* (NOWS*)		X	IMMEDIATE CYCLE COMPLETION

TABLE 5-1-C: ISA & E-ISA SIGNAL LINE OVERVIEW

BUS CONTROL SIGNALS	ISA & E-ISA		FUNCTION
	PC & AT SPECIFIC	AT SPECIFIC	
REFRESH*	X	X	REFRESH CYCLE
MASTER16*		X	16 BIT ISA MASTER
IOCHK*	X	X	ERROR ON BUS
RESET	X	X	REINITIALIZE BUS RESOURCES
BCLK	X	X	4.77 MHZ ON PC & XT 6-8 MHZ ON AT
OSC	X	X	14.31818 MHZ

TABLE 5-1-D: ISA & E-ISA SIGNAL LINE OVERVIEW

OTHER SIGNALS	ISA & E-ISA		FUNCTION
	PC & AT SPECIFIC	AT SPECIFIC	
IRQx <3-7,9>	X	X	INTERRUPT REQUEST
IRQx <10-12,14,15>		X	INTERRUPT REQUEST
DACKx*, DRQx <1-3>	X	X	DMA & ISA BUS MASTER REQUEST
DACKx*,DRQx <0,5-7>		X	DMA & ISA BUS MASTER REQUEST
TC	X	X	DMA TERMINATION DMA TO I/O RESOURCE

FIG. 5-1-E: ISA & E-ISA SIGNAL LINE OVERVIEW

OVERVIEW OF EISA COMPATIBLE SIGNAL LINES

Tables 5-2-A to 5-2-E provide a brief overview of the EISA compatible signal lines that will be discussed in this chapter. For comparison, the PC, AT, and AT signal lines have been included. EISA platforms allow PC, XT, and AT add-on slave cards to be installed.

The EISA specific signal lines are a superset of the ISA and E-ISA specific signal lines. They reflect a larger data width and address space, improved support of add-on bus owner cards (bus master functions), and improved and new access bus cycles.

ADDRESS SIGNALS	ISA & E-ISA		EISA SPECIFIC	FUNCTION
	PC & AT SPECIFIC	AT SPECIFIC		
BALE	X	X		LATCH THE ADDRESS, AENx, SBHE*
SA<0-19>	X	X		FIRST MEGABYTE OF MEMORY ADDRESS & ALL I/O ADDRESS SPACE
LA<17-23>		X	X	16 MEGABYTE MEMORY
LA<2-16>			X	I/O ADDRESS & 1ST 128K MEMORY ADDRESS SPACE
LA*<24-31>			X	4 GIGABYTE MEMORY ADDRESS SPACE
SBHE*		X		VALID DATA ON SD<8-15>
AENx	X	X	X	INACTIVE=ACCESS CYCLE ACTIVE=TRANSFER CYCLE
			X	I/O ADDRESS SLOT SPECIFIC
BE*<0-3>			X	SPECIFIC BYTE LANES USED & ADDRESS FOR 4 BYTES

TABLE 5-2-A: ISA, E-ISA, & EISA SIGNAL LINE OVERVIEW

DATA SIGNALS	ISA & E-ISA		EISA SPECIFIC	FUNCTION
	PC & AT SPECIFIC	AT SPECIFIC		
SD<0-7>	X	X	X	1ST ORDER DATA BYTE
SD<8-15>		X	X	2ND ORDER DATA BYTE
SD<16-31>			X	3RD AND 4TH ORDER DATA BYTES

TABLE 5-2-B: ISA, E-ISA, & EISA SIGNAL LINE OVERVIEW

CYCLE CONTROL SIGNALS	ISA & E-ISA		EISA SPECIFIC	FUNCTION
	PC & AT SPECIFIC	AT SPECIFIC		
SMEMR*, SMEMW*	X	X		FIRST MEGABYTE MEMORY RD/WR
MEMR*, MEMW*		X		16 MEGABYTE MEMORY RD/WR
IOR*, IOW*	X	X	X	I/O RD/WR AND DMA RD/WR
MEMCS16*		X		ACCESSED MEMORY RESOURCE IS 16 BITS
IOCS16*		X	X	ACCESSED I/O RESOURCE IS 16 BITS
IOCHRDY	X	X		WAIT STATES NEEDED
SRDY* (NOWS*)		X	X	IMMEDIATE CYCLE COMPLETION COMPRESSED CYCLE
START*		X		VALID EISA CYCLE START
CMD*		X		VALID EISA CYCLE LENGTH
W-R		X		WRITE VS READ
M-IO		X		MEMORY VS I/O
EX16*, EX32*		X		EISA COMPATIBLE 16 OR 32 RESOURCE
EXRDY		X		EISA WAIT NEEDED
SLBURST*		X		ACCESSED RESOURCE SUPPORTS BURST CYCLE
MSBURST*		X		EISA BUS MASTER SUPPORTS BURST CYCLE
LOCK*			X	INSURES RETENTION OF BUS

TABLE 5-2-C: ISA, E-ISA, & EISA SIGNAL LINE OVERVIEW

BUS CONTROL SIGNALS	ISA & E-ISA		EISA SPECIFIC	FUNCTION
	PC & AT SPECIFIC	AT SPECIFIC		
REFRESH*	X	X	X	REFRESH CYCLE
MASTER16*		X	X	16 BIT ISA MASTER / 16 OR 32 BIT EISA MASTER
IOCHK*	X	X	X	ERROR ON BUS
RESET	X	X	X	REINITIALIZE BUS RESOURCES
BCLK	X	X	X	4.77 MHZ ON PC & XT 6-8 MHZ ON AT / 6-8.33 MHZ ON EISA
OSC	X	X	X	14.31818 MHZ (VIDEO COLOR BURST)

TABLE 5-2-D: ISA, E-ISA, & EISA SIGNAL LINE OVERVIEW

OTHER SIGNALS	ISA & EISA		EISA SPECIFIC	FUNCTION
	PC & AT SPECIFIC	AT SPECIFIC		
IRQx <3-7,9>	X	X	X	INTERRUPT REQUEST
IRQx <10-12,14,15>		X	X	INTERRUPT REQUEST
DRQx, DACKx* <1-3>	X	X	X	DMA & ISA BUS MASTER REQUEST
DRQx,DACKx*<0,5-7>		X	X	DMA & ISA BUS MASTER REQUEST
TC	X	X	X	DMA TERMINATION DMA TO I/O RESOURCE ACCESSED RESOURCE TO DMA TO TERMINATE DMA CYCLE
MREQx*<1-6>			X	REQUEST BY EISA MASTER FOR BUS OWNERSHIP
MAKx*<1-6>			X	ACK. TO EISA MASTER BUS OWNERSHP

TABLE 5-2-E: ISA, E-ISA, & EISA SIGNAL LINE OVERVIEW

CONVENTIONS

The following text uses ISA to represent PC, XT, and AT. E-ISA is the same as ISA except for the improvements noted earlier. The 16 bit connector is essentially an 8 bit connector with additional signal lines attached; thus, the use of the notation 8/16 (see Chapter 14 for more information). Each signal line heading specifies whether the respective signal line resides on the 8 bit ISA or E-ISA connector used for PC and XT compatible slots or on the 8/16 ISA or E-ISA connector on AT compatible slots.

Similarly, an EISA compatible platform supports the 8 bit connectors (PC and XT) and 8/16 bit connectors (AT) within the EISA connectors. The EISA connector is essentially an ISA connector with additional signal lines attached to support the EISA specific ADDRESS, DATA, and CONTROL signal lines (see Chapter 14 for more information). Each signal line heading specifies if the respective signal line resides on the 8 bit or 8/16 bit portion of the ISA connector, or the EISA connector.

FOR ISA PLATFORMS:

ISA BUS MASTERS ARE PLATFORM CPU OR ADD-ON BUS OWNER CARDS. ISA RESOURCES ARE PLATFORM RESOURCES OR ADD-ON SLAVE CARDS.

FOR E-ISA PLATFORMS:

ISA BUS MASTERS ARE ADD-ON BUS OWNER CARDS. ISA RESOURCES ARE ADD-ON SLAVE CARDS.

E-ISA BUS MASTERS ARE PLATFORM CPU OR ADD-ON BUS OWNER CARDS. E-ISA RESOURCES ARE PLATFORM RESOURCES OR ADD-ON SLAVE CARDS.

FOR EISA PLATFORMS:

ISA OR E-ISA BUS MASTERS ARE ADD-ON BUS OWNER CARDS. ISA OR E-ISA RESOURCES ARE ADD-ON SLAVE CARDS.

EISA BUS MASTERS ARE PLATFORM CPU OR ADD-ON BUS OWNER CARDS. EISA RESOURCES ARE PLATFORM RESOURCES OR ADD-ON SLAVE CARDS.

ALL PLATFORMS:

APPLIES TO ISA OR E-ISA AND EISA (PC, XT, & AT) COMPATIBLE PLATFORMS.

ADDRESS SIGNAL LINES

In addition to the actual address lines, other lines are used that aid in delivering the correct address-related information to all resources on the bus. These other signal lines are BALE, AENx, SBHE*, and BE*.

BALE (8, 8/16 ISA or E-ISA & EISA CONNECTOR)

ISA OR E-ISA PLATFORMS

Bus address latch enable (BALE) signal line is driven by the platform CPU to indicate when the SA<0-19>, LA<17-23>, AENx, and SBHE* signal lines are valid.

EISA PLATFORMS

The BALE signal line operates in the same fashion as in an ISA or E-ISA compatible platform when an ISA or E-ISA bus master or an ISA or E-ISA accessed resource is involved in the cycle. Platform circuitry drives it as a pulse when an EISA bus master executes an E-MIX access cycle. The BALE signal line is not used by EISA bus masters interacting with EISA compatible resources.

ALL PLATFORMS

The BALE signal line is driven to a logical one by the platform circuitry when an ISA or E-ISA add-on bus owner card or the DMA controller owns the bus.

For SAFE COMPATIBILITY, the input circuitry of an add-on slave memory card should latch the LA<17-23> signal lines with the BALE signal line for either a platform CPU or an add-on bus owner card should be as shown in Figure 5-1.

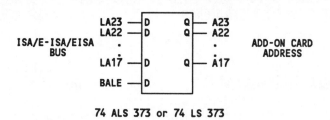

74 ALS 373 or 74 LS 373

FIGURE 5-1: INPUT ADDRESS CIRCUIT

SA<0-19> (8, 8/16 ISA or E-ISA & EISA CONNECTOR)

ISA OR E-ISA PLATFORMS

The SA signal lines are driven by the ISA or E-ISA bus master to define the lower 20 ADDRESS signal lines needed for the lower one megabyte of the memory address space. The SA<0-15> signal lines define the entire 64K address space required for the I/O address space and are driven by the ISA or E-ISA bus master. However, only the SA<0-9> signal lines are decoded by the ISA or E-ISA I/O resources on an ISA compatible platform. On an E-ISA compatible platform, the E-ISA I/O resource can decode the SA<0-11> signal lines for slot specific I/O addressing.

During refresh cycles, only the SA<0-7> signal lines are driven by the refresh controller.

EISA PLATFORMS

On an EISA platform, the SA signal lines operate in the same fashion as on an ISA or E-ISA platform when an ISA or E-ISA bus master or an ISA or E-ISA resource are involved in the cycle. The SA signal lines are not used by EISA bus masters interacting with EISA resources. For an ISA or E-ISA bus master accessing an EISA compatible resource (via an I-MIX cycle), the SA<0-16> signal lines are used by the ISA or E-ISA bus master, but are translated by the platform circuitry to the LA<2-16> and BE* signal lines for EISA resources. (The SBHE* signal line, in conjunction with the SA0 and SA1 signals, generate the BE* signal lines for I-MIX access cycles.)

For an EISA bus master accessing ISA or E-ISA resources, the SA0, and SA1 signal lines are generated from the BE* signal lines for E-MIX access cycles (see the BE* signal line section for more information).

EISA compatible platforms have expanded the definition of refresh to drive the SA<0-15> signal lines during the refresh cycle.

ALL PLATFORMS

During DMA transfer cycles, the DMA controller drives all of the SA signal lines valid.

Any SA signal line not driven floats to an indeterminate state. Some platform manufacturers attach a 10K pull-up resistor to prevent these lines from floating.

An ISA or E-ISA compatible add-on bus owner card may request a refresh cycle while it is the current bus master. During the refresh cycle, it must make the address lines inputs, because the refresh controller is driving the refresh address onto the bus.

LA < 17-23 > (8/16 ISA or E-ISA & EISA CONNECTOR)

ISA OR E-ISA PLATFORMS

The LA < 17-23 > signal lines are driven by the ISA or E-ISA bus master or DMA controller and provide the additional address lines required for the 16 megabyte memory address space. They are latched by the accessed resource and the falling edge of the BALE signal line.

EISA PLATFORMS

The LA < 17-23 > signal lines operate in the same fashion as on an ISA or E-ISA compatible platform when an ISA, E-ISA, or EISA bus master accesses an ISA or E-ISA resource. These LA signal lines are also used by EISA bus masters and the DMA controller accessing EISA compatible memory resources, and operate as outlined in the LA < 2-16 > / LA* < 24-31 > description.

ALL PLATFORMS

During a refresh cycle, the LA < 17-23 > signal lines are undefined. All resources should tri-state these lines during a refresh cycle. Any LA address lines that are not driven will float to an undefined logical state. Some platform manufacturers attach a 10K pull-up resister to prevent these lines from floating.

LA<2-16> / LA*<24-31> (EISA CONNECTOR)

EISA PLATFORMS

These latchable address (LA) signal lines are driven by the EISA bus master and work in conjunction with the LA<17-23> and BE* signal lines to address any byte in a four gigabyte memory or 64K I/O address space. The 64K I/O address space only uses the LA<2-15> signal lines. These lines, in conjunction with the LA<17-23> and BE* signal lines, are driven by the DMA controller to address any byte in the four gigabyte memory space.

The LA*<24-31> signal lines are driven with inverted logic and are pulled high by pull-up resistors. This insures that only the first 16 megabytes of the memory address space are addressed during E-MIX and I-MIX access cycles.

During I/O access cycles and refresh cycles, the LA*<24-31> signal lines are not driven. These signal lines are resistively pulled up to logical zero.

Any of the LA<2-16> signal lines not driven will float to an undefined logical state. Some platform manufacturers attach a 10K pull-up resistor to prevent these lines from floating.

SBHE* (8/16 ISA or E-ISA & EISA CONNECTOR)

ISA OR E-ISA PLATFORMS

The system byte high enable (SBHE*) signal line is driven by the ISA or E-ISA bus master to indicate that valid data resides on the SD<8-15> signal lines. This line, in conjunction with the SA0 signal line, allows the ISA or E-ISA bus master to indicate the data size requested from ISA or E-ISA compatible resources. When the SBHE* signal line is driven inactive, the data size requested is 8 data bits. When the SBHE* signal line is driven active, and the SA0 signal line is logical one, the data size requested is 8 data bits. When the SBHE* signal line is driven active, and the SA0 signal line is logical zero, the data size requested is 16 data bits. See Tables 4-3 and 4-8 for more information.

EISA PLATFORMS

On an EISA platform, the SBHE* signal line operates in the same fashion as on an ISA or E-ISA compatible platform when an ISA, E-ISA, or EISA bus master is accessing an ISA or E-ISA resource. This signal line is not used when an EISA bus master is accessing an EISA compatible resource.

The SBHE* signal line, in conjunction with the SA0 and SA1 signals, is decoded by the platform circuitry to drive the BE* signal lines for I-MIX access cycles. The BE* signal lines are decoded by the platform circuitry to drive the SBHE*, SA0, and SA1 signal lines for E-MIX access cycles. (See the BE* signal line section for more information.)

ALL PLATFORMS

The SBHE* signal line is undefined for refresh cycles because no data is actually read. If the platform circuitry does not drive this signal line it will float to an undetermined state.

AENx (8, 8/16 ISA or E-ISA & EISA CONNECTOR)

ISA OR E-ISA PLATFORMS

The address enable (AENx) signal line is driven by the platform circuitry as an indication to ISA or E-ISA I/O resources not to respond to the ADDRESS and I/O COMMAND signal lines. This signal line has no effect on memory resources.

> *The "x" suffix represents the individual versions of this signal line routed to each slot. The name without the suffix indicates that all slots receive the same signal line.*

On ISA compatible platforms, this signal line is inactive when the platform CPU or bus owner add-on card is bus master. This signal line is active only when the DMA controller is the bus owner because transfer cycles execute with the memory and the I/O COMMAND signal lines active simultaneously. The AEN signal line is the method by which I/O resources are informed that a DMA transfer cycle is occurring and that only the I/O resource with an active DACKx* signal line can respond to the I/O signal lines.

On E-ISA compatible platforms, the AENx signal lines are used for slot-specific I/O addressing and configuration space; consequently, the platform circuitry individually drives the AENx signal line to each slot. (The appended x indicates the slot number.) During a DMA transfer cycle, all of the AENx signal lines are active. During I/O access cycles executed by E-ISA bus masters, the platform circuitry decodes the I/O address and drives the appropriate AENx signal lines. If the access is to the general I/O address block, all of the AENx signal lines are inactive. ("General" is defined as the ISA compatible 768 bytes. See Chapter 2 for more information.) If the access is to a specific I/O address block of a slot, only the AENx signal line associated with the slot is inactive. See Chapter 2 for more detailed address space information, and Chapter 12 for more configuration space and slot specific I/O information.

For an ISA or E-ISA compatible platform I/O access cycle, when the platform CPU is bus owner, the AENx signal line must be inactive prior to the BALE signal line becoming active, and must remain inactive during the active period of the COMMAND lines. When an ISA or E-ISA add-on bus owner card or DMA controller is the bus owner, the AENx signal line must be inactive prior to and during the active period of the COMMAND signal lines. This requirement is because the platform circuitry drives the BALE signal line to a constant logical one for the entire cycle.

The AENx signal lines are derived from a valid decode of the SA<8,9,12-15> signal lines.

EISA PLATFORM

On an EISA platform, the AENx signal line operates in the same manner as it does on an E-ISA platform. The only two differences are when an EISA bus master is executing an EISA specific I/O access cycle or when an accessing an ISA or E-ISA compatible I/O resource via an E-MIX access cycle. During these access cycles, the AENx signal lines must be valid relative to the START* signal line being driven inactive at the point that the CMD* signal line is driven active.

The AENx signal lines are derived from a valid decode of the LA<8,9,12-15> and M-IO signal lines.

ALL PLATFORMS

When a refresh cycle is executed, the AENx signal line is active unless an add-on bus owner card requested the refresh cycle. When the ISA or E-ISA add-on bus owner card has requested a refresh, it is unclear if all platform circuitry (i.e., all chip sets) drive the AENx signal line inactive during the refresh cycle. Thus, there is no useful interpretation of this signal line during a refresh cycle and it should be ignored.

BE* <0-3> (EISA CONNECTOR)

EISA PLATFORMS

The byte enable (BE*) signal lines are driven by the EISA bus master or platform circuitry to indicate which bytes of the data signal lines are valid. BE*0 is associated with data bits <0-7>, BE*1 is associated with data bits <8-15>, and so forth. A logical low indicates that the associated byte lanes are to be used by the EISA resource. See Chapter 6 and 7 for more information.

During access cycles to ISA, E-ISA, or EISA resources, the BE* signal lines are driven by EISA bus masters. During transfer cycles, the BE* signal lines are driven by the DMA controller. The BE* signal lines replace the LA0 and LA1 address lines that are not defined as part of the EISA signal lines.

There are certain BE* patterns that are not supported. The basic criterion is that non-contiguous byte groupings are not allowed; thus, the following BE*3 to BE*0 patterns are not possible: 0010, 0100, 0101, 0110, and 1010.

When the accessed resource is ISA or E-ISA compatible, the BE* signal lines are decoded to the SA0, SA1, and SBHE* signal lines by the platform circuitry as shown in the following table.

DRIVEN BY EISA BUS MASTER OR DMA CONTROLLER				DECODED & DRIVEN BY PLATFORM CIRCUITRY		
BE*0	BE*1	BE*2	BE*3	SA0	SA1	SBHE*
0	1	1	1	0	0	INACT
1	1	0	1	0	1	INACT
1	1	1	0	1	1	ACT
1	0	1	1	1	0	ACT
1	0	0	1(1)	1	0	ACT
1	0	0	0(2)	1	0	ACT
0	0	1	1	0	0	ACT
0	0	0	1(3)	0	0	ACT
0	0	0	0(4)	0	0	ACT
1	1	0	0	0	1	ACT

TABLE 5-3: CONVERSION OF BE* SIGNAL LINES TO SA0, SA1, AND SBHE* SIGNAL LINES ON EISA COMPATIBLE PLATFORMS

NOTES:
(1) and (2) are unique in that even if the accessed resource data size is 16 data bits, the data cannot be accessed in a single cycle. Thus, the first access is 8 data bits according to 10xx (BE*0-BE*3), and the second access is 8 or 16 data bits according to the 1101 and 1100 (BE*0-BE*3) entries for (1) and (2), respectively. If the accessed resource is 8 data bits in size, multiple 8 data bit accesses are executed with the lowest order byte first.
(Please see additional notes on the following page.)

(3) and (4) are unique in that even if the accessed resource data size is 16 data bits, the data cannot be accessed in a single cycle. Thus, the first access is 16 data bits according to 00xx (BE*0-BE*3), and the second access is 8 or 16 data bits according to the 1101 and 1100 (BE*0-BE*3) entries for (3) and (4), respectively. If the accessed resource is 8 data bits in size, multiple 8 data bit accesses are executed with the lowest order byte first.

When an ISA or E-ISA bus master accesses an EISA compatible resource via an E-MIX access cycle, the SA0, SA1, SA2, and SBHE* signal lines are converted to BE* signal lines as shown in the following table.

DRIVEN BY ISA or E-ISA BUS MASTER			DECODED & DRIVEN BY PLATFORM CIRCUITRY			
SA0	SA1	SBHE*	BE*0	BE*1	BE*2	BE*3
0	0	INACT	0	1	1	1
0	1	INACT	1	1	0	1
1	1	ACT	1	1	1	0
1	0	ACT	1	0	1	1
0	0	ACT	0	0	1	1
0	0	ACT	1	1	0	0

TABLE 5-4: CONVERSION OF SA0, SA1, AND SBHE* SIGNAL LINES TO BE* SIGNAL LINES ON EISA COMPATIBLE PLATFORMS

NOTE: SA0 = 1 and SBHE* = INACTIVE is not allowed.

For maximum compatibility, the accessed resource should only drive or receive data according to the actual byte lanes specified by the BE*, SA0, and SBHE* signal lines. The platform circuitry or burst downshift bus master will always do the proper byte swapping (see Chapters 4 and 6 for further information). When data is read, the driving of the "non-specified" byte lanes may cause buffer fights with byte swapping or burst downshifting bus master circuitry.

DATA SIGNALS

SD<0-7> (8, 8/16 ISA or E-ISA & EISA CONNECTOR)
SD<8-15> (8/16 ISA or E-ISA & EISA CONNECTOR)
SD<16-31> (EISA CONNECTOR)

ISA OR E-ISA PLATFORMS

The data signal lines (SD) 0 through 7 or 8 through 15 are driven for an 8 data bit cycle and 0 through 15 are driven for a 16 data bit cycle. The SD15 signal line represents the most significant bit and SD0 the least significant bit. The platform byte swapper circuitry insures that the SD<8-15> signal lines are valid whenever the SBHE* signal line is active.

EISA PLATFORMS

The SD<16-31> signal lines are simply an extension of the SD<0-15> signal lines. For EISA specific access and DMA transfer cycles, the BE* signal lines indicate which byte lanes are valid. For I-MIX, E-MIX, DMA COMPATIBLE, and some DMA with CONVERSION cycles, the BE*, SA0, and SBHE* signal lines indicate which byte lanes are valid (see Chapters 4 and 6 for more information).

ALL PLATFORMS

The SD<0-31> signal lines are undefined for a refresh cycle. All resources should tri-state these signal lines during a refresh cycle.

Any DATA signal lines not specified as part of the cycle (by the BE, SA0, SBHE signal lines) should be tri-stated. On ISA compatible platforms, the undriven DATA signal lines float to an undetermined state. Some platform manufacturers attach a 10K pull-up resister to prevent these lines from floating. E-ISA and EISA compatible platforms pull the SA signal lines high with 8.2K pull-up resistors.*

CYCLE CONTROL SIGNALS

These signals control the address space (memory or I/O), data direction (read or write), cycle type, and cycle length.

MEMR* (8/16 ISA or E-ISA & EISA CONNECTOR)
SMEMR* (8, 8/16 ISA or E-ISA CONNECTOR & EISA CONNECTOR)

ISA OR E-ISA PLATFORMS

The memory read (MEMR*) signal line is driven by the ISA or E-ISA bus master or DMA controller to request a memory resource to drive data onto the bus during the cycle. The system memory read (SMEMR*) signal line performs the same function, and is active when the MEMR* signal line is active and the LA<20-23> signal lines indicate the first one megabyte of address space. It is driven by the platform circuitry monitoring the MEMR* and LA<20-23> signal lines; consequently, its timing lags that of the MEMR* signal line. An ISA or E-ISA add-on bus owner card drives the MEMR* signal line, never the SMEMR* signal line.

EISA PLATFORMS

When an ISA, E-ISA, or EISA bus master is accessing an ISA or E-ISA resource, the MEMR* and SMEMR* signal lines are defined as they are for the ISA or E-ISA compatible platforms. An ISA or E-ISA bus master will directly drive the MEMR* signal line. The platform circuitry will drive the SMEMR* signal line. The platform circuitry decodes the M-IO and W-R signal lines to drive the MEMR* and SMEMR* signal lines when an EISA bus master accesses an ISA or E-ISA resource. The MEMR* and SMEMR* signal lines are not defined when an EISA bus master is accessing an EISA resource.

The DMA controller drives these signal lines during COMPATIBLE transfer cycles or transfer cycles with CONVERSION.

ALL PLATFORMS

During a refresh cycle, the MEMR* signal line is driven by the refresh controller. It also drives the SMEMR* signal line active.

The purpose of the SMEMR* signal line is to maintain compatibility with 8 data bit add-on slave cards. The PC, XT, and the 8 data bit definition of the AT bus specifications do not require that the LA<20-23> signal lines be monitored. Thus, the SA<0-19> signal lines appear valid multiple times within the memory address space. The SMEMR* signal line prevents the 8 data bit resources from responding to all these multiple locations.

MEMW* (8/16 ISA or E-ISA & EISA CONNECTOR)
SMEMW* (8, 8/16 ISA or E-ISA & EISA CONNECTOR)

ALL PLATFORMS

The memory write (MEMW*) and the system memory write (SMEMW*) signal lines request the memory resource to accept data from the data lines. Otherwise, they are defined in the same fashion as the MEMR* and SMEMR* signal lines.

During a refresh cycle, these signal lines are not active. Pull-up resistors on the platform keep these signal lines from floating active.

IOR* (8, 8/16 ISA or E-ISA & EISA CONNECTOR)

ISA OR E-ISA PLATFORM

The I/O read (IOR*) signal line is driven by the ISA or E-ISA bus master or DMA controller to request an I/O resource to drive data onto the data bus during the cycle.   The I/O resource is responding to a valid address for an access cycle, or to a valid DACKx* signal line for a transfer cycle.

EISA PLATFORM

When an ISA, E-ISA, or EISA bus master is accessing an ISA or E-ISA resource, the IOR* signal line is defined the same as for the ISA or E-ISA compatible platform.   An ISA or E-ISA bus master will directly drive this signal line.   The platform circuitry decodes the M-IO and W-R signal lines and drives the IOR* signal line when an EISA bus master accesses an ISA or E-ISA compatible resource.   This signal line is not defined when an EISA bus master is accessing an EISA resource.

Because the protocol of the EISA bus only has one pair of signal lines for address space and direction (M-IO and W-R), another pair is required for DMA transfer cycles.   In the EISA bus specification for a transfer cycle, the IOR* and IOW* signal lines control the I/O resources while the M-IO and W-R signal lines control memory resources.

ALL PLATFORMS

During a refresh cycle, this signal line is not active.   Pull-up resistors on the platform keep this signal line from floating active.

IOW* (8, 8/16 ISA or E-ISA & EISA CONNECTOR)

ALL PLATFORMS

The I/O write (IOW*) signal line is driven by the ISA, E-ISA, EISA bus master, or DMA controller to request an I/O resource to accept data from the data lines. Otherwise, they are defined in the same fashion as the IOR* signal line.

MEMCS16* (8/16 ISA or E-ISA & EISA CONNECTOR)

ISA OR E-ISA PLATFORM

The memory chip select 16 (MEMCS16*) signal line is driven by the memory resource to indicate that it is an ISA or E-ISA resource that supports a 16 data bit access cycle. The ISA or E-ISA bus master may only request an 8 data bit access according to the SBHE* and SA0 signal lines. An active MEMCS16* signal line not only indicates support of 16 data bits; it also allows the ISA or E-ISA bus master to execute shorter cycles. The MEMCS16* signal results from a straight decode of the LA<17-23> signal lines without any qualification of the COMMAND signal lines. Consequently, it will be driven active also during I/O access cycles. The ISA or E-ISA bus master must ignore this line during I/O access cycles.

The MEMCS16* signal line is ignored by the DMA and refresh controller for transfer and refresh cycles, respectively.

EISA PLATFORMS

When an ISA, E-ISA, or EISA bus master is accessing an ISA or E-ISA resource, the MEMCS16* signal line is defined the same as for the ISA or E-ISA platform. This signal line is not defined when an EISA bus master is accessing an EISA resource. For an E-MIX access cycle, this signal line is sampled by the platform circuitry to determine if an E-MIX version of the EISA standard access cycle (EISA bus master data size is equal to or less than the ISA or E-ISA resource data size) or an E-ISA version of the EISA data-matching access cycle is to be executed. For an I-MIX access cycle, this signal line is driven by the platform circuitry as a translation of the EX16* and EX32* signal lines driven by the EISA compatible accessed resource.

When the EISA platform is executing a DMA COMPATIBLE transfer cycle, it is assumed that the data size of the memory resource is equal to or greater that the data size of the I/O resource; consequently, the MEMCS16* signal line is not sampled. When the DMA controller is executing a DMA TYPE A, B, or C (BURST) transfer cycle, this signal line is sampled by the DMA controller to determine if a transfer cycle with "CONVERSION" is to be executed. As with access cycles, the MEMCS16* signal line indicates to the DMA controller the data size of the memory resource and that it is ISA or E-ISA compatible. The memory resource is the only transfer cycle participant to indicate data size; the data size of the I/O participant is programmed in software.

ALL PLATFORMS

The original IBM AT does not drive the MEMCS16* signal line. Therefore, an access to the platform memory by ISA add-on bus owner cards MAY ignore an inactive MEMCS16* signal line and execute the access as a 16 bit cycle anyway. E-ISA and EISA platforms properly drive the MEMCS16* signal line when platform memory is accessed; consequently, the E-ISA add-on bus owner card must monitor the MEMCS16* signal line. See the ADD-ON BUS MASTER CARD section of Chapter 4 for more detailed information.

> *The fact that MEMCS16* is a straight decode of the LA<17-23> signal lines means that the entire 128K memory address block is either all 8 bits or all 16 bits. Problems arise if only a portion of the block is associated with a 16 data bit resource and another portion is an 8 data bit resource. When the platform CPU is the bus owner, the SA<0-16> signal lines do not become valid soon enough to allow for different bit sizes within the 128K block.*

IOCS16* (8/16 ISA or E-ISA & EISA CONNECTOR)

ISA OR E-ISA PLATFORM

The I/O chip select 16 (IOCS16*) signal line is driven by an I/O resource to indicate that it is an ISA or E-ISA compatible resource that supports a 16 data bit access cycle. The ISA or E-ISA bus master may only request an 8 data bit access according to the SBHE* and SA0 signal lines. An active IOCS16* signal line not only indicates a support of 16 data bits, it also allows the ISA or E-ISA bus master to execute shorter default cycles. IOCS16* is a straight decode of the SA<0-9> (SA<0-11> on an E-ISA compatible platform) signal lines without any qualification of the COMMAND signal lines. Consequently, the IOCS16* signal line may be driven active during memory access cycles. The bus master must ignore this line during memory access cycles.

An E-ISA resource on an E-ISA compatible platform drives the IOCS16* signal line by decoding the SA<0-11> signal lines and qualifying it with the AENx signal line.

EISA PLATFORMS

When an ISA, E-ISA, or EISA bus master is accessing an ISA or E-ISA resource, the IOCS16* signal line is defined as it is for the ISA or E-ISA compatible platform. This signal line is not defined when an EISA compatible bus master is accessing an EISA compatible resource.

For an E-MIX access cycle, this signal line is sampled by the platform circuitry to determine if an E-MIX version of the EISA standard access cycle (EISA bus master data size is equal to or less than the ISA resource data size) or an E-ISA version of the data-matching access cycle is to be executed. For an I-MIX access cycle, the EX16* signal line cannot return quickly enough to translate into the IOCS16* signal line. Thus, EISA I/O accessed resources must drive both the EX16* and IOCS16* signal lines. The EISA I/O resource (either 16 or 32 data bits in size) must drive the IOCS16* signal line under the following conditions:

- An EISA resource on an EISA platform drives the IOCS16* signal line by decoding the LA<2-11> signal lines and qualifying it with the AENx signal line.

- The result of the above decode is held in a transparent latch until an active BALE signal line ports it to the bus.

The fact that IOCS16* is a straight decode of the LA<2-11> signal lines means that the entire four byte address block is either all 8 data bits or all 16 data bits in size. Problems arise if only a portion of the block is associated with a 16 data bit resource and another portion is an 8 data bit resource.

ALL PLATFORMS

The IOCS16* signal line is ignored by the DMA and refresh controller for transfer and refresh cycles, respectively.

The original IBM AT baseboard does not drive the IOCS16* signal line because I/O platform resources were typically only accessed by the platform CPU. Consequently, some ISA add-on bus owner cards will execute 16 data bit access cycles without monitoring the IOCS16* signal line. Also, for ISA compatible platforms, the IOCS16* signal line was not qualified by the AENx signal line because no slot specific addressing was defined. For the repeated 256 byte block reflective of the platform I/O (see Chapter 2) the IOCS16* signal line may be driven during all access cycles without problems.

On E-ISA and EISA compatible platforms, the repeated 256 byte blocks are used for slot specific I/O accesses; consequently, the IOCS16* signal line must be qualified by the AENx signal line of each slot by all I/O add-on slave cards. Also, add-on bus owner cards must monitor the IOCS16* signal line. See the ADD-ON BUS MASTER CARD section of Chapter 4 for more detailed information.

IOCHRDY (8, 8/16 ISA or E-ISA & EISA CONNECTOR)

ISA OR E-ISA PLATFORM

The I/O channel ready (IOCHRDY) signal line allows resources to indicate to the ISA or E-ISA bus master that additional cycle time is required. If the IOCHRDY signal line is not driven inactive, the cycle is either a no-wait-state or a standard cycle. If the IOCHRDY signal line is driven inactive, the cycle length is extended until the line is driven active again. An inactive IOCHRDY signal line causes an active SRDY* signal to be ignored by the bus master.

On an ISA or E-ISA compatible platform, the IOCHRDY signal line must be driven inactive within a specific time of the COMMAND signal lines becoming active. When the IOCHRDY signal line is active, the cycle ends within a specific amount of time.

Both of these events occur asynchronously to the BCLK signal line on an ISA compatible platform.   On an E-ISA platform, the IOCHRDY signal line is sampled relative to the BCLK signal line in addition to supporting the previously outlined "asynchronous" support. See the IOCHRDY SIGNAL LINE ENHANCEMENT section in this chapter.

When the bus owner is either the platform CPU, an ISA or E-ISA add-on bus owner card, or the refresh controller, the increase in cycle length is measured as "wait states". The resolution of the wait states is one BCLK signal line period. When the bus owner is the DMA controller, the resolution of the wait states is two BCLK signal line periods for DMA COMPATIBLE transfer cycles. The DMA controller on an E-ISA compatible platform allows each DMA channel to be programmed for different DMA transfer cycles. Each of these cycles has a different wait state resolution. See the DMA TRANSFER CYCLE section in Chapter 6 for more detailed information.

For a DMA transfer cycle, only the memory resource can inactivate the IOCHRDY signal line; the I/O resource must be able to accept the data within the length of a default cycle.

EISA PLATFORMS

When an ISA, E-ISA, or EISA bus master is accessing an ISA or E-ISA resource, the IOCHRDY signal line is defined the same as for the ISA or E-ISA compatible platform. For an E-MIX access cycle, this signal line is sampled by the platform circuitry to determine the cycle length. For an I-MIX access cycle, this signal line is driven by the platform circuitry as a translation of the EXRDY signal line. This signal line is not defined when an EISA bus master is accessing an EISA resource.

On an EISA compatible platform, the IOCHRDY signal line is sampled relative to the BCLK signal line, in addition to supporting the previously outlined "asynchronous support".   See the IOCHRDY SIGNAL LINE ENHANCEMENT section in this chapter.

The DMA controller on an EISA compatible platform allows each DMA channel to be programmed for different DMA transfer cycle types.   Each of these cycles has a different wait state resolution. See the DMA TRANSFER CYCLE section in Chapter 6 for more detailed information.

For a DMA transfer cycle, only the memory participant can drive the IOCHRDY signal line. The I/O resource must be able to accept the data within the length of a default cycle.

ALL PLATFORMS

The IOCHRDY signal line should not remain inactive during access or transfer cycles longer than 15.6 microseconds. Otherwise, a bus refresh cycle may not occur at the appropriate time and DRAM data will be lost. The IBM Technical Reference Manual specifies 2.5 microseconds for unknown reasons. One possible explanation might be to allow other bus masters to arbitrate and execute cycles prior to a another refresh occurring.

The original IBM AT baseboard does not drive the IOCHRDY signal line. Consequently, ISA add-on bus owner cards will execute access cycles without monitoring the IOCHRDY signal line. On E-ISA and EISA platforms, the IOCHRDY signal line cannot be ignored. In order to properly access the slot specific I/O space and EISA compatible resources, all ISA or E-ISA add-on bus owner cards must monitor the IOCHRDY signal line. See the ADD-ON BUS MASTER CARD section of Chapter 4 for more detailed information.

IOCHRDY SIGNAL LINE ENHANCEMENT

As previously described, the IOCHRDY signal line must be inactive within a "specific" time after the COMMAND signal line becomes active for a ready cycle. The ready cycle is completed some time after 125 nanoseconds (120 nanoseconds for E-ISA and EISA compatible platforms) after the IOCHRDY signal line has been driven active. This timing of the IOCHRDY signal line is fairly imprecise and tends to lower performance.

In order to enhance performance, the EISA bus specification has defined a SAMPLING WINDOW that relates the IOCHRDY and BCLK signal lines. Figure 5-2 outlines this SAMPLING WINDOW as viewed by the accessed memory or I/O resource and the transfer cycle resource. The SAMPLING WINDOW can be viewed in two parts: inactive and active.

For CASES A & B, the inactive part of the INITIAL SAMPLING WINDOW is between the rising and falling edges of the BCLK signal line. An IOCHRDY signal line inactive pulse of 31 nanoseconds (for a 20 nanoseconds minimum inactive pulse at bus master) within the inactive part of the window will cause a ready cycle to be executed. For CASE C, the minimum setup time of 21 nanoseconds to the falling edge of the BCLK signal line requires the receiving platform CPU or add-on bus owner card to support an actual setup time of 10 nanoseconds. The additional 11 nanosecond loss reflects allowances for bus settling and clock tolerances.

In the active part of the INITIAL SAMPLING WINDOW, the IOCHRDY signal line is sampled at the rising clock edge at the end of the INITIAL SAMPLING WINDOW. If the IOCHRDY signal line is sampled active, the ready cycle will be completed at the end of the next BCLK period. The IOCHRDY signal line is specified as an open collector device with a 1K pull-up resistor. For an E-ISA or EISA compatible platform with an 8 MHz BCLK signal line, assume a 10 nanosecond setup time at the platform CPU or add-on bus owner card, an 11 nanosecond signal line settling time, and a 104 nanosecond rise time, then the total time is 125 nanoseconds. A minimum INITIAL SAMPLING WINDOW of 125 nanoseconds and 20 nanosecond minimum pulse width results in a one wait state ready cycle not being guaranteed. For an

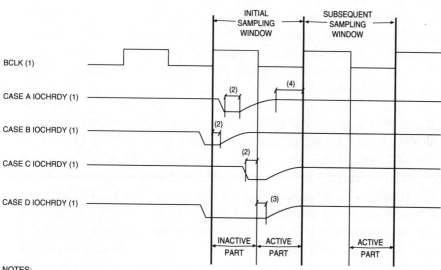

NOTES:
(1) MEASURED AT RESOURCE
    DRIVING THE IOCHRDY
    SIGNAL LINE
(2) MIN. PULSE WIDTH OF 31 NSEC
    MEASURED AT .5 VOLTS
(3) MINIMUM OF 0 NSEC.
    MEASURED AT .5 VOLTS
(4) SETUP TIME MEASURED
    AT 2.0 VOLTS (10 NSEC MEASURED AT BUS MASTER)

FIGURE 5-2:   *E-ISA AND EISA IOCHRDY REFERENCE TO THE BCLK*
                 SIGNAL LINE

E-ISA or EISA compatible platform with an 8.33 MHz BCLK signal line, the INITIAL SAMPLING WINDOW is 120 nanoseconds, the minimum inactive IOCHRDY signal line pulse width is 20 nanoseconds, and the rise time is now 104 nanoseconds. Consequently, in a fully loaded E-ISA or EISA platform, requirements for a guaranteed one wait state ready cycle are "just missed". To guarantee "conservatively" a one wait state ready cycle, the IOCHRDY signal line must be pulsed high, or a 300 ohm pull-up resistor must be used on the bus in that the rise time is only 29 nanoseconds instead of 104 nanoseconds.

If the IOCHRDY signal line is not sampled active at the end of the INITIAL SAMPLING WINDOW, SUBSEQUENT SAMPLING WINDOWS occur. These SUBSEQUENT SAMPLING WINDOWS only have an active part. The IOCHRDY signal line is sampled at the rising clock edge at the end of each sampling window. If the IOCHRDY signal line is sampled active, the ready cycle will be completed at the end of the next BCLK period. In order to insure that the IOCHRDY is sampled active, the following must be considered:

For CASE D, in order to insure only one wait state, the rise time due to a 1K resistor (for a fully loaded E-ISA or EISA backplane) of 104 nanoseconds is too long. The rise time due to a 300 ohm resistor has a rise time of 29 nanoseconds and will allow all the requirements to be met.

SRDY* (8, 8/16 ISA or E-ISA & EISA CONNECTOR) (NOWS*)

In order to maintain continuity with the ISA or E-ISA bus specification, the SRDY* and NOWS* signal line names are used interchangeably.

ISA OR E-ISA PLATFORMS

The synchronous ready (SRDY* or No-wait-state NOWS*) signal line is driven active by the accessed resource to indicate that an access cycle shorter than the standard access cycle can be executed. On an ISA compatible platform, only the platform CPU can execute a no-wait-state cycle. On the E-ISA platform, both the platform CPU and add-on bus owner card can execute a no-wait-state cycle. An inactive IOCHRDY signal line supersedes an active SRDY* signal line forcing it to be ignored.

On ISA or E-ISA compatible platforms, the SRDY* signal line is synchronized to the BCLK signal line. It must be driven active within a specific time of the COMMAND signal lines.

> *The IBM AT sampled the SRDY* signal lines during the fourth BCLK signal line period. It is not clear whether all clone platforms support the SRDY* signal line.*

An E-ISA compatible platform supports both the platform CPU and an E-ISA add-on bus owner card executing no-wait-state cycles. The E-ISA compatible platform has also expanded the number of sampling points to three for an 8 data bit accessed resource.

The SRDY* (NOWS*) signal line is ignored by the DMA and refresh controller during transfer and refresh cycles, respectively.

EISA PLATFORMS

When an E-ISA bus master is accessing an ISA or an 8 data bit EISA resource, the SRDY* signal line is defined as it is for the E-

ISA platform. For an E-MIX access cycle, this signal line is sampled by the platform circuitry to determine the length of the access cycle. For an I-MIX access cycle, the SRDY* (NOWS*) signal line is sampled by the platform circuitry when an 8 data bit EISA compatible resource is accessed.

When an EISA bus master is accessing a 16 or 32 data bit (according to the EX16* and EX32* signal lines) EISA resource, this signal line is defined differently. For the platform CPU, this signal line indicates a request to execute an EISA compressed access cycle. In the parlance of the EISA bus specification this signal is named the EISA no-wait-state (NOWS*) signal line. An EISA add-on bus owner card does not execute compressed access cycles.

On an EISA compatible accessed resource, the NOWS* signal line is a direct decode of the LA, M-IO, BE*, AENx, and W-R signal lines with a qualification of the START* signal line. The NOWS* signal line is driven inactive only after the START* signal line is inactive. If the NOWS* signal line is not driven active by an EISA 16 or 32 data bit accessed resource, the cycle is either an EISA standard, ready, data-matching, or burst access cycle.

The NOWS* signal line being driven active by the accessed resource does not automatically cause a compressed access cycle. Several conditions must be met for the access cycle to be completed as a compressed cycle. Please see Chapter 6 for more information.

Some chip sets do not support compressed cycles; consequently, in spite of the aforementioned criteria occurring, the platform circuitry will maintain the normal BCLK waveform and execute a standard access cycle.

When the EISA compatible platform is executing a DMA COMPATIBLE transfer cycle, this signal line is not sampled. When the EISA platform is executing a DMA TYPE A, B, or C (BURST), this signal line is sampled by the DMA controller when it is executing a DMA transfer cycle "WITH CONVERSION" involving an ISA or E-ISA compatible memory resource.

The NOWS* signal line cannot be driven active if the EXRDY signal line is driven inactive.

ALL PLATFORMS

The original IBM AT running the BCLK signal line at 8 MHz cannot support ISA or E-ISA no-wait-state cycles. If bus losses are assumed to be 0 nanoseconds, it appears that the add-on card has 17 nanoseconds to drive the SRDY* signal line active from an active memory COMMAND signal line. However, if 22 nanoseconds of bus losses are included (11 nanoseconds for COMMAND signal line active at the platform CPU to add-on slave and 11 nanoseconds for SRDY* to arrive at the CPU), the add-on card has -5 nanoseconds to drive the SRDY* signal line active to meet the setup time to the falling edge of the BCLK signal line. The situation is further complicated by the fact that on most AT compatible platforms the BCLK signal line is not distributed in a starburst fashion. The ability to run no-wait-state cycles at an 8 MHz BCLK signal line clock rate on original ATs is due to the "grace" of typical delay, typical settling, and typical setup times. The worst case collection of these times will cause a problem. Very few no-wait-state add-on cards have been built.

The original IBM AT running the BCLK signal line at 6 MHz can support no-wait-state cycles. If the BCLK signal line clock rate is 6 MHz, the add-on card has 16 nanoseconds (including 22 nanoseconds of bus losses) to drive the SRDY* signal line active from an active memory COMMAND signal line. As outlined above, these 16 nanoseconds disappear at an 8 MHz BCLK signal line clock rate.

E-ISA and EISA platforms have a clock rate of 8.33 MHz. These platforms must have improved COMMAND signal lines delays and setups to the falling BCLK signal line clock edge to support no-wait-state cycles. The EISA Rev. 3.12 bus specification has established a maximum delay of 16 nanoseconds from an active COMMAND signal line to the activation of the SRDY* signal line at the bus master for a 16 data bit resource. Also, the EISA bus specification has established a minimum of 10 nanoseconds to the falling edge of the BCLK signal line relative to an active SRDY* line and a 30 nanosecond COMMAND signal line active from the previous rising edge. If 22 nanoseconds of bus losses are assumed, the accessed resource has -7 nanoseconds to qualify the NOWS* signal line from the COMMAND signal line. (See the timing table in Chapter 6.)

The timing table in Chapter 6 also specifies additional time relationships between the ADDRESS signal lines and the SRDY* signal line. The adherence to these time relationships will insure that the SRDY* signal line active setup time to the BCLK signal line falling edge is met.

START* (EISA CONNECTOR)

EISA PLATFORMS

The START* signal line is driven by the EISA bus master or by the platform circuitry depending on the cycle being executed. It indicates the start of an EISA access cycle and the initial qualification of other signal lines. For the EISA compressed and data-matching access cycles, it also qualifies signal lines at several other points during these access cycles. The trailing edge indicates to the accessed resource that the LA<2:31>, M-IO, BE*<0-3>, W-R, and AENx signal lines are valid. In addition, it is used by the accessed resource to qualify other signal lines dependent on the cycle being executed.

For all access cycles, the active length of the START* signal line is one BCLK signal line period, but there are exceptions. If the platform CPU's basic clock is asynchronous to the BCLK signal line, some chip sets drive the START* signal line active asynchronously to the BCLK signal line. Also, some chip sets will drive the START* signal line active asynchronously to the BCLK signal line for ISA compatible bus masters (add-on bus owner cards) during an I-MIX access cycle. These chip sets will stretch the high and low times of the BCLK signal line. The stretching forces the active pulse width of the START* signal line to be greater than 120 nanoseconds (for an 8.33 MHz nominal BCLK signal) and the end of the active pulse to be synchronized to the BCLK signal line.

CMD* (EISA CONNECTOR)

EISA PLATFORM

The command (CMD*) signal line is driven by platform circuitry in response to an active START* signal line. The active length of the CMD* signal line is dependent on the access cycle being executed. For EISA standard, ready, data-matching, compressed, and I-MIX access cycles, the CMD* signal line provides a reference for valid read or write data. For the burst access cycle, the CMD* signal line defines the active access period for multiple accesses and transfers of the data.

> NOTE: The CMD* signal line should not be confused with the "COMMAND" signal lines. The COMMAND signal is a group name for the MEMR*, SMEMR* MEMW*, SMEMW*, IOR*, and IOW* signal lines on ISA access cycles.

Except for an I-MIX access cycle, the CMD* signal line is synchronized to the BCLK signal line. Under certain conditions, the CMD* signal line will be synchronized at the beginning of an active pulse period but not the end of an I-MIX access cycle. See Subchapter 6.3 for more information.

W-R (EISA CONNECTOR)

EISA PLATFORMS

The write-read (W-R) signal line is driven by the EISA bus master, refresh controller, DMA controller, or platform circuitry depending on the cycle executed. It indicates to the accessed resource whether to accept data from or drive data to the DATA signal lines.

For a DMA transfer cycle, this signal line is only used by the memory resource. The I/O resource uses the IOR* and IOW* signal lines in conjunction with the DACKx* signal line.

M-IO (EISA CONNECTOR)

EISA PLATFORM

The memory - input/ouput (M-IO) signal line is driven by the EISA bus master, refresh controller, DMA controller, or platform circuitry depending on the cycle executed. It indicates that the cycle is to the memory versus the I/O address space.

For a DMA transfer cycle, this signal line is only used by the memory resource. The I/O resource uses the IOR* and IOW* signal lines in conjunction with the DACKx* signal line.

EX16* and EX32* (EISA CONNECTOR)

EISA PLATFORMS

The EISA ACCESS 16 and 32 data bit (EX16* and EX32*) signal lines are driven by either the EISA resources or platform circuitry depending on the cycle being executed.

These signal lines perform two basic functions. First, they indicate if the resource supports 16 or 32 data bit EISA access cycles. If these signal lines are inactive at the sampling time, the resource being accessed is an 8 data bit EISA compatible resource or an ISA or E-ISA compatible resource. These signal lines are a direct decode of the LA<2-31> signal lines with a qualification of the address space by the M-IO and AENx signal lines.

Second, during an EISA data-matching access cycle, the EX32* signal line will be driven by the platform circuitry at the completion of the cycle. During an E-MIX access cycle, the EX16* and EX32* signal lines are driven by the platform circuitry to indicate to the EISA bus master the completion of the cycle. See Chapter 6 for more information.

When the EISA platform is executing a DMA COMPATIBLE transfer cycle, it is assumed that the data size of the memory resource is equal to or greater than the data size of the I/O resource; consequently, the EX16* and EX32* signal lines are not sampled. When the DMA controller is executing a DMA TYPE A, B, or C (BURST) transfer cycle, these signal lines are sampled by the DMA controller to determine if a transfer cycle WITH "CONVERSION" is to be executed. As with access cycles, the EX16* and EX32* signal lines indicate to the DMA controller the data size of the memory resource and that it is EISA compatible. The memory resource is the only transfer cycle participant to drive these signal lines; the data size of the I/O participant is programmed in software.

The EX16* and EX32* signal lines are a straight decode of the LA<2-31>, M-IO, and AENx signal lines, and no distinction is made between read and write cycles. The EISA resource must begin "blindly" decoding the LA<2-31>, M-IO, and AENx signal lines prior to an active START* signal line that would indicate that a valid EISA cycle is about to occur. Also, the EX16* and EX32* signal lines do not decode the BE* signal lines; consequently, the entire four byte address block is either all 16 or 32 data bits.

EXRDY (EISA CONNECTOR)

EISA PLATFORMS

The EISA ACCESS READY (EXRDY) signal line is driven by the accessed resource to indicate that additional cycle time is required. From the accessed resource viewpoint, the EXRDY signal line is a direct decode of the LA signal lines with a qualification by the M-IO, AENx, and START* signal lines. The cycle is extended until the EXRDY signal line is driven active relative to the BCLK signal line. The cycle length is extended until the EXRDY signal line is driven active again.

For E-MIX access cycles, the IOCHRDY signal line is not translated into the EXRDY signal line, but is used by platform circuitry to control the active pulse width of the CMD* signal line. For I-MIX access cycles, the EXRDY signal line is translated into the IOCHRDY signal line and controls the active pulse length of the CMD* signal line for write cycles via the platform circuitry.

For a DMA transfer cycle, only the memory participant can drive the EXRDY signal line. The I/O resource must be able to accept the data within the length of a default cycle.

The EXRDY signal line must not be driven active if the NOWS* signal line is driven active. Also, the EXRDY signal line cannot be driven inactive for longer than 2.5 microseconds.

SLBURST* & MSBURST* (EISA CONNECTOR)

EISA PLATFORMS

The slave burst (SLBURST*) and master burst (MSBURST*) signal lines are driven by the accessed EISA memory resource and the platform CPU or EISA add-on bus owner card (collectively called bus masters), respectively. An active SLBURST* signal line indicates to the EISA bus master that the accessed resource can execute a burst access cycle. The active MSBURST* signal line indicates to the accessed resource and the platform circuitry that the EISA bus master will execute a burst access cycle. A burst access cycle can only occur if both the SLBURST* and the MSBURST* signal lines are driven active.

The SLBURST* signal line is a direct decode of the LA<10-31> and M-IO signal lines. The MSBURST* signal line can only be driven active if the SLBURST* signal line has been sampled active and if the bus master can support burst cycles.

In that the SLBURST* signal line is a direct decode of the LA<10-31> signal lines, the burst access cycle can only be terminated by the bus master; consequently, the entire 1K block of memory must be part of the same accessed resource.

In addition to the above requirements that both the EISA bus master and accessed resource support burst cycles, there are three other considerations for the cycle to proceed as a BURST access cycle: If the bus master has requested a 16 bit access (using the BE* signal lines), the accessed resource must support data sizes of 16 or 32 bits (indicated by the EX16* and EX32* signal lines) ... OR ... If the bus master has requested a 32 bit access (using the BE* signal lines), an accessed resource must support data sizes of 32 bits (indicated by the EX32* signal line) ... OR ... If the EISA bus master has requested a 32 bit access and toggled the MASTER16* signal line inactive, the accessed resource must support data sizes of 16 or 32 bits (indicated by the EX16* and EX32* data lines).

For DMA transfer cycles, the SLBURST* and MSBURST* signal lines operate in a similar fashion. The only differences are: first, only the memory participant can drive the SLBURST* signal line active; and secondly, the DMA controller must respond with an active MSBURST* signal line. Finally, the I/O participant must be programmed for TYPE C transfer cycles or the DMA controller will not drive the MSBURST* signal line active.

The MSBURST* signal line is only sampled when the data is sampled; i.e., on the rising edge of the BCLK signal line after the EXRDY signal line is sampled active or the previous falling edge of the BCLK signal line.

LOCK* (EISA CONNECTOR)

EISA PLATFORM

The lock (LOCK*) signal line insures exclusive memory or I/O access by the EISA bus master that has driven it active. The LOCK* signal line cannot be driven active during EISA burst or compressed, E-MIX, and I-MIX access cycles or DMA transfer cycles. LOCK* may only be used with eight byte aligned memory or I/O addresses. Finally, memory and I/O accesses cannot be intermixed with the same active LOCK* signal line period. See Subchapter 6.4 for more information.

BUS CONTROL SIGNALS

This group of signals provides general cycle support and bus control.

REFRESH* (8, 8/16 ISA or E-ISA & EISA CONNECTOR)

ALL PLATFORMS

The memory refresh (REFRESH*) signal line is driven by the refresh controller to indicate a refresh cycle. If an ISA or E-ISA add-on bus owner card is the current bus owner, it can request a refresh cycle from the refresh controller by activating the REFRESH* signal line. In order to prevent loss of DRAM data, the refresh cycle must be requested every 15.6 microseconds. An EISA add-on bus owner card cannot request a refresh cycle. (The refresh controller can preempt the EISA add-on bus owner card to accomplish needed refresh cycles.)

MASTER16* (8, 8/16 ISA or E-ISA & EISA CONNECTOR)

ISA OR E-ISA PLATFORM

The MASTER16* signal line is only driven active by an ISA or E-ISA add-on bus owner card that has been granted bus ownership by the DMA controller. It can only be driven after the add-on card has activated the DACKx* signal line. The add-on bus owner card remains bus owner until it drives the MASTER16* signal line inactive.

During a refresh cycle requested by the ISA or E-ISA add-on bus owner card, the MASTER16* signal line is active; otherwise a platform pull-up resistor keeps the signal line inactive.

EISA PLATFORM

The MASTER16* signal line operates in the same fashion as on an ISA or E-ISA compatible platform when an ISA or E-ISA add-on bus owner card has been granted bus ownership by the DMA controller. On an EISA platform, this signal line also has an additional interpretation. The MASTER16* signal line is driven active by the platform CPU or EISA add-on bus owner card (collectively called EISA bus master) to indicate a 16 data bit bus master; an inactive MASTER16* signal line indicates a 32 data bit bus master. The EISA platform's use of this signal line is to indicate a 16 data bit bus master; consequently, the EISA bus specification has renamed the ISA MASTER* signal line to the MASTER16* signal line.

IOCHK* (8, 8/16 ISA or E-ISA & EISA CONNECTOR)

ALL PLATFORMS

The I/O channel check (IOCHK*) signal line can be driven active by any resource. It is active for a general error condition that has no specific interpretation. It can occur due to parity errors, general bus failure, and other types of errors. This signal can only be serviced by the platform CPU.

The active state of the IOCHK* signal line is latched into Port B of the platform. A non-maskable interrupt (NMI) is issued to the platform CPU if bit 3 of Port B (61H) is set to 0; otherwise, the primary CPU software must poll the IOCHK* bit in Port B.

When either the add-on bus owner, refresh controller, or DMA controller is the current bus owner, the activation of the IOCHK* channel check signal will not be acted upon immediately by the platform CPU. The platform CPU must wait until it becomes the bus owner again prior to executing any error correction software.

RESET (8, 8/16 ISA & EISA CONNECTOR)

ALL PLATFORMS

The reset (RESET) signal line is driven active by the platform circuitry. Any bus resource that senses an active RESET signal line must immediately tri-state all output drivers and enter the appropriate reset condition. See Chapter 13 for more information.

The RESET signal line can be activated at any time, by either the platform hardware or by software setting address 64H Bit 0 to a 0. The minimum pulse width is nine BCLK signal line periods. See Chapter 6 for more detailed information.

In order for software to move between protected and real mode operation, the primary CPU must be reset. This reset does not affect the condition of the RESET signal line.

BCLK (8, 8/16 ISA or E-ISA & EISA CONNECTOR)

ALL PLATFORMS

The system bus clock (BCLK) signal line is a clock driven by the platform circuitry. On ISA or E-ISA platforms, it has a 50% +/- approximately 5% (57 to 69 nanoseconds for 8.00 MHz) duty cycle of 6 to 8 MHz (+/- 500 ppm). On E-ISA or EISA platforms, the clock has a 50% +/- approximately 5% (55 to 65 nanoseconds for 8.33 MHz) duty cycle of 6 to 8.33 MHz (+/- 500 ppm). The EISA Revision 3.12 Specification has lowered the minimum frequency to 4 MHz.

On EISA compatible platforms, the EISA compressed access cycle requires a change in the BCLK signal line. The clock period changes to 1.5 times the normal period. The active high portion of the BCLK signal has a 33% duty cycle (57 to 69 nanoseconds for 8.00 MHz and 55 to 65 nanoseconds for 8.33 MHz).

OSC (8, 8/16 ISA or E-ISA & EISA CONNECTOR)

ALL PLATFORMS

The oscillator (OSC) signal line is a clock driven by the platform circuitry. It has a 45-55% duty cycle of 14.31818 MHz (+/- 500 ppm). It is not synchronized to any other bus signal line. This frequency is the color burst frequency for television, and was used to generate the composite video signal for the original CGA display cards. The widespread use of this frequency also results in the availability of large numbers of inexpensive crystals. On the platform, this clock is divided by 12 and fed to the 8254 timer.

INTERRUPT SIGNALS

The INTERRUPT signal lines allow add-on cards to request interrupt service by the platform CPU. Only the platform CPU can be notified of the interrupt by the interrupt controller.

IRQx < 3-7,9 > (8, 8/16 ISA or E-ISA & EISA CONNECTOR)
IRQx < 10-12,14,15 > (8/16 ISA or E-ISA & EISA CONNECTOR)

ISA PLATFORMS

The INTERRUPT REQUEST (IRQx) signal lines can be programmed for one type of operation on an ISA compatible platform and two types of operation on an E-ISA or EISA compatible platform. On the ISA compatible platform, the INTERRUPT signal lines are considered active by a low to high transition (edge triggered); consequently, only one add-on card can be assigned to each INTERRUPT signal line. The signal line must remain active until the platform CPU has accessed the appropriate portion of the add-on card to indicate that the interrupt is being serviced. The minimum low time between back-to-back logical highs is 125 nanoseconds.

The IBM Technical Reference manual outlines a method by which the IRQx signal can be shared even though it is edge triggered. This approach has not been universally successful; consequently the E-ISA and EISA platforms have redefined the operation of the IRQx signal line relative to shared interrupts.

E-ISA AND EISA PLATFORMS

On the E-ISA or EISA compatible platforms, the IRQx signal lines can be programmed to be edge or level triggered. When programmed to be edge triggered, their operation is the same as on an ISA compatible platform. When programmed to be level triggered, the IRQx signal lines must be driven low to be considered active. This approach allows several add-on cards to use the same IRQx signal line if the line is driven by open collector drivers. The signal line must remain active until the platform CPU has accessed the appropriate portion of the add-on card to indicate that the interrupt is being serviced.

ALL PLATFORMS

The PC, XT, and AT have defined the IRQx signal lines' operation as unshared edge triggered; consequently, add-on cards have been designed with totem pole outputs to drive the IRQx signal line. If these add-on cards are installed in an E-ISA or EISA compatible platform, they must be the only interrupt resources on that particular IRQx signal line.

The EISA Specification Rev. 3.12 has further addressed the issue of totem pole outputs sharing an IRQx signal line with open collector outputs. It recommends a 47 ohm series resistor on the open collector or the use of an open collector output that can be driven to V_{cc} without damage.

The open collector approach for a level triggered INTERRUPT signal line relies on a pull-up resistor to deactivate the interrupt request. The EISA bus specification has the largest resistor value; consequently, 500 nanoseconds are required for deactivation from an active to inactive level on the E-ISA or EISA platform.

The INTERRUPT signal lines are continuously monitored by the interrupt controller independent of the present cycle or bus owner.

DMA SIGNALS

Each DMA channel has two signal lines: DMA request and DMA acknowledge. Also, all DMA channels share the terminal count signal line. The purpose of these signal lines is to allow data to be transferred between I/O and memory resources. The platform DMA controller drives all of the control lines to execute the cycle; consequently, no control circuitry is required on the memory or I/O resource.

DRQx < 1-3 > (8, 8/16 ISA or E-ISA & EISA CONNECTOR)
DRQx < 0,5-7 > (8/16 ISA or E-ISA & EISA CONNECTOR)

ALL PLATFORMS

The DMA request (DRQx) signal lines are driven active by I/O resources to request service by the platform DMA controller. An individual DRQx signal line must remain active until the associated DMA acknowledge signal line (of the same DMA channel) is driven active. Subsequent action of the DMA controller relative to the DRQx signal line is dependent on how the DMA channel has been programmed. See Subchapter 7.4 for more information. For ISA, DRQ < 0-3 > are fixed at 8 bits; DRQ < 5-7 > are 16 bits.

The DRQx signal lines are also driven active when an ISA or E-ISA add-on bus owner card wants to own the bus. The add-on bus owner drives the MASTER16* signal line active and takes control of the bus once the appropriate DMA acknowledge signal line is driven active. See Chapter 9 for more information.

On ISA compatible platforms, the DRQx signal lines are defined to have totem pole type of outputs; thus, ISA compatible add-on cards require a jumper to attach the driver to the appropriate DRQx signal line. The EISA bus specification has defined the DRQx signal lines to have tri-state drivers; consequently, E-ISA and EISA compatible add-on cards do not need a jumper.

> *The EISA Specification Rev. 3.12 has further addressed the issue of totem pole outputs sharing a DRQx signal line with tri-state outputs. It recommends a 47 ohm series resistor on the tri-state output or the use of a tri-state output that can be driven to V_{CC} or ground without damage.*

The DRQx signal lines must be continuously monitored by the DMA controller independent of the present cycle or bus owner.

DACKx* < 1-3 > (8, 8/16 ISA or E-ISA & EISA CONNECTOR)
DACKx* < 0,5-7 > (8/16 ISA or E-ISA & EISA CONNECTOR)

ALL PLATFORMS

The DMA acknowledge (DACKx*) signal lines are driven active by the platform DMA controller to select the I/O resource that requested a DMA transfer cycle. Subsequent action of the DMA controller relative to the DACKx* signal line is dependent on how the DMA channel was programmed. See Subchapter 7.4 for more information. For ISA, DACK < 0-3 > * are fixed at 8 bits; DACK < 5-7 > * are 16 bits.

For ISA and E-ISA add-on bus owner card arbitration, the DACKx* signal lines are used to identify which add-on bus owner card has been granted bus ownership. See Chapter 9 for more information.

TC (8, 8/16 ISA or E-ISA & EISA CONNECTOR)

ISA PLATFORMS

The terminal count (TC) signal line on an ISA compatible platform is driven by the platform DMA controller to indicate that all the data has been transferred. See Chapter 7 for more information.

E-ISA AND EISA PLATFORMS

On an E-ISA or EISA compatible platform, this signal line is bi-directional. It can be programmed to be driven by the platform DMA controller in the same fashion as the ISA platform. It can also be programmed for the add-on card to drive this signal line to terminate any further data transfers. See Chapter 7 for more information.

MREQx* (EISA Connector)
MAKx* (EISA Platform)

On an EISA compatible platform, the master request (MREQx*) and master acknowledge (MAKx*) signal lines are used to determine bus ownership. An EISA add-on bus owner card can request bus ownership by driving the MREQx* (one per slot) signal line active. The platform arbiter awards bus ownership by driving the associated MAKx* (one per slot) signal line active. Not all slots are required to have an MREQx*/MAKx* signal line pair. These slots can only support ISA, E-ISA, or EISA add-on slave cards; or ISA or E-ISA add-on bus owner cards. See Chapter 9 for further information.

POWER SIGNALS

The power signal lines provide +5, -5, +12, -12, and GND to the add-on cards. All of the power values are available on 8 bit slots. The 8/16 bit slots provide one additional +5 and one additional GND connection.

The current available for each voltage is outlined in Table 5-5. Please refer to Chapter 13 for further information concerning tolerance, noise, and other associated issues.

VOLTAGE	8 BIT ISA, E-ISA	8/16 BIT ISA, E-ISA 8/16/32 BIT EISA
+5	3.0 AMPS	4.5 AMPS
+12	1.5 AMPS	1.5 AMPS
-5	1.5 AMPS	1.5 AMPS
-12	1.5 AMPS	1.5 AMPS

TABLE 5-5: CONNECTOR CURRENT

NOTE: The maximum current for each ISA or E-ISA pin is 1.5 amperes.   The maximum current for each EISA pin is .5 amperes.

Not all platforms have sufficiently large power supplies to provide the maximum current to each slot. It is required that the supply be large enough to supply a minimum of 2 amperes at 5 volts to each slot simultaneously.

Notes

CHAPTER SIX

BUS ACCESS CYCLES

This Chapter consists of the following Subchapters:

6.0 ISA SPECIFIC ACCESS CYCLES ON ISA and E-ISA PLATFORMS

INTRODUCTION

The ISA access cycles support accesses to memory and I/O resources by the platform CPU and ISA or E-ISA compatible add-on bus owner cards (also known as ISA bus masters). Table 3-1-A in Chapter 3 outlines the support level of access cycles by the various bus owners and platform CPUs.

> The term "ISA compatible platform" collectively represents PC, XT, and AT platforms.

As outlined in Chapter 3, there are three types of ISA specific access cycles. The type is determined by the exact interpretation of signal lines and the length of the cycle. The length of the cycle is dependent on the cycle's data width and the logic level of the SRDY* and IOCHRDY signal lines. The shortest cycle for a given data width is the no-wait-state cycle. The longest cycle for a given data width is the ready cycle. When both the SRDY* and the IOCHRDY signal lines are active, a no-wait-state cycle is executed. When the SRDY* signal line is inactive and the IOCHRDY signal line is active, a standard cycle is executed. The length of the standard cycle varies with data width. Finally, when the IOCHRDY signal line is inactive, a ready cycle is executed.

Most of the signal lines become active and inactive on the bus independent of the BCLK signal line. The only exception is the SRDY* signal line. From this viewpoint, the ISA bus is defined as an asynchronous bus. On an ISA platform, the CPU executes access cycles in an asynchronous fashion with a synchronized monitoring of the SRDY* signal line. The DMA, refresh, and add-on bus owner cards execute their respective cycles in an asynchronous fashion without supporting the SRDY* signal line.

The E-ISA compatible platform executes ISA bus compatible cycles in the same fashion as the ISA compatible platform. However, the E-ISA compatible platform uses an expanded interpretation of the no-wait-state cycle, and samples the IOCHRDY signal line relative to the BCLK signal line. Unlike ISA bus masters, both E-ISA platform CPUs and E-ISA add-on bus owner cards (E-ISA bus masters) can execute no-wait-state access cycles to 8 data bit resources on E-ISA compatible platforms. Additionally, on E-ISA compatible platforms the E-ISA bus masters support the IOCHRDY signal line referenced to the BCLK signal line. To support the aforementioned items, the BCLK signal line must be distributed in a "starburst" pattern to all slots on an E-ISA compatible platform. Please see Chapter 10 for more information.

The term "ISA specific access cycles" includes E-ISA specific access.

Table 6-1 has several key pieces of information. First, the "#/DET" (parameter number / detail) column relates the parameter number of the table to Figure 6-1. Second, it provides detailed information on how the number was derived. The timing numbers are affected by the settling time on the bus. The table is based on the default values for 8 slots as outlined in Chapter 10. The #/DET interpretations are shown on the page following Figure 6-1.

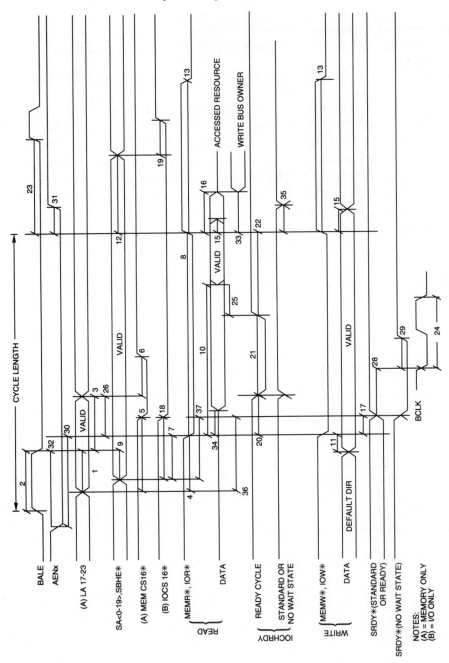

FIGURE 6-1:   ISA AND E-ISA MEMORY AND I/O ACCESS CYCLES

DETAIL	INTERPRETATION
#	NO SETTLING TIME INCLUDED.
#/A	SKEW OF TWO SIGNALS BETWEEN RESOURCES. ONE HAS A DELAY OF 0 NANOSECONDS, AND THE OTHER HAS A DELAY OF 11 NANOSECONDS.
#/B	SIGNAL IS DRIVEN BY ONE RESOURCE TO ANOTHER. THE SECOND RESOURCE MUST RESPOND BY DRIVING A SIGNAL BACK TO THE FIRST RESOURCE. # INCLUDES THE "ROUND TRIP" TIME OF 11 + 11 = 22 NANOSECONDS.
#/C	SAME AS "B", EXCEPT THE RESOURCES RELY ON A 1K OHM PULL-UP RESISTOR. # INCLUDES THE "ROUND TRIP" TIME OF 11 + 78 = 89 NANOSECONDS FOR AN ISA COMPATIBLE PLATFORM. FOR AN E-ISA OR EISA COMPATIBLE PLATFORM, THE EXTRA CAPACITANCE ADDS 26 NANOSECONDS.
#/D	SAME AS "B", EXCEPT ONE OF THE RESOURCES RELIES ON A 300 OHM PULL-UP RESISTOR. # INCLUDES THE "ROUND TRIP" TIME OF 11 + 22 = 33 NANOSECONDS FOR AN ISA COMPATIBLE PLATFORM. FOR AN E-ISA OR EISA COMPATIBLE PLATFORM, THE EXTRA CAPACITANCE ADDS 7 NANOSECONDS.
#/E	SAME AS "A", EXCEPT THE WORST CASE INTERPRETATION IS THAT BOTH SIGNALS ARE EITHER 0 NANOSECONDS OR 11 NANOSECONDS. THE NET RESULT IS A DIFFERENCE OF 0 NANOSECONDS.

"DRIVEN BY" AND "MEASURED AT" INTERPRETATION

ADD-ON	ADD-ON CARD OR PLATFORM RESOURCE
ISA-B	ISA OR E-ISA COMPATIBLE ADD-ON CARD BUS OWNER ADD-ON CARD
CPU	PLATFORM CPU
PLAT	PLATFORM CIRCUITRY

MIN. AND MAX. INTERPRETATION

ALL TIMES ARE IN NANOSECONDS WITH AN 8.00 MHZ BCLK.
THE NUMBER IN "[ ]" REFLECTS THE CALCULATED VALUE FOR AN 8.33 MHZ BCLK.

EISA INTERPRETATION

THE "EISA" ENTRIES ARE ACCORDING TO THE EISA BUS SPECIFICATION REV. 3.12

SMEMR* AND SMEMW*

SMEMR* AND SMEMW* HAVE A 21 NANOSECOND DELAY FROM MEMR* AND MEMW* SIGNAL LINES (36 NANOSECONDS IN THE EISA REV. 3.12 SPECIFICATION). THE ENTRIES IN THE TABLE ARE REFERENCED TO THE MEMR* AMD MEMW* SIGNAL LINES.

REF# /DET	DESCRIPTION OF EVENT	DRIVEN BY	MEASURED AT	MIN [8.33]	MAX	EISA
1	LA<17-23> VALID SETUP TO FALLING EDGE OF BALE	CPU	CPU	111 [104]		116
2	BALE ACTIVE TO INACTIVE	PLTFRM	PLTFRM	57 [55]		45
3	LA<17-23> VALID HOLD FROM FALLING EDGE OF BALE	CPU	CPU	15		15
4	LA<17-23> VALID SETUP TO MEMORY COMMAND ACTIVE (NOTE: FOR ISA-B 8 BITS USE #7) 16 BITS	CPU	CPU	183 [173] 120 [113]		176 112
5	MEMCS16* ACTIVE FROM VALID LA<17-23>	ADD-ON	CPU/ISA-B		102 [94]	96
5	MEMCS16* INACTIVE FROM VALID LA<17-23>	ADD-ON	CPU/ISA-B		99 [91]	96
6	MEMCS16* VALID HOLD FROM INVALID LA<17-23>	ADD-ON	CPU/ISA-B	0		0
7	SA<0-19> & SBHE* VALID TO COMMAND ACTIVE (NOTE: FOR ISA-B 8 BITS USE THIS FOR LA<17-23>) 16 BITS FOR 16 BIT I/O	CPU /ISA-B	CPU/ISA-B	102 [100] 39 [34] 102 [100]		88 24 88
8	MEMORY COMMAND ACTIVE TO INACTIVE (SEE NOTE 2) STANDARD 8 BITS 16 BITS NO-WAIT-STATE 8 BITS 16 BITS I/O COMMAND ACTIVE TO INACTIVE STANDARD 8 BITS 16 BITS NO-WAIT-STATE 8 BIT	CPU /ISA-B	CPU/ISA-B	542 [520] 235 [225] 167 [160] 110 [105] 542 [520] 167 [160] 156 [149]		530 230 166 104 530 166 166
9	SA<0-19> & SBHE* VALID TO FALLING EDGE OF BALE	CPU	CPU	40 [37]		27

TABLE 6-1-A: ACCESS CYCLE TIMINGS ... PLATFORM CPU OR ISA BUS OWNER ADD-ON CARD

REF# /DET	DESCRIPTION OF EVENT	DRIVEN BY	MEASURED AT	MIN [8.33]	MAX	EISA
10	VALID READ DATA FROM MEMORY COMMAND ACTIVE (SEE NOTE 5) STANDARD 8 BITS	ADD-ON	CPU/ISA-B		504 [482]	490
	16 BITS				195 [185]	194
	NO-WAIT-STATE 8 BITS				132 [125]	122
	16 BITS				70 [65]	70
10	VALID READ DATA FROM I/O COMMAND ACTIVE STANDARD 8 BITS	ADD-ON	CPU/ISA-B		504 [482]	490
	16 BITS				132 [125]	130
	NO-WAIT-STATE 8 BITS				132 [125]	122
11	VALID WRITE DATA SETUP TO MEMORY COMMAND ACTIVE NO-WAIT-STATE & STANDARD (SEE NOTE 12) 8 BITS	CPU /ISA-B	CPU/ISA-B	-43 [-40]		-40
	16 BITS			-43 [-40]		-40
	VALID WRITE DATA SETUP TO I/O COMMAND ACTIVE STANDARD 8 BITS			-43 [-40]		-40
	16 BITS			28 [23]		22
	NO-WAIT-STATE 8 BITS			-43 [-40]		-40
12	SA<0-19> & SBHE* VALID HOLD FROM COMMAND INACTVE (LA <17-23> FOR ISA-B) (SEE NOTE 18)	CPU /ISA-B	CPU/ISA-B	41 [41]		30

TABLE 6-1-A: ACCESS CYCLE TIMINGS ... PLATFORM CPU OR ISA BUS OWNER ADD-ON CARD (CONTINUED)

REF# /DET	DESCRIPTION OF EVENT	DRIVEN BY	MEASURED AT	MIN MAX [8.33]		EISA
13	MEMORY COMMAND INACTIVE TO MEMORY COMMAND ACTIVE 8 BITS 16 BITS I/O COMMAND INACTIVE TO I/O COMMAND ACTIVE	CPU /ISA-B CPU /ISA-B	CPU/ISA-B CPU/ISA-B	170 [163] 108 [103] 170 [163]		170 114 170
15	READ DATA VALID HOLD FROM INACTIVE MEMORY OR I/O COMMAND	ADD-ON	CPU/ISA-B	0 [0]		0
15	WRITE DATA VALID HOLD FROM INACTIVE MEMORY COMMAND (SEE NOTE 3) 8 BITS 16 BITS	CPU /ISA-B	CPU/ISA-B	20 [20] 36 [36]		9 22
15	WRITE DATA VALID HOLD FROM INACTIVE I/O COMMAND	CPU /ISA-B	CPU/ISA-B	36 [36]		22
16	COMMAND INACTIVE TO SD<0-19> TRISTATE	CPU /ISA-B	ADD-ON		41 [41]	30
17	SRDY* VALID FROM COMMAND ACTIVE (SEE NOTES 13,16) 8 BITS 16 BITS	ADD-ON	CPU/ISA-B		85 [80] 17 [15]	80 16
18	IOCS16* ACTIVE FROM VALID SA<0-11> (SEE NOTE 6)	ADD-ON	CPU/ISA-B		153 [145]	145
18	IOCS16* INACTIVE FROM VALID SA<0-11> (SEE NOTE 6)	ADD-ON	CPU/ISA-B		153 [145]	145
18	IOCS16* ACTIVE FROM VALID SA<0-11> (SEE NOTE 21)	ADD-ON	CPU/ISA-B		81 [76]	88
18	IOCS16* INACTIVE FROM VALID SA<0-11> (SEE NOTE 21)	ADD-ON	CPU/ISA-B		81 [76]	88
19	IOCS16* VALID HOLD FROM VALID SA<0-11>	ADD-ON	CPU/ISA-B	0 [0]		0

TABLE 6-1-A: ACCESS CYCLE TIMINGS ... PLATFORM CPU OR ISA BUS OWNER ADD-ON CARD (CONTINUED)

REF# /DET	DESCRIPTION OF EVENT	DRIVEN BY	MEASURED AT	MIN [8.33]	MAX	EISA
20	IOCHRDY VALID FROM ACTIVE COMMAND (See Note 10,19) 8 BITS OLD "AT"	ADD-ON	CPU/ISA-B		390 [373]	398
	16 BITS MEM				83 [78]	98
	I/O				15 [13]	24
20	IOCHRDY VALID FROM ACTIVE COMMAND (See Note 10,19) 8 BITS NEW E-ISA & EISA	ADD-ON	CPU/ISA-B		449 [430]	398
	16 BITS MEM				142 [135]	98
	I/O				74 [70]	80
21	IOCHRDY INACTIVE PULSE (SEE NOTE 4)	ADD-ON	CPU/ISA-B	125 [120]	15.6	2.5 MICROSECONDS
22	COMMAND ACTIVE HOLD FROM IOCHRDY ACTIVE	CPU /ISA-B	CPU/ISA-B	125 [120]		120
23	BALE ACTIVE FROM COMMAND INACTIVE	CPU /ISA-B	CPU/ISA-B	46 [44]		36
24	BCLK PERIOD	PLAT.	PLAT.	125 [120]		120
25	VALID READ DATA FROM IOCHRDY ACTIVE 8 BITS	ADD-ON	CPU/ISA-B		85 [80]	70
	16 BITS				85 [80]	80
26	LA<17-23> INVALID FROM COMMAND ACTIVE 8 BITS	CPU	CPU	-21 [-21]		-34
	16 BITS			41 [39]		22
28	SRDY* VALID SETUP TO THE FALLING EDGE OF BCLK (SEE NOTE 17)	ADD-ON	CPU/ISA-B	11 [11]		10
29	SRDY* VALID HOLD FROM THE FALLING EDGE OF BCLK (SEE NOTE 17)	ADD-ON	CPU/ISA-B	20 [20]		20
30	AENx VALID TO I/O COMMAND ACTIVE	PLAT.	ADD-ON	100 [100]		111
31	AENx VALID FROM I/O COMMAND INACTIVE	PLAT.	ADD-ON	30 [30]		41

TABLE 6-1-A: ACCESS CYCLE TIMINGS ... PLATFORM CPU OR ISA BUS OWNER ADD-ON CARD (CONTINUED)

REF# /DET	DESCRIPTION OF EVENT	DRIVEN BY	MEASURED AT	MIN [8.33]	MAX	EISA
32	AENx VALID TO FALLING EDGE OF BALE	PLAT.	ADD-ON	100 [100]		111
33	DATA DRIVEN IN WRITE DIRECTION FROM INACTIVE READ COMMAND	CPU /ISA-B	CPU/ISA-B	30 [30]		NOT SPEC
34	DATA DRIVEN FROM READ COMMAND ACTIVE	ADD-ON	CPU/ISA-B	0 [0]		0
35	IOCHRDY ACTIVE HOLD FROM COMMAND INACTIVE	ADD-ON	CPU/ISA-B	0 [0]		NOT SPEC
36	LA<17-23> VALID TO SRDY* ACTIVE (SEE NOTES 13,15) 8 BITS 16 BITS	CPU	CPU/ISA-B	315 [300] 190 [180]		280 156
37	SA<0-19> & SBHE* VALID TO SRDY* ACTIVE (SEE NOTES 13,14) 8 BITS 16 BITS	CPU	CPU/ISA-B		210 [200] 85 [80]	192 68

TABLE 6-1-A: ACCESS CYCLE TIMINGS ... PLATFORM CPU OR ISA BUS OWNER ADD-ON CARD (CONTINUED)

See Notes at the end of the next table.

REF# /DET	DESCRIPTION OF EVENT	DRIVEN BY	MEASURED AT	MIN [8.33]	MAX	EISA
1/A	LA<17-23> VALID SETUP TO FALLING EDGE OF BALE	CPU	ADD-ON	100 [93]		116
2/A	BALE ACTIVE TO INACTIVE	PLAT	ADD-ON	46 [44]		45
3/A	LA<17-23> VALID HOLD FROM FALLING EDGE OF BALE	CPU	ADD-ON	15		15
4/A	LA<17-23> VALID SETUP TO MEMORY COMMAND ACTIVE (NOTE: FOR ISA-B 8 BITS USE #7) 16 BITS	CPU	ADD-ON	172 [162] 109 [102]		176 112
5/B	MEMCS16* ACTIVE FROM VALID LA<17-23>	ADD-ON	ADD-ON		80 [72]	54
5/D	MEMCS16* INACTIVE FROM VALID LA<17-23> (SEE NOTE 8)	ADD-ON	ADD-ON		66 [58]	54
6/E	MEMCS16* VALID HOLD FROM INVALID LA<17-23>	ADD-ON	ADD-ON	0		0
7/A	SA<0-19> & SBHE* VALID TO COMMAND ACTIVE (NOTE: FOR ISA-B 8 BITS USE THIS FOR LA<17-23>) 16 BITS FOR 16 BIT I/O	CPU /ISA-B	ADD-ON	91 [89] 28 [23] 91 [89]		88 24 88
8/A	MEMORY COMMAND ACTIVE TO INACTIVE (2) STANDARD 8 BITS 16 BITS NO-WAIT-STATE 8 BITS 16 BITS I/O COMMAND ACTIVE TO INACTIVE (2) STANDARD 8 BITS 16 BITS NO-WAIT-STATE 8 BIT	CPU /ISA-B	ADD-ON	531 [509] 224 [214] 156 [149] 99 [94] 531 [509] 156 [149] 156 [149]		474 230 166 104 530 166 166
9/A	SA<0-19> & SBHE* VALID TO FALLING EDGE OF BALE	CPU	ADD-ON	29 [26]		27

TABLE 6-1-B: ACCESS CYCLE TIMINGS ... ACCESSED RESOURCE (PLATFORM AND ADD-ON SLAVE CARD)

REF# /DET	DESCRIPTION OF EVENT	DRIVEN BY	MEASURED AT	MIN	MAX [8.33]	EISA
10/B	VALID READ DATA FROM MEMORY COMMAND ACTIVE STANDARD (SEE NOTE 1,11)	ADD-ON	ADD-ON			
	8 BITS EVEN				482 [460]	314
	ODD				456 [434]	NOT SPEC
	16 BITS				173 [163]	182
	NO-WAIT-STATE 8 BITS EVEN				110 [103]	110
	ODD				84 [77]	NOT SPEC
	16 BITS				48 [43]	58
10/B	VALID READ DATA FROM I/O COMMAND ACTIVE (SEE NOTE 11) STANDARD	ADD-ON	ADD-ON			
	8 BITS EVEN				482 [460]	477
	ODD				456 [434]	NOT SPEC
	16 BITS				110 [103]	118
	NO-WAIT-STATE 8 BITS EVEN				110 [103]	110
	ODD				84 [77]	NOT SPEC
11/A	VALID WRITE DATA SETUP TO MEMORY COMMAND ACTIVE NO-WAIT-STATE & STANDARD (SEE NOTE 11)	CPU /ISA-B	ADD-ON			
	8 BITS EVEN			-54 [-51]		-40
	ODD			-80 [-77]		-41
	16 BITS			-54 [-51]		-40
	VALID WRITE DATA SETUP TO I/O COMMAND ACTIVE (SEE NOTE 11) STANDARD					
	8 BITS EVEN			-54 [-51]		NOT SPEC
	ODD			-80 [-77]		-41
	16 BITS			17 [22]		22

TABLE 6-1-B: ACCESS CYCLE TIMINGS ... ACCESSED RESOURCE (PLATFORM AND ADD-ON SLAVE CARD) (CONTINUED)

REF# /DET	DESCRIPTION OF EVENT	DRIVEN BY	MEASURED AT	MIN [8.33]	MAX	EISA
11/A (cont)	NO-WAIT-STATE 8 BITS EVEN ODD			-54 [-51] -80 [-77]		-41
12/A	SA<0-19> & SBHE* VALID HOLD FROM COMMAND INACTVE (LA<17-23> FOR ISA-B)	CPU /ISA-B	ADD-ON	30 [30]		30
13/A	MEMORY COMMAND INACTIVE TO MEMORY COMMAND ACTIVE 8 BITS 16 BITS	CPU /ISA-B	ADD-ON	159 [152] 97 [92]		170 114
	I/O COMMAND INACTIVE TO I/O COMMAND ACTIVE	CPU /ISA-B	ADD-ON	159 [152]		170
15	READ DATA VALID HOLD FROM INACTIVE MEMORY OR I/O COMMAND	ADD-ON	ADD-ON	0 [0]		0
15/A	WRITE DATA VALID HOLD FROM INACTIVE MEMORY COMMAND 8 BITS 16 BITS	CPU /ISA-B	ADD-ON	9 [9] 25 [25]		9 22
15/A	WRITE DATA VALID HOLD FROM INACTIVE I/O COMMAND	CPU /ISA-B	ADD-ON	25 [25]		22
16/E	COMMAND INACTIVE TO SD<0-19> TRISTATE	CPU /ISA-B	ADD-ON		30 [30]	30
17/B	SRDY* VALID FROM COMMAND ACTIVE (SEE NOTES 13,16) 8 BITS 16 BITS	ADD-ON	ADD-ON		63 [58] -5 [-7]	68 4
18/B	IOCS16* ACTIVE FROM VALID SA<0-11> (SEE NOTE 6)	ADD-ON	ADD-ON		131 [123]	103
18/D	IOCS16* INACTIVE FROM VALID SA<0-11> (SEE NOTE 6)	ADD-ON	ADD-ON		113 [105]	103
18/B	IOCS16* ACTIVE FROM VALID SA<0-11> (SEE NOTE 21)	ADD-ON	ADD-ON		59 [54]	46
18/D	IOCS16* INACTIVE FROM VALID SA<0-11> (SEE NOTE 21)	ADD-ON	ADD-ON		48 [43]	46

TABLE 6-1-B: ACCESS CYCLE TIMINGS ... ACCESSED RESOURCE (PLATFORM AND ADD-ON SLAVE CARD) (CONTINUED)

REF# /DET	DESCRIPTION OF EVENT	DRIVEN BY	MEASURED AT	MIN [8.33]	MAX	EISA
19/E	IOCS16* VALID HOLD FROM VALID SA<0-15>	ADD-ON	ADD-ON	0 [0]		0
20/B	IOCHRDY INACTIVE FROM ACTIVE COMMAND (SEE NOTE 7,10,20) 8 BITS OLD "AT" 16 BITS MEM I/O	ADD-ON	ADD-ON		368 [351] 61 [56] -7 [-9]	188 MEM 386 I/O 86 12
20/B	IOCHRDY INACTIVE FROM ACTIVE COMMAND (SEE NOTE 9,10,20) 8 BITS NEW E-ISA & EISA 16 BITS MEM I/O	ADD-ON	ADD-ON		427 [408] 120 [115] 52 [48]	188 MEM 386 I/O 86 68
20/C	IOCHRDY ACTIVE FROM ACTIVE COMMAND (SEE NOTE 7,10,20) 8 BITS OLD "AT" 1K PULL-UP 16 BITS ON PLATFORM MEM I/O	ADD-ON	ADD-ON		301 [284] -5 -10 -74 [-76]	NOT SPEC
20/C	IOCHRDY ACTIVE FROM ACTIVE COMMAND (SEE NOTE 7,10,20) 8 BITS OLD "AT" 300 PULL-UP 16 BITS ON PLATFORM MEM I/O	ADD-ON	ADD-ON		357 [340] 90 [85] -18 [-20]	NOT SPEC
20/C	IOCHRDY ACTIVE FROM ACTIVE COMMAND (SEE NOTE 9,10,20) 8 BITS NEW E-ISA & EISA 1K PULL-UP 16 BITS ON PLATFORM MEM I/O	ADD-ON	ADD-ON		334 [315] 67 [60] -41 [-45]	NOT SPEC

TABLE 6-1-B: ACCESS CYCLE TIMINGS ... ACCESSED RESOURCE (PLATFORM AND ADD-ON SLAVE CARD) (CONTINUED)

REF# /DET	DESCRIPTION OF EVENT	DRIVEN BY	MEASURED AT	MIN [8.33]	MAX	EISA
20/C	IOCHRDY ACTIVE FROM ACTIVE COMMAND (SEE NOTE 9,10,20) 8 BITS NEW E-ISA & EISA 300 PULL-UP 16 BITS ON PLATFORM MEM I/O	ADD-ON	ADD-ON		409 [390] 149 [135] 34 [30]	NOT SPEC
21	IOCHRDY INACTIVE PULSE (SEE NOTE 4)	ADD-ON	ADD-ON	125 [120]	15.6 MICROSECONDS	2.5
22/E	COMMAND ACTIVE HOLD FROM IOCHRDY ACTIVE	CPU /ISA-B	ADD-ON	125 [120]		120
23/A	BALE ACTIVE FROM COMMAND INACTIVE	CPU /ISA-B	ADD-ON	35 [33]		36
24	BCLK PERIOD	PLTFRM	ADD-ON	125		120
25/A	VALID READ DATA FROM IOCHRDY ACTIVE (SEE NOTE 11) 8 BITS EVEN ODD 16 BITS	ADD-ON	ADD-ON		74 [69] 48 [43] 74 [69]	70 49 80
26/A	LA<17-23> INVALID FROM COMMAND ACTIVE 8 BITS 16 BITS	CPU /ISA-B	ADD-ON	-32 [-32] 30 [28]		-34 22
28/B	SRDY* VALID SETUP TO THE FALLING EDGE OF BCLK	ADD-ON	ADD-ON	22 [22]		NOT SPEC
29	SRDY* VALID HOLD FROM THE FALLING EDGE OF BCLK	ADD-ON	ADD-ON	20 [20]		20
30/A	AENx VALID TO I/O COMMAND ACTIVE	PLAT.	ADD-ON	100 [100]		100
31/A	AENx VALID FROM I/O COMMAND INACTIVE	PLAT.	ADD-ON	30 [30]		25
32/A	AENx VALID TO FALLING EDGE OF BALE	PLAT.	ADD-ON	100 [100]		100
33	DATA DRIVEN IN WRITE DIRECTION FROM INACTIVE READ COMMAND	CPU /ISA-B	ADD-ON	30 [30]		
34	DATA DRIVEN FROM READ COMMAND ACTIVE	ADD-ON	ADD-ON	0 [0]		0

TABLE 6-1-B: ACCESS CYCLE TIMINGS ... ACCESSED RESOURCE (PLATFORM AND ADD-ON SLAVE CARD) (CONTINUED)

REF# /DET	DESCRIPTION OF EVENT	DRIVEN BY	MEASURED AT	MIN MAX [8.33]		EISA
35	IOCHRDY ACTIVE HOLD FROM COMMAND INACTIVE	ADD-ON	ADD-ON	0 [0]		
36/B	LA<17-23> VALID TO SRDY* ACTIVE (SEE NOTES 13,15) 8 BITS	CPU	ADD-ON	293 [278]		268
	16 BITS			169 [158]		144
37/B	SA<0-19> & SBHE* VALID TO SRDY* ACTIVE (SEE NOTES 13,14) 8 BITS	CPU	ADD-ON		188 [178]	180
	16 BITS				63 [58]	54

TABLE 6-1-B: ACCESS CYCLE TIMINGS ... ACCESSED RESOURCE (PLATFORM AND ADD-ON SLAVE CARD) (CONTINUED)

NOTES:

(1) Parameter 10 in the above table represents the numbers computed for an actual IBM platform. However, to meet the same timings when the same 8 data bit add-on memory card is part of a DMA transfer cycle, the actual time must be less. According to Parameter 24 of Table 7-1, the numbers 482 [460] should be replaced by 325 [310].   Indeed, this appears to be what was done by the EISA bus specification.   The numbers for the ODD 8 bit bytes must be reduced by 26 nanoseconds for byte swapping; the resulting numbers to replace 325 [310] are 299 [284].

(2) The entry assumes a 15 nanosecond same package skew between high/low and low/high transition with an 11 nanosecond bus delay at the beginning and a 0 nanosecond bus delay at the end. The entries in Table 6-1-A do not include the 11 nanoseconds for settling time.

(3) The first megabyte of the memory address space can be accessed with the SMEMW signal line. For the platform CPU, the numbers in the table are correct because the MEMW* and SMEMW* signal lines are driven "almost at the same time". For an ISA or E-ISA add-on bus owner card, the SMEMW* signal line is driven by the platform circuitry after the MEMW* signal line is driven active by the*

ISA or E-ISA add-on bus owner card. Consequently, the ISA or E-ISA add-on bus owner card must hold the data valid 21 nanoseconds longer than the numbers in the table for an 8 data bit memory resource when the access is to the first megabyte of the address space. The EISA Rev. 3.12 bus specification requires a 36 nanosecond number.

(4) The IBM Technical Reference Manual specifies 2.5 microseconds.

(5) The first megabyte of the memory address space can be accessed with the SMEMR* signal line. For the platform CPU, the numbers in the table are correct because the MEMR* and SMEMR* signal lines are driven "almost at the same time". For an ISA add-on bus owner card, the SMEMR* signal line is driven by the platform circuitry after the MEMR* signal line is driven active by the ISA or E-ISA add-on bus owner card. Consequently, the ISA or E-ISA add-on bus owner card must receive the data 21 nanoseconds later than the numbers in the table for an 8 data bit memory resource. The EISA Rev. 3.12 bus specification requires a 36 nanosecond number.

(6) Use this number for ISA or E-ISA add-on cards installed in E-ISA and EISA compatible platforms. If the bus master is an ISA add-on bus owner card, 153 [145] is replaced with 81 [76] in Table 6-1-A, and 113 [105] is replaced with 41 [35] in Table 6-1-B.

(7) Use this number for ISA or E-ISA add-on cards installed in ISA compatible platforms. This number assumes a 15pf per slot load.

(8) An E-ISA or EISA platform supports a 20 pf load instead of a 15 pf load per slot. Thus, for signal lines with 1K pull-up resistors, the number in the table must be decreased by 26 nanoseconds. For signal lines with 300 ohm pull-up resistors the number in the table must be decreased by 7 nanoseconds.

(9) Use this number for ISA or E-ISA add-on cards installed in E-ISA and EISA platforms (or for 8 data bit EISA memory add-on cards installed in EISA platforms). This number assumes a 20pf per slot load.

(10) If possible, use the smaller of the numbers from each section (OLD "AT" vs NEW E-ISA and EISA).

(11) The number used in the table for the ODD byte has been decreased by 26 nanoseconds from the EVEN byte numbers. This allows for byte swapping overhead if an ISA or E-ISA add-on bus owner card was executing the access and it wanted to maintain timing compatible to the platform CPU. (This Note is continued on the next page.)

(11 continued) *When the bus master is reading an odd address byte from a 16 data bit accessed resource, it can use the even address byte timing if the bus master can read directly off of the SD <8-15 > signal lines. The odd address byte timings are for an 8 bit (PC, XT) type of add-on card.*

When the bus master is writing an even address byte to a 16 data bit accessed resource, the add-on card can use the even address byte if it can accept thedata directly off of the SD <8-15 > signal lines. The odd address byte timings are for an 8 bit (PC, XT) type of add-on card.

(12) The first megabyte of the memory address space can be accessed with the SMEMW* or SMEMR* signal lines. For the platform CPU, the numbers in the table are correct because the MEMW* and SMEMW* signal lines are driven "almost at the same time". For an ISA or E-ISA add-on bus owner card, the SMEMW* and SMEMR* signal lines are driven by the platform circuitry after the MEMW* and MEMR* signal lines are driven active by the ISA or E-ISA add-on bus owner card. Consequently, the ISA or E-ISA add-on bus owner card must add 21 nanoseconds to the numbers in the table for 8 data bit memory resources. The EISA Rev. 3.12 bus specification requires a 36 nanosecond number.

(13) The entry in the table is for 3 BCLK signal line period no-wait-state access cycles. To get 4 and 5 BCLK signal period access cycles add 125 [120] and 250 [240] nanoseconds to the table, respectively. The original "AT" executed 4 BCLK signal line period no-wait-state cycles, but it is unclear if all "AT" clones did.

(14) For the original "AT", the table entries should be reduced by 54 and 21 nanoseconds for 8 and 16 data bits access cycles, respectively.

(15) For the original "AT", the table entries should be reduced by 38 nanoseconds.

(16) For the original "AT", the table entries should be reduced by 2 nanoseconds.

(17) If the BCLK signal line is distributed in a starburst fashion, the numbers in the table are possible. If not distributed in a starburst fashion, the entries in the table are reduced by 11 nanoseconds.

(18) The first megabyte of the memory address space can be accessed with the SMEMW* or SMEMR* signal lines. For the platform CPU, the numbers in the table are correct because the MEMW* and SMEMW* signal lines are driven "almost at the same time". For an ISA add-on bus owner card, the SMEMW* and SMEMR* signal lines are driven by the platform circuitry after the MEMW* and MEMR* signal lines are driven active by the ISA add-on bus owner card. Consequently, the ISA or E-ISA add-on bus owner card must hold the SA and SBHE* signal lines 21 nanoseconds longer than the numbers in the table for 8 data bit memory resources. The EISA Rev. 3.12 bus specification requires a 36 nanosecond number.

(19) The first megabyte of the memory address space can be accessed with the SMEMW* or SMEMR* signal lines. For the platform CPU, the numbers in the table are correct because the MEMW* and SMEMW* signal lines are driven "almost at the same time". For an ISA or E-ISA add-on bus owner card, the SMEMW* and SMEMR* signal lines are driven by the platform circuitry after the MEMW* and MEMR* signal lines are driven active by the ISA or E-ISA add-on bus owner card. Consequently, the ISA or E-ISA add-on bus owner card samples the IOCHRDY signal line 21 nanoseconds later than the numbers in the table for an 8 data bit memory resource. The EISA Rev. 3.12 bus specification requires a 36 nanosecond number.

(20) Parameter 20 in the above table is computed for an access cycle at the add-on memory slave card. However, to meet the same timings when the same 8 data bit add-on memory card is part of a DMA transfer cycle, the actual time must be less. According to Parameter 9 in Table 7-1-A, the entries in Table 6-1-B must be replaced as follows: (8.00[8.33] MHz) 368 [351] becomes 195 [180], 427 [408] becomes 188 [178], 301 [284] becomes 128 [113], 357 [340] becomes 174 [159], 334 [315] becomes 95 [85], and 409 [390] becomes 170 [160].

(21) Use this number for ISA or E-ISA add-on cards installed in ISA compatible platforms. This number assumes a 15 pf load. If the bus master is an E-ISA add-on bus owner card, 81 [76] is replaced with 153 [145] in Table 6-1-A and 48 [43] is replaced with 120 [112] in Table 6-1-B.

The following sections will first discuss the details for each ISA bus cycle executed in an ISA platform, and will then cover the enhancements for the E-ISA platform.

STANDARD MEMORY ACCESS CYCLE (ISA PLATFORM)

The ISA standard memory access cycle can be executed by the platform CPU or by an ISA or E-ISA add-on bus owner card (collectively called ISA bus masters). (See Figures 6-2 and 6-3.) When the platform CPU is the bus owner, the functional portion of the cycle begins by pulsing the BALE signal line to indicate that the LA, SA, AENx, and SBHE* signal lines are valid. For an ISA or E-ISA add-on bus owner card, the functional portion of the cycle begins when the COMMAND signal line is driven active. When the platform CPU is bus owner, the overall cycle is a standard cycle if the IOCHRDY signal line is active within a specific time relative to the COMMAND signal line becoming active, and if the SRDY* signal line is inactive at the center falling edge of the second clock period of the BCLK cycle (fourth clock period for an 8 data bit access). When an add-on bus owner card owns the bus, a standard cycle is dependent only upon the IOCHRDY signal line being active within a specific time relative to the COMMAND signal line becoming active.

For a 16 data bit access cycle, the ISA bus master must request a 16 data bit cycle and the accessed resource must support a 16 data bit cycle. For an 8 data bit access cycle, either the ISA bus owner must request an 8 data bit cycle or the accessed resource must be an 8 data bit resource. This is summarized in Table 6-2.

BUS MASTER			ACCESSED RESOURCE	DATA SIZE
SBHE*	SA0	DATA SIZE REQUESTED	MEMCS16*	OF CYCLE
INACT.	0	8	X (1)	8
ACT.	1	8	X (1)	8
ACT.	0	16	INACT.	8
ACT.	0	16	ACT.	16

TABLE 6-2: ISA AND E-ISA PLATFORM MEMORY CYCLE DATA SIZE

NOTE:
(1) For an odd or even address byte read, the bus master can use 16 bit timing and access cycles if it chooses. For an odd or even address byte write, the add-on card must assume valid write data timing per the 8 bit specification. Even though the add-on card indicated a 16 bit resource, there is no assurance that the bus master had begun the access cycle with 16 bit data set up to write command timing.

Once the data size is established, the ISA bus owner and the accessed resource know the minimum length of time that the COMMAND signal line is driven active. For a read cycle, the data from the accessed resource must be valid within a maximum time from the MEMR* (SMEMR*) signal line becoming active. For a write cycle, the data must be valid prior to the MEMW* (SMEMW*) signal line becoming active. The data must remain valid a minimum time after the appropriate command line is driven inactive. The COMMAND signal line becoming inactive indicates the completion of the cycle.

When the bus owner executes an access cycle, the SMEMR* and SMEMW* signal lines must be monitored by certain memory resources. If either line is active, only the first one megabyte of the memory address space is being accessed. For a memory resource in an 8/16 bit slot, the LA<20-23> signal lines are available to indicate the first one megabyte, and the MEMR* and MEMW* signal lines are also available. For a memory resource in an 8 bit slot, the LA<20-23>, MEMR*, and MEMW* signal lines are not available. Since the SMEMR* and SMEMW* signal lines are the only memory command signal lines available in an 8 bit slot, 8 bit memory resources can only reside in the first one megabyte of the address space.

The standard memory access cycle length will vary depending on the data width of the cycle. The reference point for the beginning of the cycle will vary for different bus owners. Table 6-3 summarizes the cycle length in terms of TCLK (period of BCLK). Due to bus settling times and device delays, TCLK should be considered as approximate for the "CYCLE BEGINS" column.

BUS MASTER	CYCLE BEGINS	CYCLE ENDS	CYCLE SIZE	CYCLE LENGTH
PLATFORM CPU	.5 TCLK TO ACT. BALE	END COMMAND ACT. PERIOD	8 BITS 16 BITS	6 TCLK 3 TCLK
ADD- ON	1.5 TCLK TO ACT. COMMAND	END COMMAND ACT. PERIOD	8 BITS	6 TCLK
ADD- ON	1 TCLK TO ACT. COMMAND	END COMMAND ACT. PERIOD	16 BITS	3 TCLK

TABLE 6-3: ISA AND E-ISA PLATFORM STANDARD MEMORY ACCESS CYCLE LENGTH

The above cycle description applies to E-ISA compatible add-on cards on an ISA compatible platform.

STANDARD MEMORY ACCESS CYCLE (E-ISA PLATFORM)

When a platform CPU or E-ISA compatible add-on bus owner card (collectively called E-ISA bus masters) is executing the cycle, the operation of an E-ISA standard memory access cycle is defined in the same way as for an ISA compatible platform. (See Figures 6-2 and 6-3.) Additionally, on an E-ISA compatible platform, the E-ISA bus master sampling of the IOCHRDY signal line has been enhanced. For a 16 bit cycle, the INITIAL SAMPLING WINDOW for the IOCHRDY signal line is the third BCLK cycle. For an 8 bit cycle, the INITIAL SAMPLING WINDOW for the IOCHRDY signal line is the sixth BCLK cycle. For the cycle to remain a standard cycle, the IOCHRDY signal line must be sampled active during the initial sampling window.

See Tables 6-2 and 6-3 in the STANDARD MEMORY ACCESS CYCLE (ISA PLATFORM) section for cycle data size and cycle length information, respectively. Also see this section for back to back bus cycle information.

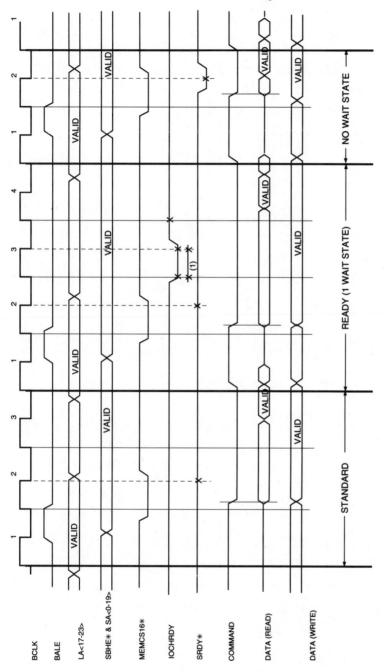

X = SAMPLING POINT
(1) = INITIAL SAMPLING WINDOW
SEE CHAPTER 5

BCLK
BALE
LA<17-23>
SBHE* & SA<0-19>
MEMCS16*
IOCHRDY
SRDY*
COMMAND
DATA (READ)
DATA (WRITE)

FIGURE 6-2-A: 16 DATA BIT ISA & E-ISA MEMORY ACCESS CYCLE. PLATFORM CPU ON ISA & E-ISA COMPATIBLE PLATFORMS AND E-ISA ADD-ON BUS OWNER CARD ON E-ISA COMPATIBLE PLATFORM

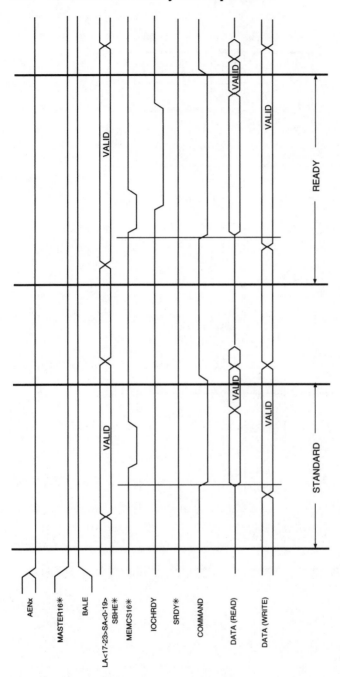

FIGURE   6-2-B: 16 DATA BIT MEMORY ACCESS CYCLES . . . ISA & E-ISA
ADD-ON BUS OWNER CARD ON ISA COMPATIBLE PLATFORMS

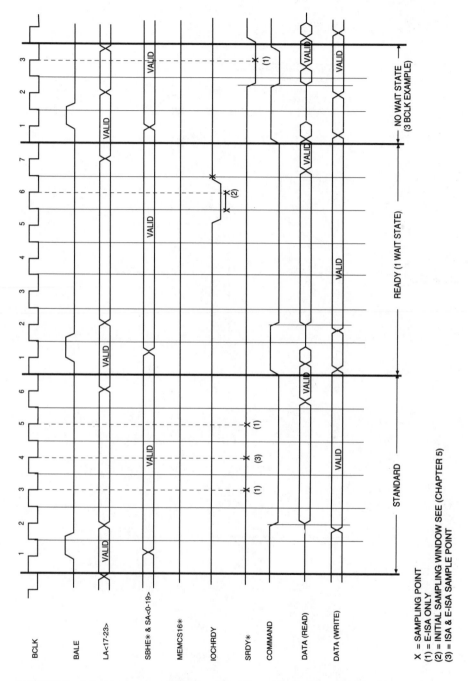

FIGURE 6-3-A: *8 DATA BIT ISA & E-ISA MEMORY ACCESS CYCLES . . .*
PLATFORM CPU ON ISA & E-ISA COMPATIBLE PLATFORMS
AND 8 DATA BIT E-ISA ADD-ON BUS OWNER CARD ON E-ISA
COMPATIBLE PLATFORM

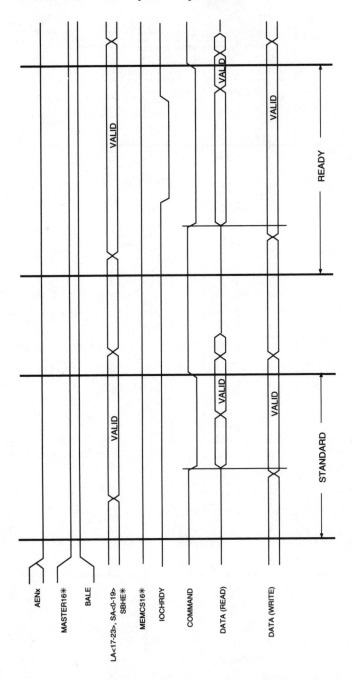

FIGURE   6-3-B: 8 DATA BIT MEMORY ACCESS CYCLES . . . ISA & E-ISA
ADD-ON BUS OWNER CARD ON ISA COMPATIBLE PLATFORMS

STANDARD I/O ACCESS CYCLE (ISA PLATFORM)

The ISA standard I/O access cycle can be executed by either a platform CPU or an ISA or E-ISA add-on bus owner card (collectively called ISA bus masters). (See Figures 6-4 and 6-5.) The standard I/O access cycle operates in the same way as a standard memory cycle, except that the LA<17-23> and the SA<10-19> signal lines are not used. When the platform CPU is the bus owner, the functional portion of the cycle begins by pulsing the BALE signal line to indicate that SA, AENx, and SBHE* signal lines are valid. For an ISA or E-ISA add-on bus owner card, the functional portion of the cycle begins when a COMMAND signal line is driven active.

When the platform CPU is bus owner, the overall cycle timings are those of a standard cycle if the IOCHRDY signal line is active and the SRDY* signal line is inactive. When the add-on bus owner card owns the bus, the cycle is a standard cycle dependent only on the IOCHRDY signal line being active within a specific time of the COMMAND signal line becoming active. For a 16 data bit access cycle, the bus owner must request a 16 data bit cycle and the accessed resource must support a 16 data bit cycle. For an 8 data bit access cycle, either the bus owner must request an 8 data bit cycle or the accessed resource must be only an 8 data bit resource. This is summarized in Table 6-4.

BUS MASTER SBHE* SAO DATA SIZE REQUESTED	ACCESSED RESOURCE IOCS16*	DATA SIZE OF CYCLE
INACT. 0 8	X (SEE NOTE FOR	8
ACT. 1 8	X TABLE 6-2)	8
ACT. 0 16	INACT.	8
ACT. 0 16	ACT.	16

TABLE 6-4: ISA AND E-ISA PLATFORM I/O ACCESS CYCLE DATA SIZE

Once the data size is established, the ISA bus master and the accessed resource know the minimum length of time that the COMMAND signal line is driven active. For a read cycle, the data from the accessed resource must be valid within a maximum amount of time from the IOR* signal line becoming active. For a write cycle, the data must be valid prior to the IOW* signal line becoming active. The data must remain valid for a minimum amount of time after the appropriate COMMAND line is driven inactive. The COMMAND signal line becoming inactive indicates the completion of the cycle.

The ISA standard I/O access cycle length will vary depending on the data width for the cycle. The reference point for the beginning of the cycle varies for different bus owners. Table 6-5 summarizes the cycle length in terms of TCLK (period of BCLK). Due to bus settling times and device delays, TCLK should be considered as approximate for the "CYCLE BEGINS" column.

BUS MASTER	CYCLE BEGINS	CYCLE ENDS	CYCLE SIZE	CYCLE LENGTH
PLATFORM CPU	.5 TCLK TO ACT. BALE	END COMMAND ACT. PERIOD	8 BITS 16 BITS	6 TCLK 3 TCLK
ADD-ON	1.5 TCLK TO ACT. COMMAND	END COMMAND ACT. PERIOD	8 BITS 16 BITS	6 TCLK 3 TCLK

TABLE 6-5: ISA AND E-ISA PLATFORM STANDARD I/O ACCESS CYCLE LENGTH

On an ISA platform, only the SA<0-9> signal lines are driven valid by the bus owner during an I/O access cycle.

The above cycle description applies to an E-ISA compatible add-on card on an ISA compatible platform.

STANDARD I/O ACCESS CYCLE (E-ISA PLATFORM)

When a platform CPU or E-ISA compatible add-on bus owner card (collectively called E-ISA bus masters) is executing a standard I/O access cycle, the operation of a standard I/O access cycle is

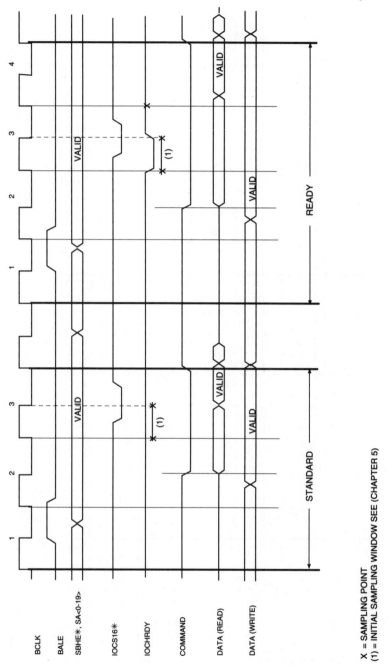

FIGURE 6-4-A: *16 DATA BIT I/O ACCESS CYCLES . . . PLATFORM CPU ON ISA OR E-ISA COMPATIBLE PLATFORMS AND 16 DATA BIT E-ISA ADD-ON BUS OWNER CARD ON E-ISA COMPATIBLE PLATFORM*

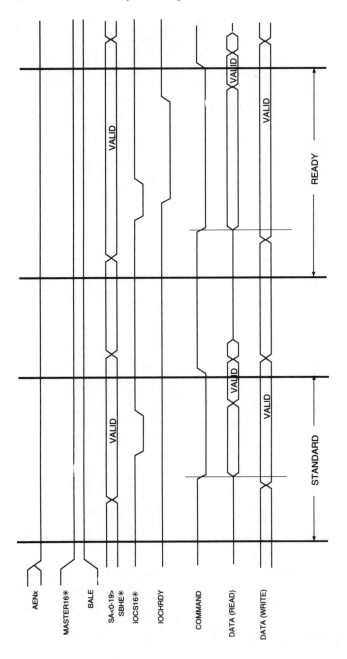

FIGURE   6-4-B: *16 DATA BIT I/O CYCLE . . . ISA & E-ISA ADD-ON BUS OWNER CARD ON ISA COMPATIBLE PLATFORMS*

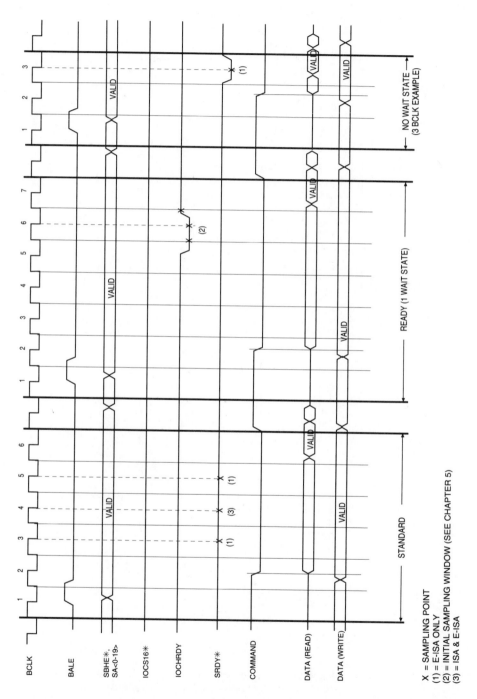

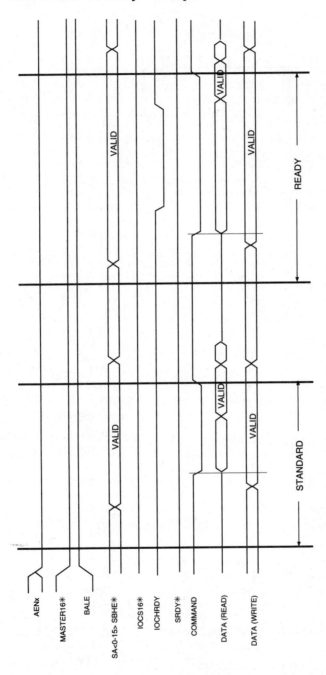

*FIGURE   6-5-B: 8 DATA BIT I/O ACCESS CYCLES . . . ISA & E-ISA ADD-ON
BUS OWNER CARD ON ISA COMPATIBLE PLATFORMS*

defined for an E-ISA compatible platform in the same way as for an ISA compatible platform. (See Figures 6-4 and 6-5.) Additionally, on an E-ISA compatible platform, the E-ISA bus master sampling of the IOCHRDY signal line has been enhanced. For a 16 bit cycle, the INITIAL SAMPLING WINDOW for the IOCHRDY signal line is the third BCLK cycle. For an 8 bit cycle, the INITIAL SAMPLING WINDOW for the IOCHRDY signal line is the sixth BCLK cycle. For the cycle to remain a standard cycle, the IOCHRDY signal line must be sampled active during the sampling window.

See Tables 6-4 and 6-5 in the STANDARD ACCESS I/O CYCLE (ISA PLATFORM) section for cycle data size and cycle length information, respectively. Also see this section for back to back bus cycle information.

An I/O access cycle executed by an E-ISA bus master must drive the SA<0-15> signal lines valid. The SA<12-15> signal lines must be driven valid during an I/O access cycle so the platform circuitry can decode the SA<8,9,12-15> value into the AENx signal lines, and SA<0-11> for decoding of the IOCS16* signal line. If an E-ISA bus master does not want to access the configuration space or slot specific I/O, only the SA<0-9> signal lines need to be driven.

READY MEMORY ACCESS CYCLE (ISA PLATFORM)

The ISA ready memory access cycle can be executed by an ISA compatible platform CPU or an ISA or E-ISA compatible add-on bus owner card (collectively called ISA bus masters). (See Figures 6-2 and 6-3.) The cycle begins in the same fashion as the standard memory access cycle. The standard memory access cycle becomes a ready memory access cycle if the IOCHRDY signal line is driven inactive by the accessed resource. The IOCHRDY signal line must be driven inactive within a "specific time" of an active COMMAND signal line. (If the SRDY* signal line is driven active when the IOCHRDY signal line is active, the SRDY* signal line is ignored.)

The COMMAND signal line remains active until the IOCHRDY signal line is driven active by the accessed resource. During a memory read cycle, the IOCHRDY signal line becoming active indicates to the ISA bus master that valid data is available. During a write cycle, the IOCHRDY signal line becoming active indicates to the ISA bus master that the accessed resource has accepted the data. For either read or write cycles, the activation of the IOCHRDY signal line is the indication to the ISA bus master to complete the cycle. The cycle is completed when the COMMAND signal line becomes inactive.

See Table 6-2 in the STANDARD MEMORY ACCESS CYCLE (ISA PLATFORM) section for cycle data size information.

The ISA ready memory access cycle length depends on when the IOCHRDY signal line is reactivated. The ready memory access cycle length is extended in increments of the BCLK period. (In order to insure refresh of memory, the longest inactive period allowed for the IOCHRDY signal line is 15.6 microseconds.) The minimum time for a ready memory access cycle is controlled by several factors: first, once the IOCHRDY signal line is reactivated, the COMMAND signal line will not be deactivated until after a minimum of one BCLK signal line period has elapsed. Second, the ISA bus master must have sufficient sampling time for the IOCHRDY signal line; consequently, the minimum inactive period of the signal is one BCLK signal line period. Finally, sufficient decode time from a COMMAND signal line going active must be allocated. These requirements collectively establish the minimum length of a ready memory access cycle. The minimum cycle length, in terms of TCLK (period of BCLK), is summarized in Table 6-6. Due to bus settling times and device delays, TCLK should be considered as approximate for the "CYCLE BEGINS" column.

BUS MASTER	CYCLE BEGINS	CYCLE ENDS	CYCLE SIZE	CYCLE LENGTH
PLATFORM CPU	.5 TCLK TO ACT. BALE	END COMMAND ACT. PERIOD	8 BITS 16 BITS	7 TCLK 4 TCLK
ADD-ON	1.5 TCLK TO ACT. COMMAND	END COMMAND ACT. PERIOD	8 BITS	7 TCLK
ADD-ON	1 TCLK TO ACT. COMMAND	END COMMAND ACT. PERIOD	16 BITS	4 TCLK

TABLE 6-6: ISA AND E-ISA PLATFORM MINIMUM READY MEMORY ACCESS CYCLE LENGTH

The above cycle description applies to an E-ISA compatible add-on card on an ISA compatible platform.

READY MEMORY ACCESS CYCLE (E-ISA PLATFORM)

When a platform CPU or E-ISA compatible add-on bus owner card (collectively called E-ISA bus masters) is executing the cycle, the operation of an E-ISA ready memory access cycle is defined by an E-ISA platform in the same way as for an ISA platform. (See Figures 6-2 and 6-3.) Refer to the READY MEMORY ACCESS CYCLE (ISA PLATFORM) section for further information. Additionally, on an E-ISA platform, the E-ISA bus master sampling of the IOCHRDY signal line has been enhanced by relating it to the BCLK signal line. See Chapter 5 for more information. For a 16 bit cycle, the INITIAL SAMPLING WINDOW for the IOCHRDY signal line is the third BCLK cycle. For an 8 bit cycle, the INITIAL SAMPLING WINDOW for the IOCHRDY signal line is the sixth BCLK cycle. For the cycle to remain a standard cycle, the IOCHRDY signal line must be sampled active during the sampling window.

See Table 6-2 in the STANDARD MEMORY ACCESS CYCLE (ISA PLATFORM) section for cycle data size information. See Table 6-6 in the READY MEMORY ACCESS CYCLE (ISA PLATFORM) section for E-ISA ready memory cycle length information.

READY I/O ACCESS CYCLE (ISA PLATFORM)

The ISA ready I/O access cycle can be executed by either an ISA compatible platform CPU or an ISA or E-ISA add-on bus owner card (collectively called ISA bus masters). (See Figures 6-4 and 6-5.) The cycle begins in the same fashion as the standard access I/O cycle. The standard access I/O cycle becomes a ready access I/O cycle if the IOCHRDY signal line is driven inactive by the accessed resource. The IOCHRDY signal line must be driven inactive within a "specific time" of an active COMMAND signal line. (If the SRDY* signal line is driven active when the IOCHRDY signal line is active, the SRDY* signal line is ignored.)

The COMMAND signal line remains active until the IOCHRDY signal line is driven active by the accessed resource. During an I/O read cycle, the IOCHRDY signal line becoming active indicates to the bus owner that valid data is available. During a write cycle, the IOCHRDY signal line becoming active indicates to the bus master that the accessed resource has accepted the data. For either read or write cycles, the activation of the IOCHRDY signal line is the indication to the bus master to complete the cycle. The cycle is completed when the COMMAND signal line becomes inactive.

See Table 6-4 in the STANDARD ACCESS I/O CYCLE (ISA PLATFORM) section for cycle data width information.

The ISA ready I/O access cycle length depends on when the IOCHRDY signal line is reactivated. The ready I/O access cycle length is extended in increments of the BCLK signal. (In order to insure memory refresh, the longest inactive period of the IOCHRDY signal line is 15.6 microseconds.) The minimum time for a ready I/O access cycle is controlled by several factors. First, once the IOCHRDY signal line is reactivated, the COMMAND signal line will not be deactivated until after a minimum of one BCLK period has elapsed. Second, the ISA bus master must have sufficient sampling time for the IOCHRDY signal line; consequently, the minimum inactive period of the signal is one

BCLK period. Finally, sufficient decode time from a COMMAND signal line going active must be allocated. These requirements

BUS MASTER	CYCLE BEGINS	CYCLE ENDS	CYCLE SIZE	CYCLE LENGTH
PLATFORM CPU	.5 TCLK TO ACT. BALE	END COMMAND ACT. PERIOD	8 BITS 16 BITS	7 TCLK 4 TCLK
ADD-ON	1.5 TCLK TO ACT. COMMAND	END COMMAND ACT. PERIOD	8 BITS	7 TCLK
ADD-ON	1.5 TCLK TO ACT. COMMAND	END COMMAND ACT. PERIOD	16 BITS	4 TCLK

TABLE 6-7: ISA AND E-ISA PLATFORM MINIMUM READY I/O ACCESS CYCLE LENGTH

collectively establish the minimum length of a ready I/O access cycle. The minimum cycle length, in terms of TCLK (period of BCLK), is summarized in Table 6-7. Due to bus settling times and device delays, TCLK should be considered as approximate for the "CYCLE BEGINS" column.

The above cycle description applies to an E-ISA compatible add-on card on an ISA compatible platform.

READY I/O ACCESS CYCLE (E-ISA PLATFORM)

When a platform CPU or E-ISA compatible add-on bus owner card (also called E-ISA bus master) is executing this cycle, the operation of an E-ISA ready I/O access cycle is defined by an E-ISA platform in the same way as for an ISA platform. (See Figures 6-4 and 6-5.) Refer to the READY I/O ACCESS CYCLE (ISA PLATFORM) Section for further information. Additionally, on an E-ISA platform, the E-ISA bus master sampling of the IOCHRDY signal line has been enhanced by relating it to the BCLK signal line. See Chapter 5 for more information. For a 16 bit cycle, the INITIAL SAMPLING WINDOW for the IOCHRDY signal line is the third BCLK cycle. For an 8 bit cycle, the INITIAL SAMPLING WINDOW for the IOCHRDY signal line is the sixth

BCLK cycle.   For the cycle to remain a standard cycle, the IOCHRDY signal line must be sampled active during the sampling window.

See Table 6-4 in the STANDARD I/O ACCESS CYCLE (ISA PLATFORM) section for cycle data size. See Table 6-7 in the READY I/O ACCESS CYCLE (ISA PLATFORM) section for E-ISA ready I/O access cycle length information.

NO-WAIT-STATE MEMORY ACCESS CYCLE (ISA PLATFORM)

The ISA no-wait-state memory access cycle can be executed when an ISA compatible platform CPU is accessing an ISA or E-ISA memory resource. (See Figure 6-3.) The cycle begins in the same fashion as the standard memory access cycle. The standard memory access cycle becomes a no-wait-state memory access cycle if the SRDY* signal line is driven active by the accessed resource within a "specific time" of an active COMMAND signal line relative to the center falling edge of the second cycle of the BCLK cycle. The cycle will be completed at the end of the same cycle. The SRDY* signal line for a 16 bit memory access is sampled only at one point of the cycle. Sampling at other points is not needed because other cycle lengths are either a standard cycle or a ready cycle. (If the IOCHRDY signal line is driven inactive during this "specific time", the SRDY* signal line is ignored.) The SRDY* signal line for an 8 bit memory access is sampled only at one point. Sampling at other points would have been possible; it simply was not done on the IBM AT.

The completion of the no-wait-state memory access cycle is the same as the standard cycle, except that the active period of the COMMAND signal line is shorter.

See Table 6-2 in the STANDARD MEMORY ACCESS CYCLE (ISA PLATFORM) Section for cycle data width information.

The ISA no-wait-state memory access cycle length is defined for the platform CPU accessing an 8 or 16 data bit memory resource. Table 6-8 summarizes the no-wait-state memory cycle length in terms of TCLK (period of BCLK). Due to bus settling times and device delays, TCLK should be considered as approximate for the "CYCLE BEGINS" column.

BUS MASTER	CYCLE BEGINS	CYCLE ENDS	CYCLE SIZE	CYCLE LENGTH
PLATFORM CPU	.5 TCLK TO ACT. BALE	END COMMAND ACT. PERIOD	16 BITS	2 TCLK
PLATFORM CPU	.5 TCLK TO ACT. BALE	END COMMAND ACT. PERIOD	8 BITS	4 TCLK

TABLE 6-8: ISA PLATFORM NO-WAIT-STATE MEMORY ACCESS CYCLE LENGTH

The original IBM PC and XT platforms defined the SRDY* signal line connector pin as a card select response from an 8 data bit slot. IBM AT platforms define this pin as the SRDY* signal line. For purposes of this book, it is assumed an 8 data bit slot and add-on card uses this connector pin for the SRDY* signal line.

The IBM "AT" supported no-wait-state access cycles to 8 data bit memory. It is unclear whether all "AT" clones support this type of cycle for this data size. The EISA Rev. 3.12 bus specification clearly identifies support; consequently, so does the E-ISA compatible platform.

NO-WAIT-STATE MEMORY ACCESS CYCLE (E-ISA PLATFORM)

The E-ISA compatible platform CPU executes an E-ISA no-wait-state memory access cycle in the same fashion as an ISA compatible platform CPU for 8 and 16 data bit memory resources. (See Figures 6-2 and 6-3.) See the NO-WAIT-STATE MEMORY ACCESS CYCLE (ISA PLATFORM) section for more information.

An E-ISA platform CPU also supports an expanded definition of accesses to 8 data bit memory resources. (See Figure 6-3.) The cycle begins in the same fashion as the standard memory access cycle. The standard memory access cycle becomes a no-wait-state access cycle if the SRDY* signal line is driven active by the accessed resource. The SRDY* signal line must be driven active within a "specific time" of an active COMMAND signal line relative to the center falling edge of the BCLK signal line. The cycle will be completed at the end of the same cycle. The SRDY* signal line for an 8 data bit memory access has been expanded to sample at three points of the cycle, which allows the cycle to complete earlier than a standard length cycle. Sampling at other points for a 16 data bit cycle is not needed because other cycle lengths are either the standard cycle or a ready cycle.

The SRDY* signal line is sampled at the falling edge of the center transition of the second cycle of the BCLK signal line for 16 data bit resources. The 8 data bit COMMAND signal line is just becoming active at the center falling edge of the second cycle of the BCLK signal line. Consequently, for an 8 data bit resource, the first valid sampling is in the third cycle. On E-ISA and EISA compatible platforms, the SRDY* (NOWS*) signal line is sampled in the third, fourth, and fifth period of the BCLK signal line. On an IBM "AT", it is sampled in the fourth period of the BCLK signal line for an 8 data bit resource.

The completion of the no-wait-state memory access cycle is the same as the standard memory cycle, except that the active period of the COMMAND signal line is shorter.

An E-ISA compatible platform supports no-wait state memory access cycles for add-on bus owner cards *because the BCLK signal line is distributed in a "starburst" pattern to all slots.* Please see Chapter 10 for more information.

See Table 6-2 in the STANDARD MEMORY ACCESS CYCLE (ISA PLATFORM) section for data width information.

The length of the no-wait-state memory access cycle is defined for the platform CPU accessing an 8 or 16 bit memory resource. Table 6-9 summarizes the no-wait-state memory cycle length in terms of TCLK (period of BCLK). Due to bus settling times and device delays, the TCLK should be considered as approximate for the "CYCLE BEGINS" column.

BUS MASTER	CYCLE BEGINS	CYCLE ENDS	CYCLE SIZE	CYCLE LENGTH
PLATFORM CPU	.5 TCLK TO ACTIVE BALE	END COMMAND ACT. PERIOD	8 BITS	3 TCLK (1)
	.5 TCLK TO ACTIVE BALE	END COMMAND ACT. PERIOD	16 BITS	2 TCLK
ADD-ON	1.5 TCLK TO ACTIVE COMMAND	END COMMAND ACT. PERIOD	8 BITS	3 TCLK
ADD-ON	1.5 TCLK TO ACTIVE COMMAND	END COMMAND ACT. PERIOD	16 BITS	2 TCLK

TABLE 6-9: E-ISA PLATFORM NO-WAIT-STATE MEMORY ACCESS CYCLE LENGTH

NOTE:
(1) Shortest no-wait-state access cycle. 4 TCLK and 5 TCLK no-wait-state access cycles are also possible.

Please see the "NOTE" in the shaded box in the NO-WAIT-STATE MEMORY ACCESS CYCLE (E-ISA PLATFORM) section.

NO-WAIT-STATE I/O ACCESS CYCLE (ISA PLATFORM)

The original IBM PC, XT, and AT platforms did not support 16 bit ISA no-wait-state I/O access cycles. The I/O command is active later in the cycle than a memory command (see Figures 6-4 and 6-5), which means that the SRDY* signal line would be sampled during the third BCLK signal line period instead of the second. However, the sampling in the third BCLK* signal line period is useless because the standard cycle length is three cycles. The standard cycle length of an 8 bit I/O access cycle is 6 cycles; consequently, defining no-wait-state cycles is possible.

The ISA no-wait-state I/O access cycle can be executed when an ISA compatible platform CPU is accessing an ISA or E-ISA 8 data bit I/O resource. (See Figure 6-5.) The cycle begins in the same fashion as the standard I/O access cycle. The standard I/O access cycle becomes a no-wait-state I/O access cycle if the SRDY* signal line is driven active by the accessed resource within a "specific time" of an active COMMAND signal line relative to the center falling edge of the second cycle of the BCLK signal line. The cycle will be completed at the end of the same cycle. The SRDY* signal line for an 8 data bit I/O access is sampled only at one point. Sampling at other points would have been possible; it simply was not done on the IBM AT. (If the IOCHRDY signal line is driven inactive during this "specific time", the SRDY* signal line is ignored.)

> *The original IBM PC and XT platforms defined the SRDY* signal line connector pin as a card select response from slot 8. IBM AT platforms define this pin as the SRDY* signal line. For purposes of this book, it is assumed that slot 8 card select response is not supported on ISA platforms.*

> *The IBM AT supported no-wait-state access cycles to 8 data bit I/O. It is unclear whether all AT clones support this type of cycle for this data size. The EISA Rev. 3.12 bus specification clearly identifies support; consequently, so does the E-ISA platform. See the E-ISA section in this chapter for more information. The EISA bus specification CLEARLY DEFINES 8 BIT NO-WAIT-STATE CYCLES. Please see the NO-WAIT-STATE I/O ACCESS CYCLE (E-ISA PLATFORM) section for more information. Please see the NOTE in the description of the SRDY* signal line section of Chapter 5 for more detailed information.*

The completion of the no-wait-state I/O access cycle is the same as the standard cycle, except that the active period of the COMMAND signal line is shorter.

See Table 6-4 in the STANDARD I/O ACCESS CYCLE (ISA PLATFORM) section for cycle data width information.

The ISA no-wait-state I/O access cycle length is defined for the platform CPU accessing an 8 data bit I/O resource. Table 6-10 summarizes the no-wait-state I/O cycle length in terms of TCLK (period of BCLK). Due to bus settling times and device delay, TCLK should be considered as approximate for the "CYCLE BEGINS" column.

BUS MASTER	CYCLE BEGINS	CYCLE ENDS	CYCLE SIZE	CYCLE LENGTH
PLATFORM CPU	.5 TCLK TO ACTIVE BALE	END COMMAND ACT. PERIOD	8 BITS	4 TCLK

TABLE 6-10-A: ISA PLATFORM NO-WAIT-STATE I/O ACCESS CYCLE LENGTH

NO-WAIT-STATE I/O ACCESS CYCLE (E-ISA PLATFORM)

The E-ISA no-wait-state I/O access cycle can be executed when an E-ISA compatible platform CPU or E-ISA add-on bus owner card (collectively called E-ISA bus masters) is accessing an 8 data bit resource. (See Figure 6-5.) The cycle begins in the same fashion as the standard I/O access cycle. The standard I/O access cycle becomes a no-wait-state I/O access cycle if the SRDY* signal line is driven active by the accessed resource. The SRDY* signal line must be driven active within a "specific time" of an active COMMAND signal line relative to the center falling edge of the third, fourth, or fifth period of the BCLK cycle. The cycle will be completed at the end of the same cycle. The E-ISA compatible platform does not support no-wait-state I/O access cycles to a 16 data bit resource for the same reasons as an ISA compatible platform. The SRDY* signal line for an 8 data bit access is sampled at three points of the cycle. The multiple sampling allows the cycle to complete earlier than a standard length cycle. (If the IOCHRDY signal line is driven inactive during this "specific time", the SRDY* signal line is ignored.)

An E-ISA platform supports no-wait state I/O access cycles for E-ISA compatible add-on bus owner cards because *the BCLK signal line is distributed in a "starburst" pattern to all slots on an E-ISA compatible platform.* Please see Chapter 10 for more information.

> *The EISA bus specification allows the first sampling of the SRDY* signal line at the center falling edge of the third clock cycle. The sampling cannot occur sooner because the 8 bit COMMAND signal line is becoming active only at the middle of the second period of the BCLK signal line.*

The completion of the no-wait-state I/O access cycle is the same as the standard cycle, except that the active period of the COMMAND line is shorter. See Table 6-4 in the STANDARD I/O ACCESS CYCLE (ISA PLATFORM) section for cycle data size.

The E-ISA no-wait-state I/O access cycle length is defined for the E-ISA bus master accessing an 8 bit I/O resource. Table 6-11 summarizes the minimum cycle length in terms of TCLK (period of

BCLK). Due to bus settling times and device delays TCLK should be considered as approximate for the "CYCLE BEGINS" column.

BUS MASTER	CYCLE BEGINS	CYCLE ENDS	CYCLE SIZE	CYCLE LENGTH
PLATFORM CPU/ADD-ON	.5 TCLK TO ACTIVE BALE	END COMMAND	8 BITS	3 TCLK (1)

TABLE 6-10-B: E-ISA PLATFORM NO-WAIT-STATE I/O ACCESS CYCLE MINIMUM LENGTH

NOTE:
(1) Shortest no-wait-state access cycle. 4 TCLK and 5 TCLK no-wait-state access cycles are also possible.

6.1 EISA SPECIFIC ACCESS CYCLES ON EISA PLATFORMS

INTRODUCTION

The EISA specific access cycles support access to memory and I/O resources by the bus owner. The two bus owners that can execute access cycles are the platform CPU and EISA compatible add-on bus owner cards (collectively called EISA bus masters). Table 3-1-B and 3-1-C in Chapter 3 outlines the support level of access cycles by the various bus owners and platform CPUs.

As described in Chapter 3, there are five types of EISA specific access cycles: standard, ready, data-matching, compressed, and burst. These cycles can only be executed on EISA compatible platforms. Like the ISA specific access cycles, the type is determined by the interpretation of the signal lines and the length of the cycles. The length of one of the cycle types is dependent on the cycle's data width and the logic level of the EXRDY and NOWS* (also called SRDY*).

EISA specific access cycles are both synchronous and asynchronous in nature. From the EISA bus master viewpoint, all of the signals are synchronous; that is, the signal lines become active and inactive relative to the BCLK signal line. From the EISA compatible accessed resource viewpoint, the access cycles are asynchronous; but, for some access cycles, some signal lines become synchronous to the BCLK signal line.

EISA specific access cycles occur on an EISA compatible platform between EISA compatible resources. On an EISA compatible platform, all bus cycles executed by the platform CPU or EISA bus owner add-on cards assume EISA access cycle compatibility. If the accessed resource is ISA compatible, the cycle proceeds as an EISA bus master to ISA compatible accessed resource cycle (also called E-MIX access cycles). E-MIX access cycles are discussed in Subchapter 6.2. If the access cycle is executed by an ISA or E-ISA bus owner add-on card, the cycles proceed as an ISA or E-ISA bus master to an EISA accessed resource (also called I-MIX access cycles). I-MIX access cycles are discussed in Subchapter 6.3.

Figure 6-6-A details standard and ready type EISA access cycle timings from the viewpoint of EISA bus masters. Figure 6-6-B details standard and ready type EISA access cycle timings from the viewpoint of EISA accessed resource. Tables 6-11-A and 6-11-B lists the values of these timing relationships for Figures 6-6-A and 6-6-B, respectively.

The EISA specific bus timings assume that the BCLK signal line is distributed in a "starburst" pattern to all slots. That is, there is a single driver with an individual line going to each of the slots; consequently, the maximum skew between all of the BCLK signal lines at each slot is less than one nanosecond. Assume that the CMD* signal line is driven from platform circuitry in a "non-starburst" pattern. That is, the platform circuitry drives a single CMD* signal line which runs in a daisy chain fashion from slot to slot; consequently the skew between any two CMD* signal lines is the bus settling time. Finally, the timings assume that there are no buffers on the data signal lines between any two slots. If swapping between data signal lines occur, the entry will note the change in the listed time.

Tables 6-11-A and 6-11-B have several key pieces of information. First, the "#/DET" (parameter number / detail) column relates the parameter number of the table to Figures 6-6-A and 6-6-B. Second, it provides detailed information on how the number was derived. The timing numbers are affected by the settling time on the bus. The table is based on the default values for 8 slots as outlined in Chapter 10. The #/DET interpretations are shown on the following page.

DETAIL	INTERPRETATION
#	NO SETTLING TIME INCLUDED.
#/A	SKEW OF TWO SIGNALS BETWEEN RESOURCES. ONE HAS A DELAY OF 0 NANOSECONDS, AND THE OTHER HAS A DELAY OF 11 NANOSECONDS.
#/B	SIGNAL IS DRIVEN FROM ONE RESOURCE TO ANOTHER. THE SECOND RESOURCE MUST RESPOND BY DRIVING A SIGNAL BACK TO THE FIRST RESOURCE. # INCLUDES THE "ROUND TRIP" TIME OF 11 + 11 = 22 NANOSECONDS.
#/D	SAME AS "B" EXCEPT ONE OF THE RESOURCES RELIES ON A 300 OHM PULL-UP RESISTOR. # INCLUDES THE "ROUND TRIP" TIME OF 11 + RC NANOSECONDS.
#/F	RC RISE TIME DUE TO A 300 OHM PULL-UP RESISTOR = 29 NANOSECONDS.

"DRIVEN BY" AND "MEASURED AT" INTERPRETATION

ADD-ON	ADD-ON CARD OR PLATFORM RESOURCE
CPU	PLATFORM CPU
PLAT	PLATFORM CIRCUITRY
EISA-B	EISA COMPATIBLE BUS OWNER ADD-ON CARD

MIN. AND MAX. INTERPRETATION

ALL TIMES ARE IN NANOSECONDS.

The "Bus Master Viewpoint" table does not contain the "Actual" vs. "EISA" columns of the other tables. The numbers used in this table are directly from the EISA Rev. 3.12 specification for an EISA master. Other tables for the EISA slaves track the EISA master numbers with the adjustment for bus settling and BCLK signal line frequency. Also, unlike the other tables, the BCLK signal line frequency is not included in the "Bus Master Viewpoint" table because the entries are simply referenced to clock edges.

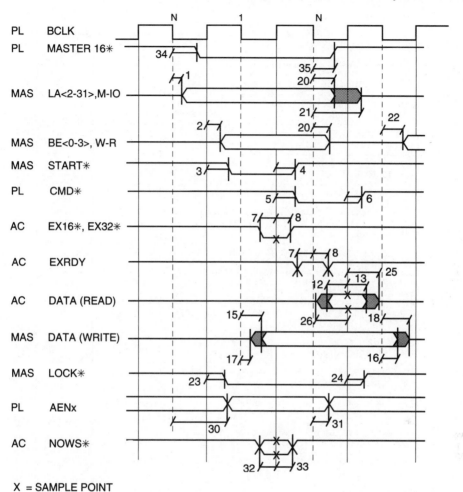

X = SAMPLE POINT

FIGURE 6-6-A: *EISA STANDARD & READY ACCESS CYCLE ... EISA BUS MASTER VIEWPOINT*

REF# /DET	DESCRIPTION OF EVENT	DRIVEN BY	MEASURED AT	MIN NSEC	MAX NSEC	NOTES
1	LA, M-IO VALID DELAY FROM FALLING EDGE OF BCLK	CPU EISA-B	CPU EISA-B		50	
2	BE*, W-R VALID DELAY FROM RISING EDGE OF BCLK	CPU EISA-B	CPU EISA-B		25	(6)
3	START* ACTIVE FROM RISING EDGE OF BCLK	CPU EISA-B	CPU EISA-B	2	25	
4	START* INACTIVE FROM RISING EDGE OF BCLK	CPU EISA-B	CPU EISA-B	2	25	
5/A	CMD* ACTIVE FROM RISING EDGE OF BCLK	PLAT	CPU EISA-B	2	36	(1) (2)
6/A	CMD* INACTIVE FROM RISING EDGE OF BCLK	PLAT	CPU EISA-B	2	36	(1) (2)
7	EX16/EX32* VALID SETUP TO RISING EDGE OF BCLK	ADD-ON	CPU EISA-B	25		
8	EX16/EX32* HOLD FROM RISING EDGE OF BCLK	ADD-ON	CPU EISA-B	55		
9	EXRDY VALID SETUP TO FALLING EDGE OF BCLK	ADD-ON	PLAT	15		
10	EXRDY HOLD FROM FALLING EDGE OF BCLK	ADD-ON	PLAT	5		
12	READ DATA VALID SETUP TO RISING EDGE OF BCLK	ADD-ON	CPU EISA-B	12		(4)
13	READ DATA VALID HOLD FROM RISING EDGE OF BCLK	ADD-ON	CPU EISA-B	4		
15	WRITE DATA VALID DELAY FROM FALLING EDGE OF BCLK	CPU EISA-B	CPU EISA-B		40	
16	WRITE DATA VALID HOLD FROM FALLING EDGE OF BCLK	CPU EISA-B	CPU EISA-B	0		
17	WRITE DATA NON-TRISTATE FROM FALLING EDGE OF BCLK	CPU EISA-B	CPU EISA-B	5		
18	WRITE DATA TRI-STATE FROM FALLING EDGE OF BCLK	CPU EISA-B	CPU EISA-B		50	(3)

TABLE 6-11-A: EISA SPECIFIC ACCESS CYCLE ... BUS MASTER VIEWPOINT (PLATFORM CPU, EISA COMPATIBLE ADD-ON BUS OWNER CARD OR PLATFORM CIRCUITRY)

REF# /DET	DESCRIPTION OF EVENT	DRIVEN BY	MEASURED AT	MIN NSEC	MAX NSEC	NOTES
20	LA<2-31>, M-IO, BE*, W-R VALID HOLD FROM FALLING EDGE OF BCLK	CPU EISA-B	CPU EISA-B	2		
21	LA<2-31>, M-IO, BE*, W-R TRISTATE DELAY FROM FALLING EDGE OF BCLK	CPU EISA-B	CPU EISA-B		50	
22	BE*, W-R VALID DELAY FROM FALLING EDGE OF BCLK	CPU EISA-B	CPU EISA-B		90	
23	LOCK* ACTIVE FROM RISING EDGE OF BCLK	CPU EISA-B	CPU EISA-B		60	
24	LOCK* INACTIVE FROM RISING EDGE OF BCLK	CPU EISA-B	CPU EISA-B	2		
25	READ DATA TRISTATE FROM RISING EDGE OF BCLK	ADD-ON	CPU EISA-B		30	
26	READ DATA NON-TRISTATE TO RISING EDGE OF BCLK	ADD-ON	CPU EISA-B	53		
30	AENx VALID FROM THE FALLING EDGE OF BCLK	PLAT	PLAT		79	(5)
31	AENx VALID HOLD FROM THE FALLING EDGE OF BCLK	PLAT	PLAT	2		
32	NOWS* VALID SETUP TO FALLING EDGE OF BCLK	ADD-ON	CPU EISA-B	15		
33	NOWS* VALID HOLD FROM FALLING EDGE OF BCLK	ADD-ON	CPU EISA-B	5		
34	MASTER16* VALID DELAY FM FALLING EDGE OF BCLK	CPU EISA-B	CPU EISA-B	2	30	
35	MASTER16* VALID HOLD FM FALLING EDGE OF BCLK	CPU EISA-B	CPU EISA-B	2	50	

TABLE 6-11-A: EISA SPECIFIC ACCESS CYCLE ... BUS MASTER VIEWPOINT (PLATFORM CPU, EISA COMPATIBLE ADD-ON BUS OWNER CARD, OR PLATFORM CIRCUITRY) (CONTINUED)

NOTES:
(1) With 11 nanosecond settling time.
(2) Platform circuitry does not "starburst" CMD* signal line to the slots.
(3) Used for back to back write to read or if BE* signal lines change.
(4)   Entry is 32 data bit or downshift. 15 nanoseconds for 16 data bit master (MASTER16* = 0).
(5) Includes 11 nanoseconds settling time plus 18 nanoseconds decode plus delay of valid address signals from the BCLK signal lines.
(6) May be driven as early as previous falling BCLK signal line.

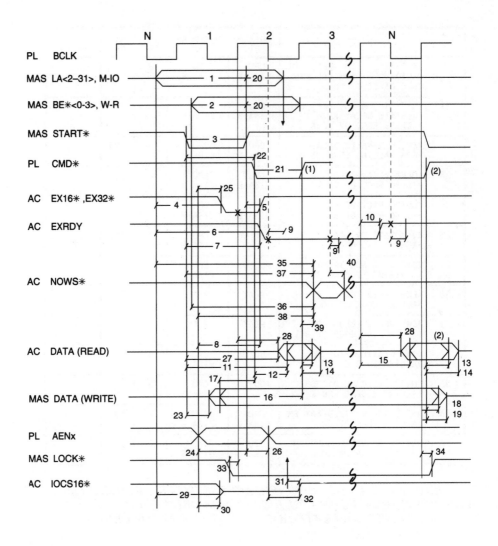

X = Location of Sample Pt.
(1) = For Standard Cycle
(2) = For Ready Cycle

*FIGURE 6-6-B: EISA STANDARD & READY ACCESS CYCLE . . . ACCESSED
RESOURCE VIEWPOINT*

REF# /DET	DESCRIPTION OF EVENT	DRIVEN BY	MEASURED AT	ACTUAL MIN NSEC [8.33]	MAX NSEC	EISA SPEC & NOTES
1/A	LA<2-31>, M-IO VALID SETUP TO START* INACTIVE	CPU EISA-B	ADD-ON	123 [116]		120
2/A	BE*<0-3>,W-R VALID SETUP TO START* INACTIVE	CPU EISA-B	ADD-ON	91 [86]		80
2/A	32 BIT MASTER TO 16 BIT SLAVE / DATA-MATCHING BE*<0-3>,W-R VALID SETUP TO START* INACTIVE	PLAT	ADD-ON	91 [86]		80
3/A	START* ACTIVE TO INACTIVE PULSE WIDTH	CPU EISA-B	ADD-ON	100 [95]		115 (5)
4/B	EX16/EX32* ACTIVE DELAY FROM LA, M-IO VALID	ADD-ON	ADD-ON		83 [76]	54
4/D	EX16/EX32* INACTIVE DELAY FROM LA, M-IO VALID	ADD-ON	ADD-ON		65 [58]	54
5	EX16/EX32* HOLD FROM START* INACTIVE	ADD-ON	ADD-ON	53 [53]		NOT SPEC
6/B	EXRDY INACTIVE DELAY FROM LA, M-IO VALID	ADD-ON	ADD-ON		164 [154]	143
6/D	EXRDY ACTIVE DELAY FROM LA, M-IO VALID	ADD-ON	ADD-ON		146 [136]	143
7/B	EXRDY INACTIVE DELAY FROM START* ACTIVE	ADD-ON	ADD-ON		120 [113]	124
7/D	EXRDY ACTIVE DELAY FROM START* ACTIVE	ADD-ON	ADD-ON		102 [95]	124
8/B	EXRDY INACTIVE DELAY FROM AENx VALID	ADD-ON	ADD-ON		134 [124]	143
8/D	EXRDY ACTIVE DELAY FROM AENx VALID	ADD-ON	ADD-ON		116 [106]	143
9	EXRDY VALID HOLD FROM FALLING EDGE BCLK	ADD-ON	ADD-ON	3 [3]		3
10/A	EXRDY INACTIVE DELAY FROM RISING EDGE BCLK	ADD-ON	ADD-ON		31 [29]	35
10/F	EXRDY ACTIVE DELAY FROM RISING EDGE BCLK	ADD-ON	ADD-ON		13 [11]	35
11/B	READ DATA VALID DELAY FROM START* ACTIVE	ADD-ON	ADD-ON		191 [181]	170 (4)
11/B	32 BIT MASTER TO 16 BIT SLAVE / DATA-MATCHING READ DATA VALID DELAY FROM START* ACTIVE	ADD-ON	ADD-ON		170 [160]	170 (2)

TABLE 6-11-B: EISA SPECIFIC ACCESS CYCLE ... ACCESSED RESOURCE VIEWPOINT (PLATFORM RESOURCES OR ADD-ON SLAVE CARD)

REF# /DET	DESCRIPTION OF EVENT	DRIVEN BY	MEASURED AT	ACTUAL MIN NSEC [8.33]	MAX NSEC	EISA SPEC & NOTES
12/B	READ DATA VALID DELAY FROM CMD* ACTIVE	ADD-ON	ADD-ON		66 [61]	50 (4)
12/B	32 BIT MASTER TO 16 BIT SLAVE / DATA-MATCHING READ DATA VALID DELAY FROM CMD* ACTIVE	ADD-ON	ADD-ON		45 [40]	47 (2)
13	READ DATA VALID HOLD FROM CMD* INACTIVE	ADD-ON	ADD-ON	2 [2]		2
14/A	READ DATA TRISTATE FROM CMD* INACTIVE	ADD-ON	ADD-ON		30 [30]	30
15/A	READ DATA VALID FROM RISING EDGE OF BCLK	ADD-ON	ADD-ON		103 [97]	80 (4)
15/A	32 BIT MASTER TO 16 BIT SLAVE / DATA-MATCHING READ DATA VALID FROM RISING EDGE OF BCLK	ADD-ON	ADD-ON		81 [76]	77 (2)
16/A	WRITE DATA VALID SETUP TO CMD* INACTIVE	CPU EISA-B	ADD-ON	133 [126]		110 (8)
16/A	32 BIT MASTER TO 16 BIT SLAVE / DATA-MATCHING WRITE DATA VALID SETUP TO CMD* INACTIVE	CPU EISA-B	ADD-ON	133 [126]		108 (1)(8)
17/A	WRITE DATA VALID SETUP TO CMD* ACTIVE	CPU EISA-B	ADD-ON	8 [6]		-10
17/A	32 BIT MASTER TO 16 BIT SLAVE / DATA-MATCHING WRITE DATA VALID SETUP TO CMD* ACTIVE	CPU EISA-B	ADD-ON	8 [6]		-10 (6)
18	WRITE DATA VALID HOLD FROM CMD* INACTIVE	CPU EISA-B	ADD-ON	25 [25]		25
19	WRITE DATA TRISTATE FROM CMD* INACTIVE	CPU EISA-B	ADD-ON		25 [25]	NOT SPEC
19	32 BIT MASTER TO 16 BIT SLAVE / DATA-MATCHING WRITE DATA TRISTATE FROM CMD* INACTIVE	CPU EISA-B	ADD-ON		25 [25]	NOT SPEC
20/A	LA, M-IO, BE*, W-R VALID HOLD FROM START* INACTIVE	CPU EISA-B	ADD-ON	21 [21]		15
20/A	32 BIT MASTER TO 16 BIT SLAVE / DATA-MATCHING LA, M-IO, BE*, W-R VALID HOLD FROM START* INACTIVE	CPU EISA-B	ADD-ON	21 [21]		15

TABLE 6-11-B: EISA SPECIFIC ACCESS CYCLE ... ACCESSED RESOURCE VIEWPOINT (PLATFORM RESOURCES OR ADD-ON SLAVE CARD) (CONTINUED)

REF# /DET	DESCRIPTION OF EVENT	DRIVEN BY	MEASURED AT	ACTUAL MIN NSEC [8.33]	MAX NSEC	EISA SPEC & NOTES
21/A	CMD* ACTIVE TO INACTIVE PULSE WIDTH	PLAT	ADD-ON	100 [95]		115 (5)
22/A	START* ACTIVE TO CMD* ACTIVE	CPU,EISA /B, PLAT	ADD-ON	100 [95]		90 (5)
23	WRITE DATA DRIVEN FROM START* ACTIVE	CPU EISA-B	ADD-ON	37 [35]		NOT SPEC
24/B	AENx VALID SETUP TO START* INACTIVE	PLAT	ADD-ON	95 [87]		95
25/B	EX16/32* ACTIVE DELAY FROM AENx VALID	ADD-ON	ADD-ON		56 [49]	34
25/D	EX16/32* INACTIVE DELAY FROM AENx VALID	ADD-ON	ADD-ON		38 [31]	34
26/A	AENx VALID HOLD FROM START* INACTIVE	PLAT	ADD-ON	21 [21]		25
27	DATA DRIVEN FROM START* ACTIVE	ADD-ON	ADD-ON	128 [118]		NOT SPEC
28	DATA DRIVEN FROM BCLK RISING	ADD-ON	ADD-ON	5 [0]		NOT SPEC
29/D	IOCS16* INACTIVE FROM LA VALID	ADD-ON	ADD-ON		55 [50]	54
29/B	IOCS16* ACTIVE FROM LA VALID	ADD-ON	ADD-ON		73 [68]	54
30/D	IOCS16* INACTIVE FROM AENx VALID	ADD-ON	ADD-ON		26 [21]	NOT SPEC
30/B	IOCS16* ACTIVE FROM AENx VALID	ADD-ON	ADD-ON		44 [39]	NOT SPEC
31	IOCS16* VALID HOLD LA INVALID	ADD-ON	ADD-ON	20		20
33/A	LOCK* ACTIVE SETUP TO RISING EDGE OF BCLK	ADD-ON	ADD-ON	52 [49]		54
34	LOCK* ACTIVE HOLD FROM RISING EDGE OF BCLK	ADD-ON	ADD-ON	2 [2]		2

TABLE 6-11-B: EISA SPECIFIC ACCESS CYCLE ... ACCESSED RESOURCE VIEWPOINT (PLATFORM RESOURCES OR ADD-ON SLAVE CARD) (CONTINUED)

NOTES:

(1) The first 16 data bit access is 126 nanoseconds. The second 16 data bit access is 105 nanoseconds.

(2) Setup to data read to platform circuitry appears to be 33 nanoseconds according to the EISA specification.

(3) The first 16 data bits of the access sequence is as stated in the table. The second access is 77 nanoseconds.

(4) Entries in the table are for a 32 data bit bus master (MASTER 16* = 1) accessing a 32 data bit resource. If a 16 data bit bus master (MASTER16* = 0) is accessing a 16 bit resource, the times in the "ACTUAL" & "EISA SPEC." column of the table must be decreased 3 nanoseconds (when no byte swapping occurs). If a 16 data bit bus master is accessing a 32 bit resource, swapping between upper and lower words must occur. The times in the "ACTUAL" and "EISA SPEC." columns of the Table must be decreased by 29 nanoseconds.

(5) If same package skew and the difference in bus settling is assumed to be 0 nanoseconds, the entry in the "ACTUAL" column of the table is increased by 23 nanoseconds. The entry in the table is for a same package skew of 12 nanoseconds with an 11 nanoseconds bus settling time.

(6) The first 16 data bits of the access sequence is as stated in the table. The second access is 15 nanoseconds max.

(7) The table entry is for a 32 data bit bus master accessing a 32 data bit resource (indicated by MASTER16* = 1). If a 16 data bit bus master is accessing a 16 bit resource, the times in the "ACTUAL" & "EISA SPEC" columns of the table must be decreased 3 nanoseconds (when no byte lane swapping occurs). If a 16 data bit bus master is accessing a 32 bit resource, swapping between upper and lower words must occur and the time in the "ACTUAL" column of the table is -31 nanoseconds.

(8) The entries in the table are for a 32 data bit bus master (MASTER16* = 1) accessing a 32 data bit resource. A 16 data bit master (MASTER16* = 0) accessing a 16 data bit resource decreases the number in the "EISA SPEC." column by 2 nanoseconds. If a 16 data bit bus master (MASTER16* = 0) is accessing a 32 bit resource, swapping between upper and lower words must occur. The times in the "ACTUAL" column of the table must be decreased by 29 nanoseconds.

EISA STANDARD MEMORY OR I/O ACCESS CYCLE (EISA PLATFORM)

The EISA standard access cycle can be executed by the EISA compatible platform CPU or add-on bus owner cards (collectively called EISA bus masters). The EISA bus master can use the EISA standard access cycle to access EISA compatible memory and I/O resources on the platform or add-on slave cards. The data size of the accessed resource must be equal to or greater than the data size requested by the EISA bus master; otherwise, an EISA data-matching access cycle must be executed. If an EISA bus master is accessing an ISA or E-ISA compatible resource, the E-MIX access cycle is executed.

From the EISA bus master viewpoint, the signal lines are synchronous to the BCLK signal line. From the accessed resource viewpoint, the signal lines are asynchronous to the BCLK signal line, but they are referenced to the change of state of other signal lines (see Figures 6-7-A & 6-7-B). The cycle begins with the EISA bus master driving the LA and M-IO signal lines valid and then driving the START* signal line active. (The MASTER16* signal line will be valid prior to and after the cycle. See Chapter 9 for more information.) The BE and W-R signal lines are driven valid simultaneously with the START* signal line being driven active. The accessed resource responds by driving the EX16*, EX32*, and EXRDY signals valid after the decoding of the LA, M-IO, and AENx signal lines. The EXRDY signal line also uses the START* signal line as a qualifier.

Due to worst case timings, the decoding of the LA, M-IO, and AENx signal lines to properly drive the EX16* and EX32* signal lines must be done by all potential accessed resources independent of the START* signal line. See the description of EX16* and EX32* in Chapter 5 for further information.

The active START* signal line indicates to the accessed resource and platform cycle control circuitry that a cycle has begun. The START* signal line active pulse width is always a minimum of one BCLK signal line period. At the end of the active START* signal line pulse width the accessed resource must latch the **LA, M-IO, BE*, W-R,** and **AENx** signal lines. Thus the accessed resource has begun the EISA standard cycle without the direct use of the **BCLK** signal line.

The access cycle continues with the EISA bus master driving the **START*** signal line inactive and sampling the **EX16*** and **EX32*** signal lines on the rising edge of the **BCLK** signal line. The platform circuitry samples the **EXRDY** signal line on the falling edge of the **BCLK** signal line. The length of the cycle is controlled by the **CMD*** signal line, which is driven by the platform circuitry. The active pulse width of this signal line is determined by the state of the **EX16*, EX32*,** and **EXRDY** signal lines. If the **EXRDY** and either **EX16*** or **EX32*** signal lines are active, the cycle length is two **BCLK** signal line periods. If both **EX16*** and **EX32*** signal lines are inactive, a longer E-MIX access cycle is executed. See other sections of this chapter and Chapter 3 for more information. If **EXRDY** is sampled inactive, the cycle becomes an EISA ready access cycle.

From the accessed resource viewpoint, data for a read cycle is driven valid a maximum time from active **START*** or **CMD*** signal lines. The **DATA** signal lines are held valid until after the **CMD*** signal line is inactive. From the EISA bus master viewpoint, the data must be valid relative to the rising edge of the **BCLK** signal line.

The use of the **CMD*** signal lines for valid read data from 16 or 32 data bit accessed resources requires very tight timing requirements. This is partly due to the delay of the **CMD*** signal line relative to the **BCLK** signal line. Also, the **CMD*** signal line might not be distributed in a starburst fashion, which introduces increased bus settling time. Since the **BCLK** signal line is distributed in a starburst pattern, it makes a better reference point than the **CMD*** signal line. These timings are included in the appropriate tables.

From the accessed resource viewpoint, data for a write cycle is driven valid by the EISA bus master prior to an active CMD* signal line. The data is held valid until after the CMD* signal line is inactive. From the EISA bus master viewpoint, the data is valid relative to falling edges of the BCLK signal line.

Thus, for an EISA standard access cycle, the cycle is synchronous to the BCLK signal line from the EISA bus master's viewpoint and asynchronous to the BCLK signal line from the accessed resource's viewpoint.

An EISA standard access cycle is executed if the data size requested by the EISA bus master (with the BE* signal lines) equals the data size of the accessed resource (indicated by the EX16* and EX32* signal lines). When a data size match occurs, the access cycle proceeds as outlined above. If the EISA bus master requests an 8 data bit access, any 16 or 32 data bit EISA compatible accessed resource can support an EISA standard access cycle. If the EISA bus master requests a 16 data bit access, the accessed resource must support either 16 or 32 data bit accesses to proceed forward as an EISA standard access cycle. Platform circuitry supports data swapping that allows cycles between EISA bus masters and accessed resources of unequal data size. Tables 6-12 and 6-13 outline the byte lanes used and the data size of a standard or ready access cycle.

If the EISA bus master is requesting a data size larger than the accessed resource data size, the cycle is completed as an EISA data-matching access cycle. See Chapter 3 and other sections of this chapter for more information. Special consideration must be given to EISA compatible accessed resources that are 8 data bits in size (as indicated by inactive EX16* and EX32* signal lines). See the E-MIX subchapter for further information.

BUS MASTER				ACCESSED RESOURCE		MAS. DRIVEN BYTE LANE				ACCESS RECEIVED BYTE LANE				BITS
BE3	BE2	BE1	BE0	EX16*	EX32*	3	2	1	0	3	2	1	0	
MAS16*=ACT.														
1	1	0	0	0	1	N	N	Y	Y	N	N	Y	Y	16
1	1	0	0	1	0	N	N	Y	Y	N	N	Y	Y	16
0	0	1	1	0	1	N	N	Y	Y	N	N	Y	Y	16
0	0	1	1	1	0	N	N	Y	Y	Y	Y	N	N	16
0	1	1	1	0	1	N	N	Y	N	N	N	Y	N	8
0	1	1	1	1	0	N	N	Y	N	Y	N	N	N	8
1	0	1	1	0	1	N	N	N	Y	N	N	N	Y	8
1	0	1	1	1	0	N	N	N	Y	N	Y	N	N	8
1	1	0	1	0	1	N	N	Y	N	N	N	Y	N	8
1	1	0	1	1	0	N	N	Y	N	N	N	Y	N	8
1	1	1	0	0	1	N	N	N	Y	N	N	N	Y	8
1	1	1	0	1	0	N	N	N	Y	N	N	N	Y	8
MAS16*=INACT.														
0	0	0	0	1	0	Y	Y	Y	Y	Y	Y	Y	Y	32
1	1	0	0	0	1	N	N	Y	Y	N	N	Y	Y	16
1	1	0	0	1	0	N	N	Y	Y	N	N	Y	Y	16
0	0	1	1	0	1	Y	Y	N	N	N	N	Y	Y	16
0	0	1	1	1	0	Y	Y	N	N	Y	Y	N	N	16
1	1	0	1	0	1	N	N	Y	N	N	N	Y	N	8
1	1	0	1	1	0	N	N	Y	N	N	N	Y	N	8
1	1	1	0	0	1	N	N	N	Y	N	N	N	Y	8
1	1	1	0	1	0	N	N	N	Y	N	N	N	Y	8
1	0	1	1	0	1	N	Y	N	N	N	Y	N	N	8
1	0	0	1	1	0	N	Y	Y	N	N	Y	Y	N	16
0	1	1	1	0	1	Y	N	N	N	N	N	Y	N	8
0	1	1	1	1	0	Y	N	N	N	Y	N	N	N	8
1	0	0	0	1	0	N	Y	Y	Y	N	Y	Y	Y	24
0	0	0	1	1	0	Y	Y	Y	N	Y	Y	Y	N	24

TABLE 6-12: EISA PLATFORM ... WRITE EISA STANDARD OR READY ACCESS CYCLE BYTE LANES. DATA SIZE REQUESTED LESS THAN OR EQUAL TO DATA SIZE OF ACCESSED RESOURCE.

BUS MASTER				ACCESSED RESOURCE		MAS. REC. BYTE LANE				ACCESS DRIVEN BYTE LANE				BITS
BE3	BE2	BE1	BE0	EX16*	EX32*	3	2	1	0	3	2	1	0	
MAS16*=ACT.														
1	1	0	0	0	1	N	N	Y	Y	N	N	Y	Y	16
1	1	0	0	1	0	N	N	Y	Y	N	N	Y	Y	16
0	0	1	1	0	1	N	N	Y	Y	N	N	Y	Y	16
0	0	1	1	1	0	N	N	Y	Y	Y	Y	N	N	16
0	1	1	1	0	1	N	N	Y	N	N	N	Y	N	8
0	1	1	1	1	0	N	N	Y	N	Y	N	N	N	8
1	0	1	1	0	1	N	N	N	Y	N	N	N	Y	8
1	0	1	1	1	0	N	N	N	Y	N	Y	N	N	8
1	1	0	1	0	1	N	N	Y	N	N	N	Y	N	8
1	1	0	1	1	0	N	N	Y	N	N	N	Y	N	8
1	1	1	0	0	1	N	N	N	Y	N	N	N	Y	8
1	1	1	0	1	0	N	N	N	Y	N	N	N	Y	8
MAS16*=INACT.														
0	0	0	0	1	0	Y	Y	Y	Y	Y	Y	Y	Y	32
1	1	0	0	0	1	N	N	Y	Y	N	N	Y	Y	16
1	1	0	0	1	0	N	N	Y	Y	N	N	Y	Y	16
0	0	1	1	0	1	Y	Y	N	N	N	N	Y	Y	16
0	0	1	1	1	0	Y	Y	N	N	Y	Y	N	N	16
1	1	0	1	0	1	N	N	Y	N	N	N	Y	N	8
1	1	0	1	1	0	N	N	Y	N	N	N	Y	N	8
1	1	1	0	0	1	N	N	N	Y	N	N	N	Y	8
1	1	1	0	1	0	N	N	N	Y	N	N	N	Y	8
1	0	1	1	0	1	N	Y	N	N	N	N	N	Y	8
1	0	1	1	1	0	N	Y	N	N	N	Y	N	N	8
0	1	1	1	0	1	Y	N	N	N	N	N	Y	N	8
0	1	1	1	1	0	Y	N	N	N	Y	N	N	N	8
1	0	0	1	1	0	N	Y	Y	N	N	Y	Y	N	16
1	0	0	0	1	0	N	Y	Y	Y	N	Y	Y	Y	24
0	0	0	1	1	0	Y	Y	Y	N	Y	Y	Y	N	24

TABLE 6-13: EISA PLATFORM ... READ EISA STANDARD OR READY ACCESS CYCLE BYTE LANES. DATA SIZE REQUESTED LESS THAN OR EQUAL TO DATA SIZE OF ACCESSED RESOURCE.

> *The "Y" in the above tables indicates that the associated byte lane contains valid data. An "N" indicates that the driving resource is NOT driving the associated byte lane and the associated driver should be tri-stated. This allows the platform byte swapping circuitry to drive the appropriate byte lanes. For a read cycle, the values of the EX16* and EX32* signal lines are known prior to the data being read. For a write cycle, the values of these signal lines are not known when the write data lines need to be active; consequently, the platform swapping circuitry must drive the appropriate byte lanes in anticipation of either the EX16* or EX32* being driven active.*

The standard memory access cycle length will vary depending on the data width of the cycle. The reference point for the beginning of the cycle will vary for different bus owners. Table 6-14 summarizes the cycle length in terms of TCLK (period of BCLK). Due to bus settling times and device delays, TCLK should be considered as approximate for the "CYCLE BEGINS" column.

BUS MASTER	CYCLE BEGINS	CYCLE ENDS	CYCLE SIZE	CYCLE LENGTH
PLATFORM CPU OR ADD-ON	ACTIVE START*	INACTIVE CMD*	16/32 BITS	2 TCLK

TABLE 6-14: EISA SPECIFIC EISA STANDARD ACCESS CYCLE LENGTH

EISA READY MEMORY OR I/O ACCESS CYCLE (EISA PLATFORM)

The EISA ready access cycle can be executed by the platform CPU or by add-on bus owner cards (collectively called EISA bus masters). The data size of the accessed resource must be equal to or greater than the data size requested by the bus master; otherwise, an EISA data-matching access cycle must be executed. If a bus master is accessing an ISA or E-ISA compatible resource, the E-MIX access cycle is executed.

From the EISA bus master viewpoint, the signal lines are synchronous to the BCLK signal line. From the accessed resource viewpoint, all the signal lines (except for the EXRDY and DATA (read) signal lines) are asynchronous to the BCLK signal line (see Figures 6-7-A & 6-7-B). The EXRDY and DATA signal lines are asynchronous at the beginning of the cycle and become partly synchronous at the end of the cycle. The reference to the BCLK signal line is needed because none of the other signal lines change state during the latter part of the cycle; consequently, there is no convenient reference point other than the BCLK signal line.

The cycle begins and operates in the same fashion as an EISA standard access cycle. If the EX16* or EX32* signal lines are active, the cycle length is dependent on the EXRDY signal line. If both EX16* and EX32* signal lines are inactive, a longer E-MIX access cycle is executed. See other sections of this chapter and Chapter 3 for more information. If EXRDY is not sampled inactive (on the falling edge of the BCLK signal line), the cycle remains an EISA standard access cycle.

For an EISA ready access cycle, the EX16* and EX32* signal lines are still driven relative to other signal lines. The EXRDY and the DATA (read) signal lines are also referenced to "other" signal lines and the BCLK signal line.

Initially, the EXRDY signal line is driven inactive by the accessed resource relative to the LA, M-IO, AENx, and START* signal lines as in the EISA standard access cycle case. The platform circuitry uses the falling edge of the BCLK signal line for the initial sampling of the EXRDY signal line. Subsequent sampling for an active EXRDY signal line by the platform circuitry is also sampled at the falling edge of the BCLK signal line. The signal lines initially used by the accessed resource to drive the EXRDY signal line are not changing state; consequently, the accessed resource must drive the EXRDY signal line relative to the BCLK signal line. The sampling of an active EXRDY signal line at a falling edge of the BCLK signal line causes the cycle to be completed.

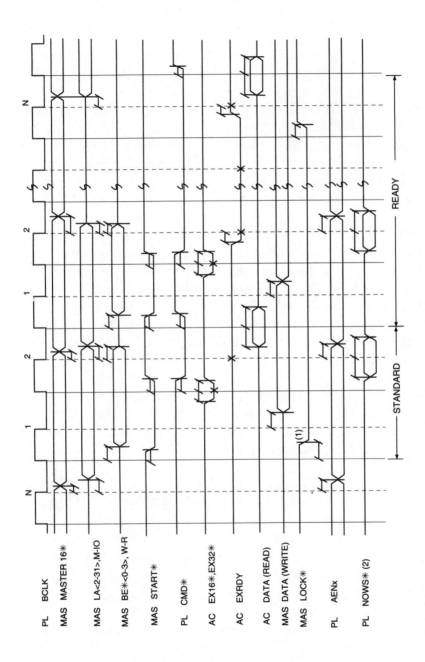

*FIGURE   6-7-A: EISA STANDARD AND READY ACCESS CYCLE . . . EISA BUS
MASTER VIEWPOINT*

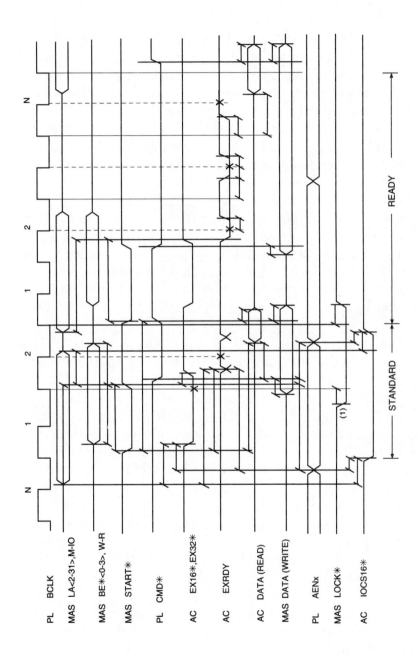

X = SAMPLE POINT
(1) = IF PLATFORM CPU IS BUS MASTER, LOCK* CAN CHANGE 1 BCLK PERIOD LATER.

FIGURE 6-7-B: EISA SPECIFIC STANDARD AND READY ACCESS CYCLE . . .
ACCESSED RESOURCE VIEWPOINT

From the accessed resource viewpoint, DATA (read) signal lines for an EISA standard access cycle are driven valid a maximum time from an active START* or CMD* signal line. For a read EISA ready access cycle, the data signal lines are driven valid relative to the falling edge of the BCLK signal line during the last clock period of the cycle. The data signal lines are held valid until after the CMD* signal line is inactive. From the EISA bus master viewpoint, the data lines are valid relative to the rising edge of the BCLK signal line.

From the accessed resource viewpoint, the DATA signal lines for a write EISA ready access cycle are driven valid by the EISA bus master prior to an active CMD* signal line and are held valid until after the CMD* signal line is inactive, as in the EISA standard access cycle case. From the EISA bus master viewpoint, the data lines are valid relative to the falling edges of the BCLK signal lines.

An EISA ready access cycle is executed if the data size requested by the EISA bus master (by the BE* signal lines) equals the size of the accessed resource (as indicated by the EX16* and EX32* signal lines). When a data size match occurs, the access cycle proceeds as outlined above. If the EISA bus master requests an 8 data bit access, any 16 or 32 data bit EISA compatible accessed resource can support an EISA ready access cycle. If the EISA bus master requests a 16 data bit access, the accessed resource must support either 16 or 32 data bit accesses to proceed forward as an EISA ready access cycle. Platform circuitry supports data swapping that allows cycles between bus masters and accessed resources of unequal data size. Tables 6-12 and 6-13 outline the byte lanes used and the data size of an EISA standard or EISA ready access cycle.

If the EISA bus master is requesting a data size access that is larger than the accessed resource data size, the cycle is completed as an EISA data-matching access cycle. See Chapter 3 and other sections of this chapter for more information. Special consideration must be given to EISA accessed resources that are 8 data bits in size (EX16* and EX32* signal lines inactive). See the E-MIX subchapter for further information.

The EISA ready access cycle length will vary depending on the data width of the cycle. The reference point for the beginning of the cycle will vary for different bus owners. Table 6-15 summarizes the minimum EISA ready access cycle length in terms of TCLK (period of BCLK). Due to bus settling times and device delays, TCLK should be considered as approximate for the "CYCLE BEGINS" column.

BUS MASTER	CYCLE BEGINS	CYCLE ENDS	CYCLE SIZE	CYCLE LENGTH
PLATFORM CPU OR ADD-ON	ACTIVE START*	INACTIVE CMD*	16/32 BITS	3 TCLK

TABLE 6-15: EISA SPECIFIC MINIMUM EISA READY ACCESS CYCLE LENGTH

EISA DATA-MATCHING MEMORY OR I/O ACCESS CYCLE (EISA PLATFORM)

The EISA data-matching access cycle can be executed by the platform CPU or by EISA compatible add-on bus owner cards (collectively called EISA bus masters). The EISA bus master can use the EISA data-matching access cycle to access EISA compatible memory and I/O resources on the platform or add-on slave cards when there is a data size mismatch. A mismatch occurs when the data size the EISA bus master requested (by the BE* signal lines) is larger than the data size of the accessed resource (according to the EX16* and EX32* signal lines). As with the EISA standard and ready access cycles, there is a special E-MIX version of EISA data-matching when the access is to an 8 data bit resource or an ISA or E-ISA compatible resource.

Figure 6-8 details the additional timings needed to define a data-matching access cycle from the EISA bus master viewpoint.

These numbers are tabulated in Table 6-16. Any EISA bus master timings not listed are the same as for an EISA standard access cycle.   The accessed resource (ISA, E-ISA, or EISA) from a functional viewpoint cannot differentiate a data-matching from other access cycles.   However, due to data assembly and data disassembly timing some "tweaks" are required. These "tweaks" are outlined in Table 6-11-B.

The EISA specific bus timings assume that the BCLK signal line is distributed in a "starburst" pattern to all slots. In this case, there is a single driver with an individual line going to each of the slots; consequently, the maximum skew between all of the BCLK signal lines at each slot is less than one nanosecond. It is also assumed that the CMD* signal line is driven from platform circuitry in a "non-starburst" pattern. That is, the platform circuitry drives a single CMD* signal line which runs in a daisy chain fashion from slot to slot; consequently, the skew between any two CMD* signal lines at any two slots is the bus settling time. Finally, the timings assume that there are no buffers on the data signal lines between any two slots. If swapping between data signal lines occur, the entry will note the change in the listed time.

Table 6-16 has several key pieces of information. First, the "#/DET" (parameter number / detail) column relates the parameter number of the table to Figures 6-8. Second, it provides detailed information on how the number was derived. The timing numbers are affected by the settling time on the bus. The table is based on the default values for eight slots as outlined in Chapter 10. The #/DET interpretations are shown in the following table.

DETAIL   INTERPRETATION

\#   NO SETTLING TIME INCLUDED.

\#/A   SKEW OF TWO SIGNALS BETWEEN RESOURCES. ONE HAS A DELAY OF
                0 NANOSECONDS, AND THE OTHER HAS A DELAY OF 10-15
                NANOSECONDS.

"DRIVEN BY" AND "MEASURED AT" INTERPRETATION

ADD-ON   ADD-ON CARD OR PLATFORM RESOURCE
ISA-B   ISA OR E-ISA COMPATIBLE ADD-ON CARD BUS OWNER ADD-ON CARD
CPU   PLATFORM CPU
PLAT   PLATFORM CIRCUITRY
EISA-B   EISA COMPATIBLE BUS OWNER ADD-ON CARD

MIN. AND MAX. INTERPRETATION

ALL TIMES ARE IN NANOSECONDS.

The "Bus Master Viewpoint" table does not contain the "Actual" vs. "EISA" columns of the other tables. The numbers used in this table are directly from the EISA Rev. 3.12 specification for an EISA master. Other tables for the EISA slaves track the EISA master numbers with the adjustment for bus settling and BCLK signal line frequency. Also, unlike the other tables, the BCLK signal line frequency is not included in the "Bus Master Viewpoint" table because the entries are simply referenced to clock edges.

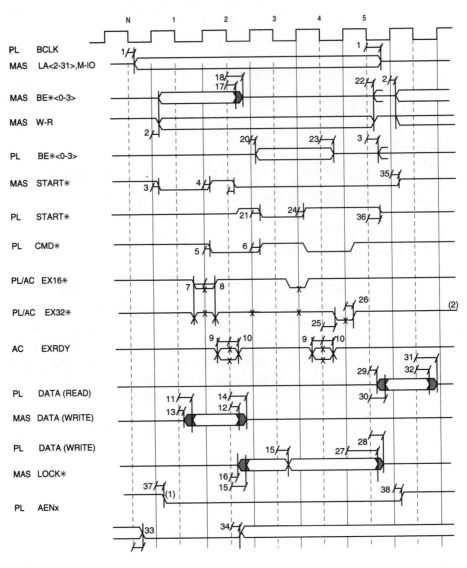

X = SAMPLE POINT
(1) = IF PLATFORM CPU IS BUS MASTER, LOCK∗ CAN CHANGE 1 BCLK PERIOD LATER
(2) = FOR 16 BIT BUS MASTER EX32∗ IS NOT USED; BUT EX16∗ IS USED.

FIGURE 6-8:   EISA DATA-MATCHING ACCESS CYCLE . . . EISA BUS MASTER
              VIEWPOINT

REF# /DET	DESCRIPTION OF EVENT	DRIVEN BY	MEASURED AT	MIN NSEC	MAX NSEC	NOTES
1	LA, M-IO VALID DELAY FROM FALLING EDGE OF BCLK	CPU EISA-B	CPU EISA-B		50	
2	BE*, W-R VALID DELAY FROM RISING EDGE OF BCLK	CPU EISA-B	CPU EISA-B		25	(6)
3	START* ACTIVE FROM RISING EDGE OF BCLK	CPU EISA-B	CPU EISA-B	2	25	
4	START* INACTIVE FROM RISING EDGE OF BCLK	CPU EISA-B	CPU EISA-B	2	25	
5/A	CMD* ACTIVE FROM RISING EDGE OF BCLK	PLAT	CPU EISA-B	2	36	(1) (2)
6/A	CMD* INACTIVE FROM RISING EDGE OF BCLK	PLAT	CPU EISA-B	2	36	(1) (2)
7	EX16/EX32* VALID SETUP TO RISING EDGE OF BCLK	ADD-ON	CPU EISA-B	25		
8	EX16/EX32* HOLD FROM RISING EDGE OF BCLK	ADD-ON	CPU EISA-B	55		
9	EXRDY VALID SETUP TO FALLING EDGE OF BCLK	ADD-ON	PLAT	15		
10	EXRDY HOLD FROM FALLING EDGE OF BCLK	ADD-ON	PLAT	5		
11	WRITE DATA VALID DELAY FROM FALLING EDGE OF BCLK	CPU EISA-B	CPU EISA-B		36	
12	WRITE DATA VALID HOLD FROM FALLING EDGE OF BCLK	CPU EISA-B	CPU EISA-B	0		(3)
13	WRITE DATA NON-TRISTATE FROM FALLING EDGE OF BCLK	CPU EISA-B	CPU EISA-B	5		
14	WRITE DATA TRISTATE FROM FALLING EDGE OF BCLK	CPU EISA-B	CPU EISA-B		50	(3)
15/A	WRITE DATA VALID DELAY FROM FALLING EDGE OF BCLK	PLAT	PLAT	2	61	(3)
16	WRITE DATA NON-TRISTATE FROM FALLING EDGE OF BCLK	PLAT	PLAT	2		(3)
17	BE* VALID HOLD FROM FALLING EDGE OF BCLK	CPU EISA-B	CPU EISA-B	2		
18	BE* TRISTATE FROM FALLING EDGE OF BCLK	CPU EISA-B	CPU EISA-B		50	

TABLE 6-16: EISA SPECIFIC DATA-MATCHING ACCESS CYCLE ... EISA BUS MASTER VIEWPOINT (PLATFORM CPU OR EISA COMPATIBLE ADD-ON BUS OWNER CARD)

REF# /DET	DESCRIPTION OF EVENT	DRIVEN BY	MEASURED AT	MIN NSEC	MAX NSEC	NOTES
19	START* INACTIVE HOLD FROM FALLING EDGE OF BCLK	CPU EISA-B	CPU EISA-B	45		
20	BE* VALID FROM RISING EDGE OF BCLK	PLAT	PLAT		34	
21	START* ACTIVE FROM RISING EDGE OF BCLK	PLAT	PLAT		25	
22	BE*, W-R VALID DELAY FROM FALLING EDGE OF BCLK	CPU EISA-B	CPU EISA-B	2	85	
23	BE* VALID HOLD FROM RISING EDGE OF BCLK	PLAT	PLAT	0		
24	START* INACTIVE FROM RISING EDGE OF BCLK	PLAT	PLAT	2	25	
25/A	EX16/EX32* ACTIVE DELAY FROM RISING EDGE OF BCLK	PLAT	CPU EISA-B		44	(8) (10)
26	EX16/EX32* HOLD FROM RISING EDGE OF BCLK	PLAT	CPU EISA-B	50		(8)
27	DATA VALID HOLD FROM RISING EDGE OF BCLK	PLAT	PLAT	57		
28	DATA TRISTATE FROM FALLING EDGE OF BCLK	PLAT	PLAT		50	NOT SPEC
29	READ DATA NON-TRISTATE FROM FALLING EDGE OF BCLK	PLAT	CPU EISA-B	0		NOT SPEC
30/A	READ DATA VALID DELAY FROM FALLING EDGE OF BCLK	PLAT	CPU EISA-B		41	(11)
31	READ DATA TRISTATE FROM RISING EDGE OF BCLK	PLAT	CPU EISA-B		50	
32	READ DATA VALID HOLD FROM RISING EDGE OF BCLK	PLAT	CPU EISA-B	2		NOT SPEC
33	AENx VALID FROM THE FALLING EDGE OF BCLK	PLAT	PLAT		79	(5)
34	AENx VALID HOLD FROM THE FALLING EGDE OF BCLK	PLAT	PLAT	2		
35	START* ACTIVE FROM FALLING EDGE OF BCLK	CPU EISA-B	CPU EISA-B	2		NOT SPEC
36	START* TRISTATE FROM FALLING EDGE OF BCLK	CPU EISA-B	CPU EISA-B		50	NOT SPEC
37	LOCK* ACTIVE FROM RISING EDGE OF BCLK	CPU EISA-B	CPU EISA-B		60	
38	LOCK* INACTIVE FROM RISING EDGE OF BCLK	CPU EISA-B	CPU EISA-B	2		

TABLE 6-16: EISA SPECIFIC DATA-MATCHING ACCESS CYCLE ... EISA BUS MASTER VIEWPOINT (PLATFORM CPU OR EISA COMPATIBLE ADD-ON BUS OWNER CARD) (CONTINUED)

NOTES:

(1) With 11 nanoseconds settling time.

(2) Platform does not starburst the CMD* signal line to the slots.

(3) The CPU, EISA-B, and platform circuitry overlap in the driving of the data signal lines.

(6) May be driven as early as the previous falling BCLK signal line.

(8) These # are used at the end of the data-matching cycle when driven by the platform circuitry.

(10) The EISA Bus Specification Rev. 3.12 states that the setup to the BCLK signal line is 15 nanoseconds, but with platform circuitry driving these signal lines only 10 nanoseconds setup to the BCLK signal line is available.

(11) The EISA Bus Specification Rev. 3.12 states that the setup to the BCLK signal line is 12 and 15 nanoseconds for 32 and 16 data bits access, respectively. However, with platform circuitry driving these signal lines, only 11 nanoseconds setup to the BCLK signal line is available.

From the EISA bus master viewpoint, the signal lines are referenced to the BCLK signal line in the same fashion as they are for an EISA standard or ready access cycle. The major difference is that some of the signal lines are driven by both the EISA bus master and the platform circuitry (see Figure 6-9). This co-driving arrangement places most of the complexity for data-matching on the platform circuitry and some on each of the individual EISA bus masters.

An EISA data-matching access cycle actually begins as an EISA standard or EISA ready access cycle. The bus master drives the LA and M-IO signal lines valid and then drives the START* signal line active. The BE* and W-R signal lines are driven valid simultaneously to the START* signal line being driven active. The EISA accessed resource responds by driving the EX16*, EX32*, and EXRDY signals valid after the decoding of the LA, M-IO, and AENx signal lines. The EXRDY signal line also uses the START* signal line as a qualifier. The cycle continues with the EISA bus master driving the START* signal line inactive and sampling the EX16* and EX32* signal lines (on the rising edge of the BCLK signal line).

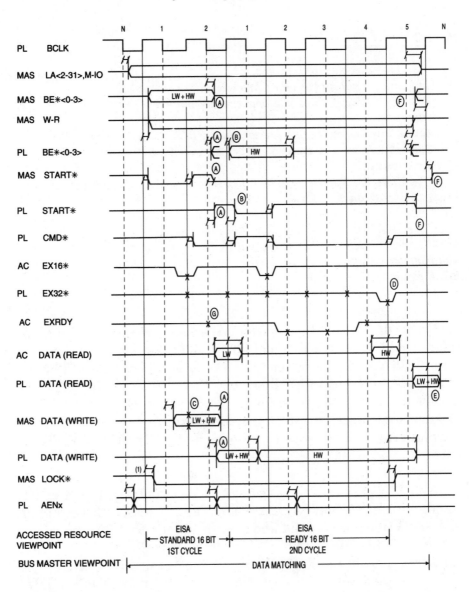

X = SAMPLE POINT
(1) = IF PLATFORM CPU IS BUS MASTER, LOCK* CAN CHANGE 1 BCLK PERIOD LATER.

*FIGURE 6-9:   EISA DATA-MATCHING ACCESS CYCLE . . . EISA BUS MASTER
VIEWPOINT*

If the EISA bus master requested (by the initial BE* signal lines) a data size that was equal to or less than the data size supported by the accessed resource (indicated by the ex16* and EX32* signal lines), an EISA standard or ready access cycle will result. If the data size requested is larger than the size of the resource, the cycle continues as an EISA data-matching access cycle. If either the EX16* or EX32* signal line is active, it is an "EISA version" of an EISA data-matching access cycle. If the EX16* and EX32* signal lines are inactive, an "E-MIX version" of the EISA data-matching cycle is executed. See other sections of this chapter and Chapter 3 for more information about an E-MIX data-matching cycle.

After the EISA bus master has determined the cycle to be an EISA data-matching access cycle, it immediately places the BE*, START*, and the DATA (for writes) signal lines into tristate mode at the next falling edge of the BCLK signal line (Point A in Figure 6-9). It continues to drive the LA, M-IO, and W-R signal lines valid for the remainder of the EISA data-matching access cycle. Simultaneously, the platform circuitry has also determined that the cycle is an EISA data-matching access cycle by sampling the BE* signal lines relative to the rising edge of the START* signal line and the EX16* and EX32* signal lines at the rising edge of the BCLK signal. The platform circuitry now drives the BE* and START* signal lines (Point A in Figure 6-9). Also, for a write access cycle, the platform circuitry becomes master of the DATA signal lines (Point A in Figure 6-9). At the subsequent rising edge of the BCLK signal line, the platform circuitry drives the BE* and START* signal lines valid (Point B in Figure 6-9). The START* signal line will not be driven active at the subsequent BCLK signal line period if the EXRDY signal line is sampled inactive (Point G in Figure 6-9). The START* signal line will be driven active at the falling edge of the BCLK signal line after the EXRDY signal line is sampled active.

If the access cycle is a write cycle, the platform circuitry will have sampled the DATA signal lines (Point C in Figure 6-9). For a write cycle, the platform circuitry will first drive the same DATA signal lines identified by the BE* signal lines driven by the EISA bus master. In the example shown in Figure 6-9, the EISA bus master identifies the low word and high word (LW and HW) via the BE* signal lines. The LW and HW are driven onto the data signal lines. Once the LW data is accepted by the accessed resource, the platform circuitry drives the START*, BE*, and CMD* signal lines active to write the HW to the accessed resource. During this "second cycle", the platform circuitry also drives the HW it latched at Point C onto to the lower bytes.

If the access cycle is a read cycle, the START*, BE*, and CMD* signal lines are operated in the same fashion as in a write cycle. The data that is read from the accessed resource is latched into a buffer by the platform circuity. During the "first cycle" the LW data is read and latched. During the "second cycle", the HW addressed by the BE* signal lines is read and latched by the platform circuitry.

The EISA data-matching write or read access cycle is completed by the platform circuity driving the EX32* signal line. The EISA bus master, knowing that it is a data-matching access cycle, monitors the EX32* signal line waiting for an indication that the cycle is complete (Point D in Figure 6-9). For a write cycle, the active EX32* signal line indicates that all data has been written. For a read cycle, the active EX32* signal line indicates that the full 32 data bits is available at the next subsequent BCLK signal line rising edge (Point E in Figure 6-9). At Point F in Figure 6-9, the ownership of the START* and BE* signal lines transfers to the EISA bus master from the platform circuitry.

The above description and Figure 6-9 discuss a 32 data bit request to a 16 data bit resource. If a 16 or 32 data bit request was made to an 8 data bit resource, the operation of the EISA data-matching access cycle is similar. This will be discussed in the E-MIX section of this chapter because there is no way to distinguish between an 8 data bit ISA , E-ISA, or EISA accessed resource.

The completion of a EISA data-matching access cycle is indicated by the platform circuitry driving the EX32* signal line active. The EISA data-matching cycle appears as a single 32 data bit access cycle to the EISA bus master. The EISA bus master has issued only one active START* signal line pulse and is waiting for an active EX32* signal line to indicate access completion. The operation of the EXRDY signal line is also ignored by the EISA bus master, but is used by the platform circuitry. The EXRDY signal line is meaningless to the EISA bus master during an EISA data-matching access cycle because until all the data is disassembled (write) or assembled (read) the access cycle is not complete.

The preceding paragraph explains why by convention an EISA bus master views an EISA data-matching access cycle as an EISA standard access cycle and not an EISA ready access cycle. Also, it explains why the EISA bus master should always monitor the CMD* signal line, and not the EXRDY signal line to determine the cycle length. There is no use of EXRDY signal line by the EISA bus master.

To the accessed resource, there is very little distinction between an EISA standard or ready access cycle versus an EISA data-matching access cycle. For the accessed resource, use the EISA standard and ready access cycles' description and timing diagram.

Tables 6-17 and 6-18 outline the byte lanes used by data-matching access cycles. "TS" in the tables indicates the tri-state condition of the output drivers. The first 16 data bits are the low word and the second are the high word. For an 8 data bit (i.e., EX16* and EX32* are inactive) accessed resource see the E-MIX section of this chapter.

CYCLE	BUS MAS. DRIVEN BYTE ENABLES BE3 BE2 BE1 BE0				PLAT DRIVEN BYTE ENABLES BE3 BE2 BE1 BE0				ACCESSED RESOURCE EX16* EX32*		DRIVEN (4) BYTE LANE 3 2 1 0				ACCESS RCVD (6) BYTE LANE BITS 3 2 1 0				
	MAS16*=INACT.																		
1	0	0	0	0	TS	TS	TS	TS	0	1	Y	Y	Y	Y	N N Y Y 16				
2	TS	TS	TS	TS	0	0	1	1	0	(2)	Y	Y	Y	Y	N N Y Y 16(1)				
1	0	0	0	1	TS	TS	TS	TS	0	1	Y	Y	Y	N	N N Y N 8				
2	TS	TS	TS	TS	0	0	1	1	0	(2)	Y	Y	Y	Y	N N Y Y 16(1)				
1	1	0	0	0	TS	TS	TS	TS	0	1	N	Y	Y	Y	N N Y Y 16				
2	TS	TS	TS	TS	1	0	1	1	0	(2)	N	Y	N	Y	N N N Y 8(1)				
1	1	0	0	1	TS	TS	TS	TS	0	1	N	Y	Y	N	N N Y N 8				
2	TS	TS	TS	TS	1	0	1	1	0	(2)	N	Y	N	Y	N N N Y 8(1)				

TABLE 6-17: EISA PLATFORM WRITE DATA-MATCHING ACCESS CYCLE BYTE LANES

CYCLE R = REDRIVE	BUS MAS. DRIVEN BYTE ENABLES BE3 BE2 BE1 BE0				PLAT DRIVEN BYTE ENABLES BE3 BE2 BE1 BE0				ACCESSED RESOURCE EX16* EX32*		DRIVEN (5) BYTE LANE 3 2 1 0				ACCESS DRVN (7) BYTE LANE BITS 3 2 1 0				
	MAS16*=INACT.																		
1	0	0	0	0	TS	TS	TS	TS	0	1	N	N	Y	Y	N N Y Y 16				
2	TS	TS	TS	TS	0	0	1	1	0	(2)	(8)	(8)	Y	Y	N N Y Y16(3)				
R	TS	TS	TS	TS	X	X	X	X	1	1	Y	Y	Y	Y	N N N N				
1	1	0	0	0	TS	TS	TS	TS	0	1	N	N	Y	Y	N N Y Y 16				
2	TS	TS	TS	TS	1	0	1	1	0	(2)	N	(8)	N	Y	N N N Y 8(3)				
R	TS	TS	TS	TS	X	X	X	X	1	1	N	Y	Y	Y	N N N N				
1	0	0	0	1	TS	TS	TS	TS	0	1	N	N	Y	N	N N Y N 8				
2	TS	TS	TS	TS	0	0	1	1	0	(2)	N	(8)	N	Y	N N Y Y16(3)				
R	TS	TS	TS	TS	X	X	X	X	1	1	Y	Y	Y	N	N N N N				
1	1	0	0	1	TS	TS	TS	TS	0	1	N	N	Y	N	N N Y N 8				
2	TS	TS	TS	TS	1	0	1	1	0	(2)	N	(8)	N	Y	N N N Y 8(3)				
R	TS	TS	TS	TS	X	X	X	X	1	1	N	Y	Y	Y	N N N N				

TABLE 6-18: EISA PLATFORM READ DATA-MATCHING ACCESS CYCLE BYTE LANES

Please see the Notes on the following page.

NOTES:

(1) Bytes are swapped from upper to lower byte lanes.
(2) EX32* is active at this time and is driven by platform circuitry.
(3) Bytes are swapped from lower to upper byte lanes.
(4) First cycle by the EISA bus master and second cycle by the platform circuity.
(5) Driven by the platform circuitry on "redrive" and perhaps second cycle. Driven by accessed resource on first cycle.
(6) Byte lanes from which the accessed resource "accepts" data.
(7) Byte lanes onto which the accessed resource "drives" data.
(8) This byte lane MAY NOT be driven, because the platform circuitry is accumulating bytes to be "redriven".

The "Y" in the above tables indicate that the associated byte lane contains valid data. An "N" indicates that the driving resource is NOT driving the associated byte lane and the associated driver should be tri-stated. This allows the platform byte swapping circuitry to drive the appropriate byte lanes. For a read cycle, the values of the EX16* and EX32* signal lines are known prior to the data being read. For a write cycle, the values of these signal lines are not known when the write data lines need to be active; consequently, the platform swapping circuitry must drive the appropriate byte lanes in anticipation of either the EX16* or EX32* being driven active.

EISA COMPRESSED MEMORY OR I/O ACCESS CYCLE (EISA PLATFORM)

Figures 6-10-A and 6-10-B outline the EISA compressed access cycle timings from the viewpoint of the platform CPU and the EISA compatible accessed resource (add-on slave card), respectively. Tables 6-20-A and 6-20-B list the values of these timing relationships for Figures 6-10-A and 6-10-B, respectively.

> The EISA specific bus timings assume that the BCLK signal line is distributed in a "starburst" pattern to all slots. That is, there is a single driver with an individual line going to each of the slots; consequently, the maximum skew between all of the BCLK signal lines at each slot is less than one nanosecond. It is also assumed that the CMD* signal line is driven from platform circuitry in a "non-starburst" pattern. That is, the platform circuitry drives a single CMD* signal line which runs in a daisy chain fashion from slot to slot; consequently, the skew between any two CMD* signal lines at any two slots is equal to the bus settling time. Finally, the timings assume that there are no buffers on the data signal lines between any two slots. If swapping between data signal lines occur, the entry will note the change in the listed time.

Tables 6-20-A and 6-20-B have several key pieces of information. First, the "#/DET" (parameter number / detail) column relates the parameter number of the table to Figures 6-10-A and 6-10-B. Second, it provides detailed information on how the number was derived. The timing numbers are affected by the settling time on the bus. The table is based on the default values for eight slots as outlined in Chapter 10. The #/DET interpretations follow.

DETAIL	INTERPRETATION
#	NO SETTLING TIME INCLUDED.
#/A	SKEW OF TWO SIGNALS BETWEEN RESOURCES. ONE HAS A DELAY OF 0 NANOSECONDS, AND THE OTHER HAS A DELAY OF 10-15 NANOSECONDS.
#/B	SIGNAL IS DRIVEN FROM ONE RESOURCE TO ANOTHER. THE SECOND RESOURCE MUST RESPOND BY DRIVING A SIGNAL BACK TO THE FIRST RESOURCE. # INCLUDES THE "ROUND TRIP" TIME OF 11 + 11 = 22 NANOSECONDS.
#/D	SAME AS "B" EXCEPT ONE OF THE RESOURCES RELIES ON A 300 OHM PULL-UP RESISTOR. # INCLUDES THE "ROUND TRIP" TIME OF 11 + RC NANOSECONDS = 40 NANOSECONDS.

"DRIVEN BY" AND "MEASURED AT" INTERPRETATION

ADD-ON	ADD-ON CARD OR PLATFORM RESOURCE
CPU	PLATFORM CPU
PLAT	PLATFORM CIRCUITRY

MIN. AND MAX. INTERPRETATION

ALL TIMES ARE IN NANOSECONDS.

The "Bus Master Viewpoint" table does not contain the "Actual" vs. "EISA" columns of the other tables. The numbers used in this table are directly from the EISA Rev. 3.12 specification for an EISA master. Other tables for the EISA slaves track the EISA master numbers with the adjustment for bus settling and BCLK signal line frequency. Also, unlike the other tables, the BCLK signal line frequency is not included in the "Bus Master Viewpoint" table because the entries are simply referenced to clock edges.

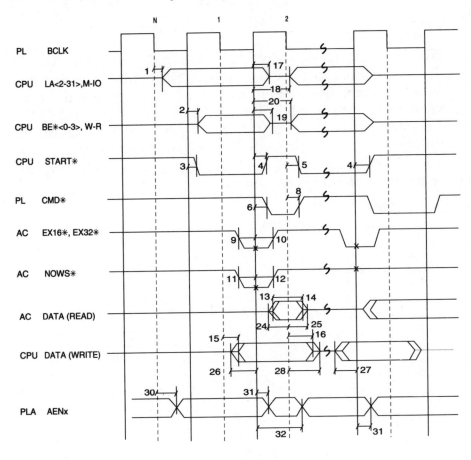

*FIGURE 6-10-A: EISA COMPRESSED ACCESS CYCLE ... PLATFORM CPU
VIEWPOINT*

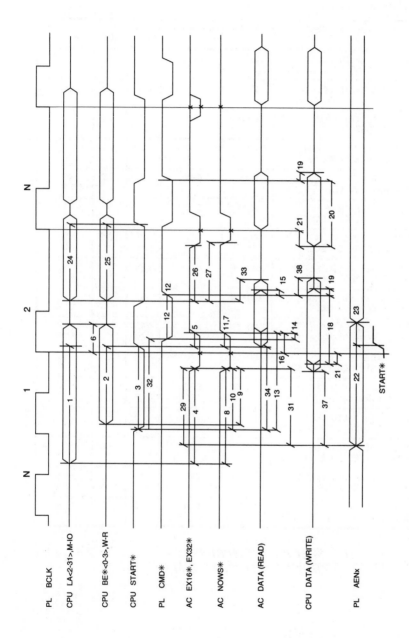

*FIGURE 6-10-B: EISA COMPRESSED ACCESS CYCLE . . . ADD-ON SLAVE
CARD (ACCESSED RESOURCE) VIEWPOINT*

REF# /DET	DESCRIPTION OF EVENT	DRIVEN BY	MEASURED AT	MIN NSEC	MAX NSEC	NOTES
1	LA, M-IO VALID DELAY FROM FALLING EDGE OF BCLK	CPU	CPU		50	
2	BE*, W-R VALID DELAY FROM RISING EDGE OF BCLK	CPU	CPU		25	(6)
3	START* ACTIVE FROM RISING EDGE OF BCLK	CPU	CPU	2	25	
4	START* INACTIVE FROM RISING EDGE OF BCLK	CPU	CPU	2	25	
5	START* ACTIVE FROM FALLING EDGE OF BCLK	CPU	CPU	2	25	NOT SPEC (3)
6/A	CMD* ACTIVE FROM RISING EDGE OF BCLK	PLAT	CPU	2	36	(1) (2)
8/A	CMD* INACTIVE FROM FALLING EDGE OF BCLK	PLAT	CPU	2	36	(1) (2)
9	EX16/EX32* VALID SETUP TO RISING EDGE OF BCLK	ADD-ON	CPU	25		
10	EX16/EX32* HOLD FROM RISING EDGE OF BCLK	ADD-ON	CPU	55		
11	NOWS* VALID SETUP TO RISING EDGE OF BCLK	ADD-ON	CPU	15		
12	NOWS* ACTIVE HOLD FROM RISING EDGE OF BCLK	ADD-ON	CPU	5		
13	READ DATA VALID SETUP TO FALLING EDGE OF BCLK	ADD-ON	CPU	15		
14	READ DATA VALID HOLD FROM FALLING EDGE OF BCLK	ADD-ON	CPU	4		
15	WRITE DATA VALID DELAY FROM FALLING EDGE OF BCLK	CPU	CPU		40	
16	WRITE DATA VALID HOLD FROM FALLING EDGE BCLK	CPU	CPU	61		
17	LA,M-IO VALID HOLD FROM RISING EDGE OF BCLK	CPU	CPU	20		

TABLE 6-20-A: EISA SPECIFIC COMPRESSED ACCESS CYCLE ... BUS MASTER VIEWPOINT (PLATFORM CPU ONLY)

REF# /DET	DESCRIPTION OF EVENT	DRIVEN BY	MEASURED AT	MIN NSEC	MAX NSEC	NOTES
18	LA<2-31>, M-IO VALID DELY FROM RISING OF BCLK	CPU	CPU		50	
19	BE*<0-3>, W-R VALID HOLD FROM RISING EDGE OF BCLK	CPU	CPU	20		
20	BE*<0-3>, W-R VALID DELAY FROM RISING EDGE OF BCLK	CPU	CPU		85	
24	READ DATA NON-TRISTATE TO RISING EDGE OF BCLK	ADD-ON	CPU	53		
25	READ DATA TRISTATE FROM RISING EDGE OF BCLK	ADD-ON	CPU		30	
26	WRITE DATA NON TRISTATE FROM FALLING EDGE OF BCLK	CPU	CPU	5		
27	WRITE DATA SETUP TO RISING EDGE OF BCLK	CPU	CPU	15		
28	WRITE DATA TRISTATE FROM FALLING EDGE OF BCLK	CPU EISA-B	CPU EISA-B		50	(4)
30	AENx VALID FROM THE FALLING EGDE OF BCLK	PLAT	PLAT		79	(5)
31	AENx VALID HOLD FROM THE RISING EDGE OF BCLK	PLAT	PLAT	20		
32	AENx VALID DELAY FROM THE RISING EDGE OF BCLK	PLAT	PLAT		79	(5)

TABLE 6-20-A: EISA SPECIFIC COMPRESSED ACCESS CYCLE ... BUS MASTER VIEWPOINT (PLATFORM CPU ONLY) (CONTINUED)

NOTES:

(1) With 11 nanosecond settling time.

(3) Not specified in Intel 350DT chip set or EISA Rev. 3.12. Assume same as Parameter 3.

(2) The platform circuitry does not starburst the CMD* signal line.

(4) Used for back to back write to read or if BE* signal lines change.

(5) Includes 11 nanosecond settling time plus 18 nanoseconds decode plus delay of valid address signals from the BCLK signal lines.

(6) May be driven as early as previous falling BCLK signal line.

REF# /DET	DESCRIPTION OF EVENT	DRIVEN BY	MEASURED AT	ACTUAL MIN NSEC [8.33]	MAX NSEC	EISA SPEC & NOTES
1/A	LA<2-31>, M-IO VALID SETUP TO START* INACTIVE	CPU	ADD-ON	123 [116]		120 (2)
2/A	BE*<0-3>, W-R VALID SETUP TO START* INACTIVE	CPU	ADD-ON	91 [86]		80 (2)
3/A	START* ACTIVE TO INACTIVE PULSE WIDTH	CPU	ADD-ON	100 [95]		115 (1)
4/B	EX16/EX32* ACTIVE DELAY FROM LA, M-IO VALID	ADD-ON	ADD-ON		83 [76]	54 (2)
4/D	EX16/EX32* INACTIVE DELAY FROM LA, M-IO VALID	ADD-ON	ADD-ON		65 [58]	54 (2)
5	EX16/EX32* HOLD FROM START* INACTIVE	ADD-ON	ADD-ON	53 [53]		NOT SPEC
6	LA<2-31>, M-IO, BE*<0-3>, W-R HOLD FROM RISING BCLK	CPU	ADD-ON	20 [20]		20
7	NOWS* VALID HOLD FROM START* INACTIVE	ADD-ON	ADD-ON	1 [1]		1
8/B	NOWS* ACTIVE DELAY FROM LA, M-IO VALID	ADD-ON	ADD-ON		95 [88]	78 (2)
8/D	NOWS* INACTIVE DELAY FROM LA, M-IO VALID	ADD-ON	ADD-ON		77 [70]	78 (2)
9/B	NOWS* ACTIVE DELAY FROM BE*<0-3>, W-R VALID	ADD-ON	ADD-ON		63 [58]	63 (2)
9/D	NOWS* INACTIVE DELAY FROM BE*<0-3>, W-R VALID	ADD-ON	ADD-ON		45 [40]	63 (2)
10/B	NOWS* ACTIVE DELAY FROM START* ACTIVE	ADD-ON	ADD-ON		65 [60]	68 (2)
10/D	NOWS* INACTIVE DELAY FROM START* ACTIVE	ADD-ON	ADD-ON		47 [42]	68 (2)
11	NOWS* TRISTATE FROM START* INACTIVE	ADD-ON	ADD-ON		30 [30]	30
12/A	CMD* ACTIVE TO INACTIVE	PLAT	ADD-ON	34 [32]		50 (1)
13/B	READ DATA VALID DELAY FROM START* ACTIVE	ADD-ON	ADD-ON		120 [113]	150
14/B	READ DATA VALID DELAY FROM CMD* ACTIVE	ADD-ON	ADD-ON		-5 [-7]	4 (3)

TABLE 6-20-B: EISA SPECIFIC COMPRESSED ACCESS CYCLE ...
ACCESSED RESOURCE VIEWPOINT (ADD-ON SLAVE CARD)

REF# /DET	DESCRIPTION OF EVENT	DRIVEN BY	MEASURED AT	ACTUAL MIN NSEC [8.33]	MAX NSEC	EISA SPEC & NOTES
15	READ DATA VALID HOLD FROM CMD* INACTIVE	ADD-ON	ADD-ON	2 [2]		NOT SPEC
16/A	READ DATA VALID DELAY FROM RISING EDGE OF BCLK	ADD-ON	ADD-ON		31 [29]	30 (6)
18/A	WRITE DATA VALID SETUP TO CMD* INACTIVE	CPU	ADD-ON	76 [71]		85 (1)
19/A	WRITE DATA VALID HOLD FROM CMD* INACTIVE	CPU	ADD-ON	25 [25]		25
20/A	WRITE DATA VALID SETUP TO CMD* INACTIVE	CPU	ADD-ON	66 [61]		85 (1,5)
21/A	WRITE DATA VALID SETUP TO RISING EDGE OF BCLK	CPU	ADD-ON	6 [4]		15
22/B	AENx VALID SETUP TO START* INACTIVE	PLAT	ADD-ON	95 [87]		95
23/A	AENx VALID HOLD FROM START* INACTIVE	PLAT	ADD-ON	21 [21]		25
24/A	LA, M-IO VALID SETUP TO START* INACTIVE	CPU	ADD-ON	123 [116]		120
25/A	BE*<0-3>, W-R VALID SETUP TO START* INACTIVE	CPU	ADD-ON	86 [81]		80
26/B	EX16/EX32* ACTIVE DELAY FROM LA, M-IO VALID	ADD-ON	ADD-ON		85 [78]	54
26/D	EX16/EX32* INACTIVE DELAY FROM LA, M-IO VALID	ADD-ON	ADD-ON		67 [60]	54
27/B	NOWS* ACTIVE FROM LA<2-31>, M-IO VALID	ADD-ON	ADD-ON		95 [88]	78
27/D	NOWS* INACTIVE FROM LA<2-31>, M-IO VALID	ADD-ON	ADD-ON		77 [70]	78
27/B	NOWS* ACTIVE DELAY FROM BE*<0-3>, W-R VALID	ADD-ON	ADD-ON		62 [53]	63
27/D	NOWS* INACTIVE DELAY FROM BE*<0-3>, W-R VALID	ADD-ON	ADD-ON		40 [35]	63

TABLE 6-20-B: EISA SPECIFIC COMPRESSED ACCESS CYCLE ...
ACCESSED RESOURCE VIEWPOINT (ADD-ON SLAVE CARD)
(CONTINUED)

REF# /DET	DESCRIPTION OF EVENT	DRIVEN BY	MEASURED AT	ACTUAL MIN NSEC [8,33]	ACTUAL MAX NSEC	EISA SPEC & NOTES
29/B	EX16/32* ACTIVE DELAY FROM AENx VALID	ADD-ON	ADD-ON		56 [49]	34
29/D	EX16/32* INACTIVE DELAY FROM AENx VALID	ADD-ON	ADD-ON		38 [31]	34
31/B	NOWS* ACTIVE DELAY FROM AENx VALID	ADD-ON	ADD-ON		65 [59]	NOT SPEC
31/D	NOWS* INACTIVE DELAY FROM AENx VALID	ADD-ON	ADD-ON		48 [41]	NOT SPEC
32/A	START* ACTIVE TO CMD* ACTIVE	CPU,EISA /B, PLAT	ADD-ON	100 [95]		90 (5)
33/A	READ DATA TRISTATE FROM CMD* INACTIVE	ADD-ON	ADD-ON		30 [30]	30
34	DATA DRIVEN FROM START* ACTIVE	ADD-ON	ADD-ON	125 [118]		NOT SPEC
37	WRITE DATA DRIVEN FROM START* ACTIVE	CPU EISA-B	ADD-ON	37 [35]		NOT SPEC.
38	WRITE DATA TRISTATE FROM CMD* INACTIVE	CPU EISA-B	ADD-ON		30 [30]	NOT SPEC
38	32 BIT MASTER TO 16 BIT SLAVE / DATA-MATCHING WRITE DATA TRISTATE FROM CMD* INACTIVE	CPU EISA-B	ADD-ON		25 [25]	NOT SPEC

TABLE 6-20-B: EISA SPECIFIC COMPRESSED ACCESS CYCLE ...
ACCESSED RESOURCE VIEWPOINT (ADD-ON SLAVE CARD)
(CONTINUED)

NOTES:

(1) If same package skew for the CMD signal line is assumed to be 0 nanoseconds, the entry in the "ACTUAL" column of the table is increased by 23 nanoseconds. The entry in the table is for same package skew of 12 nanoseconds with an 11 nanosecond bus settling time.*
(2) Used for the first access at the beginning of a sequence of compressed access cycles. Subsequent accesses use Parameters 24, 25, 26, and 27.
(3) This timing relationship does not work when full settling time is considered.
(5) Used for the subsequent accesses after the first in the sequence of compressed access cycles.

The EISA compressed access cycle can be executed only by the platform CPU to access 16 and 32 data bit EISA compatible memory and I/O compatible resources on the platform or add-on slave cards. An 8 data bit EISA compatible resource or ISA compatible resource cannot be accessed with an EISA compressed access cycle. From the platform CPU viewpoint, the cycle timing is referenced to the BCLK signal line (see Figure 6-11-A). From the accessed resource viewpoint, the cycle timing is referenced to the change of state of the signal lines (see Figure 6-11-B). The reference to the signal lines is possible because the LA, M-IO, BE*, W-R, START*, CMD*, and AENx change during the sequence of cycles. This allows the EX16*, EX32*, NOWS* (also known as SRDY*), and DATA signal lines to change relative to the aforementioned signal lines without the use of the BCLK signal line.

The cycle begins in the same fashion as an EISA standard access cycle with the platform CPU driving the LA and M-IO signal lines valid and then driving the START* signal line active. The BE* and W-R signal lines are driven valid simultaneously to the START* signal line being driven active. The accessed resource responds by driving the EX16* and EX32* signal lines valid after the decoding of the LA, M-IO, and AENx signal lines. The EISA standard access cycle becomes an EISA compressed access cycle if the accessed resource drives the NOWS* signal line active after decoding the LA, M-IO, BE*, W-R, and AENx signal lines. The NOWS* signal line also uses the START* signal line as a qualifier.

The platform CPU began the access cycle with the LA and M-IO signal lines valid relative to the falling edge of the BCLK signal line, the START* signal line valid relative to a full BCLK signal line period, and the BE* and W-R signal lines valid relative to the rising edge of the BCLK signal line (see Figure 6-11-A). Also, at the beginning of the access cycle, the platform circuitry drove the BCLK signal line symmetrically and the CMD* signal line in period increments of the BCLK signal line. Once an EISA compressed access cycle is established, the LA, M-IO, BE*, and W-R signal lines collectively become valid and invalid relative to the

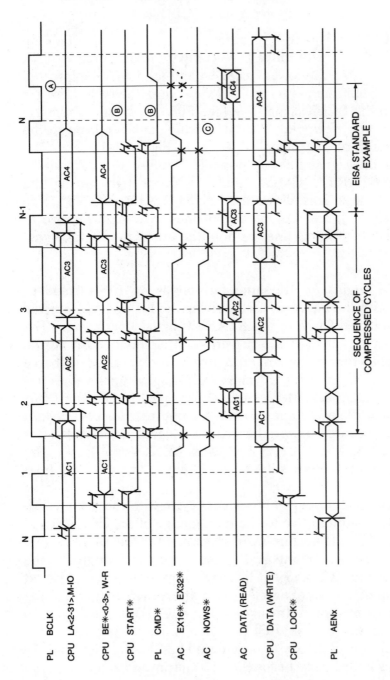

FIGURE 6-11-A: EISA COMPRESSED ACCESS CYCLE . . . PLATFORM
                  CPU VIEWPOINT

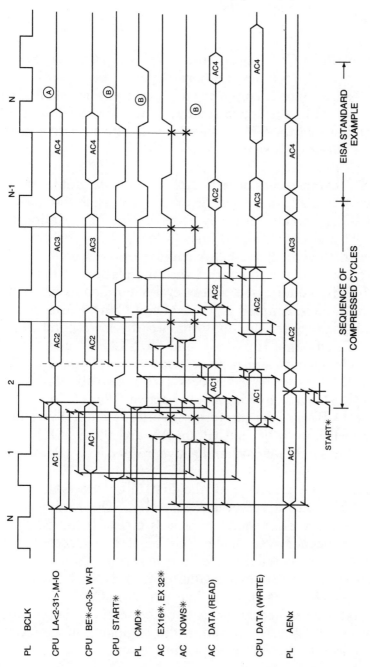

FIGURE 6-11-B: *EISA COMPRESSED ACCESS CYCLE . . . ADD-ON SLAVE*
                    CARD VIEWPOINT

rising edges of the BCLK signal line. The BCLK signal line is driven with a period 1.5 times the normal period by extending the low portion. Also, once a compressed access cycle is established, the START* signal line is active relative to the low portion of the BCLK signal line, and the CMD* signal line is active relative to the high portion of the BCLK signal line.

The EISA compressed access cycle continues until, at the discretion of the platform circuitry or the accessed resource, it becomes an EISA standard or ready access cycle. The relationship of the START* and CMD* signal lines to the BCLK signal line can instantly return to that of an EISA standard access cycle by the platform circuitry working in concert with the platform CPU. The sequence of EISA compressed access cycles terminates when the NOWS* signal line is sampled inactive (Point C in Figures 6-11-A and 6-11-B), which causes the platform circuitry to respond with a normal BCLK signal line (Point A), and the START* and CMD* signal lines held inactive and active, respectively (Point B). The sequence of EISA compressed access cycles can also terminate when the NOWS* signal line is sampled active (Point C in Figures 6-11-A and 6-11-B) but the platform circuitry unilaterally returns the BCLK signal line to normal (Point A), and the START* and CMD* signal lines held inactive and active, respectively (Point B).

In Figures 6-11-A and 6-11-B, the first three accesses (AC#) were done as EISA compressed access cycles. The fourth access (AC4) is done as an EISA standard access cycle. If the EXRDY signal line had been driven active, the EISA ready access cycle would have been executed for the fourth access. Similarly, the fourth access could also be the beginning of an EISA burst access cycle or an E-MIX access cycle. The platform CPU can switch from EISA compressed access cycles to other access cycles because from the accessed resource viewpoint the beginning of the cycles are not referenced to the BCLK signal line.

The change of the aforementioned signal lines relative to the BCLK signal line, and the change in the BCLK signal line itself, allows for several things to occur in an EISA compressed access cycle: First, data can be accessed every 1.5 times the normal BCLK signal line period with a unique address and data direction. Second, from the accessed resource viewpoint, the change in the LA, M-IO, BE*, W-R, EX16*, EX32*, and NOWS* signal lines are all relative to the START* signal line and not to the BCLK signal line or to each other (see Figure 6-11-B). Third, also from the accessed resource viewpoint, the data is valid relative to the START* and CMD* signal lines. Thus the accessed resource can support an access cycle asynchronous relative to the BCLK signal line.

From the accessed resource viewpoint, data for a read cycle is driven valid by the accessed resource a maximum time from the START* signal lines becoming active. Valid read data cannot be referenced to the CMD* signal line driven active because the CMD* signal line active pulse width is too short in a compressed access cycle. The data is held valid until after the CMD* signal line is inactive.

From the accessed resource viewpoint, data for a write cycle is driven valid by the platform CPU prior to an active CMD* signal line. The data is held valid until after the CMD* signal line is inactive.

The accessed resource that activates the NOWS* signal line must be able to operate with EISA standard access cycle timings. Several conditions must be met to execute an EISA compressed access cycle: First, the bus master must be the platform CPU and the accessed resource must be EISA compatible. Second, the accessed resource drives the NOWS* signal line active at the sampling points. Third, the data size of the access (indicated by the BE* signal lines) must be equal to or smaller than the data size of the accessed resource (indicated by the EX16* and EX32* signal lines). If these criteria are met, the platform circuitry can increase the BCLK signal line low time to twice the low time of the normal BCLK waveform to begin an EISA compressed access cycle.

Tables 6-12 and 6-13 in the EISA standard access cycle section outline the byte lanes used and the data size of an EISA compressed access cycle. Platform circuitry supports data swapping that allows cycles between the platform CPU and accessed resources of unequal data size. Please see Chapter 3 for further information. If the platform CPU is requesting a 24 or 32 data bit access and the accessed resource only supports EISA 16 bit accesses, the cycle is completed as an EISA data-matching access cycle.

The EISA compressed access cycle length is fixed, and the EXRDY signal line cannot be used to extend the access. Table 6-21 summarizes the compressed access cycle length in terms of TCLK (period of BCLK). Due to bus settling times and device delays, TCLK should be considered as approximate for the "CYCLE BEGINS" column.

BUS MASTER	CYCLE BEGINS	CYCLE ENDS	CYCLE SIZE	CYCLE LENGTH
PLATFORM CPU OR	ACTIVE START*	INACTIVE CMD*	16/32 BITS	1.5 TCLK

TABLE 6-21: EISA PLATFORM ... EISA COMPRESSED ACCESS CYCLE LENGTH

BURST MEMORY ACCESS CYCLE (EISA PLATFORM)

Figures 6-12-A and 6-12-B outline the EISA burst access cycle timings from the viewpoint of the platform CPU or by EISA compatible add-on bus owner cards (collectively called EISA bus masters) and the EISA compatible accessed resource (platform and add-on slave cards), respectively. Tables 6-21-A and 6-21-B list the values of these timing relationships for Figures 6-12-A and 6-12-B, respectively.

The EISA specific bus timings assume that the BCLK signal line is distributed in a "starburst" pattern to all slots. That is, there is a single driver with an individual line going to each of the slots; consequently, the maximum skew between all of the BCLK signal lines at each slot is less than one nanosecond. It is also assumed that the CMD* signal line is driven from platform circuitry in a "non-starburst" pattern. That is, the platform circuitry drives a single CMD* signal line which runs in a daisy chain fashion from slot to slot; consequently, the skew between any two CMD* signal lines at any two slots is equal to the bus settling time. Finally, the timings assume that there are no buffers on the data signal lines between any two slots. If swapping between data signal lines occur, the entry will note the change in the listed time.

Tables 6-21-A and 6-21-B have several key pieces of information. First, the "#/DET" (parameter number / detail) column relates the parameter number of the table to Figures 6-12-A and 6-12-B. Second, it provides detailed information on how the number was derived. The timing numbers are affected by the settling time on the bus. The table is based on the default values for 8 slots as outlined in Chapter 10. The #/DET interpretations are shown in the following table.

DETAIL	INTERPRETATION
#	NO SETTLING TIME INCLUDED.
#/A	SKEW OF TWO SIGNALS BETWEEN RESOURCES. ONE HAS A DELAY OF 0 NANOSECONDS, AND THE OTHER HAS A DELAY OF 11 NANOSECONDS.
#/B	SIGNAL IS DRIVEN FROM ONE RESOURCE TO ANOTHER. THE SECOND RESOURCE MUST RESPOND BY DRIVING A SIGNAL BACK TO THE FIRST RESOURCE. # INCLUDES THE "ROUND TRIP" TIME OF 11+11= 22 NANOSECONDS.
#/D	SAME AS "B", EXCEPT ONE OF THE RESOURCES RELIES ON A 300 OHM PULL-UP RESISTOR. # INCLUDES THE "ROUND TRIP" TIME OF 11 + RC = 40 NANOSECONDS.
#/F	RC RISE TIME 300 OHMS = 29 NANOSECONDS.
#/I	INCLUDES A SETTLING TIME OF 15 NSEC.

"DRIVEN BY" AND "MEASURED AT" INTERPRETATION

ADD-ON	ADD-ON CARD OR PLATFORM RESOURCE
CPU	PLATFORM CPU
PLAT	PLATFORM CIRCUITRY
EISA-B	EISA COMPATIBLE BUS OWNER ADD-ON CARD

MIN. AND MAX. INTERPRETATION

ALL TIMES ARE IN NANOSECONDS.

The "Bus Master Viewpoint" table does not contain the "Actual" vs. "EISA" columns of the other tables. The numbers used in this table are directly from the EISA Rev. 3.12 specification for an EISA master. Other tables for the EISA slaves track the EISA master numbers with the adjustment for bus settling and BCLK signal line frequency. Also, unlike the other tables, the BCLK signal line frequency is not included in the "Bus Master Viewpoint" table because the entries are simply referenced to clock edges.

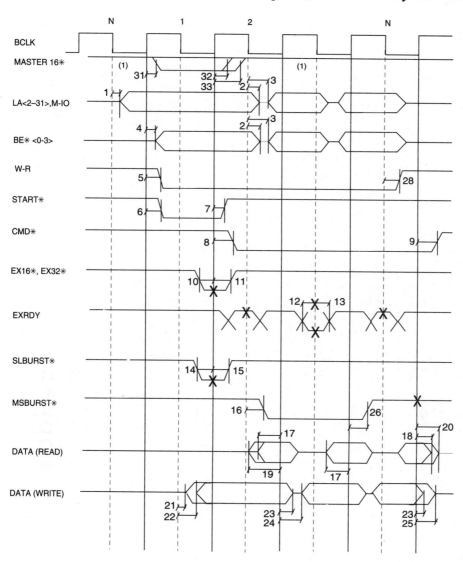

X = SAMPLE POINT
(1) = LOW ENTIRE TIME FOR 16 BIT BURST BUS MASTER

FIGURE 6-12-A: EISA BURST ACCESS CYCLE . . . EISA BUS MASTER
VIEWPOINT

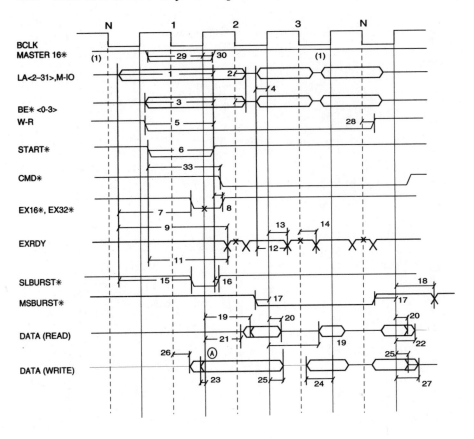

X = SAMPLE POINT
(1) = LOW ENTIRE TIME FOR 16 BIT BURST BUS MASTER

*FIGURE 6-12-B: EISA BURST ACCESS CYCLE ... EISA ACCESSED
RESOURCE VIEWPOINT*

REF# /DET	DESCRIPTION OF EVENT	DRIVEN BY	MEASURED AT	MIN NSEC	MAX NSEC	NOTES
1	LA<2,31>,M-IO VALID DELAY FROM FALLING EDGE BCLK	CPU EISA-B	CPU EISA-B		50	
2	LA<2-31>, M-IO, BE* VALID HOLD FRM FALL. EDGE BCLK	CPU EISA-B	CPU EISA-B	2		
3	LA<2-31>, M-IO, BE* VALID DELAY FRM FALL. EDGE BCLK	CPU EISA-B	CPU EISA-B		44	
4	BE*<0-3>, VALID DELAY FROM RISING EDGE OF BCLK	CPU EISA-B	CPU EISA-B		25	(6)
5	W-R VALID DELAY FROM RISING EDGE OF BCLK	CPU EISA-B	CPU EISA-B		25	(6)
6	START* ACTIVE FROM RISING EDGE OF BCLK	CPU EISA-B	CPU EISA-B	2	25	
7	START* INACTIVE FROM RISING EDGE OF BCLK	CPU EISA-B	CPU EISA-B	2	25	
8/A	CMD* ACTIVE FROM RISING EDGE OF BCLK	PLAT	CPU EISA-B	2	36	(1,2)
9/A	CMD* INACTIVE FROM RISING EDGE OF BCLK	PLAT	CPU EISA-B	2	36	(1,2)
10	EX16/EX32* VALID SETUP TO RISING EDGE OF BCLK	ADD-ON	CPU EISA-B	25		
11	EX16/EX32* HOLD FROM RISING EDGE OF BCLK	ADD-ON	CPU EISA-B	55		
12	EXRDY VALID SETUP TO FALLING EDGE OF BCLK	ADD-ON	PLAT	15		
13	EXRDY HOLD FROM FALLING EDGE OF BCLK	ADD-ON	PLAT	5		
14	SLBURST* VALID SETUP TO RISING EDGE OF BCLK	ADD-ON	CPU EISA-B	15		
15	SLBURST* ACTIVE HOLD FROM RISING EDGE OF BCLK	ADD-ON	CPU EISA-B	55		
16	MSBURST* ACTIVE DELAY FROM FALLING EDGE OF BCLK	CPU EISA-B	CPU EISA-B		35	
17	READ DATA VALID SETUP TO RISING EDGE OF BCLK	ADD-ON	CPU EISA-B	15		(7)
18	READ DATA VALID HOLD FROM RISING OR FALLING EDGE OF BCLK (SEE NOTE 9)	ADD-ON	CPU EISA-B	5		

TABLE 6-21-A: EISA SPECIFIC BURST ACCESS CYCLE ... BUS MASTER VIEWPOINT (PLATFORM CPU OR EISA COMPATIBLE ADD-ON BUS OWNER CARD)

REF# /DET	DESCRIPTION OF EVENT	DRIVEN BY	MEASURED AT	MIN NSEC	MAX NSEC	NOTES
19	READ DATA NON-TRISTATE TO RISING EDGE OF BCLK	ADD-ON	CPU EISA-B	53		NOT SPEC
20	READ DATA TRISTATE FROM RISING EDGE OF BCLK	ADD-ON	CPU EISA-B		30	NOT SPEC
21	WRITE DATA NON-TRISTATE FROM FALLING EDGE OF BCLK	CPU EISA-B	CPU EISA-B	5		
22	WRITE DATA VALID DELAY FROM FALLING EDGE OF BCLK	CPU EISA-B	CPU EISA-B		40	
23	WRITE DATA VALID HOLD FROM RISING EDGE OF BCLK (SEE NOTE 10)	CPU EISA-B	CPU EISA-B	5		
24	WRITE DATA VALID DELAY FROM RISING EDGE OF BCLK	CPU EISA-B	CPU EISA-B		40	(8)
25	WRITE DATA TRISTATE FROM RISING EDGE OF BCLK	CPU EISA-B	CPU EISA-B		50	NOT SPEC (3)
26	MSBURST* ACTIVE HOLD FROM FALLING EDGE OF BCLK	CPU EISA-B	CPU EISA-B	35		
28	W-R VALID HOLD FROM FALLING EDGE OF BCLK	CPU EISA-B	CPU EISA-B	2		
31	MASTER16* ACTIVE DELAY FROM RISING EDGE OF BCLK	CPU EISA-B	CPU EISA-B		50	
32	MASTER16* ACTIVE HOLD FROM RISING EDGE OF BCLK	CPU EISA-B	CPU EISA-B	3		
33	MASTER16* TRISTATE FROM RISING EDGE OF BCLK	CPU EISA-B	CPU EISA-B		40	

TABLE 6-21-A: EISA SPECIFIC BURST ACCESS CYCLE ... BUS MASTER VIEWPOINT (PLATFORM CPU OR EISA COMPATIBLE ADD-ON BUS OWNER CARD) (CONTINUED)

NOTES:

(1) With 11 nanosecond settling time.

(2) The platform circuitry does not "starburst" the CMD* signal line to the slots.

(3) Used for back to back write to read or if the BE* signal lines change.

(6) May be driven as early as previous falling BCLK signal line.

(7) The entry in the table is for 32 data bits (MASTER16* = 1). For 16 data bits use 13 nanoseconds (MASTER16* = 0).

(8) The entry in the table is for 32 data bits or downshift to 16 data bits (according to MASTER16*). For 16 data bits in non-downshift mode use 38 nanoseconds.

(9) The time relative to the falling edge is only used for the EMB access cycle.

(10) For ENHANCED MASTER BURST access cycle the minimum time is 7 nsec to reflect clock skew. The "normal" EISA burst access cycles should also adhere to this longer hold time.

REF# /DET	DESCRIPTION OF EVENT	DRIVEN BY	MEASURED AT	ACTUAL MIN NSEC [8.33]	MAX NSEC	EISA SPEC & NOTES
1/A	LA<2-31>, M-IO VALID SETUP TO START* INACTIVE	CPU EISA-B	ADD-ON	123 [116]		120
2	LA<2-31>, M-IO, BE*<0-3> HELD FROM FALLING BCLK	CPU EISA-B	ADD-ON	2 [2]		2
3/A	BE*<0-3> VALID SETUP TO START* INACTIVE	CPU EISA-B	ADD-ON	91 [86]		80
4/A	LA<2-31>, M-IO, BE*<0-3> VLID SETUP TO RISING BCLK	CPU EISA-B	ADD-ON	2 [0]		5
5/A	W-R VALID SETUP TO START* INACTIVE	CPU EISA-B	ADD-ON	91 [86]		80
6/A	START* ACTIVE TO INACTIVE PULSE WIDTH	CPU EISA-B	ADD-ON	100 [95]		115 (4)
7/B	EX16/EX32* ACTIVE DELAY FROM LA, M-IO VALID	ADD-ON	ADD-ON		83 [76]	54
7/D	EX16/EX32* INACTIVE DELAY FROM LA, M-IO VALID	ADD-ON	ADD-ON		65 [58]	54
8	EX16/EX32* HOLD FROM START* INACTIVE	ADD-ON	ADD-ON	53 [53]		NOT SPEC
9/B	EXRDY INACTIVE DELAY FROM LA, M-IO VALID	ADD-ON	ADD-ON		164 [154]	143
9/D	EXRDY ACTIVE DELAY FROM LA, M-IO VALID	ADD-ON	ADD-ON		146 [136]	143
11/B	EXRDY INACTIVE DELAY FROM START* ACTIVE	ADD-ON	ADD-ON		120 [113]	124
11/D	EXRDY ACTIVE DELAY FROM START* ACTIVE	ADD-ON	ADD-ON		102 [95]	124
12/B	EXRDY INACTIVE DELAY FROM LA, BE* VALID	ADD-ON	ADD-ON		44 [39]	NOT SPEC
12/D	EXRDY ACTIVE DELAY FROM LA, BE* VALID	ADD-ON	ADD-ON		26 [21]	NOT SPEC
13/A	EXRDY INACTIVE DELAY FROM RISING EDGE OF BCLK	ADD-ON	ADD-ON		31 [29]	35
13/F	EXRDY ACTIVE DELAY FROM RISING EDGE OF BCLK	ADD-ON	ADD-ON		13 [11]	35
14	EXRDY INACTIVE OR ACTIVE HOLD FROM FALL. EDGE BCLK	ADD-ON	ADD-ON	5 [5]		5
15/B	SLBURST* ACTIVE FROM LA<2-31>, M-IO VALID	ADD-ON	ADD-ON		95 [88]	55

TABLE 6-21-B: EISA SPECIFIC BURST ACCESS CYCLE ... ACCESSED RESOURCE VIEWPOINT (EISA COMPATIBLE PLATFORM OR ADD-ON SLAVE CARD)

REF# /DET	DESCRIPTION OF EVENT	DRIVEN BY	MEASURED AT	ACTUAL MIN NSEC [8,33]	ACTUAL MAX NSEC	EISA SPEC & NOTES
15/D	SLBURST* INACTIVE FROM LA<2-31>, M-IO VALID	ADD-ON	ADD-ON		77 [70]	55
16	SLBURST* ACTIVE HOLD START* INACTIVE	ADD-ON	ADD-ON	55 [55]		55
17/A	MSBURST* VALID SETUP TO RISING EDGE OF BCLK	CPU EISA-B	ADD-ON	11 [9]		14
18	MSBURST* VALID HOLD FROM RISING EDGE OF BCLK	CPU EISA-B	ADD-ON	47 [45]		45
19/A	READ DATA VALID DELAY FROM RISING EDGE OF BCLK	ADD-ON	ADD-ON		73 [68]	65 (1)
20	READ DATA VALID HOLD FROM RISING EDGE OF BCLK	ADD-ON	ADD-ON	5 [5]		3
21	READ DATA NON-TRISTATE FROM RISING EDGE OF BCLK	ADD-ON	ADD-ON		72 [67]	NOT SPEC
22	READ DATA TRISTATE FROM RISING EDGE OF BCLK	ADD-ON	ADD-ON		30 [30]	50
23/A	WRITE DATA VALID SETUP TO RISING EDGE OF BCLK	CPU EISA-B	ADD-ON	-20 [-22]		NOT SPEC (5)
24/A	WRITE DATA VALID SETUP TO RISING EDGE OF BCLK	CPU EISA-B	ADD-ON	48 [43]		55 (2)
25	WRITE DATA VALID HLD FROM RISING OR FALLING EDGE OF BCLK (SEE NOTE 9)	CPU EISA-B	ADD-ON	5 [5]		5
26	WRITE DATA NON-TRISTATE FROM FALLING EDGE OF BCLK	CPU EISA-B	ADD-ON	5 [5]		5
27	WRITE DATA TRI-STATE FROM RISING EDGE OF BCLK	CPU EISA-B	ADD-ON		50 [50]	50 (3)
28	W-R VALID HOLD FROM FALLING EDGE OF BCLK	CPU EISA-B	ADD-ON	2 [2]		2
29/A	MASTER16* VALID SETUP TO RISING EDGE OF BCLK	CPU EISA-B	ADD-ON	63 [59]		NOT SPEC
30	MASTER16* VALID HOLD FROM RISING EDGE OF BCLK	CPU EISA-B	ADD-ON	3 [3]		NOT SPEC
33/A	START* ACTIVE TO CMD* ACTIVE	CPU,EISA -B, PLAT	ADD-ON	100 [95]		90 (4)

TABLE 6-21-B: EISA SPECIFIC BURST ACCESS CYCLE ... ACCESSED RESOURCE VIEWPOINT (EISA COMPATIBLE PLATFORM OR ADD-ON SLAVE CARD) (CONTINUED)

NOTES:

(1) The table entry in the "ACTUAL" column is for 32 data bits (MASTER16* = 1) or downshift. For 16 data bits (MASTER16* = 0), use 70 nanoseconds. The EISA Bus Specification Rev. 3.12 for 16 data bits is 69 nanoseconds.
(2) The table entry in the "ACTUAL" column is for 32 data bits (MASTER16* = 1) or downshift. For 16 data bits (MASTER16* = 0), use 45 nanoseconds. The EISA Bus Specification Rev. 3.12 for 16 data bits is 51 nanoseconds.
(3) Used for back to back write to read or if the BE* signal lines change.
(4)   If same package skew is assumed to be 0 nanoseconds, the entry in the "ACTUAL" column of the table is increased by 23 nanoseconds.
(5)   The table entry is for 32 data bits (MASTER16* = 1). For 16 data bits (MASTER16* = 0), the entry is -20 nanoseconds.
(9) The time relative to the falling edge is only used for the ENHANCED MASTER BURST access cycle.

The EISA burst access cycle can be executed by the platform CPU or by EISA compatible add-on bus owner cards (collectively called EISA bus masters). This cycle can only be used to access 16 and 32 data bit (determined by the EX16* and EX32* signal lines) EISA compatible memory resources. EISA compatible I/O, 8 data bit EISA compatible memory resources, or ISA compatible resources cannot be accessed with an EISA burst access cycle. From the EISA bus master viewpoint, the cycle timing is referenced to the BCLK signal line (see Figure 6-13-A). From the accessed resource viewpoint, the cycle timing is referenced to the change of state of the signal lines and to the BCLK signal line (see Figure 6-13-B).

The EISA burst access cycle begins as an EISA standard access cycle. The initial LA, M-IO, BE*, and W-R signal lines are valid relative to the START* signal line, and the initial EXRDY signal line is decoded from the LA, M-IO, and AENx signal lines and qualified by the START* signal line. After the access cycle becomes an EISA burst access cycle, the accessed resource references the LA, BE*, and EXRDY signal lines to the BCLK signal line instead of to the START* signal line. The AENx signal line is not shown in the figures because only memory resources can participate in burst cycles.

> *The first data to be written in the burst sequence is valid for more than one BCLK signal line period. If the EXRDY signal line is inactive during this time, the valid data period extends in increments of BCLK signal line periods. As seen in Table 6-21-B, Parameter 23 is negative which prevents the data to be accepted on the rising edge of the BCLK signal line (Point A in Figure 6-12-B).*

The EISA burst access cycle differs from other access cycles in several ways. First, the burst access cycle only accesses EISA compatible memory resources. Second, the entire cycle must be all reads or writes; consequently it is academic if the M-IO or W-R signal lines change logic level, although it is advisable that these signal lines remain valid for an entire EISA burst access cycle. Third, an EISA compressed access cycle allows the accessed resource to terminate the cycle, whereas an EISA burst access cycle cannot be terminated by the accessed resource. The SLBURST* signal line, driven by the accessed resource, is only sampled once. Only the EISA bus master can terminate the EISA burst access cycle by driving the MSBURST* signal line inactive. Fourth, the EX16* and EX32* signal lines are only sampled once during the sequence of burst access cycles. Finally, also unlike the compressed cycle, a burst access cycle cannot execute across page boundaries. (A page boundary is a 1K address multiple.)

The value of the LA<10-31> signal lines must be the same for the entire burst cycle. The LA<2-9> and the BE*<0-3> signal lines are the only things that change during the burst access cycle. When a page boundary is encountered, the cycle must be terminated by the EISA bus master driving the MSBURST* signal line inactive.

The EISA burst access cycle begins in the same fashion as an EISA standard access cycle with the EISA bus master driving the LA and M-IO signal lines valid and then driving the START* signal line active. The BE* and W-R signal lines are driven valid simultaneously to the START* signal line being driven active. The accessed resource responds by driving the EX16*, EX32*, and EXRDY* signal lines valid in response to the LA, M-IO, and START* signal lines. The EISA standard access cycle becomes an EISA burst access cycle if the EISA bus master samples the SLBURST* signal line active and responds by driving the MSBURST* signal line active. The SLBURST* signal line is driven by the accessed resource in response to the LA and M-IO signal lines. If either the SLBURST* or MSBURST* signal lines is sampled inactive, the cycle proceeds as one of the other access cycle types. The accessed resource must be also be able to run the other cycle types in the event that the MSBURST* signal line is not driven active by the EISA bus master.

Once the SLBURST* and MSBURST* signal lines have been driven active, the accessed resource references the LA, BE*, EXRDY, and DATA signal lines to the BCLK signal line (see Figure 6-13-B). The reference to the BCLK signal line is needed because none of the other signal lines change state during the remainder of the burst access cycle; consequently, there is no convenient reference point. From the accessed resource and EISA bus master viewpoints, the DATA signal lines are driven and held valid relative to rising edges of the BCLK signal line.

The data can be read or written by the EISA bus master at each rising edge of the BCLK signal line. The requirement for valid data at each rising edge of the BCLK signal line can be "waived" by the accessed resource. If the EXRDY signal line is sampled inactive at the falling edge of the BCLK signal line, the data is not valid at the subsequent rising edge. When the EXRDY signal line is sampled active, the data is sampled at the subsequent rising edge of the BCLK signal line. A side effect of the EXRDY signal line being driven inactive is the longer valid period of the LA and BE* signal lines. The LA and BE* signal lines will change to the next address at the same time that the EXRDY signal line is sampled. Thus, simultaneously to the EXRDY signal line being sampled inactive (Point B in Figures 6-13-A and 6-13-B) the LA and BE* signal lines are changing to the next address (Point C in Figures 6-13-A and 6-13-B). The net effect is that the LA and BE* signal lines will not change at the next EXRDY signal line sample point (Point D in Figures 6-13-A and 6-13-B), because it references the same address and the previous EXRDY signal line sample point (Point B in Figures 6-13-A and B).

The EISA burst access cycle terminates when the EISA bus master drives the MSBURST* signal line inactive. When an accessed resource samples the MSBURST* signal line active at the DATA signal line sample point, the burst access cycle continues to the next data access. If the MSBURST* signal line is sampled inactive at the data access time (Point A of Figures 6-13-A and 6-13-B), the EISA burst access cycle does not continue to the next data access.

The EISA burst access cycle is essentially a series of individual access cycles. Each individual access cycle can be lengthened by the accessed resource driving the EXRDY signal line inactive. The minimum length of each individual access cycle is a BCLK signal line period (except for the initial access at the beginning of the EISA burst access cycle).

An additional consideration for EISA burst access cycles relates to data sizing. When the data size requested by the EISA bus master (using the initial BE* signal lines) equals the size of the accessed memory resource (indicated by the EX16* and EX32* signal lines), the EISA burst cycle proceeds as outlined above. If the EISA bus master is requesting a 16 data bit access and the memory resource is a 32 data bit resource, the EISA burst access cycle also proceeds as outlined above. The accessed memory resource that has driven the EX32* signal line active must drive and receive data over the DATA signal lines identified by the BE* signal lines (see Tables 6-22 and 6-23). The platform circuitry will swap upper and lower words accordingly.

If a 32 data bit EISA bus master (MASTER16* signal line inactive) requests an access to a 16 data bit resource, the cycle normally would proceed as an EISA data-matching access cycle. However, a class of burst compatible EISA bus masters called "downshift" EISA bus masters are able to execute EISA burst access cycles under certain conditions. An EISA bus master that can execute as a downshift EISA bus master indicates such by driving the MASTER16* signal line active when the START* signal line is active. If the EX16* signal line is active, the cycle proceeds forward as a downshift burst access cycle. A downshift EISA bus master must swap the high and low words internally without the help of the platform byte swapper circuitry.

> *The EISA Rev. 3.12 specification actually uses an inactive EX32* signal line to indicate a 16 data bit EISA resource, although the use of the EX16* signal line seems more appropriate.*

> *If the 32 data bit EISA bus master has pulsed the MASTER16* signal line low to indicate downshift support, the platform byte swapping circuitry will begin monitoring the SLBURST* signal line. If the platform circuitry samples the SLBURST* signal line active, it will assume a downshift EISA bus master and will not do byte swapping. Thus, even if the EISA bus master does not drive the MSBURST* signal line active to execute an EISA burst access cycle, it is now responsible for all byte swapping and latching.*

Figure 6-13 outlines the basic downshift bus master cycle for a data write cycle. The bus master drives the data bytes specified by the initial BE*<0-3> signal lines. The platform byte swapping circuitry immediately copies the high word to the low word in anticipation of a 16 data bit EISA resource. Once the SLBURST* signal line is sampled active the EISA bus master (redundantly) drives the low word and the platform byte swapping circuitry tri-states the low word. For a brief period of time, both the EISA bus master and the platform byte swapping circuitry are driving the low word.

After the initial redundant data driving, the EISA bus master can execute additional data accesses, but must do its own byte swapping. The data must be received by (or driven by) the downshift EISA bus master on the lower byte lanes (BE* < 0:1 > = 00). For a downshift read access cycle (or a write access cycle with initial BE* signal lines driving both lower bytes) there is no redundant data driving. All of the signal line relationships, timings, and EXRDY signal line support are the same as the regular EISA burst access cycle.

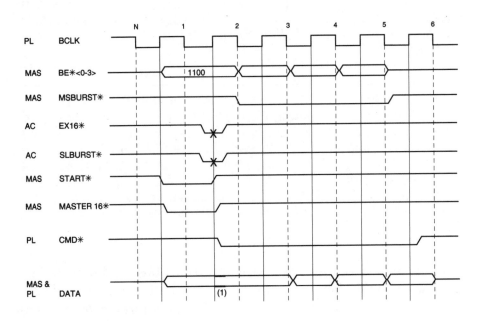

(1) DRIVEN BY BUS MASTER AND PLATFORM

FIGURE 6-13   BUS MASTER & PLATFORM DATA DRIVE

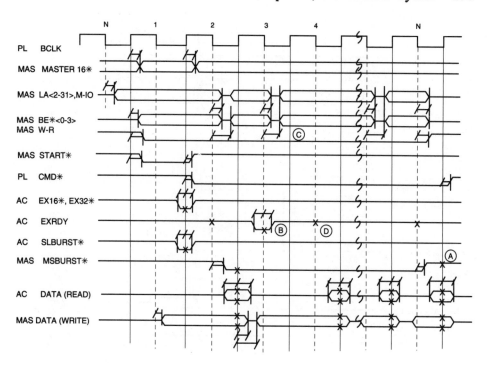

X = SAMPLE POINT

FIGURE 6-13-A: EISA BURST CYCLE ... EISA BUS MASTER VIEWPOINT

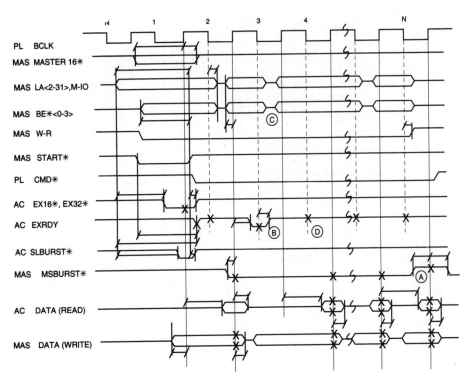

X = SAMPLE POINT

FIGURE 6-13-B: EISA BURST CYCLE ... ACCESSED RESOURCE VIEWPOINT

BUS MASTER					ACCESSED RESOURCE		MAS. DRIVEN BYTE LANE				ACCESS RECEIVED BYTE LANE				BITS
BE3	BE2	BE1	BE0		EX16*	EX32*	3	2	1	0	3	2	1	0	
MAS16*=ACT.															
1	1	0	0		0	1	N	N	Y	Y	N	N	Y	Y	16
1	1	0	0		1	0	N	N	Y	Y	N	N	Y	Y	16
0	0	1	1		0	1	N	N	Y	Y	N	N	Y	Y	16
0	0	1	1		1	0	N	N	Y	Y	Y	Y	N	N	16
0	1	1	1		0	1	N	N	Y	N	N	N	Y	N	8
0	1	1	1		1	0	N	N	Y	N	Y	N	N	N	8
1	0	1	1		0	1	N	N	N	Y	N	N	N	Y	8
1	0	1	1		1	0	N	N	N	Y	N	Y	N	N	8
1	1	0	1		0	1	N	N	Y	N	N	N	Y	N	8
1	1	0	1		1	0	N	N	Y	N	N	N	Y	N	8
1	1	1	0		0	1	N	N	N	Y	N	N	N	Y	8
1	1	1	0		1	0	N	N	N	Y	N	N	N	Y	8
MAS16*=INACT.															
0	0	0	0	(1)	0	1	Y	Y	Y	Y	N	N	Y	Y	16(8)
0	0	0	0		1	0	Y	Y	Y	Y	Y	Y	Y	Y	32
1	1	0	0	(1)	0	1	N	N	Y	Y	N	N	Y	Y	16
1	1	0	0		1	0	N	N	Y	Y	N	N	Y	Y	16
0	0	1	1	(1)	0	1	*	*	Y	Y	N	N	Y	Y	16
0	0	1	1		1	0	Y	Y	N	N	Y	Y	N	N	16
1	1	0	1		0	1	N	N	Y	N	N	N	Y	N	8
1	1	0	1		1	0	N	N	Y	N	N	N	Y	N	8
1	1	1	0		0	1	N	N	N	Y	N	N	N	Y	8
1	1	1	0		1	0	N	N	N	Y	N	N	N	Y	8
1	0	1	1	(1)	0	1	N	*	N	Y	N	N	N	Y	8
1	0	1	1		1	0	N	Y	N	N	N	Y	N	N	8
0	1	1	1	(1)	0	1	*	N	Y	N	N	N	Y	N	8
0	1	1	1		1	0	Y	N	N	N	Y	N	N	N	8
1	0	0	1	(1)	0	1	N	Y	Y	N	N	N	Y	N	8(2)
1	0	0	1		1	0	N	Y	Y	N	N	Y	Y	N	16
0	0	0	1	(1)	0	1	Y	Y	Y	N	N	N	Y	N	8(3)
0	0	0	1		1	0	Y	Y	Y	N	Y	Y	Y	N	24
1	0	0	0	(1)	0	1	N	Y	Y	Y	N	N	Y	Y	16(4)
1	0	0	0		1	0	N	Y	Y	Y	N	Y	Y	Y	24

TABLE 6-22: EISA PLATFORM ... WRITE EISA BURST ACCESS CYCLE BYTE LANES

BUS MASTER				ACCESSED RESOURCE		MAS. REC. BYTE LANE				ACCESS DRIVEN BYTE LANE				BITS
BE3	BE2	BE1	BE0	EX16*	EX32*	3	2	1	0	3	2	1	0	
MAS16*=ACT.														
1	1	0	0	0	1	N	N	Y	Y	N	N	Y	Y	16
1	1	0	0	1	0	N	N	Y	Y	N	N	Y	Y	16
0	0	1	1	0	1	N	N	Y	Y	N	N	Y	Y	16
0	0	1	1	1	0	N	N	Y	Y	Y	Y	N	N	16
0	1	1	1	0	1	N	N	Y	N	N	N	Y	N	8
0	1	1	1	1	0	N	N	Y	N	Y	N	N	N	8
1	0	1	1	0	1	N	N	N	Y	N	N	N	Y	8
1	0	1	1	1	0	N	N	N	Y	N	Y	N	N	8
1	1	0	1	0	1	N	N	Y	N	N	N	Y	N	8
1	1	0	1	1	0	N	N	Y	N	N	N	Y	N	8
1	1	1	0	0	1	N	N	N	Y	N	N	N	Y	8
1	1	1	0	1	0	N	N	N	Y	N	N	N	Y	8
MAS16*=INACT.														
0	0	0	0 (1)	0	1	N	N	Y	Y	N	N	Y	Y	16(9)
0	0	0	0	1	0	Y	Y	Y	Y	Y	Y	Y	Y	32
1	1	0	0 (1)	0	1	N	N	Y	Y	N	N	Y	Y	16
1	1	0	0	1	0	N	N	Y	Y	N	N	Y	Y	16
0	0	1	1 (1)	0	1	*	*	Y	Y	N	N	Y	Y	16
0	0	1	1	1	0	Y	Y	N	N	Y	Y	N	N	16
1	1	0	1	0	1	N	N	Y	N	N	N	Y	N	8
1	1	0	1	1	0	N	N	Y	N	N	N	Y	N	8
1	1	1	0	0	1	N	N	N	Y	N	N	N	Y	8
1	1	1	0	1	0	N	N	N	Y	N	N	N	Y	8
1	0	1	1 (1)	0	1	N	*	N	Y	N	N	N	Y	8
1	0	1	1	1	0	N	Y	N	N	N	Y	N	N	8
0	1	1	1 (1)	0	1	*	N	Y	N	N	N	Y	N	8
0	1	1	1	1	0	Y	N	N	N	Y	N	N	N	8
1	0	0	1 (1)	0	1	N	N	Y	N	N	N	Y	N	8(5)
0	0	0	1 (1)	0	1	N	N	Y	N	N	N	Y	N	8(6)
1	0	0	0 (1)	0	1	N	N	Y	Y	N	N	Y	Y	16(7)
1	0	0	1	1	0	N	Y	Y	N	N	Y	Y	N	16
0	0	0	1	1	0	Y	Y	Y	N	Y	Y	Y	N	24
1	0	0	0	1	0	N	Y	Y	Y	N	Y	Y	Y	24

TABLE 6-23: EISA PLATFORM ... READ EISA BURST ACCESS CYCLE BYTE LANES

NOTES for Tables 6-22 & 6-23:

A "*" in the above tables indicates that byte swapping is done internally by the EISA downshift bus master, but does not necessarily appear on the bus for a read access cycle. It does appear for a write cycle.

(1) Only possible with a downshift burst master, and it must do all byte swapping internally.

(2) THROUGH (9) The platform circuitry does not do byte swapping. The burst downshift bus master must execute the following subsequent cycles:

NOTE #	BUS MASTER BE3 BE2 BE1 BE0	ACCESSED RESOURCE EX16* EX32*	MAS. DRIVEN BYTE LANE 3 2 1 0	ACCESS RECEIVED BYTE LANE BITS 3 2 1 0
(2)	1 0 1 1	0 1	N * N Y	N N N Y 8
(3)	0 0 1 1	0 1	* * Y Y	N N Y Y 16
(4)	1 0 1 1	0 1	N * N Y	N N N Y 8
(8)	0 0 1 1	0 1	* * Y Y	N N Y Y 16

NOTES TO TABLE 6-22

NOTE #	BUS MASTER BE3 BE2 BE1 BE0	ACCESSED RESOURCE EX16* EX32*	MAS. RECEIVE BYTE LANE 3 2 1 0	ACCESS DRIVEN BYTE LANE BITS 3 2 1 0
(5)	1 0 1 1	0 1	N * N Y	N N N Y 8
(6)	0 0 1 1	0 1	* * Y Y	N N Y Y 16
(7)	1 0 1 1	0 1	N * N Y	N N N Y 8
(9)	0 0 1 1	0 1	* * Y Y	N N Y Y 16

NOTES TO TABLE 6-23

NOTE:

A "*" in the above tables indicates that byte swapping is done internally by the EISA downshift bus master, but does not necessarily appear on the bus for a read access cycle. It does appear for a write cycle.

A "Y" in the above tables indicates that the associated byte lane contains valid data. An "N" indicates that the driving resource is not driving the associated byte lane and the associated driver should be tri-stated. This allows the EISA burst bus master to drive the appropriate byte lanes.

NOTE: If the EISA bus master has indicated it supports downshifting and the SLBURST* signal is not driven active, the other access cycle types are executed. These other access cycle types assume a 32 data bit EISA bus master. It is only the EISA accessed slave that requests a burst access that monitors the MASTER16* signal line during the active START* pulse.

6.2 EISA BUS MASTER ACCESS CYCLES TO ISA and E-ISA RESOURCES (EISA PLATFORMS)

INTRODUCTION

The E-MIX access cycle is a mixture of ISA and EISA specific cycles executed either by the EISA compatible platform CPU or EISA compatible add-on bus owner cards (collectively called EISA bus masters). ISA and E-ISA compatible accessed resources reside on the EISA bus only as add-on cards; all other platform resources on the EISA compatible platforms are EISA compatible. Access cycles between the EISA bus masters and other EISA compatible platform resources and add-on slave cards operate with EISA compatible cycles without the use of E-MIX access cycles.

There are several unique issues relative to E-MIX access cycles:

FIRST:

The EISA bus only supports EX16* and EX32* signal lines which indicate EISA compatibility and data size. There is NO EX8* signal line to indicate that the accessed resource is 8 data bits in size and is EISA compatible. Consequently, the EISA bus master and platform circuitry must assume that any access that is not a data size of 16 or 32 bits (indicated by MEMCS16*, IOCS16*,

EX16*, or EX32*) is an access to an 8 data bit resource that is either ISA, E-ISA, or EISA compatible.

Another side effect of the EISA bus specification not supporting an EX8* signal line (that would have identified an EISA compatible 8 data bit resource) is that the NOWS* (also called SRDY*) signal line cannot be used to support EISA compressed access cycles with 8 data bit resources. Thus, the NOWS* signal line on an 8 data bit EISA compatible resource operates in the same fashion as an 8 data bit E-MIX resource, and can only be used as part of the E-MIX access cycle.

The end result of the above is that an 8 data bit EISA compatible memory resource is equivalent to an ISA or E-ISA compatible resource. That is, an 8 data bit EISA compatible memory add-on card can only respond to ISA compatible access cycles. It is indistinguishable from an ISA or E-ISA compatible add-on memory card. Finally, an 8 data bit EISA compatible I/O resource appears equivalent to an ISA or E-ISA compatible resource, but is not.

SECOND:

Notice that it is not possible to define an 8 data bit EISA bus master. The MASTER16* signal line can only define a 16 or 32 data bit EISA bus master. Either of these EISA bus masters can act like an 8 data bit EISA bus master by enabling only one of the BE* signal lines. At the beginning of an access cycle, the data size of the EISA bus master can only be defined as 16 or 32 data bits.

THIRD:

The ISA or E-ISA and EISA compatible resources use only the ISA and EISA compatible signal lines, respectively. Consequently, the EISA bus master must assume that the accessed resource is EISA compatible, and relies on the platform circuitry to translate between ISA and EISA signal lines if the accessed resource is ISA or E-ISA compatible.

The E-MIX access cycle can be executed by the EISA bus master to access 8 and 16 data bit ISA or E-ISA compatible add-on memory and I/O slave cards.   From the EISA bus master viewpoint, the cycle timing is referenced to the BCLK signal line and appears as an EISA standard or data-matching access cycle. From a 16 data bit ISA, E-ISA, or EISA compatible accessed resource viewpoint, it appears to be a standard, ready, or no-wait state ISA compatible access cycle (see Figures 6-14-A and 6-14-B). From an 8 data bit ISA, E-ISA, or EISA compatible memory resource's viewpoint, it appears to be a standard, ready, or no-wait state ISA compatible access cycle. (See Figures 6-14-C and 6-14-D.) For an EISA compatible accessed resource, the operation of the NOWS* signal line is defined like an E-ISA compatible platform.

For an E-MIX access cycle, the accessed resource sees everything in its native mode. As shown in Figures 6-14-A to 6-14-D, the ISA compatible signal lines (SA, SBHE*, BALE, and COMMAND (MEMR*, MEMW*, IOR*, and IOW*)) must be available simultaneously with the EISA compatible signal lines (LA, M-IO, W-R, BE*, START*, and CMD*). The ISA or E-ISA compatible accessed resource only drives the ISA compatible signal lines (MEMCS16*, IOCS16*, IOCHRDY, SRDY*, and DATA). The EISA bus master only needs to generate and monitor EISA compatible signal lines; the ISA compatible signal lines are translated by the platform circuitry to EISA compatible signal lines. The timing of the EISA compatible signal lines is compatible to the EISA standard access cycle discussed at the beginning of this sub-chapter.   The timing of the ISA compatible signal lines is the responsibility of the platform circuitry and must be compatible to the ISA specific access timing discussed at the beginning of this sub-chapter.

The E-MIX access cycle for an 8 data bit EISA compatible I/O resource actually uses the EISA compatible signal lines.   The beginning of the E-MIX access cycle is identical to an EISA standard access cycle. The platform circuitry monitors the NOWS* and the EXRDY signal lines to determine when the CMD* signal line should be driven inactive to complete the cycle. As will be explained later, the NOWS* and EXRDY signal lines are sampled at special points for the access cycle to the 8 data bit EISA compatible I/O resource.

Figures 6-14-A to D do not show the timing relationships of the E-MIX version of the data-matching access cycle. The operation of this type of cycle appears to the EISA bus master as the previously-described for EISA data-matching access cycles in Figures 6-8 and 6-9.

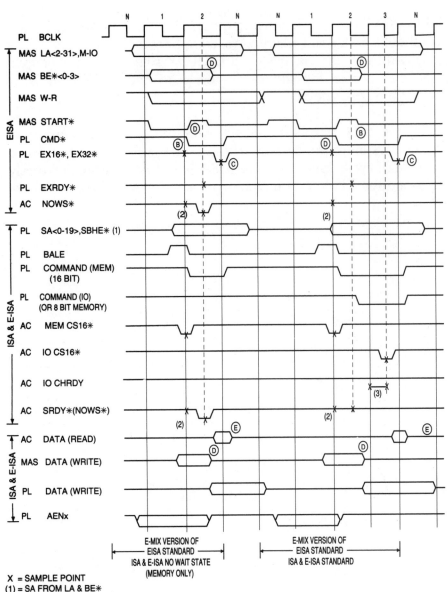

X = SAMPLE POINT
(1) = SA FROM LA & BE∗
(2) = If active a compressed cycle will occur
      (command has to qualify for ISA)
(3) = SAMPLE WINDOW

FIGURE 6-14-A: E-MIX VERSION OF EISA STANDARD 16 DATA BIT ACCESS CYCLE TO ISA OR E-ISA 16 DATA BIT ADD ON SLAVE CARD (MASTER16∗ = 0)

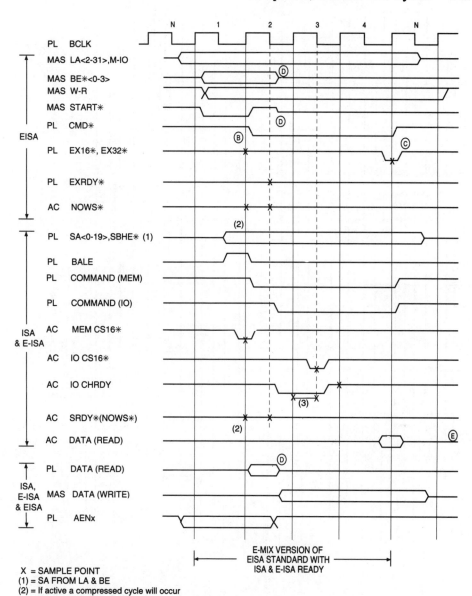

FIGURE 6-14-B: *E-MIX VERSION OF EISA STANDARD 16 DATA BIT ACCESS CYCLE TO ISA OR E-ISA 16 DATA BIT ADD-ON SLAVE CARD (MASTER16* = 0)*

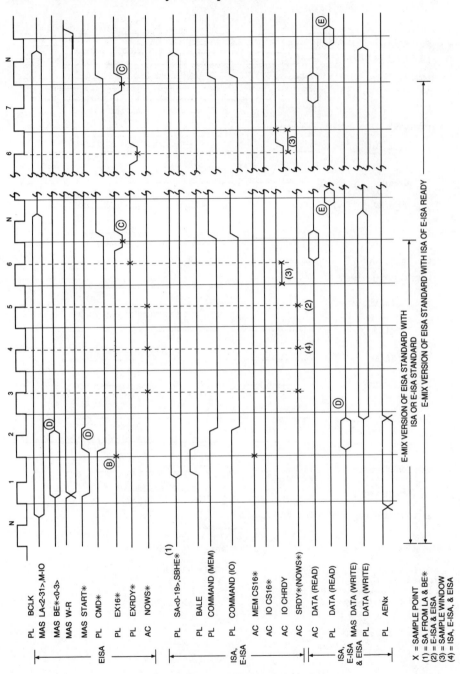

*FIGURE 6-14-C: E-MIX VERSION OF EISA STANDARD 8 DATA BIT ACCESS
CYCLE TO ISA OR E-ISA 8 DATA BIT ADD-ON SLAVE CARD
(MASTER16* = 0 OR 1)*

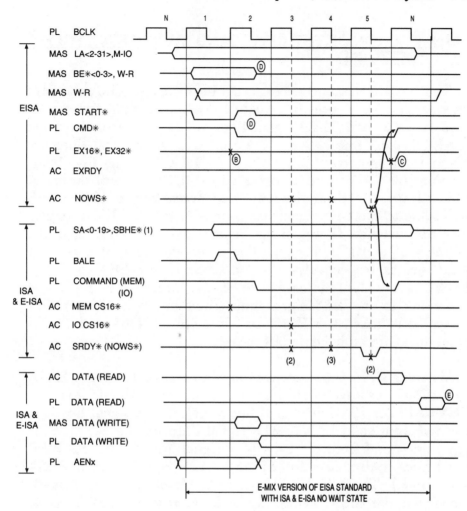

FIGURE 6-14-D: *E-MIX VERSION OF EISA STANDARD 8 DATA BIT ACCESS CYCLE TO ISA OR E-ISA 8 DATA BIT ADD-ON SLAVE CARD (MASTER16* = 0 OR 1)*

E-MIX VERSION OF THE EISA STANDARD ACCESS CYCLE (EISA PLATFORM)

The E-MIX standard access cycle begins as an EISA standard access cycle (see Figures 6-7-A and 6-7-B). The EISA bus master drives the LA and M-IO signal lines valid, and then drives the START* signal line active. The BE* and W-R signal lines are driven valid simultaneously with the START* signal line being driven active. The cycle becomes an E-MIX version of the EISA standard access cycle if the requested access size is 16 data bits (according to the BE* signal lines), the EX16* and EX32* signal lines are inactive (Point B in Figures 6-14-A to D), and the MEMCS16* or IOCS16* signal line is driven active for a memory or I/O access, respectively. Also, the cycle is an E-MIX version of the EISA standard access cycle if the access size requested (according to the BE* signal lines) and the accessed resource (indicated by inactive MEMCS16*, IOCS16*, EX16*, and EX32* signal lines) are both 8 data bits in size.

When an EISA bus master requests an access, the ISA or E-ISA compatible resource indicates its data size by driving the MEMCS16* or IOCS16* signal line valid. These signal lines are decoded from valid LA<17-23> signal lines for the MEMCS16* signal lines, and from the SA<0-9> signal lines for the IOCS16* signal line. (Also, SA<10-11> and AENx signal lines, if E-ISA compatible.) The MEMCS16* signal line could be sampled early enough for the EISA bus master to know it is an E-MIX access cycle. The IOCS16* signal line cannot be sampled early enough. Thus, by convention, once the EX16* and EX32* signal lines are sampled inactive, an E-MIX access cycle is assumed.

The EISA bus master must tri-state the BE*, START*, and DATA (for write) signal lines for the possibility that an E-MIX version of the EISA data-matching access cycle may occur (Point D in Figures 6-14-A to D). The timings for the BE* and START* signal lines are as shown in Figure 6-8, and the associated tables. For a write cycle, the DATA signal lines are driven by the platform circuitry. Also, the EISA bus master holds the LA, M-IO, and W-R signal lines valid until cycle completion according to the EISA data-matching access cycle timings in Figures 6-8 and the associated tables. The ISA or E-ISA accessed resource does not need the LA signal lines held valid; it is only required in the anticipation that an E-MIX version of the EISA data-matching access cycle will be executed.

There is a similar problem with the NOWS* (SRDY*) and IOCHRDY signal lines. These signal lines are driven by the ISA compatible accessed resource too late for the platform circuitry to correctly drive the EXRDY signal line. Thus, as with the data-matching access cycle, the EISA bus master must not sample the EXRDY signal line, it must rely on the platform circuitry controlling cycle length via the CMD* signal line.

The end result of the aforementioned cycle operation is that the LA, M-IO, BE*, W-R, and DATA (write) signal lines operate in the same fashion as an EISA data-matching access cycle, even if the data size requested does not need multiple byte assembly and disassembly.

For read access cycles, the platform circuitry will drive the EX16* and EX32* signal lines active simultaneously with driving the CMD* signal line inactive and the accessed resource driving the DATA signal lines valid. For write access cycles, the EISA bus master had to tri-state the data signal lines in anticipation of a data-matching cycle. Thus, the platform circuitry has to drive the data signal lines valid for the remainder of the cycle. The data is written to the accessed resource simultaneously to the platform circuitry driving the EX16* and EX32* signal lines active and driving the CMD* signal line inactive. In either case, the EISA bus master must only monitor the EX16*, EX32*, and CMD* signal lines to complete the cycle.

At the end of the cycle, the BE*, START*, and DATA (for writes) signal lines are tri-stated by the platform circuitry as outlined in the EISA data-matching access cycle (see Figure 6-8 and associated tables).

When the cycle begins, the data size of the EISA bus master is known from the MASTER16* signal line. If the EISA bus master is 32 data bits in size (MASTER16* = 1), then independent of the actual access size (according to the BE* signal lines) the DATA (read) signal lines will be redriven by the platform circuitry one BCLK signal line after the CMD* signal line is driven inactive. In Figures 6-14-A and B, if the EISA bus master data size is 32 bits (MASTER16* = 1), the data read is redriven by the platform circuitry at Point E. If the EISA bus master is 16 data bits in size (MASTER16* = 0) and the accessed resource is 16 data bits in size (from MEMCS16* or IOCS16* signal lines active), the DATA (read) signal lines are NOT redriven. Finally, for a 16 data bit EISA bus master (MASTER16* = 0) accessing an 8 data bit resource (EX16*, EX32*, MEMCS16* and IOCS16* signal lines active), the DATA (read) signal lines are redriven one BCLK signal line period after the CMD* signal line is driven inactive. This occurs even if the data size actually requested (by the BE* signal lines) is 8 data bits in size.

There are several important issues to remember relative to the E-MIX version of the EISA standard access cycle:

As shown in Figure 6-14-A, the EXRDY signal line is not driven active; the platform circuitry uses the EX16* or EX32* signal line to indicate the completion of the cycle. Thus, by definition, the cycles outlined in this figure are E-MIX VERSIONS OF THE EISA STANDARD ACCESS CYCLES ... they are NOT defined as E-MIX versions of the EISA ready access cycle because the EXRDY signal line is not used.

Also note that the IOCHRDY signal line is monitored by the platform circuitry NOT to drive the EXRDY signal line, but to determine when to drive the EX16* and EX32* signal lines active and the CMD* signal line inactive.

For ISA, E-ISA, and EISA accessed resources of 8 data bits in size, the SRDY* (also known as NOWS*) signal line is sampled by the platform circuitry in the 3rd, 4th, and 5th BCLK signal line periods. If the SRDY* signal line is sampled active, the cycle is immediately completed. (See Figure 6-14-D.)

For EISA accessed resources of 8 data bits in size, the IOCHRDY signal line is not sampled until the 6th BCLK signal line period. (See Figure 6-14-C.) Because it is not known if it is an 8 data bit ISA, E-ISA, or EISA I/O resource, the EXRDY signal line is also sampled by platform circuitry. The "earliest" point that the EXRDY signal line is sampled is the sixth BCLK signal line period.

If the accessed resource is an ISA or E-ISA compatible 16 data bit memory resource, the SRDY* (also known as NOWS*) signal line will be sampled in the 2nd BCLK signal line period. If the SRDY* signal line is sampled active, the cycle is immediately completed (see Figure 6-14-A).

> *Please see Subchapter 3.2 concerning slight differences in the operation of the E-MIX access cycle if the EISA bus master is the platform CPU.*

Tables 6-24 and 6-25 define the byte lanes used and the byte swapping needed for the E-MIX version of the EISA standard access cycle.

BUS MAS. DRIVEN BYTE ENABLES BE3 BE2 BE1 BE0	ACCESSED RESOURCE EX16* EX32*		DRIVEN (4) BYTE LANE 3 2 1 0				ACCESS RECEIVED(5) BYTE LANE 3 2 1 0				BITS
MAS16*=INACT. MEMCS16* & IOCS16*=INACT. 1 1 1 0	(2)	(2)	N	N	N	Y	N	N	N	Y	8
1 1 0 1	(2)	(2)	N	N	Y	Y	N	N	N	Y	8(1)
1 0 1 1	(2)	(2)	N	Y	N	Y	N	N	N	Y	8(1)
0 1 1 1	(2)	(2)	Y	N	N	Y	N	N	N	Y	8(1)
MAS16*=INACT. MEMCS16* OR IOCS16*= ACT. 1 1 0 0	(2)	(2)	N	N	Y	Y	N	N	Y	Y	16
0 0 1 1	(2)	(2)	Y	Y	Y	Y	N	N	Y	Y	16(1)
MAS16*=ACT MEMCS16* & IOCS16*=INACT. 1 1 1 0	(2)	(2)	N	N	N	Y	N	N	N	Y	8
1 1 0 1	(2)	(2)	N	N	Y	Y	N	N	N	Y	8(1)
1 0 1 1	(2)	(2)	N	N	N	Y	N	N	N	Y	8
0 1 1 1	(2)	(2)	N	N	Y	Y	N	N	N	Y	8(1)
MAS16*=ACT. MEMCS16* OR IOCS16*= ACT. 1 1 0 0	(2)	(2)	N	N	Y	Y	N	N	Y	Y	16
0 0 1 1	(2)	(2)	N	N	Y	Y	N	N	Y	Y	16

TABLE 6-24: EISA PLATFORM ... E-MIX VERSION OF THE EISA STANDARD WRITE ACCESS CYCLE BYTE LANES

Please see the NOTES on the next page.

BUS MAS. DRIVEN BYTE ENABLES BE3 BE2 BE1 BE0	ACCESSED RESOURCE EX16* EX32*	RECEIVED (4) BYTE LANE 3 2 1 0	ACCESS DRIVEN(6) BYTE LANE BITS 3 2 1 0	DATA REDRIVEN 1 BCLK AFTER CMD* INACTIVE
MAS16*=INACT. MEMCS16* & IOCS16*=INACT.				
1 1 1 0	(2) (2)	N N N Y	N N N Y 8	YES
1 1 0 1	(2) (2)	N N (7) Y	N N N Y 8(3)	YES
1 0 1 1	(2) (2)	N (7) N Y	N N N Y 8(3)	YES
0 1 1 1	(2) (2)	(7) N N Y	N N N Y (3)	YES
MAS16*=INACT. MEMCS16* OR IOCS16*= ACT.				
1 1 0 0 0 0 1 1	(2) (2) (2) (2)	N N Y Y (7)(7) Y Y	N N Y Y 16 N N Y Y 16(3)	YES YES
MAS16*=ACT MEMCS16* & IOCS16*=INACT.				
1 1 1 0	(2) (2)	N N N Y	N N N Y 8	YES
1 1 0 1	(2) (2)	N N (7) Y	N N N Y 8(3)	YES
1 0 1 1	(2) (2)	N N N Y	N N N Y 8	YES
0 1 1 1	(2) (2)	N N (7) Y	N N N Y 8(3)	YES
MAS16*=ACT. MEMCS16* OR IOCS16*= ACT.				
1 1 0 0	(2) (2)	N N Y Y	N N Y Y 16	NO
0 0 1 1	(2) (2)	N N Y Y	N N Y Y 16	NO

TABLE 6-25: EISA PLATFORM ... E-MIX VERSION OF THE EISA STANDARD READ ACCESS CYCLE BYTE LANES

NOTES:

(1) Bytes are swapped from upper to lower byte lanes.

(2) EX16* or EX32* is active at this time. If the EISA bus master is an EISA add-on bus owner card, these signal lines are driven at the end of the cycle. They are not driven if the EISA bus master is the platform CPU.

(3) Bytes are swapped from lower to upper byte lanes.

(4) Driven by both the EISA bus master or accessed resource, and in some cases platform byte swapping circuitry.

(5) Byte lanes from which the accessed resource accepts data.

(6) Byte lanes onto which the accessed resource drives data.

(7) This byte lane MAY NOT be driven because the platform circuitry is accumulating the bytes to be redriven.

A "Y" in the above tables indicates that the associated byte lane contains valid data. An "N" indicates that the driving resource is NOT driving the associated byte lane and the associated driver should be tri-stated. This allows the platform byte swapping circuitry to drive the appropriate byte lanes. For read cycles, the values of the MEMCS16* and IOCS16* signal lines are known prior to the data being read. For write cycles, the values of these signal lines are not known when the write data needs to be active; consequently, the platform byte swapping circuitry must drive the appropriate byte lanes in anticipation of either MEMCS16* (for memory access) or IOCS16* (for I/O access) signal line being active.

SPECIAL CONSIDERATION:
E-MIX VERSION OF THE EISA STANDARD ACCESS CYCLE
TO AN 8 DATA BIT EISA I/O RESOURCE

As previously mentioned, an 8 data bit EISA I/O resource used the EISA compatible signal lines. The access cycle begins as an EISA standard access cycle that turns into an E-MIX version of this cycle when the EX16* and EX32* signal lines are sampled inactive. When the platform circuitry has determined that it is an 8 data bit I/O resource, it monitors the SRDY* (NOWS*), IOCHRDY, and EXRDY signal lines.

The beginning of the access cycle is the same as an EISA standard access cycle (see Figure 6-14-E). The timings are the same as an EISA standard access cycle tabulated in Table 6-11-B. Some of the signal lines have additional "timings" relative to the cycle length of the no-wait-state access cycle. In keeping with the philosophy of EISA, the accessed resource does not have to reference the BCLK signal line except for EISA ready and burst access cycles. Consequently, different length versions of parameters 11, 12, and 16 can be defined. (See the Table 6-11-B Addendum.) It is also possible to use the parameters usually used by an EISA ready access cycle (15, 28, 13, 18, 19). Finally, the use of the DATA and EXRDY signal lines are defined in the same fashion as an EISA ready access cycle (15, 28, 13, 9, 18, 19).

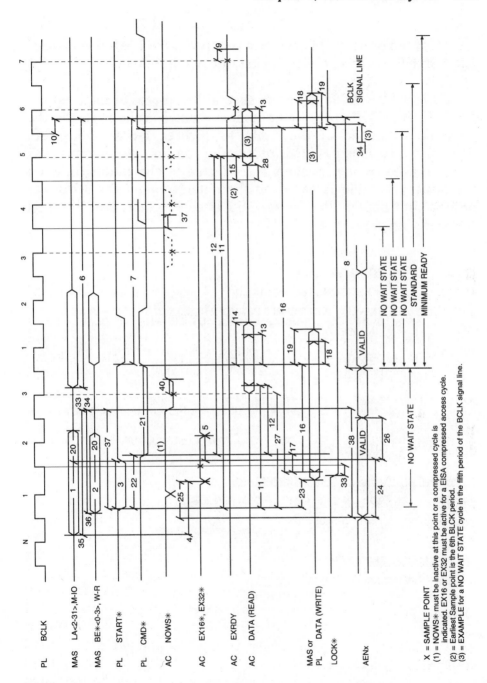

FIGURE   6-14-E   E-MIX ACCESS CYCLE 8 DATA BIT EISA I/O RESOURCE
VIEWPOINT

All of the previous information relative to the E-MIX version of EISA standard access cycles applies, including redrive.

Table 6-11-B Addendum has several key pieces of information. First, the "#/DET" (parameter number / detail) column relates the parameter number of the table to Figures 6-6-A and 6-6-B. Second, it provides detailed information on how the number was derived. The timing numbers are affected by the settling time on the bus. The table is based on the default values for 8 slots as outlined in Chapter 10. The #/DET interpretations are shown on the following page.

DETAIL	INTERPRETATION
#	NO SETTLING TIME INCLUDED.
#/A	SKEW OF TWO SIGNALS BETWEEN RESOURCES. ONE HAS A DELAY OF 0 NANOSECONDS, AND THE OTHER HAS A DELAY OF 11 NANOSECONDS.
#/B	SIGNAL IS DRIVEN FROM ONE RESOURCE TO ANOTHER. THE SECOND RESOURCE MUST RESPOND BY DRIVING A SIGNAL BACK TO THE FIRST RESOURCE. # INCLUDES THE "ROUND TRIP" TIME OF 11 + 11 = 22 NANOSECONDS.
#/D	SAME AS "B" EXCEPT ONE OF THE RESOURCES RELIES ON A 300 OHM PULL-UP RESISTOR. # INCLUDES THE "ROUND TRIP" TIME OF 11 + RC NANOSECONDS.
#/F	RC RISE TIME DUE TO A 300 OHM PULL-UP RESISTOR = 29 NANOSECONDS.

"DRIVEN BY" AND "MEASURED AT" INTERPRETATION

ADD-ON	ADD-ON CARD OR PLATFORM RESOURCE
CPU	PLATFORM CPU
PLAT	PLATFORM CIRCUITRY
EISA-B	EISA COMPATIBLE BUS OWNER ADD-ON CARD

MIN. AND MAX. INTERPRETATION

ALL TIMES ARE IN NANOSECONDS.

REF# /DET	DESCRIPTION OF EVENT	DRIVEN BY	MEASURED AT	ACTUAL MIN NSEC. [8.33]	MAX NSEC.	EISA SPEC & NOTES
6/B	16/32 BIT MAS. TO 8 BIT SLAVE / E-MIX NOWS* ACTIVE THIRD BCLK EXRDY INACTIVE DELAY FROM LA, M-IO VALID	ADD-ON	ADD-ON	289 [274]		NOT SPEC (4)
6/D	16/32 BIT MAS. TO 8 BIT SLAVE / E-MIX NOWS* ACTIVE THIRD BCLK EXRDY ACTIVE DELAY FROM LA, M-IO VALID	ADD-ON	ADD-ON	271 [256]		NOT SPEC (4)
7/B	16/32 BIT MAS. TO 8 BIT SLAVE / E-MIX NOWS* ACTIVE THIRD BCLK EXRDY INACTIVE DELAY FROM START* ACTIVE	ADD-ON	ADD-ON	245 [233]		NOT SPEC (4)
7/D	16/32 BIT MAS. TO 8 BIT SLAVE / E-MIX NOWS* ACTIVE THIRD BCLK EXRDY ACTIVE DELAY FROM START* ACTIVE	ADD-ON	ADD-ON	227 [215]		NOT SPEC (4)
8/B	16/32 BIT MAS. TO 8 BIT SLAVE / E-MIX EXRDY INACTIVE DELAY FROM AENx VALID	ADD-ON	ADD-ON	259 [244]		NOT SPEC (4)
8/D	16/32 BIT MAS. TO 8 BIT SLAVE / E-MIX EXRDY ACTIVE DELAY FROM AENx VALID	ADD-ON	ADD-ON	241 [226]		
11/B	16/32 BIT MAS. TO 8 BIT SLAVE / E-MIX NOWS* ACTIVE THIRD BCLK READ DATA VALID DELAY FROM START* ACTIVE	ADD-ON	ADD-ON		295 [280]	(2) (4)
12/B	16/32 BIT MAS. TO 8 BIT SLAVE / E-MIX NOWS* ACTIVE THIRD BCLK READ DATA VALID DELAY FROM CMD* ACTIVE	ADD-ON	ADD-ON		170 [160]	(2) (4)
15/A	16/32 BIT MASTER TO 8 BIT SLAVE / E-MIX READ DATA VALID FROM RISING EDGE OF BCLK	ADD-ON	ADD-ON		81 [76]	(2)

TABLE 6-11-B ADDENDUM: E-MIX ACCESS CYCLE TO AN 8 DATA BIT EISA I/O RESOURCE... ACCESSED RESOURCE VIEWPOINT (PLATFORM RESOURCES OR ADD-ON SLAVE CARD)

REF# /DET	DESCRIPTION OF EVENT	DRIVEN BY	MEASURED AT	ACTUAL MIN NSEC. [8.33]	MAX NSEC.	EISA SPEC & NOTES
16/A	16/32 BIT MAS. TO 8 BIT SLAVE / E-MIX NOWS* ACTIVE THIRD BCLK WRITE DATA VALID SETUP TO CMD* INACTIVE	CPU EISA-B	ADD-ON	258 [246]		(1) (4)
21/A	16/32 BIT MAS. TO 8 BIT SLAVE / E-MIX NOWS* ACTIVE THIRD BCLK CMD* ACTIVE TO INACTIVE PULSE WIDTH	PLAT	ADD-ON	225 [215]		NOT SPEC (4)
35/D	NOWS* INACTIVE DELAY FROM LA, M-IO VALID THIRD BCLK	ADD-ON	ADD-ON		275 [260]	NOT SPEC (4)
35/B	NOWS* ACTIVE DELAY FROM LA, M-IO VALID THIRD BCLK	ADD-ON	ADD-ON		293 [278]	NOT SPEC (4)
36/D	NOWS* INACTIVE DELAY FROM BE*<0-3>, W-R VALID THIRD BCLK	ADD-ON	ADD-ON		232 [220]	NOT SPEC (4)
36/B	NOWS* ACTIVE DELAY FROM BE*<0-3>, W-R VALID THIRD BCLK	ADD-ON	ADD-ON		250 [238]	NOT SPEC (4)(5)
37/D	NOWS* INACTIVE DELAY FROM FROM START* ACTIVE THIRD BCLK	ADD-ON	ADD-ON		232 [220]	NOT SPEC (4)
37/B	NOWS* ACTIVE DELAY FROM FROM START* ACTIVE THIRD BCLK	ADD-ON	ADD-ON		250 [238]	NOT SPEC (4)
38/B	NOWS* ACTIVE DELAY FROM AENx VALID	ADD-ON	ADD-ON		264 [249]	NOT SPEC
38/D	NOWS* INACTIVE DELAY FROM AENx VALID	ADD-ON	ADD-ON		246 [231]	NOT SPEC
39/A	NOWS* ACTIVE DELAY FROM RISING EDGE OF BCLK	ADD-ON	ADD-ON		36 [34]	NOT SPEC
39/F	NOWS* INACTIVE DELAY FROM RISING EDGE OF BCLK	ADD-ON	ADD-ON		18 [16]	NOT SPEC
40	NOWS* VALID HOLD FROM FALLING EDGE OF BCLK	ADD-ON	ADD-ON	20 [20]		NOT SPEC

TABLE 6-11-B ADDENDUM: E-MIX ACCESS CYCLE TO AN 8 DATA BIT EISA I/O RESOURCE... ACCESSED RESOURCE VIEWPOINT (PLATFORM RESOURCES OR ADD-ON SLAVE CARD) (CONTINUED)

NOTES:

(1) The first 8 data bits of the access sequence is as stated in the table. The 2nd, 3rd, and 4th 8 data bit access is 21 nanoseconds.

(2) Setup to data read to platform circuitry appears to be 33 nanoseconds according to the EISA Rev. 3.12 specification.

(3) The first 8 data bits of the access sequence is as stated in the table. The 2nd, 3rd, and 4th 8 data bit access is 77 nanoseconds.

(4) The table entry is for sampling in the 3rd BCLK period of the access cycle. For the 4th BCLK period add 120 nanoseconds, and for the 5th BCLK period add 240 nanoseconds to the table entry. For a standard access cycle add 360 nanoseconds to the table entry. The times are for an 8.33 MHz BCLK signal line. For an 8.00 MHz BCLK signal line, 120 becomes 125 nanoseconds, 240 becomes 250 nanoseconds, and 360 becomes 375 nanoseconds.

(5) The table entry is for an EISA standard or the first access of a data-matching access cycle. For the 2nd, 3rd, and 4th 8 data bit accesses of data-matching access cycles add the 120, 240, and 360 nanoseconds as outlined in Note 4 above, and subtract 9 nanoseconds. The times are for an 8.33 MHz BCLK signal line. For an 8.00 MHz signal line, 120 becomes 125 nanoseconds, 240 becomes 250 nanoseconds, and 360 becomes 375 nanoseconds.

(6) The first 8 data bits of the access sequence is as stated in the table. The 2nd, 3rd, and 4th 8 data bit access is -15 nanoseconds max.

E-MIX VERSION OF THE EISA DATA-MATCHING ACCESS CYCLE

The E-MIX data-matching access cycle begins as an EISA standard access cycle (see Figures 6-7-A and 6-7-B). The EISA bus master drives the LA and M-IO signal lines valid and then drives the START* signal line active. The BE* and W-R signal lines are driven valid simultaneously to the START* signal line being driven active. The cycle becomes an E-MIX version of the EISA data-matching access cycle under the following conditions: First, the EX16* and EX32* signal lines are inactive (Point B in Figures 6-14-A to D). Second, the access data size is 32 data bits (according to the BE* signal lines)   OR   The access size is 16 data bits (according to the BE* signal lines), and the MEMCS16* and IOCS16* signal lines are NOT driven active for a memory or I/O access, respectively.

The EISA bus master executes an E-MIX version of the data-matching cycle in a similar fashion to the E-MIX version of the EISA standard access cycle. In both cases, the EISA bus master is sampling the EX16* or EX32* signal lines for cycle completion and not the EXRDY signal line. The platform circuitry executes the E-MIX version of the data-matching access cycle differently from the E-MIX version of the EISA standard access cycle in the following ways:

- The platform circuitry must execute a series of "sub access cycles" to assemble and disassemble the data bytes.

- The platform circuitry will drive the BE* and START* lines that had been tri-stated by the EISA bus master.

- For a read access cycle, the data is redriven by the platform circuitry one BCLK signal line period after the CMD* signal line is driven inactive. This is true for all read cycles, without exception.

The E-MIX version of the data-matching access cycle operates as the "regular" EISA data-matching access cycle shown in Figure 6-9-A and associated timing tables. The only difference is that the ISA compatible signal lines must be used as outlined for the E-MIX version of the EISA standard access cycle.

Tables 6-26 and 6-27 show the byte lanes used and the byte swapping needed for the E-MIX version of the EISA data-matching access cycle to an 8 data bit resource.

CYCLE	BUS MAS. DRIVEN BYTE ENABLES				PLAT DRIVEN BYTE ENABLES				ACCESSED RESOURCE		DRIVEN (4) BYTE LANE				ACCESS RCVD (6) BYTE LANE BITS				
	BE3	BE2	BE1	BE0	BE3	BE2	BE1	BE0	EX16*	EX32*	3	2	1	0	3	2	1	0	
	MAS16*=INACT. MEMCS16* & IOCS16*=INACT.																		
1	1	1	0	0	TS	TS	TS	TS	1	1	N	N	Y	Y	N	N	N	Y	8
2	TS	TS	TS	TS	1	1	0	1	(2)	(2)	N	N	Y	Y	N	N	N	Y	8(1)
1	1	0	0	1	TS	TS	TS	TS	1	1	N	Y	Y	Y	N	N	N	Y	8(1)
2	TS	TS	TS	TS	1	0	1	1	(2)	(2)	N	Y	N	Y	N	N	N	Y	8(1)
1	0	0	1	1	TS	TS	TS	TS	1	1	Y	Y	N	Y	N	N	N	Y	8(1)
2	TS	TS	TS	TS	0	1	1	1	(2)	(2)	Y	N	N	Y	N	N	N	Y	8(1)
1	1	0	0	0	TS	TS	TS	TS	1	1	N	Y	Y	Y	N	N	N	Y	8
2	TS	TS	TS	TS	1	1	0	1	1	1	N	N	Y	Y	N	N	N	Y	8(1)
3	TS	TS	TS	TS	1	0	1	1	(2)	(2)	N	Y	N	Y	N	N	N	Y	8(1)
1	0	0	0	1	TS	TS	TS	TS	1	1	Y	Y	Y	Y	N	N	N	Y	8(1)
2	TS	TS	TS	TS	1	0	1	1	1	1	N	Y	N	Y	N	N	N	Y	8(1)
3	TS	TS	TS	TS	0	1	1	1	(2)	(2)	Y	N	N	Y	N	N	N	Y	8(1)
1	0	0	0	0	TS	TS	TS	TS	1	1	Y	Y	Y	Y	N	N	N	Y	8
2	TS	TS	TS	TS	1	1	0	1	1	1	N	N	Y	Y	N	N	N	Y	8(1)
3	TS	TS	TS	TS	1	0	1	1	1	1	N	Y	N	Y	N	N	N	Y	8(1)
4	TS	TS	TS	TS	0	1	1	1	(2)	(2)	Y	N	N	Y	N	N	N	Y	8(1)
	MAS16*=INACT. MEMCS16* OR IOCS16*=ACT.																		
1	0	0	0	0	TS	TS	TS	TS	1	1	Y	Y	Y	Y	N	N	Y	Y	16
2	TS	TS	TS	TS	0	0	1	1	(2)	(2)	Y	Y	Y	Y	N	N	Y	Y	16(1)
1	0	0	0	1	TS	TS	TS	TS	1	1	Y	Y	Y	N	N	N	Y	N	8
2	TS	TS	TS	TS	0	0	1	1	(2)	(2)	Y	Y	Y	Y	N	N	Y	Y	16(1)
1	1	0	0	0	TS	TS	TS	TS	1	1	N	Y	Y	Y	N	N	Y	Y	16
2	TS	TS	TS	TS	1	0	1	1	(2)	(2)	N	Y	N	Y	N	N	N	Y	8(1)
1	1	0	0	1	TS	TS	TS	TS	1	1	N	Y	Y	N	N	N	Y	N	8
2	TS	TS	TS	TS	1	0	1	1	(2)	(2)	N	Y	N	Y	N	N	N	Y	8(1)
	MAS16*=ACT MEMCS16* & IOCS16*=INACT.																		
1	1	1	0	0	TS	TS	TS	TS	1	1	N	N	Y	Y	N	N	N	Y	8
2	TS	TS	TS	TS	1	1	0	1	(2)	(2)	N	N	Y	Y	N	N	N	Y	(1)8
1	0	0	1	1	TS	TS	TS	TS	1	1	N	N	Y	Y	N	N	N	Y	(1)8
2	TS	TS	TS	TS	0	1	1	1	(2)	(2)	N	N	Y	Y	N	N	N	Y	(1)8

TABLE 6-26: EISA PLATFORM E-MIX DATA-MATCHING WRITE ACCESS CYCLE BYTE LANES

See NOTES on next page.

CYCLE	BUS MAS. DRIVEN BYTE ENABLES BE3 BE2 BE1 BE0				PLAT DRIVEN BYTE ENABLES BE3 BE2 BE1 BE0				ACCESSED RESOURCE EX16* EX32*		DRIVEN (5) BYTE LANE 3 2 1 0				ACCESS DRVN (7) BYTE LANE 3 2 1 0				BITS
R = REDRV	MAS16*=INACT. MEMCS16* & IOCS16*=INACTIVE																		
1	1	1	0	0	TS	TS	TS	TS	1	1	N	N	N	Y	N	N	N	Y	8
2	TS	TS	TS	TS	1	1	0	1	(2)	(2)	N	N	(8)	Y	N	N	N	Y	8(3)
R	X	X	X	X	X	X	X	X	1	1	N	N	Y	Y	N	N	N	N	
1	1	0	0	1	TS	TS	TS	TS	1	1	N	N	(8)	Y	N	N	N	Y	8(3)
2	TS	TS	TS	TS	1	0	1	1	(2)	(2)	N	(8)	N	Y	N	N	N	Y	8(3)
R	X	X	X	X	X	X	X	X	1	1	N	Y	Y	N	N	N	N	Y	
1	0	0	1	1	TS	TS	TS	TS	1	1	N	(8)	N	Y	N	N	N	Y	8(3)
2	TS	TS	TS	TS	0	1	1	1	(2)	(2)	(8)	N	N	Y	N	N	N	Y	8(3)
R	X	X	X	X	X	X	X	X	1	1	Y	Y	N	N	N	N	N	N	
1	1	0	0	0	TS	TS	TS	TS	1	1	N	N	N	Y	N	N	N	Y	8
2	TS	TS	TS	TS	1	1	0	1	1	1	N	N	(8)	Y	N	N	N	Y	8(3)
3	TS	TS	TS	TS	1	0	1	1	(2)	(2)	N	(8)	N	Y	N	N	N	Y	8(3)
R	X	X	X	X	X	X	X	X	1	1	N	Y	Y	Y	N	N	N	N	
1	0	0	0	1	TS	TS	TS	TS	1	1	N	N	(8)	Y	N	N	N	Y	8(3)
2	TS	TS	TS	TS	1	0	1	1	1	1	N	(8)	N	Y	N	N	N	Y	8(3)
3	TS	TS	TS	TS	0	1	1	1	(2)	(2)	(8)	N	N	Y	N	N	N	Y	8(3)
R	X	X	X	X	X	X	X	X	1	1	Y	Y	Y	N	N	N	N	N	
1	0	0	0	0	TS	TS	TS	TS	1	1	N	N	N	Y	N	N	N	Y	8
2	TS	TS	TS	TS	1	1	0	1	1	1	N	N	(8)	Y	N	N	N	Y	8(3)
3	TS	TS	TS	TS	1	0	1	1	1	1	N	(8)	N	Y	N	N	N	Y	8(3)
4	TS	TS	TS	TS	0	1	1	1	(2)	(2)	(8)	N	N	Y	N	N	N	Y	8(3)
R	X	X	X	X	X	X	X	X	1	1	Y	Y	Y	Y	N	N	N	N	
	MAS16*=INACT. MEMCS16* OR IOCS16*=ACTIVE																		
1	0	0	0	0	TS	TS	TS	TS	1	1	N	N	Y	Y	N	N	Y	Y	16
2	TS	TS	TS	TS	0	0	1	1	(2)	(2)	(8)	(8)	Y	Y	N	N	Y	Y	16(3)
R	X	X	X	X	X	X	X	X	1	1	Y	Y	Y	Y	N	N	N	N	
1	0	0	0	1	TS	TS	TS	TS	1	1	N	N	Y	N	N	N	Y	N	8
2	TS	TS	TS	TS	0	0	1	1	(2)	(2)	(8)	(8)	Y	Y	N	N	Y	Y	16(3)
R	X	X	X	X	X	X	X	X	1	1	Y	Y	Y	Y	N	N	N	N	
1	1	0	0	0	TS	TS	TS	TS	1	1	N	N	Y	Y	N	N	Y	Y	16
2	TS	TS	TS	TS	1	0	1	1	(2)	(2)	N	(8)	N	Y	N	N	N	Y	8(3)
R	X	X	X	X	X	X	X	X	1	1	N	Y	Y	Y	N	N	N	N	
1	1	0	0	1	TS	TS	TS	TS	1	1	N	N	Y	N	N	N	Y	N	8
2	TS	TS	TS	TS	1	0	1	1	(2)	(2)	N	(8)	N	Y	N	N	N	Y	8(3)
R	X	X	X	X	X	X	X	X	1	1	N	Y	Y	N	N	N	N	N	
	MAS16*=ACT MEMCS16* & IOCS16*=INACTIVE																		
1	1	1	0	0	TS	TS	TS	TS	1	1	N	N	N	Y	N	N	N	Y	8
2	TS	TS	TS	TS	1	1	0	1	(2)	(2)	N	N	(8)	Y	N	N	N	Y	8(3)
R	X	X	X	X	X	X	X	X	1	1	N	N	Y	Y	N	N	N	N	
1	0	0	1	1	TS	TS	TS	TS	1	1	N	(8)	N	Y	N	N	N	Y	(3)8
2	TS	TS	TS	TS	0	1	1	1	(2)	(2)	(8)	N	N	Y	N	N	N	Y	(3)8
R	X	X	X	X	X	X	X	X	1	1	Y	Y	N	N	N	N	N	N	

TABLE 6-27: EISA PLATFORM ... E-MIX DATA-MATCHING READ ACCESS CYCLE BYTE LANES

NOTES:
TS = Tristate, X = DON'T CARE
(1) Bytes are swapped from upper to lower byte lanes
(2) EX16* or EX32* is active at this time. If the EISA bus master is an EISA add-on bus owner card, these signal lines are driven at the end of the cycle. They are not driven if the EISA bus master is the platform CPU.
(3) Bytes are swapped from lower to upper byte lanes
(4) First cycle by the EISA bus master and in some cases by platform byte swapping circuitry. Subsequent cycles driven by the platform circuity.
(5) First cycle driven by the accessed resource and in some cases by the platform byte swapping circuitry. Driven by platform circuitry at the end of the cycle for REDRIVE.
(6) Byte lanes from which the accessed resource accepts data.
(7) Byte lanes onto which the accessed resource drives data.
(8) This byte lane MAY NOT be driven because the platform circuitry is accumulating the bytes to be redriven.

A "Y" in the above tables indicates that the associated byte lane contains valid data. An "N" indicates that the driving resource is NOT driving the associated byte lane and the associated driver should be tri-stated. This allows the platform byte swapping circuitry to drive the appropriate byte lanes. For read cycles, the values of the MEMCS16* and IOCS16* signal lines are known prior to the data being read. For write cycles, the values of these signal lines are not known when the write data needs to be active; consequently, the platform byte swapping circuitry must drive the appropriate byte lanes in anticipation of either MEMCS16* (for memory access) or IOCS16* (for I/O access) signal line being active.

SPECIAL CONSIDERATION:
E-MIX VERSION OF THE EISA DATA-MATCHING ACCESS
CYCLE TO AN 8 DATA BIT EISA I/O RESOURCE

When the requested data size is larger than the 8 data bit size of the EISA I/O resource, an E-MIX version of the EISA data-matching access cycle is executed. The timings are the same as those discussed for the E-MIX version of the EISA standard access cycle. The execution of the cycle proceeds as described in the previous section, including redrive protocol.

6.3 ISA AND E-ISA BUS MASTER ACCESS CYCLES TO EISA RESOURCES (EISA PLATFORMS)

INTRODUCTION

The I-MIX access cycle is a mixture of ISA and EISA specific cycles. ISA and E-ISA compatible bus masters (collectively called ISA bus masters) only reside on the EISA bus as add-on cards. The EISA resources reside both on the platform and on the EISA bus as add-on cards. Access cycles between the ISA bus masters and other ISA and E-ISA compatible add-on slave cards operate as ISA compatible cycles without the use of I-MIX access cycles.

Figure 6-15 outlines the I-MIX access cycle timing from the platform's viewpoint. Table 6-28 lists the values of these timing relationships.

The EISA specific bus timings assume that the BCLK signal line is distributed in a "starburst" pattern to all slots. That is, there is a single driver with an individual line going to each of the slots; consequently, the maximum skew between all of the BCLK signal lines at each slot is less than one nanosecond. It is also assumed that the CMD* signal line is driven from platform circuitry in a "non-starburst" pattern. That is, the platform circuitry drives a single CMD* signal line which runs in a daisy chain fashion from slot to slot; consequently, the skew between any two CMD* signal lines at any two slots is equal to the bus settling time. Finally, the timings assume that there are no buffers on the data signal lines between any two slots. If swapping between data signal lines occur, the entry will note the change in the listed time.

Table 6-28 has several key pieces of information. First, the "#/DET" (parameter number / detail) column relates the parameter number of the table to Figure 6-15. Second, it provides detailed information on how the number was derived. The timing numbers are affected by the settling time on the bus. The table is based on the default values for eight slots as outlined in Chapter 10. The #/DET interpretations are shown on the following page.

DETAIL	INTERPRETATION
#	NO SETTLING TIME INCLUDED.
#/A	SKEW OF TWO SIGNALS BETWEEN RESOURCES. ONE HAS A DELAY OF 0 NANOSECONDS, AND THE OTHER HAS A DELAY OF 11 NANOSECONDS.
#/B	SIGNAL IS DRIVEN FROM ONE RESOURCE TO ANOTHER. THE SECOND RESOURCE MUST RESPOND BY DRIVING A SIGNAL BACK TO THE FIRST RESOURCE. # INCLUDES THE "ROUND TRIP" TIME OF 11 + 11 = 22 NANOSECONDS.
#/D	SAME AS "B" EXCEPT ONE OF THE RESOURCES RELIES ON A 300 OHM PULL-UP RESISTOR. # INCLUDES THE "ROUND TRIP" TIME OF 11 + 29 = 40 NANOSECONDS. (ASSUMES 20 PF LOAD PER SLOT.)
#/E	SAME AS "A", EXCEPT THE WORST CASE INTERPRETATION IS THAT BOTH SIGNALS ARE EITHER 0 NANOSECONDS OR 11 NANOSECONDS. THE NET RESULT IS A DIFFERENCE OF 0 NANOSECONDS.
#/H	RC RISE TIME DUE TO A 1K PULL-UP RESISTOR = 104 NANOSECONDS.

"DRIVEN BY" AND "MEASURED AT" INTERPRETATION

ADD-ON	ADD-ON CARD OR PLATFORM RESOURCE
ISA-B	ISA OR E-ISA COMPATIBLE ADD-ON CARD BUS OWNER ADD-ON CARD
CPU	PLATFORM CPU
PLAT	PLATFORM CIRCUITRY

MIN. AND MAX. INTERPRETATION

THE NUMBERS IN THE TABLE ARE CALCULATED FOR AN 8.33 MHZ BCLK.

EISA INTERPRETATION

THE "EISA" ENTRIES ARE ACCORDING TO THE EISA BUS SPECIFICATION REV. 3.12

SMEMR* AND SMEMW*

SMEMR* AND SMEMW* HAVE A 21 NANOSECOND DELAY FROM MEMR* AND MEMW* SIGNAL LINES (36 NANOSECONDS IN THE EISA REV. 3.12 SPECIFICATION). THE ENTRIES IN THE TABLE ARE REFERENCED TO THE MEMR* AMD MEMW* SIGNAL LINES.

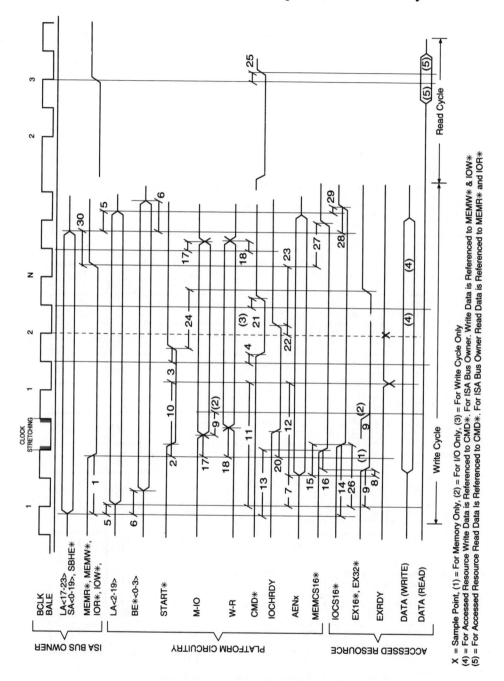

FIGURE 6-15: *I-MIX ACCESS CYCLE . . . ISA OR E-ISA BUS OWNER ADD-ON CARD TO EISA ACCESSED RESOURCE*

REF# /DET	DESCRIPTION OF EVENT	DRIVEN BY	MEASURED AT	ACTUAL MIN NSEC. [8,33]	ACTUAL MAX NSEC.	EISA SPEC & NOTES
1/A	SA, SBHE*, LA VALID SETUP TO COMMAND ACTIVE	ISA-B	ADD-ON			
	8 BITS			91 [89]		88
	16 BITS			28 [23]		24
	FOR 16 BIT I/O			91 [89]		88
2	START* ACTIVE DELAY FROM TO COMMAND ACTIVE	PLAT	ADD-ON		(1)	
3/A	START* INACTIVE DELAY FROM BCLK RISING EDGE	PLAT	ADD-ON		36 [36]	25
4/A	CMD* ACTIVE DELAY FROM BCLK RISING EDGE	PLAT	ADD-ON		36 [36]	25
5/B	LA<2-19> VALID DELAY FROM SA<2-19> VALID	PLAT	ADD-ON	0	37 [37]	15
6/B	BE*<0-3> VALID DELAY FROM SA0 & SBHE* VALID	PLAT	ADD-ON	0	82 [82]	NOT SPEC (2)
7/A	AENx VALID DELAY FROM LA <8-9,11-15> VALID	PLAT	ADD-ON		29 [29]	18
8/B	EX16* & EX32* ACTIVE DELAY FROM AENx VALID	ADD-ON	ADD-ON		56 [49]	34
8/D	EX16* & EX32* INACTIVE DELAY FROM AENx VALID	ADD-ON	ADD-ON		38 [31]	34
9/B	EX16* & EX32* ACTIVE DELY FRM LA,M/I-O VALID	ADD-ON	ADD-ON		83 [76]	54
9/D	EX16* & EX32* INACTIVE DELY FRM LA,M/I-O VALID	ADD-ON	ADD-ON		65 [58]	54
10/D	EXRDY ACTIVE DELAY FROM START* ACTIVE	ADD-ON	ADD-ON		102 [95]	124
10/B	EXRDY INACTIVE DELAY FROM START* ACTIVE	ADD-ON	ADD-ON		120 [113]	124
11/D	EXRDY ACTIVE DELAY FROM LA<2-19> VALID	ADD-ON	ADD-ON		146 [136]	143
11/B	EXRDY INACTIVE DELAY FROM LA<2-19> VALID	ADD-ON	ADD-ON		164 [154]	143
12/D	EXRDY ACTIVE DELAY FROM AENx VALID	ADD-ON	ADD-ON		116 [106]	143
12/B	EXRDY INACTIVE DELAY FROM AENx VALID	ADD-ON	ADD-ON		134 [124]	143

TABLE 6-28: I-MIX ACCESS CYCLE TIMINGS

REF# /DET	DESCRIPTION OF EVENT	DRIVEN BY	MEASURED AT	ACTUAL MIN NSEC. [8.33]	MAX NSEC.	EISA SPEC & NOTES
14/B 14	IOCS16* ACTIVE DELAY FROM SA<0-11> VALID	ADD-ON ADD-ON	ADD-ON ISA-B		131 [123] 153 [145]	103 * 145 *,(4)
14/D 14	IOCS16* INACTIVE DELAY FROM SA<0-11> VALID	ADD-ON ADD-ON	ADD-ON ISA-B	106 [98]	153 [145]	103 * 145 *,(4)
15/B 15	IOCS16* ACTIVE DELAY FROM AENx VALID	ADD-ON ADD-ON	ADD-ON ISA-B		44 [39] 66 [61]	NOT SPEC
15/D 15	IOCS16* INACTIVE DELAY FROM AENx VALID	ADD-ON ADD-ON	ADD-ON ISA-B		26 [21] 66 [61]	NOT SPEC
16/B	MEMCS16* ACTIVE DELAY FROM EX16/32* VALID	PLAT	ISA-B		37 [37]	15
16/D	MEMCS16* INACTIVE DELAY FROM EX16/32* VALID	PLAT	ISA-B		15 [15]	15
17/B	M-IO VALID DELAY FROM IOR* & IOW* VALID	PLAT	ADD-ON		62 [62]	NOT SPEC (2)
18/B	W-R VALID DELAY FROM MEMORY OR I/O CMD VALID	PLAT	ADD-ON		82 [82]	NOT SPEC (2)
19/D	EXRDY ACTIVE DELAY FROM M/I-O VALID	ADD-ON	ADD-ON		146 [136]	143
19/B	EXRDY INACTIVE DELAY M/I-O VALID	ADD-ON	ADD-ON		164 [154]	143
20/B	IOCHRDY INACT. DELY FROM MEMORY OR I/O CMD VALID	PLAT	ISA-B		82 [82]	NOT SPEC (2)
21/A	CMD* INACTIVE DELAY FROM BCLK RISING EDGE	PLAT	ADD-ON		36 [36]	25
22/H	IOCHRDY ACTIVE DELY FROM BCLK FALLING EDGE	PLAT	ISA-B		119 [119]	NOT SPEC(2,3)
23/E	COMMAND INACTIVE FROM IOCHRDY ACTIVE	PLAT	ISA-B	125 [120]		
24	EX16/32* VALID HOLD FROM START* INACTIVE	ADD-ON	ADD-ON	53 [53]		NOT SPEC
25	CMD* INACTIVE DELAY FRM READ COMMAND INACTIVE	PLAT	ADD-ON	0 [0]		NOT SPEC (2)

TABLE 6-28: I-MIX ACCESS CYCLE TIMINGS (CONTINUED)

REF# /DET	DESCRIPTION OF EVENT	DRIVEN BY	MEASURED AT	ACTUAL MIN NSEC. [8,33]	MAX NSEC.	EISA SPEC & NOTES
26/B	IOCS16* ACTIVE DELAY FROM LA<2-11> VALID	ADD-ON	ADD-ON		73 [68]	54 *
		ADD-ON	PLAT		95 [90]	NOT SPEC
26/D	IOCS16* INACTIVE DELAY FROM LA<2-11> VALID	ADD-ON	ADD-ON		55 [50]	54 *
		ADD-ON	PLAT & ISA-B		95 [90]	NOT SPEC
27/E	MEMCS16* VALID HOLD FROM INVALID LA<17-23>	ADD-ON	ADD-ON	0 [0]		0
		ADD-ON	ISA-B	0		0
28/E	IOCS16* VALID HOLD FROM VALID SA<0-11>	ADD-ON	ADD-ON	0 [0]		0
29/E	IOCS16* VALID HOLD FROM VALID LA<2-11>, AENx	ADD-ON	ADD-ON	0 [0]		0
30	SA<0-19> & SBHE* VALID HOLD FROM COMMAND INACTVE (LA<17-23> FOR ISA-B)	ISA-B	ADD-ON	30 [30]		30

TABLE 6-28: I-MIX ACCESS CYCLE TIMINGS (CONTINUED)
NOTES:
"*" Please see Table 6-11- Notes 6 and 21.
(1) Not specified because of the synchronization of the COMMAND to the BCLK and START* signal lines. See the text for further information.
(2) Data from Intel 82358DT.
(3) The entry is for a 1K pull-up resistor. If a 300 ohm pull-up resistor is used, the entry is 44 nanoseconds.
(4) Use this number for ISA or E-ISA add-on cards installed in E-ISA and EISA compatible platforms. If the bus master is an ISA add-on bus owner card, 153 [145] is replaced with 81 [76] in Table 6-1-A, and 113 [105] is replaced with 41 [35] in Table 6-1-B..

The I-MIX access cycle can be executed only by an ISA or E-ISA add-on bus owner card (collectively called ISA bus master). The ISA bus master can use the I-MIX access cycle to access EISA compatible memory and I/O resources. The execution of the I-MIX access cycle requires extensive assistance from the platform circuitry. The ISA bus master executes cycles in its native ISA mode independent of the EISA control signal lines. The EISA compatible accessed resource executes cycles in its native EISA mode independent of the ISA control signal lines. The only signal lines used during the actual access cycle by both protocols in an I-MIX access cycle are the SA<0-15>, LA<17-23>, IOCS16* and SRDY* (NOWS*) signal lines.

The implementation of the I-MIX access cycle is very ad-hoc in nature. The ISA bus master does not operate synchronously to the BCLK signal line (except for the SRDY* and IOCHRDY signal lines), unlike an EISA bus master. The signals generated by the ISA bus master must be translated into equivalent EISA bus master signals. The address and data exchanged between the two resources must satisfy both the ISA and EISA bus cycle protocols. To these ends, the operation of the I-MIX access cycles can best be viewed as follows:

First, the ISA bus master executes ISA ready access cycles to EISA 16 data bit memory and I/O resources, and EISA 8 data bit I/O resources. The operation of the EISA accessed resources is as described for EISA standard and ready access cycles on EISA compatible platforms.

Second, an ISA bus master requesting a 16 data bit access to an 8 bit resource does not require the platform circuitry to assemble the data into a 16 bit word; consequently, there is no concept of data-matching. Similarly, an access to a 32 data bit resource simply requires byte swapping by the platform circuitry to complete the cycle.

Third, accesses to 8 data bit EISA compatible resources cannot be distinguished from accesses to 8 data bit ISA compatible resources. This condition will be discussed separately at the end of this sub-chapter.

Finally, the only unique timings associated with the I-MIX access cycle are those required to link ISA and EISA protocols. Any signal line relationship not discussed in the subsequent section are defined in the previous ISA and EISA sections. Some of these timings are repeated here to help explain the I-MIX access cycles.

FIRST PART OF THE I-MIX ACCESS CYCLE

The I-MIX access cycle to 16 or 32 data bit EISA compatible resources begins as an ISA standard access cycle after the obtain portion of an ISA arbitration has been executed. The platform circuitry drives the AENx signal line inactive and the BALE signal line active (see Chapter 9 for more information about arbitration cycles). The platform circuitry also drives the W-R signal line to be in the default read mode (see Figures 6-16-A and B). The ISA bus master drives the LA<17-23>, SA<0-19>, and SBHE* signal lines valid. The platform circuitry converts the SA<0-1>, SBHE*, and SA<2-16> signal lines to the BE*<0-3> and LA<2-16> signal lines, respectively. The platform circuitry also drives the AENx signal line valid. The accessed resource responds by driving the EX16*, EX32*, and IOCS16* (for I/O resource) signal lines valid.

There are unique requirements during the first portion of the cycle because the ISA bus protocol establishes a minimum time from valid unique ISA ADDRESS (LA<17-23>, SA<0-19>, SBHE*) signal lines to COMMAND (MEMR*, MEMW*, IOR*, and IOW*) signal lines active. Also, the ISA bus protocol establishes a maximum time from valid ISA ADDRESS (except SBHE*) signal lines and valid MEMCS16* and IOCS16* signal lines. In order to address these requirements, the following protocol has been established:

First, the EISA unique ADDRESS (LA<2-16> and BE*<0-3>) signal lines are a straight translation of the ISA ADDRESS signal lines (SA<0-16> and SBHE*) without any qualification by the BCLK signal line.

Second, the EX16*, EX32*, AENx, and IOCS16* signal lines decode from the EISA ADDRESS signal lines independent of address space (memory vs I/O) and the direction of data flow (read vs. write). The EX16* and EX32* signal lines decode the LA<2-23> signal lines (as well as the LA<24-31>* signal lines which are inactive). The AENx signal line is driven by the platform circuitry

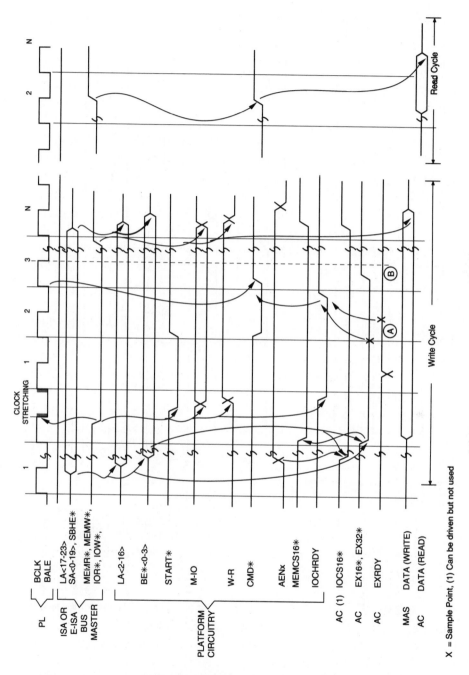

FIGURE 6-16-A: *I-MIX ACCESS CYCLE . . . ISA OR E-ISA BUS OWNER CARD TO 16 DATA BIT EISA ACCESSED RESOURCE*

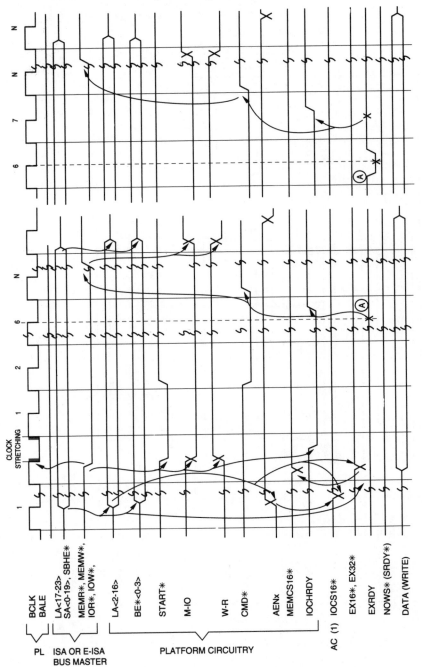

CLOCK
STRETCHING

BCLK	
BALE	PL
LA<17-23>	
SA<0-19>, SBHE*	ISA OR E-ISA
MEMR*, MEMW*,	BUS MASTER
IOR*, IOW*,	
LA<2-16>	
BE*<0-3>	
START*	
M-IO	
W-R	PLATFORM CIRCUITRY
CMD*	
AENx	
MEMCS16*	
IOCHRDY	
IOCS16*	AC (1)
EX16*, EX32*	
EXRDY	
NOWS* (SRDY*)	
DATA (WRITE)	

X = Sample Point, (1) Can be driven but not used

*FIGURE 6-16-B: I-MIX ACCESS CYCLE . . . ISA OR E-ISA BUS OWNER CARD
TO 8 DATA BIT EISA I/O ACCESSED RESOURCE
(WRITE EXAMPLE)*

and is a decode of the LA<8, 9, 12-15> signal lines. The IOCS16* signal line must be driven by the EISA compatible accessed resource to insure that it is valid in the time established by the ISA access cycle protocol. The IOCS16* signal line decodes from the LA<2-11> and AENx signal lines.

Third, the MEMCS16* signal line does not need the AENx signal as a qualifier, and is translated by the platform circuitry from the EX16* and EX32* signal lines.

DETERMINATION OF RESOURCE TYPE

First, at the beginning of the cycle, the M-IO signal line indicates a memory access. It does not change to indicate an I/O access until after the COMMAND signal lines are driven active. If the EX16* and EX32* signal lines remain inactive, the access is not to an EISA compatible memory resource. The platform circuitry does not have further participation with this cycle.

Second, with the M-IO signal line initially indicating a memory access, EISA compatible resources could possibly drive the EX16* and EX32* signal lines even when the ISA bus master is accessing an ISA or E-ISA compatible I/O resource. The activation of the EX16* and EX32* signal lines will incorrectly indicate an EISA resource. Similarly, EX16* and EX32* signal lines will be valid too late as a reasonable indicator of an EISA compatible I/O resource. Thus, the I-MIX access cycle is always executed by the platform circuitry when the IOR* or IOW* signal line is driven active by the ISA bus master even if it is an ISA or E-ISA compatible resource.

An ISA bus master access to an EISA compatible I/O resource, as indicated by active EX16* and EX32* signal lines, is clearly an I-MIX access cycle. The fact that the IOCS16* signal line is driven by the EISA compatible I/O resource is simply for timing reasons. If the EISA compatible I/O resource is 8 data bits in size it cannot be distinguished from an ISA or E-ISA compatible I/O resource, but can use all of the EISA compatible control lines. The platform circuitry simply monitors the EXRDY signal line in order to control the IOCHRDY and CMD* signal lines. The fact that 8 data bit ISA, E-ISA, and EISA compatible I/O resources are indistinguishable from each other allows the EISA compatible resource to use the NOWS* (SRDY*) signal line. Consequently, an 8 data bit EISA compatible I/O resource can execute no-wait-state cycles as if it were an ISA or E-ISA compatible resource.

Third, notice that an 8 data bit EISA compatible memory resource cannot indicate to the platform circuitry that it is an EISA resource. Without the activation of the EX16* and EX32* signal lines, the I-MIX access cycle is not executed; consequently, the EISA bus control signal lines are not used by the accessed resource, and the EXRDY signal line is not monitored by platform circuitry. The ISA bus master must "directly" access the EISA 8 data bit memory resource as if it is an ISA compatible resource. An EISA bus master accessing the same resource will do so with an E-MIX access cycle. Even though an 8 data bit memory resource COULD use EISA specific signal lines (LA, BE*), there is NO assurance that the platform circuitry will drive the START* and CMD signal lines; consequently, it must respond to ISA compatible signal lines. Also, for an ISA or E-ISA compatible memory resource, the address spaces may overlap with the EISA compatible resources. Thus, for all intents and purposes, an EISA compatible 8 data bit memory resource must operate as, and is identical to, an ISA compatible 8 data bit memory resource. It is accessed by the ISA or E-ISA bus master without the use of the I-MIX access cycle.

CONTINUATION OF THE I-MIX ACCESS CYCLE

The I-MIX access cycle continues with the ISA bus master driving the COMMAND signal lines asynchronously to the BCLK signal line. In order for the platform circuitry to mimic the EISA bus master protocol, the asynchronous COMMAND signal lines must be translated into synchronous START* and CMD* signal lines. To effect this translation, the START* signal line will be driven active asynchronously to the BCLK signal line when one of the COMMAND signal lines is driven active. The platform circuitry then stretches the low and high period of the BCLK signal line to insure that the driving point for the START* signal line going inactive and an active CMD* signal line are synchronized to the BCLK signal line.

Once the COMMAND signal lines are driven active, the platform circuitry drives the IOCHRDY signal line inactive. The IOCHRDY signal line remains inactive until Point A in Figure 6-16-A and B. At Point A, the EXRDY signal line may be driven inactive by the EISA compatible resource if an EISA ready access cycle is needed. If the EXRDY signal line remains active, the platform circuitry will drive the CMD* and IOCHRDY signal lines inactive and active, respectively. The resulting cycle resembles an EISA standard access cycle to the accessed resource, but resembles an ISA ready access cycle to the ISA bus master. The earliest BCLK signal line period that the EXRDY signal line is sampled is the falling edge of the first period and fifth period of the active CMD* signal line for 16 and 8 data bit resources, respectively.

If the SRDY* (NOWS*) signal line was monitored active by the ISA bus master, it would still execute a standard or ready access cycle. The SRDY* (NOWS*) signal line is ignored when the IOCHRDY signal line is inactive.

If the accessed I/O resource was actually ISA compatible, and is executing an ISA ready access cycle, the IOCHRDY signal line continues to be driven inactive by the accessed resource.

Once the CMD* signal line is driven active, the I-MIX cycle proceeds as an EISA compatible standard or ready cycle relative to the accessed resource. An EISA standard access cycle is exemplified in the write cycle portion of Figure 6-16-A. Obviously, the cycle is extended if the EXRDY signal line is driven active as required by the EISA bus protocol, as shown in Figure 6-16-B.

The ISA bus protocol only establishes a minimum time from an active IOCHRDY signal line and an inactive COMMAND signal line; consequently, there is an indeterminate time for the cycle to complete. For a write cycle, the data is received by the EISA compatible resource at the end of the active period of the CMD* signal line; thus, the COMMAND signal lines (MEMW*, IOW*, and SMEMW*) can be driven inactive after the CMD* signal line is driven inactive. For a read cycle, the data is received by the ISA bus master when it drives the COMMAND signal lines (MEMR*, SMEMR*, and IOR*) inactive; thus, the CMD* signal line must be held active until after the MEMR* or IOR* signal lines are driven inactive.

During an I-MIX access cycle, the LA* <24-31> signal lines are high due to pull-up resistors on the bus. These address lines are defined as containing the inverted address; consequently, only the lower 16 megabytes of the memory address space can be accessed. For an ISA compatible add-on bus owner card, the I/O address space is a subset of the EISA I/O address space; the ISA bus master can drive only the SA<0-9> signal lines. For an E-ISA compatible add-on bus owner card, the I/O address space by definition is the same as the EISA I/O addresss space.

As described in Chapters 3 and 5, the original IBM AT did not support MEMCS16, IOCS16*, or IOCHRDY signal lines for a non-platform CPU access to platform resources. Due to this condition, "ill-behaved" ISA bus masters as add-on bus owner cards did not monitor these signal lines and always executed 16 data bit memory access cycles. As outlined above, the I-MIX access cycle relies on the ISA bus master to execute an ISA ready access cycle to both 8 and 16 data bit EISA resources. This requires the ISA bus master to be "well-behaved" and to monitor the MEMCS16*, IOCS16* and IOCHRDY signal lines. Given these restrictions, an ill-behaved ISA bus master can only access certain ISA compatible add-on slave cards in an EISA system. Only a well-behaved ISA bus master can access EISA compatible platform or add-on slave card resources.*

6.4 LOCK CYCLES

The platform CPU or EISA add-on bus owner card (collectively called EISA bus masters) can access an EISA memory or I/O resource with a locking feature. The EISA bus master can access a semaphore on an accessed resource while preventing other resources from accessing the same semaphore. The rules for activating the LOCK* signal line are as follows:

1. The accessed resource must be EISA memory and I/O compatible.

2. A maximum of 8 bytes of memory or I/O address locations can be accessed during a single active LOCK* signal line pulse. The access must be within an eight byte alignment boundary.

3. The byte access must be done in a read-modify-write fashion.

4. All of the access within a single active LOCK* signal line pulse must be all memory or all I/O.

5. The EISA bus master must not drive the LOCK* signal line active if the associated MAKx* signal line is inactive.

6. An EISA bus master must not drive the LOCK* signal line active if an 8 data bit EISA memory is accessed. An 8 data bit EISA memory resource uses ISA compatible signal lines, including the IOCHRDY signal line. If the MAKx* signal line is inactive just after the LOCK* signal line is driven inactive, it is possible that the entire read-modify-write sequence cannot be completed before a bus time out has occurred.

7. Independent of the bus master or accessed resource data size, sufficient access cycles (single or multiple) are needed to access the entire semaphore size.

8. An active LOCK* signal line can occur for any access cycle EXCEPT for EISA compressed or burst, E-MIX, and I-MIX access cycles.

If the LOCK* signal line is sampled active at the last rising edge of the BCLK signal line when the START* signal line is active, the cycle is locked. A sequence of locked cycles also occurs if the bus master is the platform CPU and the LOCK* signal line is sampled active at the first rising edge of the BCLK signal line when the CMD* signal line is active. The sequence of locked cycles is terminated under two conditions: (1) The LOCK* signal line is sampled inactive at the last rising edge of the BCLK signal line of an active CMD* signal line pulse, OR (2) the LOCK* signal line is sampled inactive at the last rising edge of the BCLK signal line when the START* signal line is active.

6.5 BACK TO BACK PROTOCOL

There are timing restrictions from the end of one access cycle to the beginning of the next. Table 6-29 outlines an EISA bus master accessing bus resources. The entries in the table represent the number of BCLK signal line periods between an inactive CMD* signal line of the present cycle to an active START* signal line of the next cycle.

EISA BUS MASTER BACK TO BACK TIMING		BCLK SIGNAL LINE PERIODS NEXT CYCLE		
		EISA MEM, I/O	EISA DATA-MATCHING MEM, I/O	E-MIX STANDARD AND DATA-MATCHING MEM, I/O
PRESENT CYCLE	EISA MEM, I/O	0	0	0
	EISA DATA-MATCHING MEM, I/O	1	1	1
	E-MIX STANDARD AND DATA-MATCHING MEM, I/O	1	1	1

TABLE 6-29: EISA BUS MASTER BACK TO BACK TIMING

NOTES:

For the data-matching cycle, the "internal" cycles have a CMD* signal line inactive to START* signal line active.
The START* signal line active is relative to the rising edge of the BCLK signal line.
The BCLK signal line period is defined as 120 nanoseconds.

Table 6-30 shows the case of an ISA or E-ISA bus master accessing bus resources. The entries in the table represent the number of BCLK signal line periods between an inactive COMMAND signal line of the present cycle to an active COMMAND signal line of the next cycle. (COMMAND signal lines are SMEMR*, SMEMW*, MEMR*, MEMW*, IOR*, and IOW*.)

ISA OR E-ISA BUS MASTER BACK TO BACK TIMING		BCLK SIGNAL LINE PERIODS NEXT CYCLE	
		ISA, E-ISA, I-MIX MEMORY	ISA, E-ISA, I-MIX I/O
PRESENT CYCLE	ISA, E-ISA, I-MIX MEMORY	1.5 (1)	1.5
	ISA, E-ISA, I-MIX I/O	1.5 (1)	2.5

TABLE 6-30: ISA OR E-ISA BUS MASTER BACK TO BACK TIMING

Please see the Notes on the next page.

NOTES:

(1) If the next cycle is to a 16 data bit memory resource, the entry is one (1) BCLK signal line period.

The BCLK signal line period is defined as 120 nanoseconds.

Some chip sets allow longer programmable minimum back to back timings for I/O to I/O resources. This programmability allows for the support of older PC and XT add-on cards that may need additional time.   The 2.5 number in Table 6-30 reflects the EISA Rev. 3.12 specification. For E-MIX I/O cycles in Table 6-29, the "1" number for CMD* to START* results in a "2.5" number for IOW* and IOR* signal lines.

Notes

Notes

CHAPTER SEVEN

DMA TRANSFER BUS CYCLES

This Chapter consists of the following Subchapters:

7.0 GENERAL INFORMATION
7.1 DMA TRANSFER CYCLES ON ISA and E-ISA
     PLATFORMS
7.2 DMA TRANSFER CYCLES ON EISA PLATFORMS
7.3 DMA MODES
7.4 DRQx AND TC CONSIDERATIONS

7.0 GENERAL INFORMATION

The DMA transfer cycles are only executed by the platform DMA controller to transfer data between memory and I/O resources.

On an ISA compatible platform, signal lines during transfer cycles become active and inactive independent of the BCLK signal line. Only one type of transfer cycle, COMPATIBLE, is supported on an ISA compatible platform. As described in Chapter 4, specific DACKx* signal lines are defined for 8 data bit I/O resources, and others are specific for 16 data bit I/O resources. The memory resource for a transfer cycle with an 8 data bit I/O resource can be either 8 or 16 data bits in width. The platform circuitry will swap the bytes between high and low DATA signal lines as needed. The memory resource for a 16 data bit I/O resource must always be a 16 data bit resource.

On an E-ISA compatible platform, some of the signal lines are referenced to the BCLK signal line. COMPATIBLE transfer cycles are executed between ISA and E-ISA resources in the same fashion as the ISA compatible platform. However, the E-ISA platform can execute two additional types of transfer cycles between ISA or E-ISA add-on I/O cards and platform memory resources. These two additional types of transfer cycles are TYPE A and TYPE B. Each channel can be programmed for COMPATIBLE, TYPE A, or TYPE B transfer cycles and an 8 or 16 bit I/O resource, and the direction of the TC signal line.

On an EISA compatible platform, some of the signal lines become active and inactive independent of the BCLK signal line, and some do not. The EISA platform executes COMPATIBLE transfer cycles between ISA or E-ISA resources in the same fashion as on an ISA or E-ISA compatible platform. The EISA platform also executes TYPE A and TYPE B transfer cycles between ISA or E-ISA add-on I/O cards and platform memory resources in the same fashion as on an E-ISA compatible platform. As on the E-ISA compatible platform, each channel can be programmed for COMPATIBLE, TYPE A, or TYPE B transfer cycles, an 8 or 16 bit I/O resource and the direction of the TC signal line.

The EISA compatible platform also supports transfer cycle features beyond those possible on ISA and E-ISA compatible platforms. First, TYPE A, and TYPE B transfer cycles are supported between ISA or E-ISA memory and I/O add-on slave cards. Second, COMPATIBLE, TYPE A, and TYPE B transfer cycles are supported between ISA I/O add-on slave cards and EISA memory add-on slave cards and platform memory. Third, the EISA compatible platform defines an additional transfer cycle, called TYPE C (also called BURST) between EISA compatible memory and I/O resources. Fourth, the data size of the memory resource can be smaller than the data size of the I/O resource.

Each type of transfer cycle for any of the platforms comes in two versions: standard and ready. The difference between the two versions is the length of the cycle, which is controlled through the use of the IOCHRDY or EXRDY signal lines.

There are two ways to execute transfer cycles: fly-by and non-fly-by. In a fly-by operation, data is read from the source at the same time it is written to the destination. The data in a fly-by operation is never held or modified by the DMA controller. The fly-by transfer cycle only supplies a single value on the ADDRESS signal lines during each transfer cycle. This address is only valid for the memory resource of the cycle. The I/O resources receive only an active DACKx* signal line to indicate which I/O resource participates in the cycle. This is in contrast to a non-fly-by transfer where data is read from the source by the DMA controller, and subsequently, the DMA controller executes a separate cycle to write data to the destination. Between the two cycles, the DMA controller holds the data and can view or modify it. The two individual cycles allow separate valid values on the ADDRESS signal lines; consequently, transfer cycles between memory and memory, and memory and I/O can be supported. The ISA, E-ISA, EISA platforms only execute the fly-by transfer cycles.

On an EISA compatible platform, when the data size of the memory resource is smaller than the I/O resource, data is "held" by the platform circuitry as part of the "CONVERSION" operation. Even though data is "held", by definition only fly-by transfers between memory and I/O resources are supported.

Finally, transfer cycles on all the platforms can be executed under four modes of the DMA controller: single mode, block mode, demand mode, or cascade mode.

7.1 DMA TRANSFER CYCLE ON ISA and E-ISA PLATFORMS

The basic transfer cycle is focused on the I/O resource. It is assumed that the memory resource operates in the same fashion during a transfer cycle as it does during an access cycle. Thus, all of the memory parameters listed in Table 7-1-A are from Tables 6-1-A and 6-1-B with a few exceptions.

Table 7-1-A has several key pieces of information. First, the "#/DET" (parameter number / detail) column relates the parameter number of the table to Figure 7-1. Second, it defines the detail information on how the number was derived. The timing numbers are affected by the settling time on the bus. The table is based on the default values for 8 slots as outlined in chapter 10. The #/DET interpretations are shown on the page following Figure 7-1-A.

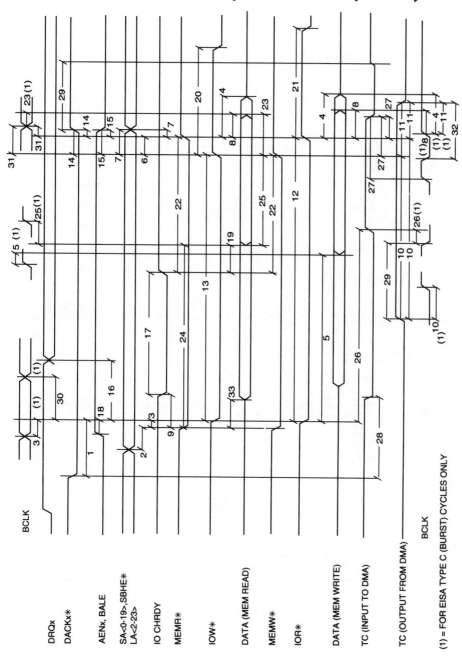

FIGURE 7-1-A TRANSFER CYCLE

DETAIL	INTERPRETATION
#	NO SETTLING TIME INCLUDED.
#/A	SKEW OF TWO SIGNALS BETWEEN RESOURCES. ONE HAS A DELAY OF 0 NANOSECONDS, AND THE OTHER HAS A DELAY OF 11 NANOSECONDS.
#/B	SIGNAL IS DRIVEN BY ONE RESOURCE TO ANOTHER. THE SECOND RESOURCE MUST RESPOND BY DRIVING A SIGNAL BACK TO THE FIRST RESOURCE. # INCLUDES THE "ROUND TRIP" TIME OF 11 + 11 = 22 NANOSECONDS.
#/C	SAME AS "B", EXCEPT THE RESOURCES RELY ON A 1K OHM PULL-UP RESISTOR. # INCLUDES THE "ROUND TRIP" TIME OF 11 + 78 = 89 NANOSECONDS FOR AN ISA COMPATIBLE PLATFORM. FOR AN E-ISA OR EISA COMPATIBLE PLATFORM, THE EXTRA CAPACITANCE ADDS 26 NANOSECONDS.
#/D	SAME AS "B", EXCEPT ONE OF THE RESOURCES RELIES ON A 300 OHM PULL-UP RESISTOR. # INCLUDES THE "ROUND TRIP" TIME OF 11 + 22 = 33 NANOSECONDS FOR AN ISA COMPATIBLE PLATFORM. FOR AN E-ISA OR EISA COMPATIBLE PLATFORM, THE EXTRA CAPACITANCE ADDS 7 NANOSECONDS.
#/E	SAME AS "A", EXCEPT THE WORST CASE INTERPRETATION IS THAT BOTH SIGNALS ARE EITHER 0 NANOSECONDS OR 11 NANOSECONDS. THE NET RESULT IS A DIFFERENCE OF 0 NANOSECONDS.

"DRIVEN BY" AND "MEASURED AT" INTERPRETATION

ADD-ON	ADD-ON CARD OR PLATFORM RESOURCE
PLAT	PLATFORM CIRCUITRY
SOURCE	ADD-ON CARD OR PLATFORM RESOURCE THAT PROVIDES THE DATA
DESTIN	ADD-ON CARD OR PLATFORM RESOURCE THAT ACCEPTS THE DATA
DMA	PLATFORM DMA CONTROLLER.

MIN. AND MAX. INTERPRETATION

ALL TIMES ARE IN NANOSECONDS WITH AN 8.00 MHZ BCLK.
THE NUMBER IN "[ ]" REFLECTS THE CALCULATED VALUE FOR AN 8.33 MHZ BCLK.

EISA INTERPRETATION

THE "EISA" ENTRIES ARE ACCORDING TO THE EISA REV. 3.12 BUS SPECIFICATION.

SMEMR* AND SMEMW*

SMEMR* AND SMEMW* SIGNAL LINES HAVE A 21 NANOSECOND DELAY FROM MEMR* AND MEMW* SIGNAL LINES (36 NANOSECONDS ACCORDING TO THE EISA REV. 3.12 BUS SPECIFICATION). THE ENTRIES IN THE TABLE ARE REFERENCED TO THE MEMR* AND MEMW* SIGNAL LINES.

REF# /DET	DESCRIPTION OF EVENT	DRIVEN BY	MEASURED AT	MIN [8.33]	MAX [8.33]	EISA
1/A	DACKx* ACTIVE TO IOR* ACTIVE	DMA	SOURCE	67 [62]		66
	DACKx* ACTIVE TO IOW* ACTIVE	DMA	DESTIN	316 [301]		306
2/A	ADDRESS VALID TO MEMORY COMMAND ACTIVE	DMA	SOURCE DESTIN			
	8 BIT			91 [89]		88
	16 BIT			28 [23]		24
3/A	IOR* ACTIVE TO MEMW* ACTIVE	DMA	SOURCE DESTIN	244 [234]		NOT SPEC
	MEMR* ACTIVE TO IOW* ACTIVE (SEE NOTE 1)	DMA	SOURCE DESTIN	-26 [-26]		
4	DATA FLOAT FROM ACTIVE READ COMMAND	SOURCE	SOURCE		50 [50]	50
5/B	DATA VALID FROM IOR* ACTIVE	SOURCE	SOURCE		220 [215]	218
5		SOURCE	DESTIN		242 [237]	
6/A	IOR* COMMAND ACTIVE HOLD FROM MEMW* COMMAND INACTIVE (SEE NOTE 1)	DMA	SOURCE DESTIN	31 [29]		NOT SPEC
6/A	MEMR* COMMAND ACTIVE HOLD FROM IOW* COMMAND INACTIVE (SEE NOTE 1)	DMA	SOURCE DESTIN	31 [29]		NOT SPEC
7	LA<17-23>, SA<0-19>, & SBHE* VALID HOLD FROM MEMORY COMMAND INACTIVE	DMA	SOURCE DESTIN	30 [30]		30
8	READ DATA VALID HOLD FROM INACTIVE MEMORY COMMAND	SOURCE	SOURCE	0 [0]		0
9	IOCHRDY VALID FROM MEM. COMMAND ACTIVE (SEE NOTE 2) 8 BITS OLD "AT"	SOURCE DESTIN	DMA		217 [202]	NOT SPEC
	16 BITS				83 [78]	

TABLE 7-1-A: COMPATIBLE TRANSFER CYCLE TIMINGS

REF# /DET	DESCRIPTION OF EVENT	DRIVEN BY	MEASURED AT	MIN	MAX [8,33]	EISA
9	IOCHRDY VALID FROM MEM. COMMAND ACTIVE (SEE NOTE 2) 8 BITS NEW E-ISA & EISA 16 BITS	SOURCE DESTIN	DMA		210 [200] 142 [135]	NOT SPEC
9/B	IOCHRDY INACTIVE FROM MEM. ACTIVE COMMAND (SEE NOTE 2,4) 8 BITS OLD "AT" 16 BITS	SOURCE DESTIN	SOURCE DESTIN		195 [180] 61 [56]	188 86
9/B	IOCHRDY INACTIVE FROM MEM. ACTIVE COMMAND (SEE NOTE 2,5) 8 BITS NEW E-ISA & EISA 16 BITS	SOURCE DESTIN	SOURCE DESTIN		188 [178] 120 [115]	188 86
9/C	IOCHRDY ACTIVE FROM MEM. ACTIVE COMMAND (SEE NOTE 2,4) 8 BITS OLD "AT" 1K PULL-UP 16 BITS ON PLATFORM	SOURCE DESTIN	SOURCE DESTIN		128 [113] 34 [29]	NOT SPEC
9/D	IOCHRDY ACTIVE FROM MEM. ACTIVE COMMAND (SEE NOTE 2,4) 8 BITS OLD "AT" 300 PULL-UP 16 BITS ON PLATFORM	SOURCE DESTIN	SOURCE DESTIN		174 [159] 90 [85]	NOT SPEC
9/C	IOCHRDY ACTIVE FROM MEM. ACTIVE COMMAND (SEE NOTE 2,5) 8 BITS NEW E-ISA & EISA 1K PULL-UP 16 BITS ON PLATFORM	SOURCE DESTIN	SOURCE DESTIN		95 [85] 67 [60]	NOT SPEC

TABLE 7-1-A: COMPATIBLE TRANSFER CYCLE TIMINGS (CONTINUED)

REF# /DET	DESCRIPTION OF EVENT	DRIVEN BY	MEASURED AT	MIN [8,33]	MAX	EISA
9/D	IOCHRDY ACTIVE FROM MEM. ACTIVE COMMAND (SEE NOTE 2,5) 8 BITS NEW E-ISA & EISA 300 PULL-UP 16 BITS ON PLATFORM	SOURCE DESTIN	SOURCE DESTIN		170 [160] 149 [135]	NOT SPEC
10/A	TC ACTIVE SETUP TO IOW* INACT. (OUTPUT FROM DMA) (SEE NOTE 7)	DMA	SOURCE DESTIN	500 [500]		500
11	TC ACTIVE HOLD FROM IOW* INACT. (OUTPUT FROM DMA) (SEE NOTE 7)	DMA	SOURCE DESTIN	60 [60]		60
12/A	IOR* ACTIVE TO INACTIVE (SEE NOTE 1)	DMA	SOURCE	781 [749]		755
13/A	IOW* ACTIVE TO INACTIVE (SEE NOTE 1)	DMA	DESTIN	474 [454]		455
14/A	DACKx* ACTIVE HOLD FROM IOR* INACTIVE DACKx* ACTIVE HOLD FROM IOW* INACTIVE	DMA DMA	SOURCE DESTIN	94 [89] 151 [144]		94 150
15/A	AENx & BALE VALID FROM I/O COMMAND INACTIVE	PLAT	SOURCE DESTIN	30 [30]		
16/B	DRQx VALID DELAY FROM IOR* ACTIVE	SOURCE DESTIN	SOURCE DESTIN		558 [533]	540
16/B	DRQx VALID DELAY FROM IOW* ACTIVE	SOURCE DESTIN	SOURCE DESTIN		308 [293]	300
17	IOCHRDY INACTIVE PULSE	SOURCE DESTIN	SOURCE DESTIN	125 [120]	1.56 MICROSECONDS	
18/A	AENx AND BALE VALID TO COMMAND ACTIVE	PLAT	SOURCE DESTIN	100 [95]		NOT SPEC
19/A	VALID MEMORY READ DATA FROM IOCHRDY ACTIVE (SEE NOTE 3) 8 BITS EVEN ODD 16 BITS	SOURCE	SOURCE		74 [69] 48 [43] 74 [69]	70 49 80

TABLE 7-1-A: COMPATIBLE TRANSFER CYCLE TIMINGS (CONTINUED)

REF# /DET	DESCRIPTION OF EVENT	DRIVEN BY	MEASURED AT	MIN [8,33]	MAX	EISA
19	8 BITS EVEN	SOURCE	DESTIN		85 [80]	70
	ODD				85 [80]	70
	16 BITS				85 [80]	80
20/A	IOW* INACTIVE TO ACTIVE (SEE NOTE 1)	DMA	DESTIN	474 [454]		455
21/A	IOR* INACTIVE TO ACTIVE (SEE NOTE 1)	DMA	DESTIN	156 [149]		165
22/E	MEMORY COMMAND ACTIVE HOLD FROM IOCHRDY ACTIVE	DMA	SOURCE DESTIN	125 [120]		120
23/A	WRITE DATA VALID HOLD FROM INACTIVE I/O COMMAND	SOURCE	DESTIN	25 [25]		22
24/B	VALID READ 8 BITS EVEN DATA FROM MEMORY COMMAND ODD ACTIVE (NOTES 3,6) 16 BITS	SOURCE	SOURCE		325 [310] 299 [284] 173 [165]	NOT SPEC
24	VALID READ DATA 8 BITS FROM MEMORY COMMAND ACTIVE 16 BITS (SEE NOTE 6)	SOURCE	DESTIN		347 [332] 195 [185]	NOT SPEC
25/B	DATA VALID TO IOW* INACTIVE (SEE NOTE 6,12)	SOURCE	DESTIN	138 [133]		140
26/B	TC VALID FROM IOR* ACTIVE (INPUT TO DMA) (SEE NOTE 7)	SOURCE	SOURCE		560 [560]	560
	TC VALID FROM IOW* ACTIVE (INPUT TO DMA)(7)	DESTIN	DESTIN		320 [320]	320
27	TC VALID HOLD FROM IOR* INACTIVE (INPUT TO DMA)	SOURCE	SOURCE	91 [88]		80
27	TC VALID HOLD FROM IOW* INACT (INPUT TO DMA) (9)	DESTIN	DESTIN	90 [90]		90
29/A	TC ACT/INACT FROM DACKx* INACT.	SOURCE DESTIN	SOURCE DESTIN		40	40
33	DATA DRIVEN FROM READ COMMAND ACTIVE	SOURCE	DESTIN	0 [0]		0

TABLE 7-1-A: COMPATIBLE TRANSFER CYCLE TIMINGS (CONTINUED)
(PARAMETERS 28, 30, 31, AND 32 ARE IN TABLE 7-9, PAGE 396.)

REF#/DET	DESCRIPTION OF EVENT	DRIVEN BY	MEASURED AT	TYPE A MIN [8.33]	TYPE A MAX [8.33]	EISA	TYPE B MIN [8.33]	TYPE B MAX [8.33]	EISA
1/A	DACKx* ACTIVE TO IOR* ACTIVE	DMA	SOURCE	67 [62]		66	67 [62]		66
	DACKx* ACTIVE TO IOW* ACTIVE	DMA	DESTIN	191 [181]		186	191 [181]		186
4	DATA FLOAT FROM ACTIVE READ COMMAND	SOURCE	SOURCE		50 [50]	50		50 [50]	50
5	DATA VALID FROM IOR* ACTIVE	SOURCE	DESTIN		306 [296]	280		186 [176]	160
5/B		SOURCE	SOURCE		294 [284]			173 [163]	
8	READ DATA VALID HOLD FROM INACTIVE CMD*	SOURCE	SOURCE	2 [2]		2	2 [2]		2
10/A	TC ACT. SETUP TO IOR* INACT(OUTPUT FRM DMA) (SEE NOTE 7,11)	DMA	SOURCE DESTIN	300 [300]		300	200 [200]		200
11	TC ACT. HOLD FRM IOR* INACT(OUTPUT FRM DMA) SEE NOTE 7 FOR TYPE A	DMA	SOURCE DESTIN	60 [60]		60	-25 [-25]		-31
10/A	TC ACT. SETUP TO IOW* INACT.(OUT. FROM DMA) (SEE NOTE 7)	DMA	SOURCE DESTIN	240 [240]		240	180 [180]		180
11	TC ACT. HOLD FRM IOW* INACT.(OUT. FROM DMA) (SEE NOTE 7)	DMA	SOURCE DESTIN	60 [60]		60	-31 [-31]		-31
12/A	IOR* ACT. TO INACTIVE (SEE NOTES 1, 10)	DMA	SOURCE	531 [509]		395	406 [389]		275
13/A	IOW* ACT. TO INACTIVE (SEE NOTE 1)	DMA	DESTIN	349 [334]		335	211 [201]		215
14/A	DACKx* ACT. HOLD FROM IOR* INACTIVE	DMA	SOURCE	94 [89]		94	94 [89]		29
	DACKx* ACT. HOLD FROM IOW* INACTIVE	DMA	DESTIN	151 [144]		150	151 [144]		94
15/A	AENx VALID FROM I/O COMMAND INACTIVE	PLAT	SOURCE DESTIN	30 [30]					NOT SPEC

TABLE 7-1-B: TYPE A AND B TRANSFER CYCLE TIMINGS

REF# /DET	DESCRIPTION OF EVENT	DRIVEN BY	MEASURED AT	TYPE A MIN [8.33]	MAX	EISA	TYPE B MIN [8.33]	MAX	EISA
16/B	DRQx VALID DELAY FROM IOR* ACTIVE	SOURCE DESTIN	SOURCE DESTIN		308 [293]	300		183 [173]	180
16/B	DRQx VALID DELAY FROM IOW* ACTIVE	SOURCE DESTIN	SOURCE DESTIN		183 [173]	180		58 [53]	60
18/A	AENx VALID TO I/O COMMAND ACTIVE	PLAT	SOURCE DESTIN	100 [95]		NOT SPEC	100 [95]		NOT SPEC
20/A	IOW* INACTIVE TO ACT. (SEE NOTE 1)	DMA	DESTIN	349 [334]		335	224 [214]		215
21/A	IOR* INACTIVE TO ACT. (SEE NOTE 1)	DMA	DESTIN	156 [149]		165	31 [29]		50
23/A	WRITE DATA VALID HOLD FROM INACT. I/O CMND	SOURCE	DESTIN	25 [25]		20	25 [25]		20
25/A	DATA VALID TO IOW* INACTIVE	SOURCE	DESTIN	258 [246]		240	133 [126]		130
26/B	TC VALID FROM IOR* ACTIVE (INPUT TO DMA) (SEE NOTE 7)	SOURCE	SOURCE		320 [320]	320		180 [180]	180
26/B	TC VALID FROM IOW* ACTIVE (INPUT TO DMA) (SEE NOTE 7)	DESTIN	DESTIN		200 [200]	200		60 [60]	60
27	TC VALID HLD FRM IOR* INACT. (INPUT TO DMA) SEE NOTE 7 FOR TYPE B	SOURCE	SOURCE	91 [87]		80	18 [18]		18
27	TC VALID HLD FRM IOW* INACT. (INPUT TO DMA) SEE NOTE 7 FOR TYPE B SEE NOTE 9 FOR TYPE A	DESTIN	DESTIN	90 [90]		90	80 [80]		80
29/A	TC ACT/INACT FROM DACKx* INACT.	SOURCE DESTIN	SOURCE DESTIN		40	40		40	40

TABLE 7-1-B: TYPE A AND B TRANSFER CYCLE TIMINGS (CONTINUED)
(PARAMETERS 28, 30, 31, AND 32 ARE IN TABLE 7-9, PAGE 396.)

NOTES for TABLE 7-1-A and 7-1-B:

(1) The entry assumes a 15 nanosecond same package skew between high/low and low/high transitions with an 11 or 22 nanosecond bus delay. If same package skew is 0 nanoseconds, the entries increase by 15 nanoseconds.

(2) If possible, use the smaller of the numbers from each section (OLD "AT" vs NEW E-ISA and EISA).

(3) The number used in the table for the ODD byte has been decreased by 26 nanoseconds from the EVEN byte number. This allows for byte swapping overhead.

(4) Use this number for ISA or E-ISA add-on cards installed in ISA platforms. This number assumes a 15 pf per slot load.

(5) Use this number for ISA or E-ISA add-on cards installed in E-ISA and EISA platforms (or for 8 data bit EISA memory add-on cards installed in EISA platforms). This number assumes a 20pf per slot load.

(6) The 8 bit entries in the table would be 157 nanoseconds longer except for the requirement to meet parameter 25.

(7) The entry in the table is the one required by the EISA Rev. 3.12 bus specification. The Intel 358DT chip set provides more "liberal" timing.

(9) The entry in the table is the one required by the EISA Rev. 3.12 bus specification. The Intel 358DT chip set requires 148 [143] nanoseconds.

(10) For conversion cycles (if supported by the platform), the IOR* signal line active pulse will be shortened as follows: 531 [509] becomes 406 [389], and 406 [389] becomes 281 [269].

(11) For conversion cycles (if supported by the platform), the IOR* signal line active pulse will be shortened; consequently, the TC setup time is shortened as follows: 388 [371] becomes 263 [251], and 263 [251] becomes 138 [131].

(12) For a 16 data bit transfer only, the numbers would be 290 [280]. Traditionally, however, no distinction has been made between 8 and 16 data bit transfers, so the entries in the table apply to both.

STANDARD VERSION OF THE COMPATIBLE TRANSFER CYCLE ON AN ISA PLATFORM

The standard version of the COMPATIBLE transfer cycle (abbreviated here to COMPATIBLE transfer cycle) is executed only by the platform DMA controller. The data transfer can be from I/O to memory (see Figure 7-1-B) or from memory to I/O (see Figure 7-1-C). The resource providing the data is defined as the "source". The resource receiving the data is defined as the "destination".

Figures 7-1-B and 7-1-C define how the DMA controller and platform circuitry view COMPATIBLE transfer cycles. There is no corresponding figure or table to relate the "timing marks" to actual numbers because the DMA controller is a unique part of the platform circuitry. Figures 7-1-A, B, and C and 7-3 in conjunction with Table 7-1-A provide the appropriate information to understand COMPATIBLE transfer cycles and the design requirements for an add-on card. The key concepts for COMPATIBLE transfer cycles are as follows: the memory resource operates with the timings and control lines in the native mode of the memory resource (see Table 7-1-A for some exceptions); the I/O resource operates independent of the BCLK signal line as outlined in the following paragraphs.

The request for a COMPATIBLE transfer cycle must be made by the I/O add-on slave card activating one of the DRQx signal lines. At some unspecified time later, the DMA controller will acknowledge the beginning of a series of transfer cycles with the I/O resource by activating the associated DACKx* signal line. (See Figures 7-1-B, C and 7-3.) Before the series of COMPATIBLE transfer cycles can begin, the AENx and BALE signal lines must be driven active by the platform circuitry. An

X = SAMPLE DATA, (1) = FOR INPUT TO DMA CONTROLLER, (2) = SAMPLE WINDOW E-ISA & EISA ONLY
(3) = NEEDED FOR BYTE SWAPPING, (4) = PER EISA SPEC, (5) EISA COMPATIBLE PLATFORM ONLY, (6) = PER "AT"

FIGURE 7-1-B: *ISA, E-ISA & EISA STANDARD AND READY COMPATIBLE TRANSFER CYCLE . . . DMA CONTROLLER AND PLATFORM CIRCUITRY VIEWPOINT*

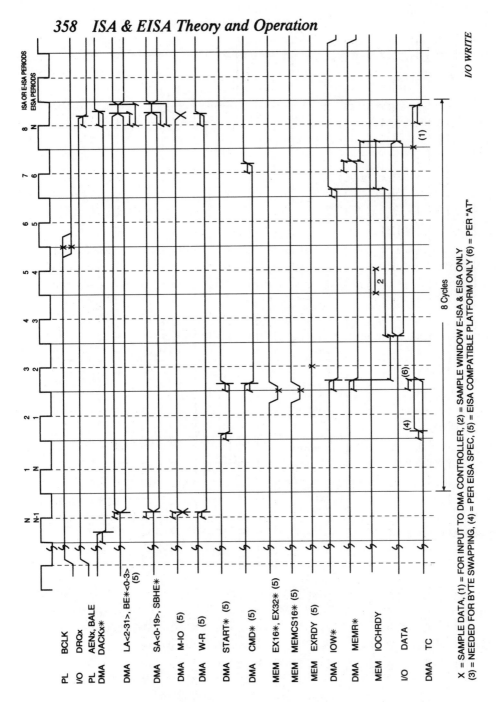

FIGURE   7-1-C: ISA, E-ISA, & EISA STANDARD AND READY COMPATIBLE
TRANSFER CYCLE . . . DMA CONTROLLER AND PLATFORM
CIRCUITRY VIEWPOINT

active AENx signal line indicates to all other I/O resources that the forthcoming activity on the ADDRESS and COMMAND (IOR* and IOW*) signal lines must be ignored.

Only the I/O resource that receives the active DACKx* signal line may participate in the transfer, and may respond to an active COMMAND signal line. The memory resource that participates in the COMPATIBLE transfer cycle is identified by a valid value on the ADDRESS signal lines. An active BALE signal line allows the input circuitry of the add-on memory slave card to receive the valid address. (See the BALE signal line definition in Chapter 5 for more information.)

After the AENx, BALE, and DACKx* signal lines have been driven active, the series of COMPATIBLE transfer cycles can begin. To begin a standard transfer cycle on an ISA compatible platform, the SA<0-19>, LA<17-23>, and SBHE* signal lines are driven by the DMA controller. (NOTE: Because the DMA controller is a unique portion of the platform circuitry by definition, all ADDRESS and some of the ISA CONTROL signal lines are driven by the DMA controller.) Programming of the DMA controller determines the COMPATIBLE transfer direction and data width for the cycle. As described in Chapter 5, specific DACKx* lines are defined for 8 bit I/O resources, and others are specific for 16 bit I/O resources.

The activation of the memory COMMAND signal lines by the DMA controller indicates the direction of the transfer, and that the ADDRESS signal lines are valid. The focus of a transfer cycle is the I/O resource. When the transfer is from the memory to the I/O resource, the data must be valid relative to the deactivation of the IOW* signal line.   The memory resource must match this timing. When the transfer is from the I/O resource to the memory resource, the data must be valid within a specific time of the IOR* signal line active The memory resource must match this timing.

A memory resource in an 8 bit slot must monitor the SMEMR* and SMEMW* signal lines. If either line is active, only the first one megabyte of the memory address space is being accessed. For a memory resource in an 8/16 bit slot, the LA<20-23>, MEMR*, and MEMW* signal lines are available to address the memory address space beyond the first megabyte.

The cycle length of the standard COMPATIBLE transfer cycle that actually transfers data is independent of the width of the data transferred. The SRDY* signal line (NOWS*) is not monitored. Table 7-3 outlines the approximate cycle lengths for the portion of the standard version of the COMPATIBLE transfer cycle that actually transfers data for different platforms. The minimum cycle length, in terms of TCLK (period of BCLK) is also summarized. Due to bus settling times and device delays, TCLK should be considered as approximate for the "CYCLE BEGINS" column.

PLAT.	CYCLE TYPE	CYCLE BEGINS	CYCLE ENDS	CYCLE LENGTH(2)	CYCLE LENGTH(3)	ADD-ON SLAVE CARD
ISA	COMPAT.	IOR* ACT. OR	1 TCLK AFTER IOR* INACT. OR	8 TCLK	9 TCLK	MEM, I/O
E-ISA	COMPAT.	2 TCLK TO IOW* ACT.	2 TCLK AFTER IOW* INACT.	8 TCLK	9 TCLK	MEM, I/O
E-ISA	TYPE A	IOR* ACT. OR	1 TCLK AFTER IOR* INACT. OR	6 TCLK	7 TCLK	I/O
E-ISA	TYPE B	1 TCLK TO IOW* ACT.	2 TCLK AFTER IOW* INACT.(1)	4 TCLK	6 TCLK	I/O

TABLE 7-3: CYCLE LENGTH OF STANDARD TRANSFER CYCLES

Please see the Notes on the following page.

NOTES:
(1) For TYPE B, IOR* is inactive for one TCLK after IOW* inactive.
(2) For the repetitive portions of demand and block transfers.
(3) For the initial cycle of demand and block modes or a single transfer cycle.

The actual number of cycles in which data is transferred for a given DMA session is dependent on how the channel is programmed and the relative activity of the of the DRQx and DACKx* signal lines. Please see Sub-chapter 7.3, DMA MODES, for further information.

When all of the data bytes that were programmed to be transferred have been transferred, the DMA controller drives the TC signal line active. The I/O resource monitors the TC signal line relative to the IOR* or IOW* signal line. For an ISA platform the TC signal line can only be driven by the DMA controller.

Another important consideration of COMPATIBLE transfer cycles on an ISA compatible platform is that the data size of the participants must match. The data size of the memory resource must be equal to or greater than the data size of the I/O resource. The MEMCS16* and IOCS16* signal lines are not used to determine data sizing. The data size of the I/O resource is programmed into the DMA controller prior to the transfer cycle beginning, with the software assuming properly matched resources.

Table 7-4 provides a summary of key attributes of a transfer cycle on an ISA platform. (This is a reprint of the same table in Chapter 3 ... it is reprinted here for convenience).

PLATFORM	PARTICIPANTS MEMORY : I/O	TRANSFER TYPES COMP	"A"	"B"	"C"	TC (1)	RESOURCE SIZE MEM:I/O		TRANSFER SIZE	DEMAND & BLOCK TRANSFER INTERRUPTIBLE
PC, XT	PC,XT : PC,XT	YES	NO	NO	NO	UNI	8	8	8	NO
AT	PC,XT : PC,XT	YES	NO	NO	NO	UNI	8	8	8	NO
	PC,XT : AT	YES	NO	NO	NO	UNI	8	8	8	NO
	AT : PC,XT	YES	NO	NO	NO	UNI	8/16	8	8	NO
	AT : AT	YES	NO	NO	NO	UNI	8/16	8	8	NO
							16	16	16	NO

TABLE 7-4: ISA COMPATIBLE PLATFORM DMA TRANSFER CYCLES

NOTES:
(1) TC = Terminal Count; UNI = UNIdirectional ... DMA controller to I/O resource; BI = BIdirectional.

STANDARD VERSIONS OF THE COMPATIBLE, TYPE A, AND TYPE B TRANSFER CYCLES ON AN E-ISA PLATFORM

The E-ISA compatible platform has expanded the different types of transfer cycles that can be executed. In addition to the previously described COMPATIBLE transfer cycle, there are also TYPE A and B. As outlined in Chapter 3, TYPE A and TYPE B transfer cycles are simply shorter versions of the COMPATIBLE transfer cycle.

The E-ISA platform distributes the BCLK signal in a "starburst" pattern like the EISA platform. Thus, additional signal lines can be referenced to the BCLK signal lines.

For clarity, Figure 7-2 and Table 7-5 have been included. These are additional timing relationships that are specific to understanding transfer cycles on E-ISA and EISA platforms, and will be useful for gaining a more complete understanding.

DETAIL   INTERPRETATION

\#   NO SETTLING TIME INCLUDED.

\#/A   SKEW OF TWO SIGNALS BETWEEN RESOURCES. ONE HAS A DELAY OF
                  0 NANOSECONDS, AND THE OTHER HAS A DELAY OF 11
                  NANOSECONDS.

"DRIVEN BY" AND "MEASURED AT" INTERPRETATION

SOURCE   ADD-ON CARD OR PLATFORM RESOURCE THAT PROVIDES THE DATA.
DESTIN   ADD-ON CARD OR PLATFORM RESOURCE THAT ACCEPTS THE DATA.
DMA   PLATFORM DMA CONTROLLER.

MIN. AND MAX. INTERPRETATION

ALL TIMES ARE IN NANOSECONDS

EISA INTERPRETATION

THE "EISA" ENTRIES ARE ACCORDING TO THE EISA REV. 3.12 BUS SPECIFICATION.

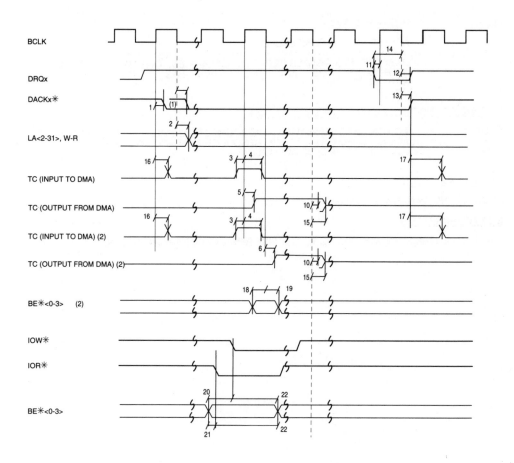

X = SAMPLE POINT

(1) = DACK✻ WILL OCCUR ON FALLING EDGE FOR DMA.

DACK✻ WILL OCCUR ON RISING EDGE FOR ISA MASTER

(2) = BURST TRANSFER CYCLES

(3) = FOR TYPE A & B TRANSFER CYCLE (OR FIRST PART OF BURST BEFORE BURST IS DETERMINED)

NOTE: ANY TIMING RELATIONSHIPS NOT LISTED ARE THE SAME AS FOR ACCESS TIMING

*FIGURE 7-2:   TRANSFER CYCLE . . . ADDITIONAL TIMING RELATIONSHIPS
ON E-ISA AND EISA COMPATIBLE PLATFORMS*

REF# /DET	DESCRIPTION OF EVENT	DRIVEN BY	MEASURED AT	MIN	MAX	EISA
1	DACKx* ACTIVE FROM BCLK RISING OR FALLING EDGE	DMA	DMA		50	50
1/A		DMA	SRCE/DEST		60	
2	LA<2-31>, W-R, BE*<0-3> VALID FROM BCLK RISING EDGE (EISA PLAT. ONLY)	DMA	DMA		50	50
2/A		DMA	SOURCE/ DESTIN.		61	
3	TC VALID SETUP TO BCLK RISING EDGE	SOURCE/ DESTIN.	DMA	15		15
3/A		SOURCE/ DESTIN.	SOURCE/ DESTIN.	26		
4	TC VALID HOLD FROM BCLK RISING EDGE	SOURCE/ DESTIN.	DMA	15		25
4		SOURCE/ DESTIN.	SOURCE/ DESTIN.	15		
5	TC VALID DELAY FROM BCLK RISING EDGE	DMA	DMA		40	35
5/A		DMA	SOURCE/ DESTIN.		51	
6	TC VALID DELAY FROM BCLK FALLING EDGE	DMA	DMA		40	35
6/A		DMA	SOURCE/ DESTIN.		51	
10	TC VALID HOLD FROM BCLK FALLING EDGE	DMA	DMA	2		5
10		DMA	SOURCE/ DESTIN.	2		
11/A	DRQx INACTIVE SETUP TO BCLK RISING EDGE	SOURCE/ DESTIN.	SOURCE/ DESTIN.	26		15
11		SOURCE/ DESTIN.	DMA	15		
12	DRQx INACTIVE HOLD FROM BCLK FALLING EDGE	SOURCE/ DESTIN.	SOURCE/ DESTIN.	2	35	2/ 35
12		SOURCE/ DESTIN.	DMA	2	35	
13	DACKx* ACTIVE HOLD FROM BCLK FALLING EDGE	DMA	DMA	10		5
13		DMA	SOURCE/ DESTIN.	10		

TABLE 7-5: ADDITIONAL TRANSFER CYCLE TIMING RELATIONSHIPS ON E-ISA AND EISA COMPATIBLE PLATFORMS

REF# /DET	DESCRIPTION OF EVENT	DRIVEN BY	MEASURED AT	MIN MAX 8.00 & 8.33 MHZ		EISA
14/A	DRQx INACTIVE SETUP TO BCLK FALLING EDGE	SOURCE/ DESTIN.	SOURCE/ DESTIN.	91		
14		SOURCE/ DESTIN.	DMA	80		80
15	TC INACTIVE DELAY FROM BCLK FALLING EDGE	DMA	DMA	35	35	
15		DMA	SOURCE/ DESTIN.	35	35	
16	TC DRIVEN INACTIVE FROM DACKx* ACTIVE (NOTE 1)	SOURCE/ DESTIN.	SOURCE/ DESTIN.	30	120	NOT SPEC(3)
17	TC DRIVEN INACTIVE FROM DACKx* INACTIVE (NOTE 2)	DMA	SOURCE/ DESTIN.	120		120 (3)
18/A	BE* VALID SETUP TO FALLING EDGE OF BCLK	DMA	SOURCE/ DESTIN.	59		60 (4)
19	BE* VALID HOLD FROM FALLING EDGE OF BCLK	DMA	SOURCE/ DESTIN.	2		2
20/A	BE* VALID SETUP TO IOW* ACTIVE	DMA	DESTIN.	116		100 (5)
21/A	BE* VALID SETUP TO IOR* ACTIVE	DMA	SOURCE	-4		5 (5)
22	BE* VALID HOLD FROM IOR* OR IOW* ACTIVE	DMA	SOURCE/ DESTIN.	30		30

TABLE 7-5: ADDITIONAL TRANSFER CYCLE TIMING RELATIONSHIPS ON E-ISA AND EISA COMPATIBLE PLATFORMS (CONTINUED)

NOTES:
(1) When the TC signal line is programmed as an input to the DMA controller, the DMA controller will float the TC signal line. The DMA source/destination must initially drive the TC signal line inactive.
(2) When the TC signal line is programmed as an input to the DMA controller, the DMA source/destination must float it after the DACKx* signal line is driven inactive.
(3) For BCLK signal line at 8.00 MHz, 120 nanoseconds becomes 125 nanoseconds.
(4) For BCLK signal line at 8.00 MHz, 59 nanoseconds becomes 64 nanoseconds.
(5) For BCLK signal line at 8.00 MHz, 116 nanoseconds becomes 123 and -4 becomes -2 nanoseconds. For a TYPE C (BURST) transfer cycle, BE* <0-3> signal lines valid set to IOW* signal line inactive is 7 nanoseconds for an 8.33 MHz BCLK signal line. For an 8.00 MHz BCLK signal line, the number is 9 nanoseconds. Also, for a TYPE C (BURST) transfer cycle, BE* <0-3> signal line hold from IOW* signal line inactive is 30 nanoseconds.

The execution protocol of transfer cycles on an E-ISA compatible platform has been expanded over the protocol on an ISA platform for both memory and I/O add-on slave cards. The E-ISA compatible memory add-on slave cards can operate with COMPATIBLE transfer cycles. The E-ISA compatible platform supports referencing the IOCHRDY signal line to the BCLK signal line. As with E-ISA ready access cycles, establishing this relationship between these signal lines potentially improves performance. Please see the READY VERSION OF THE COMPATIBLE, TYPE A, AND TYPE B TRANSFER CYCLE ON AN E-ISA PLATFORM section for more information. Other than the IOCHRDY signal line enhancement, the E-ISA memory add-on slave card executes a COMPATIBLE transfer in the same fashion as one executed for an ISA memory add-on slave card.

The E-ISA compatible platform has expanded the DMA transfer cycle definition for E-ISA I/O add-on slave cards. The E-ISA compatible platform supports the following transfer cycle enhancements:

- The DRQx and DACKx* signal lines are referenced to the BCLK signal line. (Please see Figure 7-2 and Table 7-5.)

- Three types of DMA transfer cycles are supported: COMPATIBLE, TYPE A and TYPE B. (Please see Figures 7-1-A, B, C, 7-4-A, B, C and Tables 7-1-A and B.)

- The TC signal line is bi-directional. (Please see Figures 7-2, 7-1-A, B, C, 7-4-A, B, C, and Tables 7-5-A and B.)

Other than the previously listed transfer enhancements, the E-ISA platform executes transfer cycles in the same fashion as an ISA platform. The two new transfer cycle types (TYPE A and TYPE B) operate in the same fashion as the COMPATIBLE transfer cycle. As outlined in Chapter 3, a TYPE A or B transfer has shorter active I/O COMMAND signal line pulse widths, less data setup time to an active IOW* signal line, and the IOW* signal line becomes active earlier in the cycle. Table 7-3 summarizes the various cycle lengths for the various standard transfer cycles. Table 7-6 is a summary of the three types of transfer cycles on an E-ISA platform. As Table 7-6 indicates, the COMPATIBLE cycle can be executed by either an ISA or an E-ISA compatible platform. Any ISA add-on memory slave card can only participate in a COMPATIBLE transfer cycle. The reason the EISA bus specification introduced TYPE A and TYPE B transfer cycles is that ISA add-on I/O slave cards can transfer data faster than COMPATIBLE cycles can transfer data. The concepts are: all ISA add-on I/O slave cards can support COMPATIBLE cycles, most can support a TYPE A transfer cycle, and some can support a TYPE B transfer cycle. E-ISA add-on I/O slave cards can execute

COMPATIBLE, TYPE A, or TYPE B transfer cycles, as programmed in their respective configuration spaces.

Only the COMPATIBLE transfer cycle allows the direct transfer between ISA add-on I/O slave and memory slave cards. For TYPE A and TYPE B transfer cycles it is required that the E-ISA platform memory is the memory resource. An E-ISA compatible platform also allows each individual DMA channel to be programmed for 8 or 16 data bit transfer cycles. Finally, as with an ISA compatible platform, on an E-ISA compatible platform the data size of the memory resource must be equal to or greater than the data size of the I/O resource. Table 7-6 outlines the transfer cycles on the E-ISA platform. (This is a reprint of the same table in Chapter 3 ... it is reprinted here for convenience.)

PLATFORM	PARTICIPANTS MEMORY : I/O	TRANSFER TYPES COMP	"A"	"B"	"C"	TC (1)	RESOURCE SIZE MEM: I/O		TRANSFER SIZE	DEMAND & BLOCK TRANSFER INTERRUPTIBLE
E-ISA	PC,XT :PC,XT,AT	YES	NO	NO	NO	UNI	8	8	8	NO
	AT : PC,XT	YES	NO	NO	NO	UNI	8,16	8	8	NO
	AT : AT	YES	NO	NO	NO	UNI	8,16 16	8 16	8 16	NO
	PC,XT : E-ISA	YES	NO	NO	NO	BI	8	8	8	NO
	AT : E-ISA	YES	NO	NO	NO	BI	8,16 16	8 16	8 16	NO
	E-ISA : PC,XT (2)	YES	NO	NO	NO	UNI	8,16	8	8	NO
	E-ISA : AT (2)	YES	NO	NO	NO	UNI	8,16 16	8 16	8 16	NO
	E-ISA : E-ISA (2)	YES	NO	NO	NO	BI	8,16 16	8 16	8 16	NO
	E-ISA : PC,XT (3) (4)	YES	YES	YES	NO	UNI	8,16	8	8	YES (5)
	E-ISA : AT (3) (4)	YES	YES	YES	NO	UNI	8,16 16	8 16	8 16	YES (5)
	E-ISA : E-ISA (3) (4)	YES	YES	YES	NO	BI	8,16 16	8 16	8 16	YES (5)

TABLE 7-6: E-ISA PLATFORM DMA TRANSFER CYCLES
Please see the Notes on the next page.

NOTES:
(1)   TC = Terminal Count; UNI = UNIdirectional ... DMA controller to I/O resource; BI = BIdirectional.
(2)   E-ISA memory is an add-on slave card ONLY.
(3)   E-ISA memory is the platform memory ONLY.
(4)   MOST AT, PC, and XT DMA add-on slave cards support the TYPE A transfer cycle.   SOME AT, PC, and XT DMA add-on slave cards support the TYPE B transfer cycle.
(5)   "NO", if DMA COMPATIBLE transfer cycle.

READY VERSION OF THE COMPATIBLE TRANSFER CYCLE ON AN ISA PLATFORM

The ready version of the COMPATIBLE transfer cycle begins in the same fashion as the standard version of the COMPATIBLE transfer cycle. (Please see Figures 7-1-B, C, and 7-3.) The standard version of the COMPATIBLE transfer cycle becomes a ready version of the COMPATIBLE transfer cycle if the IOCHRDY signal line is driven inactive by the memory resource. The IOCHRDY signal line must be driven inactive within a specific time of an active memory COMMAND signal line. Other than the operation of the IOCHRDY signal line, the standard and ready versions of the COMPATIBLE transfer cycle operate in the same fashion.

As previously mentioned, the focal point of a transfer cycle is the I/O resource. On an ISA compatible platform, the cycle length is controlled only by the memory resource; consequently, data must be valid relative to active I/O COMMAND signal lines. It is the responsibility of the memory resource to control the IOCHRDY signal line to insure valid data timing during the transfer. It is the responsibility of the I/O resource to always be able to execute according to the standard version of the COMPATIBLE transfer cycle timings.

The COMMAND signal lines remain active until the IOCHRDY signal line is driven active by the memory resource. During a memory read transfer cycle, the active IOCHRDY signal line indicates to the DMA controller that valid data setup time to an inactive IOW* signal line can be met. During a write cycle, it is an indication to the DMA controller that the accessed resource has accepted the data. For either memory read or write transfer cycles, the activation of the IOCHRDY signal line is the indication to the DMA controller to complete the cycle. The transfer cycle is completed when both the memory and the I/O COMMAND signal lines are driven inactive.

The length of the ready COMPATIBLE transfer cycle is increased in increments of two BCLK signal line periods. Table 7-7 outlines the types of ready transfer cycles supported for various platforms. The minimum cycle length in terms of TCLK (period of BCLK) is also summarized. The table also shows the minimum increments of the ready cycle. See Table 7-3 for the "CYCLE BEGINS" and "CYCLE ENDS" reference points.

PLAT.	CYCLE TYPE	MIN. CYCLE LENGTH	INCREMENTS OF CYCLE	ADD-ON SLAVE CARD
ISA	COMPATIBLE	10 TCLK	2 TCLK	MEM, I/O
E-ISA	COMPATIBLE	10 TCLK	2 TCLK	MEM, I/O
E-ISA	TYPE "A"	7 TCLK	1 TCLK	I/O
E-ISA	TYPE "B"	5 TCLK	1 TCLK	I/O

TABLE 7-7: CYCLE LENGTH OF READY TRANSFER CYCLES

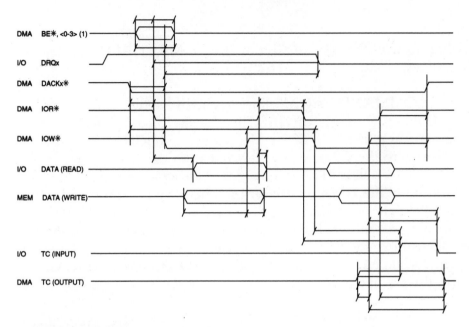

DMA   BE✳, <0-3> (1)

I/O   DRQx

DMA   DACKx✳

DMA   IOR✳

DMA   IOW✳

I/O   DATA (READ)

MEM   DATA (WRITE)

I/O   TC (INPUT)

DMA   TC (OUTPUT)

NOTE: MEMORY RESOURCE
USES SAME RELATIONSHIPS
AS IN ACCESS CYCLES

(1) FOR TYPE "A" AND "B" ON EISA
COMPATIBLE PLATFORMS ONLY

*FIGURE 7-3:   ISA, E-ISA & EISA STANDARD AND READY COMPATIBLE TYPES
A AND B TRANSFER CYCLE . . .   DMA I/O ADD-ON SLAVE CARD
RESOURCE VIEWPOINT*

READY VERSIONS OF THE COMPATIBLE, TYPE A, AND TYPE B TRANSFER CYCLES ON AN E-ISA PLATFORM

The ready versions of the various transfer cycles begin in the same fashion as the standard versions of the COMPATIBLE, TYPE A, and TYPE B transfer cycles on an E-ISA compatible platform. (Please see Figures 7-1-B and C, 7-3, and 7-4-A, B, and C.) The standard versions become ready versions if the IOCHRDY signal line is driven inactive within a specific time of an active memory COMMAND signal line. Other than the operation of the IOCHRDY signal line, the standard and ready versions operate in the same fashion.

> NOTE: Because TYPE A and TYPE B transfer cycles can only be implemented by platform memory, the IOCHRDY signal line may not be driven inactive on the bus. However, the execution of the cycle is still as defined.

Although the focal point of a transfer cycle is the I/O resource, the transfer requires both a memory resource and an I/O resource. On an E-ISA platform, the cycle length is controlled only by the memory resource; consequently, data must be valid relative to active I/O COMMAND signal lines. It is the responsibility of the memory resource to control the IOCHRDY signal line to insure valid data timing during the transfer. It is the responsibility of the I/O resource to always be able to execute according to the standard version of the various transfer cycle timings.

The COMMAND signal lines remain active until the IOCHRDY signal line is driven active by the memory resource. During a memory read transfer cycle, the active IOCHRDY signal line indicates to the DMA controller that valid data setup time to

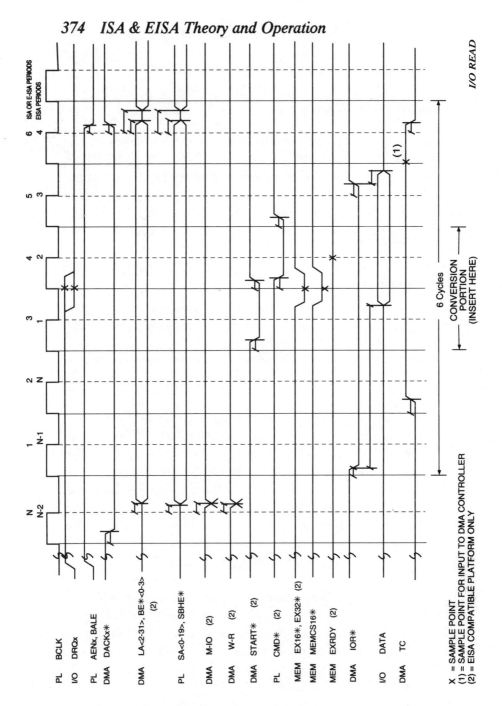

FIGURE   7-4-A: E-ISA & EISA STANDARD AND READY TYPE A TRANSFER
CYCLE (NO CONVERSION)... DMA CONTROLLER AND
PLATFORM CIRCUITRY VIEWPOINT

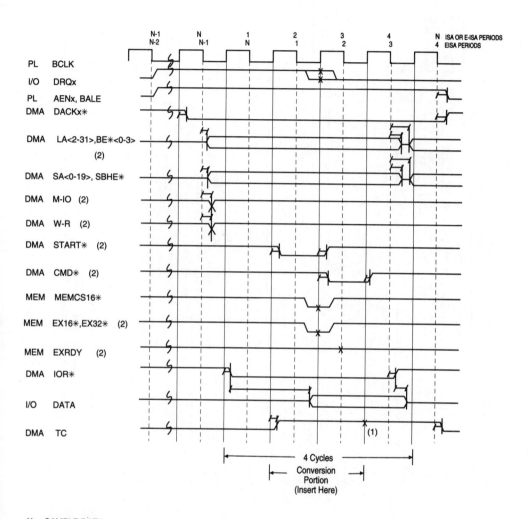

X = SAMPLE DATA
(1) = SAMPLE POINT FOR INPUT TO DMA CONTROLLER
(2) = EISA COMPATIBLE PLATFORM ONLY

I/O READ

FIGURE   7-4-B: *E-ISA & EISA STANDARD AND READY TYPE B TRANSFER*
                  CYCLE (NO CONVERSION) . . . DMA CONTROLLER AND
                  PLATFORM CIRCUITRY VIEWPOINT

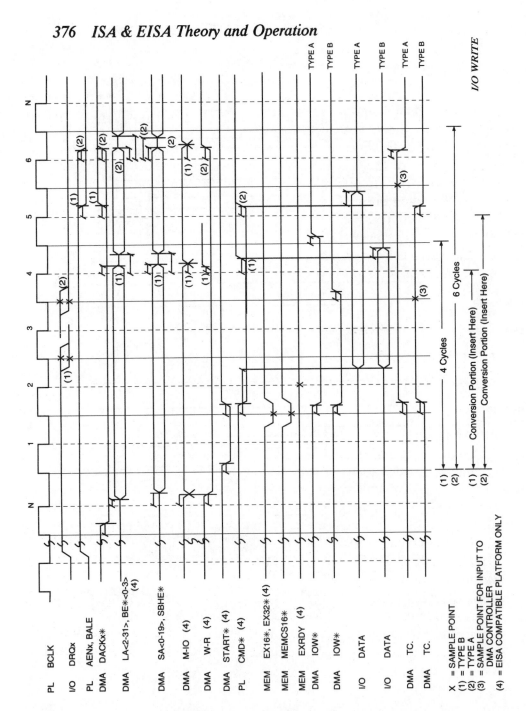

FIGURE 7-4-C: E-ISA & EISA STANDARD AND READY TYPE A AND B
TRANSFER CYCLE (NO CONVERSION) . . . DMA CONTROLLER
AND PLATFORM CIRCUITRY VIEWPOINT

an inactive IOW* signal can be met. During a write cycle, it is an indication to the DMA controller that the accessed resource has accepted the data. For either memory read or write transfer cycles, the activation of the IOCHRDY signal line is the indication to the DMA controller to complete the cycle. The transfer cycle is completed when both the memory and the I/O COMMAND signal lines are driven inactive.

The various ready transfer cycles have different cycle lengths and increments of cycle lengths. These differences are outlined in Table 7-7.

7.2 DMA TRANSFER CYCLES ON EISA PLATFORMS

INTRODUCTION

There are four types of standard and ready transfer cycles on an EISA compatible platform: COMPATIBLE, TYPE A, TYPE B, and TYPE C. The COMPATIBLE, TYPE A, and TYPE B transfer cycles are the same as those used for E-ISA compatible platforms except for the support of "CONVERSION". The TYPE C (also called BURST) transfer cycle is unique on the EISA platform and only used with EISA compatible resources. The data transfer can be from memory to I/O resources or from I/O to memory resources in a fly-by fashion. As in the ISA and E-ISA platforms, the resource providing the data is defined as the "source" and the resource receiving the data is defined as the "destination".

For COMPATIBLE, TYPE A, and TYPE B transfer cycles, the signal lines used by the I/O resource are referenced to each other and not to the BCLK signal line (see Figure 7-3). As with the E-ISA compatible platform, the DRQx, DACKx*, IOCHRDY, and TC signal lines are referenced to the BCLK signal line (see Figure 7-2 and Table 7-5). For the TYPE C (BURST) transfer cycle, additional signal lines are referenced to the BCLK signal line; these will be discussed in a later section.

The operation of the COMPATIBLE, TYPE A, and TYPE B transfer cycles WITHOUT the use of an EISA add-on memory slave card or without "CONVERSION" are the same as for the E-ISA platform. Please see those previous sections for further information. There are three areas of transfer cycle operation on an EISA platform that require additional discussion: First, the INCREMENTAL SUPPORT required for transfer cycles that include a EISA compatible memory or I/O resource. Second, support of "CONVERSION" for TYPE A and TYPE B transfer cycles is provided. Third, the execution of TYPE C (BURST) transfer cycles with and without "CONVERSION".

Table 7-8 provides a summary of the transfer cycle support on an EISA platform. In the table, the "RESOURCE SIZE" of the memory participant is identified by active MEMCS16*, EX16*, and EX32* signal lines. The "RESOURCE SIZE" of the I/O participant is programmed into the DMA controller.

PARTICIPANTS MEMORY: I/O	COMP	"A"	"A"/W CONV (1)	"B"	"B"/W CONV (1)	"C" (7)(8)	"C"/W CONV (1,7)(6)	TC (2)	RESOURCE SIZE MEM	RESOURCE SIZE I/O	TRANSFER SIZE (5)	DEMAND & BLOCK XFER INTERRUPTIBLE
PC,XT:PC,XT (3)	YES	NO	YES	NO	YES	NO	NO	UNI	8	8	8	YES
PC,XT : AT (3)	YES	NO	YES	NO	YES	NO	NO	UNI	8	8	8	
	NO	NO	YES	NO	YES	NO	NO	UNI	8	16	2x8 MULT	
PC,XT:E-ISA	YES	NO	YES	NO	YES	NO	NO	BI	8	8	8	
	NO	NO	YES	NO	YES	NO	NO	BI	8	16	2x8 MULT	
AT, E-ISA :PC,XT (3)	YES	NO	YES	NO	YES	NO	NO	UNI	8,16	8	8	
AT, E-ISA :E-ISA	YES	NO	YES	NO	YES	NO	NO	BI	8,16	8	8	
AT,E-ISA:AT (3)	YES	NO	YES	NO	YES	NO	NO	UNI	8,16	8	8	
	YES	NO	YES	NO	YES	NO	NO	UNI	16	16	16	
	NO	NO	YES	NO	YES	NO	NO	UNI	8	16	2x8 MULT	
AT, E-ISA :E-ISA	YES	NO	YES	NO	YES	NO	NO	BI	8,16	8	8	
	YES	NO	YES	NO	YES	NO	NO	BI	16	16	16	
	NO	NO	YES	NO	YES	NO	NO	BI	8	16	2x8 MULT	
PC,XT : EISA	YES	NO	YES	NO	YES	NO	YES	BI	8	8	8	
	NO	NO	YES	NO	YES	NO	YES	BI	8	16	2x8 MULT	
	NO	NO	YES	NO	YES	NO	YES	BI	8	32	4x8 MULT	
EISA : PC,XT (3)	YES	NO	YES	NO	YES	NO	NO	UNI	8	8	8	
	YES	YES	NO	YES	NO	NO	NO	UNI	16,32	8	8	
AT, E-ISA :EISA	YES	NO	YES	NO	YES	NO	YES	BI	8,16	8	8	
	YES	NO	YES	NO	YES	NO	YES	BI	16	16	16	
	NO	NO	YES	NO	YES	NO	YES	BI	8	16	2x8 MULT	
	NO	NO	YES	NO	YES	NO	YES	BI	8	32	4x8 MULT	
	NO	NO	YES	NO	YES	NO	YES	BI	16	32	2x16MULT	
EISA : AT (3)	YES	NO	YES	NO	YES	NO	NO	UNI	8	8	8	
	YES	YES	NO	YES	NO	NO	NO	UNI	16,32	8	8	
	NO	NO	YES	NO	YES	NO	NO	UNI	8	16	2x8 MULT	
	YES	YES	NO	YES	NO	NO	NO	UNI	16,32	16	16	
EISA:E-ISA	YES	NO	YES	NO	YES	NO	NO	BI	8	8	8	
	YES	YES	NO	YES	NO	NO	NO	BI	16,32	8	8	
	NO	NO	YES	NO	YES	NO	NO	BI	8	16	2x8 MULT	
	YES	YES	NO	YES	NO	NO	NO	BI	16,32	16	16	

TABLE 7-8: EISA COMPATIBLE PLATFORM DMA TRANSFER CYCLES

PARTICIPANTS MEMORY : I/O	COMP	"A"	"A"/W CONV (1)	"B"	"B"/W CONV (1)	"C" (7)(8)	"C"/W CONV (1,7)(6)	TC (2)	RESOURCE SIZE MEM:I/O	TRANSFER SIZE (5)	DEMAND & BLOCK XFER INTERUPTIBLE
EISA : EISA	YES	NO	YES	NO	YES	YES	YES	BI	8 8	8	YES
	YES	YES	NO	YES	NO	YES	YES	BI	16,32 8	8	
	YES	YES	NO	YES	NO	YES	YES	BI	16,32 16	16	
	YES	YES	NO	YES	NO	YES	YES	BI	32 32	32	
	NO	NO	YES	NO	YES	NO	YES	BI	8 16	2x8 MULT	
	NO	NO	YES	NO	YES	NO	YES	BI	8 32	4x8 MULT	
	NO	NO	YES	NO	YES	NO	YES	BI	16 32	2x16MULT	
PLAT. EISA MEMORY: EISA	YES	YES	NO	YES	NO	YES	YES	BI	8 8	8	
	YES	YES	NO	YES	NO	YES	YES	BI	16,32 8	8	
	YES	YES	NO	YES	NO	YES	YES	BI	16,32 16	16	
	YES	YES	NO	YES	NO	YES	YES	BI	32 32	32	
	NO	NO	YES	NO	YES	NO	YES	BI	8 16	2x8 MULT	
	NO	NO	YES	NO	YES	NO	YES	BI	8 32	4x8 MULT	
	NO	NO	YES	NO	YES	NO	YES	BI	16 32	2x16MULT	
PLAT. EISA MEMORY:PC,XT (3)	YES	YES	NO	YES	NO	NO	NO	UNI	8 8	8	
	YES	YES	NO	YES	NO	NO	NO	UNI	16,32 8	8	
PLAT. EISA MEMORY:AT (3)	YES	YES	NO	YES	NO	NO	NO	UNI	8 8	8	
	YES	YES	NO	YES	NO	NO	NO	UNI	16,32 16	16	
	YES	NO	YES	NO	YES	NO	NO	UNI	8 16	2x8 MULT	
PLAT. EISA MEMORY :E-ISA	YES	YES	NO	YES	NO	NO	NO	BI	8 8	8	
	YES	YES	NO	YES	NO	NO	NO	BI	16,32 16	16	
	YES	NO	YES	NO	YES	NO	NO	BI	8 16	2x8 MULT	

TABLE 7-8: EISA COMPATIBLE PLATFORM DMA TRANSFER CYCLES (CONTINUED)

NOTES:
"/W CONV" means "WITH CONVERSION"
Demand and Block transfers are interruptible EXCEPT when DMA COMPATIBLE transfer cycles are executed.
(1) A "YES" in this column, when the memory data size is greater than or equal to the I/O data size indicates a "SINGLE CONVERSION" cycle without multiple reads or writes of the memory resource. From the I/O resource's viewpoint, the timing is that of a compatible transfer cycle. Otherwise, a "MULTIPLE CONVERSION" cycle is executed.
(2) TC = Terminal Count; UNI = UNIdirectional ... DMA controller to I/O resource; BI = BIdirectional.

(3) MOST XT, PC, and AT DMA add-on slave cards can support the TYPE A transfer cycle, and SOME XT, PC, and AT DMA add-on slave cards can support the TYPE B transfer cycle.

(5) MULT = "MULTIPLE CONVERSION" ... when the memory resource data size is smaller than the I/O resource, multiple assembly/disassembly will occur.

(6) A "YES" in this column when an EISA compatible memory resource is involved indicates that the memory data size is greater than or equal to the I/O data size, and the memory resource did not drive the SLBURST* signal line active.

(7) All transfer cycle types support single, demand, and block DMA modes, except TYPE C and TYPE C WITH CONVERSION, which only supports demand and block DMA modes.

(8) A "YES" in this column indicates that the memory resource drove the SLBURST* signal line active.

INCREMENTAL SUPPORT

The memory or I/O resource for DMA cycles on an EISA platform can be an ISA, E-ISA, or EISA add-on slave card. The platform memory is by definition EISA compatible. The memory resource that participates in the transfer is identified by a valid value on the ADDRESS signal lines. The various memory resources (as add-on slave cards) operate in their respective modes; consequently, redundant memory control signal lines are driven active. To insure support for ISA and E-ISA compatible memory resources the BALE signal line is driven active to allow the input circuitry to receive the valid address. (See the BALE signal line definition in Chapter 5 for more information.)

For an EISA memory resource, the ISA and E-ISA compatible signal lines are ignored, and the LA, BE*, M-IO, W-R, START*, and CMD* signal lines are driven by the platform circuitry and DMA controller in an EISA compatible fashion. In addition, the

SA, SBHE*, MEMR*, and MEMW* signal lines are driven to support ISA or E-ISA compatible memory resources. (See Figures 7-1-A, B, and C, and 7-4-A, B, and C.)

ISA and E-ISA compatible add-on I/O slave cards on an EISA platform operate in the same fashion as on ISA and E-ISA platforms. The IOR* and IOW* signal lines are driven by the DMA controller in an ISA and E-ISA compatible fashion. On an EISA compatible platform, the EISA compatible I/O resource (either add-on slave card or platform) also uses the IOR* and IOW* signal lines. An EISA compatible I/O resource uses the IOR* and IOW* signal lines for control because the M-IO and W-R signal lines are used by the memory resource.

Also note that in order to support both an EISA and ISA or E-ISA compatible memory resource, the EXRDY and IOCHRDY signal lines are monitored, respectively. As with the E-ISA compatible platform, the standard transfer cycle becomes a ready transfer cycle if the appropriate ready signal line is not active.

Prior to any transfer cycle, the software has programmed the associated DMA channel to operate with COMPATIBLE, TYPE A or TYPE B transfer cycle timing. The COMPATIBLE transfer cycle supports transfers between ISA, E-ISA, and EISA compatible memory and I/O resources. Without "CONVERSION", the TYPE A and TYPE B transfer cycles only support transfers between EISA compatible memory and ISA, E-ISA, or EISA compatible I/O resources. Please see Table 7-8 for more information.

For a COMPATIBLE I/O read transfer cycle, the MEMW* signal line is driven active after the ADDRESS, START*, M-IO W-R, and the IOR* signal lines are valid (see Figure 7-1-B). If the

EXRDY or IOCHRDY signal lines are sampled inactive when the CMD* and MEMW* signal lines are active, the standard transfer cycle becomes a ready transfer cycle. The transfer cycle completes when the CMD* or MEMW* signal lines are driven inactive before the IOR* signal line is driven inactive. This insures a minimum hold time of valid data at the memory resource.

For a COMPATIBLE I/O write transfer cycle, the IOW*, MEMR*, and CMD* signal lines are driven active after the ADDRESS, START*, M-IO and W-R signal lines are valid (see Figure 7-1-C). If the EXRDY or IOCHRDY signal lines are sampled inactive when the CMD* or MEMR* signal line is active (similar to the access cycle specification for memory), the standard transfer cycle becomes a ready transfer cycle. The transfer cycle completes with the IOW* signal line driven inactive before the CMD* or MEMR* signal lines are driven inactive. This insures a minimum hold time of valid data at the I/O resource.

The identification of the memory resource type, ISA or E-ISA versus EISA, is determined by an active EX16*, EX32*, or MEMCS16*. Thus, even though the MEMCS16* signal line was not monitored on the ISA or E-ISA compatible platform, it is monitored on the EISA platform. Also note that if neither the EX16*, EX32*, nor MEMCS16* signal lines are active, the memory resource must be an 8 data bit ISA or EISA compatible resource. However, an EISA compatible 8 data bit memory resource can only execute ISA compatible cycles using ISA compatible signal lines.

The TYPE A and TYPE B transfer cycles on an EISA compatible platform support transfers between EISA compatible memory resources (EISA platform memory or add-on slave card) and ISA, E-ISA, or EISA compatible I/O resources. If a TYPE A or TYPE B transfer cycle is attempted with an ISA or E-ISA compatible memory add-on slave card, the cycle can only be completed with "CONVERSION". Please see the next section for more information about "CONVERSION".

The TYPE A and TYPE B transfer cycles operate in the same fashion as the previously described COMPATIBLE transfer cycle (see Figures 7-4-A, B, and C). The only difference is that the MEMR* and MEMW* signal lines are not driven active at the first part of the transfer cycle as with COMPATIBLE transfer cycles. The MEMR* and MEMW* signal lines are not driven until the "CONVERSION PORTION" of the "CONVERSION" version of the TYPE A and TYPE B transfer cycles.

TYPE A AND TYPE B TRANSFER CYCLES WITH CONVERSION ON EISA PLATFORMS

The TYPE A and TYPE B transfer cycles on an EISA compatible platform are different from those on an E-ISA compatible platform in two ways: First, the E-ISA platform only supports TYPE A and TYPE B transfer cycles when the memory resource is the platform memory. An EISA compatible platform supports TYPE A and TYPE B transfer cycles when the memory resource is either an ISA, E-ISA or EISA compatible memory add-on slave card, or the platform memory. Second, the E-ISA platform only supports TYPE A and TYPE B transfer cycles when the data size of the memory resource is larger than or equal to the data size of the I/O resource. An EISA compatible platform supports TYPE A and TYPE B transfer cycles in the same fashion as on the E-ISA platform when the data size of the memory resource is greater than or equal to the data size of the I/O resource. The EISA compatible platform also supports TYPE A and TYPE B transfer cycles when the memory resource data size is less than the I/O resource data size. The EISA compatible platform supports these two enhancements over the E-ISA compatible platform through the use of "CONVERSION".

The EISA compatible platform executes a "CONVERSION" version of the TYPE A and TYPE B transfer cycle as outlined in Table 7-8. To determine if a "CONVERSION" version of the transfer cycle is required, the type and size of the memory resource must be determined from the EX16*, EX32*, and MEMCS16* signal lines. If none of these signal lines are driven active, the memory is an 8 data bit ISA or EISA compatible resource. The data size of the I/O resource is preprogrammed by the software prior to the transfer cycle.

If a TYPE A or B transfer cycle is programmed for the I/O resource, the memory resource must be EISA compatible for the transfers to proceed as a "regular" TYPE A or B transfer cycle. If the memory resource is ISA or E-ISA compatible, the "SINGLE CONVERSION" version of the TYPE A or B transfer cycle will be executed. The key concept of a "SINGLE CONVERSION" is that the type of transfer programmed into the I/O resource cannot be supported by the memory resource. From the memory resource's viewpoint, the transfer cycle will be executed in the memory resource's native mode. From the I/O resource's viewpoint, the transfer cycle is executed as programmed.

If the data size of the memory resource is greater than or equal to the data size of the I/O resource, either a "regular" or a "SINGLE CONVERSION" version of the transfer cycle occurs. If the data size of the I/O resource is greater than the data size of the

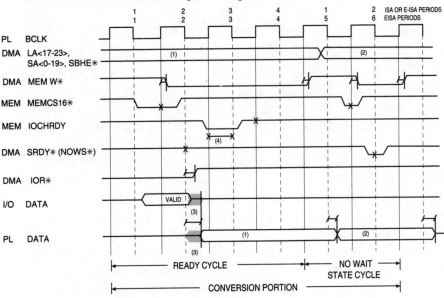

X = SAMPLE DATA
(1) = ADDRESS & DATA FOR LOWER BYTES
(2) = ADDRESS & DATA DRIVEN FROM UPPER TO LOWER BYTE
(3) = DRIVEN BY BOTH I/O RESOURCE & PLATFORM CIRCUITRY
(4) = SAMPLE WINDOW

I/O READ

FIGURE   7-5-A: *CONVERSION PORTION OF TYPE A OR B TRANSFER CYCLE*
WITH ISA AND E-ISA MEMORY (16 DATA BIT MEMORY TO 32
DATA BIT I/O EXAMPLE) . . . DMA CONTROLLER AND PLATFORM
CIRCUITRY VIEWPOINT (EISA COMPATIBLE PLATFORM ONLY)

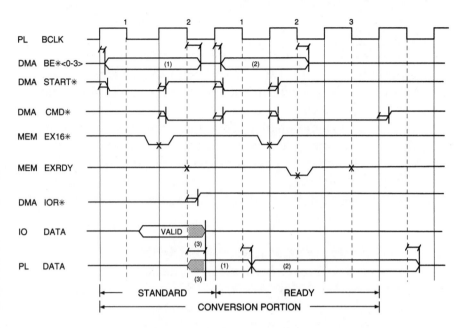

X = SAMPLE DATA
(1) = DATA FOR LOWER BYTES LANES
(2) = DATA DRIVEN FROM UPPER TO LOWER BYTE LANES
(3) = DRIVEN BY BOTH I/O RESOURCE & PLATFORM CIRCUITRY   *I/O READ*

*FIGURE 7-5-B: CONVERSION PORTION OF TYPE A OR B TRANSFER CYCLE
WITH EISA MEMORY (16 DATA BIT MEMORY TO 32 DATA
BIT I/O EXAMPLE) . . . DMA CONTROLLER AND PLATFORM
CIRCUITRY VIEWPOINT (EISA COMPATIBLE PLATFORM ONLY)*

memory resource, a "MULTIPLE CONVERSION" version of the transfer cycle occurs. For a read from the I/O resource, the data signal lines are valid from the beginning, and the "conversion" activity must disperse this data with multiple memory accesses. For a write to the I/O resource, the data signal lines must be valid relative to the end of the active period of the IOW* signal line. To achieve this, the memory resource will be read multiple times as part of the "conversion" activity within the active period of the IOW* line.

For I/O read transfer cycles, the CONVERSION PORTION in Figures 7-4-A and 7-4-B are replaced by the CONVERSION PORTION in Figure 7-5-A for ISA or E-ISA memory resources and Figure 7-5-B for EISA memory resources. The memory resource will operate in its native modes and timings for an access cycle. For either SINGLE or MULTIPLE CONVERSION transfer cycles, the IOR* signal line is driven inactive early. The platform circuitry, which has latched the data, "redrives" the DATA signal lines in conjunction with the DMA controller driving the MEMW*, START*, and CMD* signal lines (depending on the memory resource). At this point either single or multiple transfers can be executed. For a MULTIPLE CONVERSION I/O read transfer cycle, the platform circuitry and DMA controller will disperse the data latched from the I/O resource to memory resource by driving the MEMW* or CMD* signal line active multiple times. At the beginning of the CONVERSION PORTION, the appropriate data size for the memory resource (lower bytes first) is driven by the platform circuitry.

For I/O write transfer cycles, the CONVERSION PORTION in Figure 7-4-C is replaced by the CONVERSION PORTION in

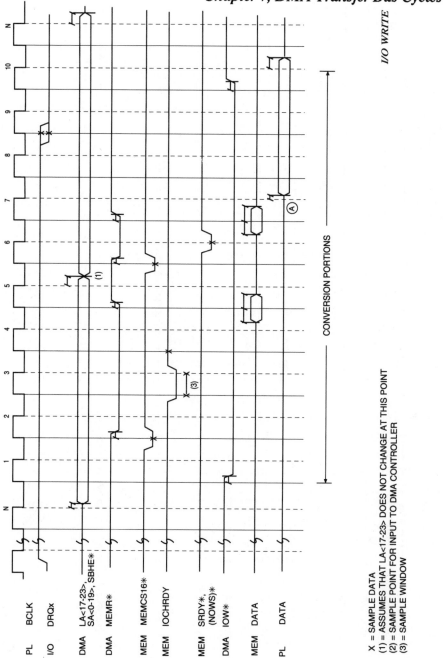

I/O WRITE

CONVERSION PORTIONS

X = SAMPLE DATA
(1) = ASSUMES THAT LA<17-23> DOES NOT CHANGE AT THIS POINT
(2) = SAMPLE POINT FOR INPUT TO DMA CONTROLLER
(3) = SAMPLE WINDOW

PL	BCLK	
I/O	DRQx	
DMA	LA<17-23>, SA<0-19>, SBHE*	
DMA	MEMR*	
MEM	MEMCS16*	
MEM	IOCHRDY	
MEM	SRDY*, (NOWS)*	
DMA	IOW*	
MEM	DATA	
PL	DATA	

FIGURE 7-6-A: CONVERSION PORTION TYPE A TRANSFER CYCLE WITH ISA & E-ISA MEMORY (16 DATA BIT MEMORY TO 32 DATA BIT I/O EXAMPLE) . . . DMA CONTROLLER AND PLATFORM CIRCUITRY VIEWPOINT (EISA COMPATIBLE PLATFORM ONLY)

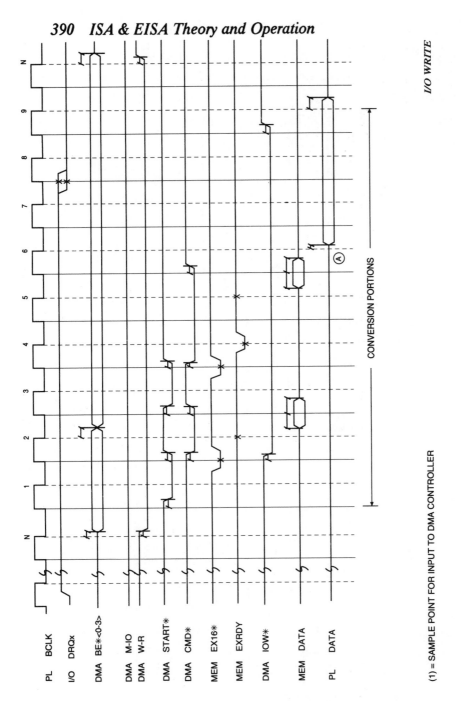

FIGURE   7-6-B: CONVERSION PORTION TYPE A TRANSFER CYCLE WITH EISA
MEMORY (16 DATA BIT MEMORY TO 32 DATA BIT I/O
EXAMPLE) . . . DMA CONTROLLER AND PLATFORM CIRCUITRY
VIEWPOINT (EISA COMPATIBLE PLATFORM ONLY)

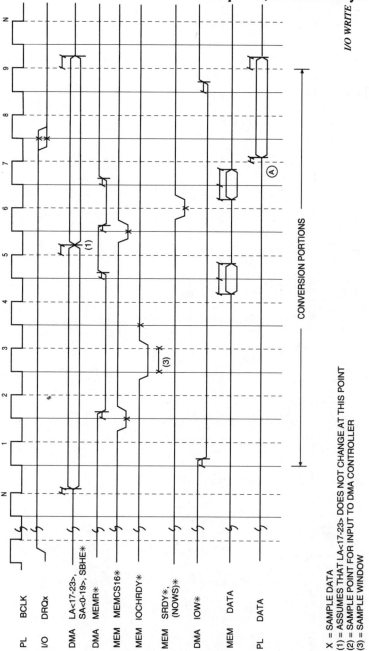

PL BCLK

I/O DRQx

DMA LA<17-23>,
SA<0-19>, SBHE*

DMA MEMR*

MEM MEMCS16*

MEM IOCHRDY*

MEM SRDY*,
(NOWS)*

DMA IOW*

MEM DATA

PL DATA

I/O WRITE

CONVERSION PORTIONS

X = SAMPLE DATA
(1) = ASSUMES THAT LA<17-23> DOES NOT CHANGE AT THIS POINT
(2) = SAMPLE POINT FOR INPUT TO DMA CONTROLLER
(3) = SAMPLE WINDOW

FIGURE 7-7-A: *CONVERSION PORTION TYPE B TRANSFER CYCLE WITH ISA
AND E-ISA MEMORY (16 DATA BIT MEMORY TO 32 DATA BIT I/O
EXAMPLE) . . . DMA CONTROLLER AND PLATFORM CIRCUITRY
VIEWPOINT (EISA COMPATIBLE PLATFORM ONLY)*

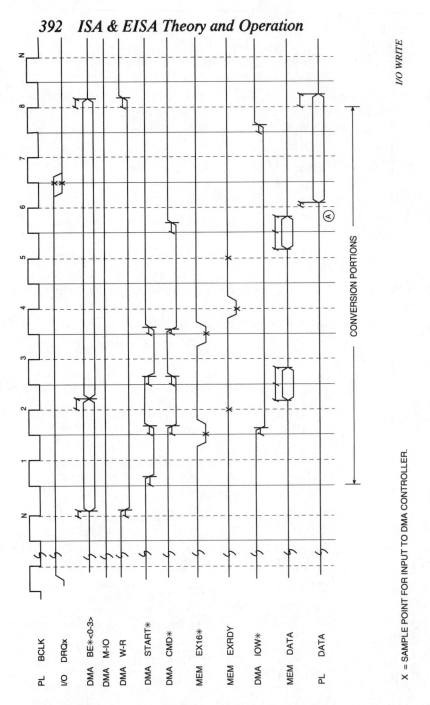

I/O WRITE

CONVERSION PORTIONS

X = SAMPLE POINT FOR INPUT TO DMA CONTROLLER.

PL	BCLK
I/O	DRQx
DMA	BE*<0-3>
DMA	M-IO
DMA	W-R
DMA	START*
DMA	CMD*
MEM	EX16*
MEM	EXRDY
DMA	IOW*
MEM	DATA
PL	DATA

FIGURE 7-7-B: *CONVERSION PORTION TYPE B TRANSFER CYCLE WITH EISA MEMORY (16 DATA BIT MEMORY TO 32 DATA BIT I/O EXAMPLE) ... DMA CONTROLLER AND PLATFORM CIRCUITRY VIEWPOINT (EISA COMPATIBLE PLATFORM ONLY)*

Figures 7-6-A and 7-7-A for ISA or E-ISA memory resources and Figures 7-6-B and 7-7-B for EISA memory resources. The operation of the memory resource of the transfer cycle is according to its native modes and timings. For either SINGLE or MULTIPLE CONVERSION transfer cycles, the DMA controller will drive the MEMR*, START*, and CMD* signal lines (depending on the memory resource), while holding the IOW* signal line active. For MULTIPLE CONVERSION transfer cycles, the DMA controller drives either the MEMW* or CMD* signal line active multiple times. The IOW* signal line is held active while the DMA controller in conjunction with the platform circuit try assembles data from the multiple accesses to the memory resources, the lower order bytes first. At the end of the data the assembled data is redriven by the platform circuitry in conjunction with the DMA controller driving the IOW* signal line inactive (Point A in Figures 7-6-A and B and 7-7-A and B).

TYPE C (BURST) TRANSFER CYCLES ON EISA PLATFORMS

The EISA compatible platform supports one additional transfer cycle type not supported on the ISA or E-ISA compatible platforms called the TYPE C (or BURST) transfer cycle. The TYPE C DMA transfer cycle is slightly different from the other transfer cycles. The TYPE C transfer cycle I/O resource synchronizes some of the signal lines to the BCLK signal line. Like the TYPE A and TYPE B transfer cycles, a CONVERSION version of the TYPE C transfer cycle is also supported.

Figures 7-1-A and 7-2 include references of the signal lines to the BCLK signal line for the TYPE C transfer cycle. Table 7-9 provides additional timing information to Table 7-1. Also see Table 7-5 for additional TYPE C related timings in Figure 7-2.

First, the "#/DET" (parameter number / detail) column relates the
parameter number of the table to Figure 7-1-A. Second, it defines
the detail information for how the number was derived. The timing
numbers are affected by the settling time on the bus. The table is
based on the default values for 8 slots as outlined in chapter 10.
The #/DET interpretations are shown on the following page.

DETAIL   INTERPRETATION

\#   NO SETTLING TIME INCLUDED.

\#/A   SKEW OF TWO SIGNALS BETWEEN RESOURCES. ONE HAS A DELAY OF
              0 NANOSECONDS, AND THE OTHER HAS A DELAY OF 11
              NANOSECONDS.

\#/E   SAME AS "A", EXCEPT THE WORST CASE INTERPRETATION IS THAT
              BOTH SIGNALS ARE EITHER 0 NANOSECONDS OR 11 NANOSECONDS.
              THE NET RESULT IS A DIFFERENCE OF 0 NANOSECONDS.

"DRIVEN BY" AND "MEASURED AT" INTERPRETATION

SOURCE   ADD-ON CARD OR PLATFORM RESOURCE THAT PROVIDES THE DATA.
DESTIN   ADD-ON CARD OR PLATFORM RESOURCE THAT ACCEPTS THE DATA.
DMA   PLATFORM DMA CONTROLLER

MIN. AND MAX. INTERPRETATION

ALL TIMES ARE IN NANOSECONDS WITH AN 8.00 MHZ BCLK.
THE NUMBER IN "[ ]" REFLECTS THE CALCULATED VALUE FOR AN 8.33 MHZ BCLK.

EISA INTERPRETATION

THE "EISA" ENTRIES ARE ACCORDING TO THE EISA REV. 3.12 BUS SPECIFICATION.

REF# /DET	DESCRIPTION OF EVENT	DRIVEN BY	MEASURED AT	TYPE C (BURST) [8.33]		EISA
				MIN	MAX	
1/A	DACKx* ACTIVE TO IOR* ACTIVE	DMA	SOURCE	67 [62]		66
	DACKx* ACTIVE TO IOW* ACTIVE	DMA	DESTIN	191 [181]		186
3/A	IOR* ACTIVE FROM BCLK FALLING EDGE	DMA	SOURCE		41 [41]	36
	IOW* ACTIVE FROM BCLK RISING EDGE	DMA	DESTIN		36 [36]	36
4	DATA FLOAT FROM BCLK RISING EDGE (READ OF I/O)	SOURCE	SOURCE		50 [50]	
5	DATA VALID FROM BCLK RISING EDGE (READ OF I/O)	SOURCE	SOURCE		38 [38]	38
5/A		SOURCE	DESTIN		49 [49]	
8	DATA HOLD FROM BCLK RISING EDGE (READ OF I/O)	SOURCE	SOURCE	5		5
		SOURCE	DESTIN	5		5
10/A	TC ACTIVE SETUP TO BCLK RISING EDGE	DMA	SOURCE DESTIN	6 [4]		15
11	TC ACTIVE HOLD FROM BCLK RISING EDGE	DMA	SOURCE DESTIN	60 [55]		55
14/A	DACKx* ACTIVE HOLD FROM IOR* INACTIVE	DMA	SOURCE	86 [81]		94
	DACKx* ACTIVE HOLD FROM IOW* INACTIVE	DMA	DESTIN	21 [18]		30
23/E	WRITE DATA VALID HOLD FROM BCLK RISING EDGE (WRITE OF I/O)	SOURCE	DESTIN	5 [5]		5
25/A	DATA VALID TO BCLK RISING EDGE(WRITE TO I/O)	SOURCE	DESTIN	13 [13]		13
26/A	TC VALID FROM BCLK FALLING EDGE	SOURCE	SOURCE			34
		DESTIN	DESTIN		34 [31]	
27	TC VALID HOLD FROM BCLK RISING EDGE	SOURCE	SOURCE	15 [15]		25
28	TC TRISTATE FROM DACK* INACTIVE	SOURCE DESTIN	SOURCE DESTIN		40 [40]	40

TABLE 7-9: TYPE C (BURST) TRANSFER CYCLE TIMINGS

REF# /DET	DESCRIPTION OF EVENT	DRIVEN BY	MEASURED AT	TYPE C (BURST) MIN [8.33]	MAX	EISA
29/A	TC ACTIVE SETUP TO BCLK RISING EDGE	DMA	SOURCE/ DESTIN.	84 [79]		75
30/A	IOR* ACTIVE SETUP TO BCLK RISING EDGE	SOURCE	SOURCE	16 [17]		19
30/A	IOW* ACTIVE SETUP TO BCLK FALLING EDGE	DESTIN.	DESTIN.	16 [14]		20
31/A	IOR* INACTIVE SETUP TO BCLK RISING EDGE	SOURCE	SOURCE	16 [14]		19
31/A	IOW* INACTIVE SETUP TO BCLK FALLING EDGE	DESTIN.	DESTIN.	16 [14]		20
32	TC HOLD FROM BCLK FALLING EDGE	DMA	SOURCE/ DESTIN.	120		120

TABLE 7-9: TYPE C (BURST) TRANSFER CYCLE TIMINGS (CONTINUED)

TYPE C (BURST) TRANSFER CYCLE WITHOUT CONVERSION

The TYPE C DMA transfer cycles without CONVERSION supports transfers only between EISA compatible memory resources (on the EISA platform memory or add-on slave card) and EISA compatible I/O resources. Additionally, both the MSBURST* and SLBURST* signal lines must be driven active.

Prior to any transfer cycle, the software will have programmed the associated DMA channel to operate with TYPE C transfer cycle timing. The TYPE C transfer cycle begins in the same fashion as the other transfer cycles (see Figures 7-8-A and 7-8-B). The DMA controller operates in the same fashion as for the other transfer cycle types.

Unlike the other transfer cycles, the I/O resource drives the DRQx, DATA, and TC signal lines relative to the BCLK signal lines. The I/O resource drives the DRQx signal line active. The platform circuitry drives the AENx and BALE signal lines active. The DMA controller then drives the appropriate DACKx* signal line active. Subsequently, the LA, BE*, M-IO, W-R, IOR* (for I/O read), and IOW* (for I/O write) signal lines are driven active. Up to this point, the cycle resembles the other transfer cycles. For a TYPE C transfer cycle, however, the subsequent cycles are unique.

The DMA controller drives the START* signal line active for one BCLK signal line period. If the transfer is programmed to be a read of the I/O resource, the platform circuitry drives the EXRDY signal line inactive for 1/2 a BCLK signal line period. The platform DMA controller and platform circuitry monitors the SLBURST*, EX16*, and EX32* signal lines. If the SLBURST* signal line is active and the data size of the memory resource is larger or equal to the data size of the I/O resource, the transfer cycle proceeds as a TYPE C without CONVERSION transfer cycle. If the SLBURST* signal line is active and the data size of the memory resource is less than the data size of the I/O resource, the cycle proceeds as a TYPE C transfer cycle with CONVERSION. In either case, if the DMA controller does not respond with an active MSBURST* signal line, the TYPE C transfer cycle with conversion is executed.

The TYPE C transfer cycle continues with the CMD* and MSBURST* signal lines driven by the platform circuitry, and IOW* (for I/O write) driven by the DMA controller. The CMD*, IOR*, IOW*, and MSBURST* signal lines remain valid for the

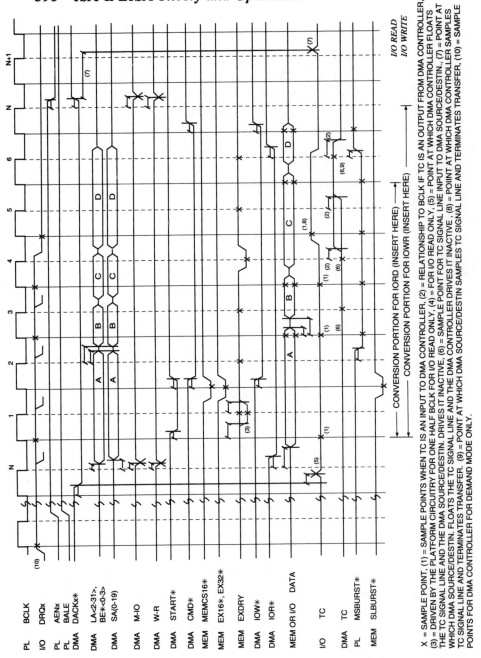

FIGURE   7-8-A: EISA STANDARD AND READY TYPE C (BURST) TRANSFER
CYCLE . . . DMA CONTROLLER AND PLATFORM CIRCUITRY
VIEWPOINT (EISA COMPATIBLE PLATFORM ONLY)

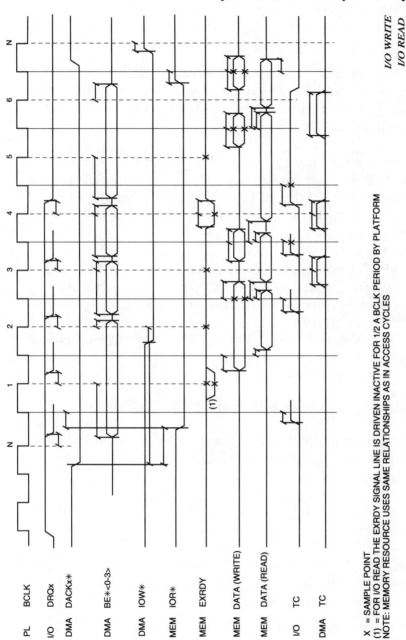

PL BCLK

I/O DRQx

DMA DACKx*

DMA BE*<0-3>

DMA IOW*

MEM IOR*

MEM EXRDY

MEM DATA (WRITE)

MEM DATA (READ)

I/O TC

DMA TC

I/O WRITE
I/O READ

X = SAMPLE POINT
(1) = FOR I/O READ THE EXRDY SIGNAL LINE IS DRIVEN INACTIVE FOR 1/2 A BCLK PERIOD BY PLATFORM
NOTE: MEMORY RESOURCE USES SAME RELATIONSHIPS AS IN ACCESS CYCLES

*FIGURE   7-8-B: EISA STANDARD AND READY TYPE C (BURST) TRANSFER
                     CYCLE . . . DMA I/O (ADD-ON SLAVE CARD) RESOURCE
                     VIEWPOINT (EISA COMPATIBLE PLATFORM ONLY)*

balance of the transfer. On each subsequent BCLK signal line rising pulse, data is transferred between resources. A transfer on a BCLK signal line is delayed if the memory resource drives the EXRDY signal line inactive.

During the transfer, the LA <10-31> signal lines do not change because the transfer must remain within a 1K page boundary. The other BE* and other LA signal lines change at the BCLK signal line falling edge when the EXRDY* signal line is first sampled for a given data transfer.

The TYPE C transfer cycle terminates when the MSBURST* signal line is driven inactive when the final data is transferred. Because the data is transferred relative to the BCLK signal line, the CMD* and IOW* signal lines are driven inactive simultaneously. Similarly, the IOR* signal line is driven inactive prior to the CMD* signal line driven inactive.

TYPE C (BURST) TRANSFER CYCLE WITH CONVERSION

As outlined above, the TYPE C (or BURST) transfer cycle will execute as a TYPE C WITHOUT CONVERSION under the following conditions:

- The memory and I/O resources are both EISA compatible.

- The data size of the memory resource must be greater than or equal to the data size of the I/O resource.

- The memory resource drives the SLBURST* signal line active and the DMA controller has driven the MSBURST* signal line active.

- The I/O resource supports TYPE C transfer as programmed into the DMA controller by the software. The DMA controller indicates such programming by driving MSBURST* signal line active in conjunction with an active SLBURST* signal line.

If the above conditions are NOT MET, the transfer cycle proceeds as a CONVERSION version of the TYPE C transfer cycle. The CONVERSION version of the TYPE C transfer cycle operates in the same fashion as the SINGLE and MULTIPLE CONVERSION version of the TYPE A and TYPE B transfer cycles.

For I/O read transfer cycles, the CONVERSION PORTION in Figure 7-8-A is replaced by the CONVERSION PORTION in Figure 7-9-A for ISA or E-ISA memory resources and Figure 7-9-B for EISA memory resources. The memory resource will operate in its native modes and timings for an access cycle. For either a SINGLE or MULTIPLE CONVERSION transfer cycle to an ISA or E-ISA memory resource, the IOR* signal line is driven inactive early. The platform circuitry "redrives" the DATA signal lines in conjunction with the DMA controller driving the MEMW* signal line. At this point either a single or multiple transfer can be executed. For MULTIPLE CONVERSION transfer cycles to an EISA memory resource, the IOR* signal line is driven inactive early. The platform circuitry "redrives" the DATA signal lines in conjunction with the DMA controller driving the CMD* signal line. At this point multiple transfers can be executed.

For MULTIPLE CONVERSION I/O read transfer cycles, the platform circuitry and DMA controller will disperse the data read from the I/O resource to memory resource by byte swapping from the latched data. Consequently, at the beginning of the CONVERSION PORTION, the IOR* signal line is driven inactive. Immediately, the appropriate data size for the memory resource (lower bytes first) are driven by the platform circuitry.

For I/O write transfer cycles, the CONVERSION PORTION in Figure 7-8-A is replaced by the CONVERSION PORTION in Figures 7-10-A for ISA or E-ISA memory resources and Figure 7-10-B for EISA memory resources. The operation of the memory resource of the transfer cycle are according to their native modes and timings for a memory access cycle. For a SINGLE CONVERSION transfer cycle to an ISA or E-ISA compatible memory resource, the DMA controller will drive the MEMR* signal line active while holding the IOW* signal line active. For MULTIPLE CONVERSION transfer cycles with ISA, E-ISA, and EISA memory resources, the DMA controller drives either the MEMW* or CMD* signal line active multiple times. The IOW* signal line is held active while the DMA controller, in conjunction with the platform circuitry, assembles data from the memory resources - the lower order bytes first. At the end of the data, the assembled data is redriven by the platform circuitry in conjunction with the DMA controller driving the IOW* signal line inactive.

> When the TYPE C transfer cycle is executed with CONVERSION, the basic reason for this cycle (transfer of data on every BCLK signal line rising edge) is lost. Multiple transfers with a single active IOW* and IOR* signal line does occur.

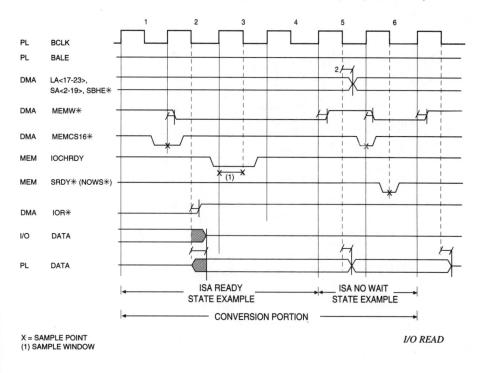

X = SAMPLE POINT
(1) SAMPLE WINDOW

I/O READ

FIGURE 7-9-A: *CONVERSION PORTION EISA STANDARD AND READY TYPE C (BURST) TRANSFER CYCLE WITH ISA & E-ISA MEMORY (16 DATA BIT MEMORY TO 32 DATA BIT I/O EXAMPLE) . . . DMA CONTROLLER & PLATFORM CIRCUITRY VIEWPOINT (EISA COMPATIBLE PLATFORM ONLY)*

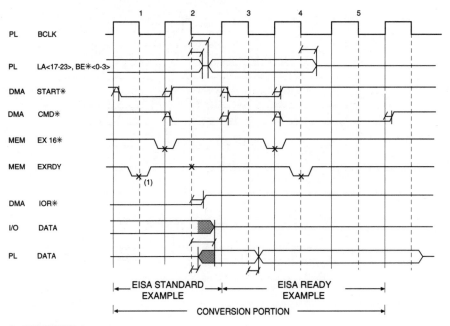

PL	BCLK
PL	LA<17-23>, BE✳<0-3>
DMA	START✳
DMA	CMD✳
MEM	EX 16✳
MEM	EXRDY
DMA	IOR✳
I/O	DATA
PL	DATA

EISA STANDARD EXAMPLE

EISA READY EXAMPLE

CONVERSION PORTION

X = SAMPLE POINT
(1) DRIVEN BY PLATFORM CIRCUITRY

I/O READ

FIGURE 7-9-B: CONVERSION PORTION EISA STANDARD AND READY TYPE C (BURST) TRANSFER CYCLE WITH EISA MEMORY (16 DATA BIT MEMORY TO 32 DATA BIT I/O EXAMPLE) . . . DMA CONTROLLER & PLATFORM CIRCUITRY VIEWPOINT (EISA COMPATIBLE PLATFORM ONLY)

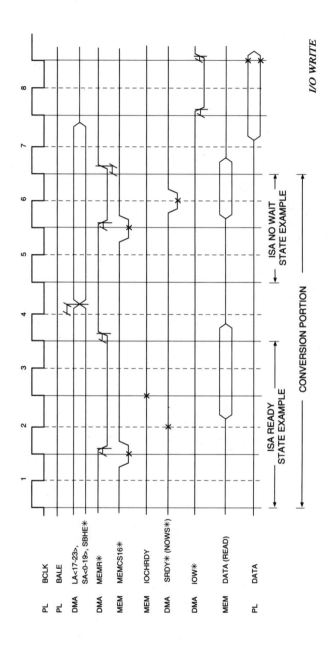

*FIGURE 7-10-A: CONVERION PORTION EISA STANDARD AND READY TYPE C
(BURST) TRANSFER CYCLE WITH ISA & E-ISA MEMORY (16
DATA BIT MEMORY TO 32 DATA BIT I/O EXAMPLE) . . . DMA
CONTROLLER AND PLATFORM CIRCUITRY VIEWPOINT
(EISA COMPATIBLE PLATFORM ONLY)*

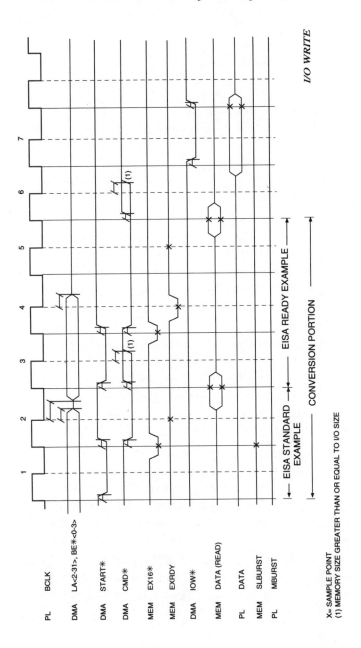

FIGURE   7-10-B: CONVERSION PORTION EISA STANDARD AND READY TYPE C
(BURST) TRANSFER CYCLE WITH EISA MEMORY (16 DATA
BIT MEMORY TO 32 DATA BIT I/O EXAMPLE) . . . DMA
CONTROLLER AND PLATFORM CIRCUITRY VIEWPOINT
(EISA COMPATIBLE PLATFORM ONLY)

7.3 DMA MODES

Each channel of the DMA controller can be programmed for four modes of DMA operation: single, block, demand, or cascade.

The cascade DMA mode is used for channels that need to support an add-on bus owner card. Refer to Chapter 9 for more detailed information.

The single DMA mode allows only a single transfer cycle for each time the DACKx* signal line becomes active. Once the DACKx* signal line is active, the DRQx signal line can become inactive. At this point there are two possible scenarios. Scenario One: If the DRQx signal line is sampled active at the sampling point (see Figures 7-1-B, 7-1-C, 7-4-A, 7-4-B, and 7-4-C), the DMA controller will only do the cycles required to transfer the data bits of the "single" data size requested and drive the DACKx* signal line inactive. The DMA controller will immediately request ownership of the bus in response to the active DRQx signal line. Once bus ownership is awarded, another "single" data transfer occurs.

Scenario Two: If the DRQx signal line is sampled inactive at the sampling point, the transfer proceeds as described above without the immediate request for bus ownership by the DMA controller at the end of the "single" transfer. The DMA controller will wait for another active DRQx signal line before requesting bus ownership and executing another transfer. In either case, the I/O resource (platform or add-on slave card) requesting service must wait until the DACKx* signal line becomes active again before the next transfer cycle.

> *The single DMA mode is supported by all DMA TYPE transfer cycles except for TYPE C with CONVERSION.*

The block DMA mode allows sequential block transfer cycles. The I/O resource (platform or add-on slave card) requests service by driving the DRQx signal line active. The DMA controller responds by obtaining bus ownership and driving the appropriate DACKx* signal line active. Once the DACKx* signal line is driven active, the I/O resource can drive the DRQx signal line inactive. The I/O resource can also continue to drive the DRQx signal line active throughout the transfer sequence. The transfer cycles continue until the preprogrammed byte, word, or double word count is completed. The TC (Terminal Count) signal line is driven active by the DMA controller to indicate to the I/O resource when the last portion of the data block has been transfered. If the I/O resource is E-ISA or EISA compatible and is operating on an E-ISA or EISA platform, the I/O resource can also terminate the transfer sequence by driving the TC signal line active.

> *A DMA COMPATIBLE transfer cycle cannot be interrupted, and therefore refresh cycles may be missed. Any long block transfers programmed for a channel programmed for the DMA COMPATIBLE may cause refresh problems. On an E-ISA or EISA compatible platform DMA TYPE A, TYPE B, and TYPE C transfer cycles can be interrupted during a Block transfer sequence.*

Indication of interruption of a block transfer sequence is the DACKx* signal line being driven inactive. The DMA controller will relinquish bus ownership to the central arbiter and will immediately request bus ownership. Once the DMA controller is awarded bus ownership, it redrives the DACKx* signal line active and continues the transfer sequence. During and after the interruption the DRQx signal line is not sampled.

The demand DMA mode is similar to the block mode, except it allows the sequential transfer to be broken into smaller parts. The demand DMA mode begins with the I/O resource (platform or add-on slave card) driving the DRQx signal line active and the DMA controller responding by driving the DACKx* signal line active. The sequential transfer continues until the DRQx signal line is sampled inactive (See Figures 7-1-B and C, 7-4-A, B, and C, and 7-8-A and B). At this time, the present single transfer is completed and the DACKx* signal line is driven inactive. When the I/O resource is ready, it redrives the DRQx signal line active. The transfer continues once the DMA controller becomes bus owner and drives the DACKx* signal line active.

As with the block DMA mode, the demand DMA mode will continue until the preprogrammed byte, word, or double word count is completed. The TC (Terminal Count) signal line is driven active by the DMA controller to indicate to the I/O resource when the last portion of the data has been transfered. If the I/O resource is E-ISA or EISA compatible and is operating on an E-ISA or EISA platform, the I/O resource can also terminate the transfer sequence by driving the TC signal line active.

A DMA COMPATIBLE transfer cycle cannot be interrupted, and therefore refresh cycles may be missed. Any long transfers for a channel programmed for the DMA COMPATIBLE transfer cycle may cause refresh problems. On an E-ISA or EISA compatible platform, DMA TYPE A, TYPE B, and TYPE C transfer cycles can be interrupted during a Demand transfer sequence.

Indication of an interruption of a demand transfer sequence is the DACKx* signal line being driven inactive. The DMA controller will relinquish bus ownership to the central arbiter. If the DRQx signal line is still driven by the I/O resource, the DMA controller will immediately request bus ownership. Once the DMA controller is awarded bus ownership it redrives the DACKx* signal line active and continues the transfer sequence. If the DRQx signal is driven inactive at the interruption point, the DMA controller will wait for the DRQx signal to be driven active to continue the sequence.

The cascade DMA mode does not actually cause a transfer cycle to occur. It simply monitors the DRQx signal line and acknowledges bus ownership with an active DACKx* signal line. An ISA or E-ISA compatible add-on bus owner card uses the cascade mode to obtain bus ownership. See Chapter 9 for more information.

7.4 DRQx and TC CONSIDERATIONS

The sampling points of the DRQx and TC signal lines (when the TC is programmed as an input to the DMA controller) is outlined in Figures 7-1-B and C, 7-4-A, B, and C, and 7-8-A and B have the following considerations:

For DMA COMPATIBLE, TYPE A, and TYPE B transfer cycles, the DRQx signal line is sampled at points referenced in the figures relative to the end of the cycle where the ADDRESS signal lines will change (driven invalid or to the next address). The sample points for the DRQ* and TC signal lines during a CONVERSION cycle are relative to the change in the LA signal lines at the end of the cycle. During CONVERSION, the LA signal lines remain constant; it is the BE*<0-3>, SA0, SA1, and SBHE* signal lines that change. Similarly, the DRQx* and TC signal line sample points for a ready transfer cycle are also sampled relative to the change in the LA signal lines at the end of the cycle. For COMPATIBLE and TYPE A transfer cycles, the DRQx signal line is sampled two and one-half BCLK signal line periods before the LA signal lines change. For TYPE B transfer cycles, the DRQx signal line is sampled one and one-half BCLK signal line periods before the LA signal lines change. The DMA controller sampling point for the TC signal line is one-half of a BCLK signal line period prior to the change in the LA signal lines at the end of the cycle. Consequently, the aforementioned sample points occur later in a ready or CONVERSION transfer cycle relative to a standard non-CONVERSION transfer cycle.

For TYPE C (BURST) transfer cycles, the following applies: When the TC signal line is an input to the DMA controller, it is sampled on the rising edge of the BCLK signal (one-half BCLK signal line period after the address has changed). The TC signal line must be driven active during the next to last data transfer (data "C" in Figure 7-8-A and B) based on decoding the last address (address "D" in Figure 7-8-A and B). The TC signal line must remain active until the first falling edge of the BCLK signal line of the last transfer.

When the TC signal line is an input to the DMA source/destination in Figure 7-8-A and B, it is sampled on the falling edge of the BCLK signal line whenever the IOR* or IOW* signal line is active and the EXRDY signal line was active at the previous falling edge of the BCLK signal line. The sampling of an active TC signal line indicates that the present data is the last to be transferred (data "D" in Figure 7-8-A and B).

The DRQx signal line is not sampled by the DMA controller until the end of the transfer for block transfer cycles.

For TYPE C (BURST) demand mode transfer cycles, the following applies: The TC signal line for demand mode operates in the same fashion as for the block mode transfer. The DRQx signal line is sampled by the DMA controller on the rising edge of the BCLK signal line. For a single transfer, the DRQx signal line must be sampled inactive at the first rising edge of the BCLK after the DACKx* signal line is driven active. Otherwise, the DRQx signal line is sampled at the rising edge of the BCLK signal line under the following conditions:

(1) Except for the aforementioned single transfer point, the sample point is the first rising edge of the BCLK signal line for each data transfer when the IOW* or IOR* signal lines are active and one-half a BCLK signal line period after the address has changed.

(2) If the transfer cycle is terminated by the TC signal line being driven active, the DRQx signal line should be driven inactive at the next falling edge of the BCLK signal line after the TC signal line is sampled active by the input circuitry (DMA controller or DMA source/destination).

CHAPTER EIGHT

REFRESH CYCLES

INTRODUCTION

The refresh cycle is the simplest cycle that is executed on the ISA, E-ISA, or EISA bus. The purpose of the refresh cycle is to refresh bus DRAM memory resources. During the bus refresh cycle, the platform memory may also be refreshed.

One of the platform timer channels is used to generate a request for a refresh cycle to the platform refresh controller every 15.6 microseconds. How quickly the actual refresh cycle occurs depends on the arbiter protocol of a particular platform, the other bus masters requesting bus ownership, and the time since the last refresh cycle. The considerations for when the refresh cycle actually occurs can be summarized as follows:

On ISA compatible platforms, the refresh cycle is usually executed immediately when requested by the timer. Most chip sets either place the platform CPU into a "hold" state, or allow the refresh controller to operate concurrently with the platform CPU. If the bus owner is the DMA controller, the refresh cycle is not executed until the DMA controller relinquishes control of the bus. The refresh cycle is held off because the original Intel 8237 DMA controller did not allow the transfer cycle to be interrupted. The one exception to a refresh cycle not being executed when the DMA controller owns the bus is when an ISA compatible add-on bus owner card "subleases" the DMA channel from the DMA controller to become a bus owner. While it is subleasing the bus, it can request a refresh cycle.

The refresh protocol on an E-ISA compatible platform is the same as that for an ISA compatible platform. Indeed, the E-ISA compatible add-on bus owner card subleases the DMA channel for bus ownership in the same way as its ISA compatible counterpart. The only difference in the refresh protocol on an E-ISA compatible platform is found when the DMA controller is executing a DMA DEMAND or BLOCK type of transfer cycle. These DMA transfer cycle types can be interrupted by the refresh controller; consequently, there is no risk of missing refresh cycles.

During the refresh cycles on ISA and E-ISA compatible platforms, the SA<0-7> signal lines are driven with the refresh address.

The refresh protocol on an EISA compatible platform is almost the same as on the E-ISA compatible platform. There are only three differences. First, the EISA compatible add-on bus owner card obtains bus ownership directly from the arbiter and not the DMA controller. Also, the EISA bus specification has established a preemption protocol. These two items allow the refresh controller to preempt the EISA compatible add-on bus owner card when needed to execute a refresh cycle.

Second, the EISA bus specification has defined that the refresh cycles can be queued up. The refresh controller queues up to four refreshes. When one refresh cycle is executed, another one (when the queue is not empty) is immediately done if no there are no other requests for bus ownership pending. The ISA and E-ISA compatible chip sets could also be designed to queue up refresh requests in a similar fashion.

Third, the refresh address is driven onto SA<0-15>, LA<2-15>, and the BE* signal lines (the BE* signal lines can be translated into the equivalent of LA0 and LA1).

Table 8-1 outlines the refresh cycle timings for Figures 8-1 and 8-2.

DETAIL	INTERPRETATION (SEE CHAPTER 10 FOR MORE DETAILED INFORMATION)
#	NO SETTLING TIME INCLUDED.
#/A	SKEW OF TWO SIGNALS BETWEEN RESOURCES. ONE HAS A DELAY OF 0 NANOSECONDS, AND THE OTHER HAS A DELAY OF 11 NANOSECONDS.

"DRIVEN BY" AND "MEASURED AT" INTERPRETATION

ADD-ON	ADD-ON ACCESSED RESOURCE
REF	REFRESH CONTROLLER
ISA-B	ISA OR E-ISA ADD-ON BUS OWNER CARD

MIN. AND MAX. INTERPRETATION

ALL TIMES ARE IN NANOSECONDS WITH AN 8.00 MHZ BCLK.
THE NUMBER IN "[ ]" REFLECTS THE CALCULATED VALUE FOR AN 8.33 MHZ BCLK.

EISA INTERPRETATION

THE "EISA" ENTRIES ARE ACCORDING TO THE EISA REV. 3.12 BUS SPECIFICATION

SMEMR* AND SMEMW*

SMEMR* AND SMEMW* SIGNAL LINES HAVE ESSENTIALLY ZERO SKEW RELATIVE TO THE MEMR* AND MEMW* SIGNAL LINES BECAUSE ALL ARE DRIVEN BY THE REFRESH CONTROLLER.

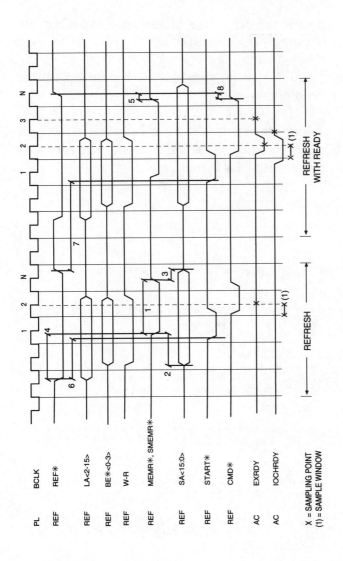

FIGURE 8-1:   REFRESH CYCLE TIMING

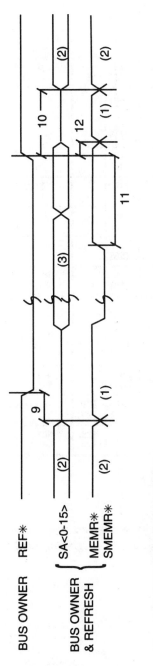

FIGURE   8-2:   ISA OR E-ISA ADD-ON BUS OWNER CARD REFRESH REQUEST

REF# /DET	DESCRIPTION OF EVENT	DRIVEN BY	MEASURED AT	MIN [8.33]	MAX	EISA
1/A	MEMR* ACTIVE TO INACTIVE (SEE NOTE 1)	REF.	ADD-ON	224 [214]		235
2/A	SA ADDRESS VALID SETUP TO MEMR* ACTIVE	REF.	ADD-ON	66 [61]		70
3/A	SA ADDRESS HOLD TO MEMR* INACTIVE	REF.	ADD-ON	16 [14]		22
4/A	REF* ACTIVE SETUP TO MEMR* ACTIVE (SEE NOTE 2)	REF.	ADD-ON	118 [111]		120
5/A	REF* ACTIVE HOLD FROM MEMR* INACTIVE	REF.	ADD-ON	17 [15]		20
6/A	REF* ACTIVE SETUP TO START* ACT. (SEE NOTE 2)	REF.	ADD-ON	61 [56]		55
7/A	REF* INACTIVE SETUP TO START* ACTIVE(SEE NOTE 3)	REF.	ADD-ON	10 [10]		10
8/A	REFRESH* HOLD FROM CMD* INACTIVE	REF.	ADD-ON	-30 [-30]		20
9	ADD-ON BUS OWNER TRISTATE OF SA & MEMR* BEFORE REFRESH* ACTIVE	ISA-B	ISA-B	0 [0]		NOT SPEC
10	SA AND MEMR* DRIVEN FROM REFRESH* INACTIVE	ISA-B	ISA-B	250 [240]		NOT SPEC
11	REFRESH* ACTIVE HOLD FROM MEMR* INACT. (SEE NOTE 4)	ISA-B	ISA-B	20 [20]	239 [229]	20
12	MEMR* AND SA TRISTATE FROM REFRESH* INACTIVE	REF.	ISA-B		125 [120]	NOT SPEC

TABLE 8-1: REFRESH CYCLES

NOTES:

(1) The entry assumes a 15 nanosecond same package skew between high/low and low/high transition with 11 nanosecond bus delay at the beginning and 0 nanosecond bus delay at the end.

(2) Parameters 4 and 6 seem to be in conflict. Parameter 6 seems to reflect the fact that perhaps the START* signal line is driven 1/2 a BCLK signal period sooner than the MEMR* signal line.
(3) The EISA bus specification allows for a one BCLK signal period between active REFRESH* signal line pulses that are queued up. As observed in NOTE (2) the START* signal line appears to go active 1/2 BCLK signal line sooner than needed.
(4) On the "AT" platform, if the REFRESH* signal line is held active by the add-on bus owner card beyond the maximum number, extra refresh cycles will be executed.

Table 8-1 does not contain all of the timing numbers needed for the signal lines in Figure 8-1. Any numbers not listed are available in Table 6-1-B for access cycles.

REFRESH CYCLE

The ADDRESS and CONTROL signal lines must be tri-stated prior to allowing the refresh controller to become the bus owner. (See Chapter 9 for more information.) On an EISA compatible platform, the refresh controller begins the cycle by driving the REFRESH* signal line active, driving the SA, LA, and BE* signal lines with the valid refresh address, the W-R signal line low, and subsequently driving the MEMR* and START* signal lines active.

As the refresh cycle progresses, the START* and CMD* signal lines are driven inactive and active, respectively. The cycle will be a standard refresh cycle if the IOCHRDY and EXRDY signal lines remain active. For a standard access cycle, the MEMR* and the combination of START* and CMD* are driven active for two BCLK signal line periods. The cycle will be a ready refresh cycle, with length increases in increments of the BCLK signal line period if the IOCHRDY or EXRDY signal line is driven inactive. The refresh cycle ends when the CMD* and MEMR* signal lines are driven inactive.

The address mapping of the refresh addresses relative to the LA and SA signal lines are outlined in Table 8-2.

REFRESH	0	1	2	3	4	5	6	7	0	1	8	9	10	11	12	13
LA,SA	0	1	2	3	4	5	6	7	8	9	10	11	12	13	14	15

TABLE 8-2: REFRESH ADDRESS MAPPING

SPECIAL CONSIDERATIONS FOR ISA AND E-ISA PLATFORMS

The above description is for an EISA compatible platform. For ISA and E-ISA compatible platforms, the refresh signal line operates in the same fashion except for the EISA specific signal lines. For an ISA or E-ISA compatible platform, the only signal lines involved in a refresh cycle are the BCLK, REFRESH*, MEMR*, SMEMR*, SA, and IOCHRDY signal lines.

An EISA add-on bus owner card can be preempted by the refresh controller for the bus ownership. An ISA or E-ISA add-on bus owner card cannot be preempted independent of the platform. The ISA or E-ISA add-on bus owner card must request a refresh cycle during the period it owns the bus. The bus owner card should request a refresh cycle every 15.6 microseconds.   Figure 8-2 outlines how a refresh cycle can be requested by an ISA or E-ISA add-on bus owner card. The bus owner card first tri-states the SA and MEMR* signal lines. It then drives the REFRESH* signal line active.   The refresh controller will drive the MEMR*,

SMEMR*, and SA signal lines and monitor the IOCHRDY signal line in order to execute a refresh cycle. If the platform is EISA compatible, the aforementioned EISA specific signal lines are also driven and monitored. When the refresh cycle is completed, the MEMR* and SMEMR* signal lines are driven inactive and the bus owner must respond and drive the REFRESH* signal line inactive.

> *On an IBM AT platform, if the REFRESH* signal line is not driven inactive within a specific amount of time, another refresh cycle will be started by the refresh controller.*

Notes

CHAPTER NINE

ARBITRATION CYCLES

INTRODUCTION

ISA, E-ISA, and EISA compatible platforms allow add-on cards to become the bus owners. The add-on card must execute an arbitration cycle to obtain bus ownership. The arbitration takes place between add-on bus owner cards, the DMA controller, the refresh controller, and the platform CPU.

The central arbiter on ISA and E-ISA compatible platforms is the DMA controller. The ISA and E-ISA add-on bus owner cards "sublease" a DMA channel through the use of DRQx and DACKx* signal lines. The DMA controller behaves as though it is "leasing" the bus to another DMA controller according to the definition of the cascade mode of the DMA controller. In reality, the ISA or E-ISA compatible add-on bus owner card is executing access cycles.

On EISA compatible platforms, the ISA and E-ISA add-on bus owner cards still use the DMA controller as their central arbiter. The DMA controller in turn arbitrates with other EISA resources on EISA compatible platforms through platform arbitration circuitry. EISA add-on bus owner cards arbitrate directly with the platform arbitration circuitry through the use of the MREQx* and MAKx* signal lines.

Table 9-1 summarizes the timing parameters for Figure 9-1. This table has several key pieces of information. First, the "#/DET" (parameter number / detail) column relates the parameter number of the table to Figure 9-1. Second, it provides detailed information on how the number was derived. The timing numbers are affected by the settling time on the bus. The table is based on the default values for eight slots as outlined in Chapter 10. The #/DET interpretations are shown below.

DETAIL	INTERPRETATION
#	NO SETTLING TIME INCLUDED. (SEE CHAPTER 10 FOR MORE DETAILED INFORMATION.)
#/A	SKEW OF TWO SIGNALS BETWEEN RESOURCES. ONE HAS A DELAY OF 0 NANOSECONDS, AND THE OTHER HAS A DELAY OF 11 NANOSECONDS.
#/B	SIGNAL IS DRIVEN BY ONE RESOURCE TO ANOTHER. THE SECOND RESOURCE MUST RESPOND BY DRIVING A SIGNAL BACK TO THE FIRST RESOURCE. # INCLUDES THE "ROUND TRIP" TIME OF 11 + 11 = 22 NANOSECONDS.

"DRIVEN BY" AND "MEASURED AT" INTERPRETATION

ADD-ON	ADD-ON ACCESSED RESOURCE
ISA-B	ISA OR E-ISA COMPATIBLE ADD-ON CARD BUS OWNER
CPU	PLATFORM CPU
PLAT	PLATFORM CIRCUITRY

MIN. AND MAX. INTERPRETATION

ALL TIMES ARE IN NANOSECONDS WITH AN 8.00 MHZ BCLK.
THE NUMBER IN "[ ]" REFLECTS THE CALCULATED VALUE FOR AN 8.33 MHZ BCLK.

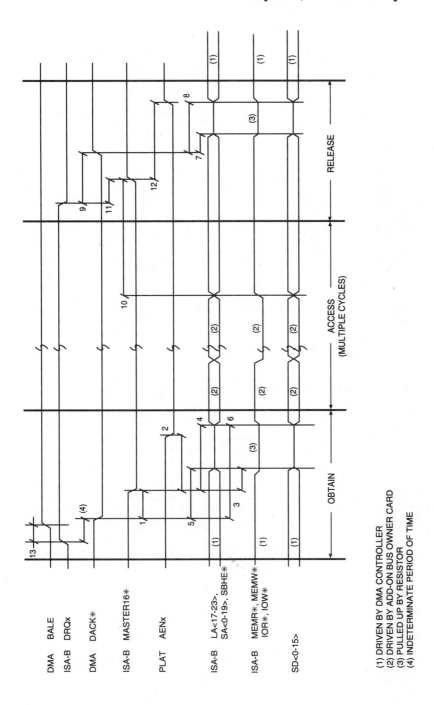

FIGURE 9-1: *ISA AND E-ISA ADD-ON BUS OWNER CARD ARBITRATION PROTOCOL*

REF# /DET	DESCRIPTION OF EVENT	DRIVEN BY	MEASURED AT	MIN [8,33]	MAX	EISA
1	MASTER* ACTIVE FROM DACKx ACTIVE	ISA-B	ISA-B	0 [0]		
2/B	AENx INACTIVE FROM MASTER* ACTIVE	PLAT	ADD-ON	0 [0]	71 [71]	
3/A	ADDRESS, COMMAND, & DATA LINES TRI-STATED FROM MASTER* ACTIVE (NOTE 1)	PLAT	ISA-B	0 [0]	60 [60]	
4	ISA-B DRIVES ADDRESS, COMMAND, & DATA LINES FROM MASTER* ACTIVE	ISA-B	ISA-B	125 [120]		
5	ADDRESS, COMMAND, & DATA LINES TRI-STATED FROM DACKx* ACTIVE (NOTE 1)	PLAT	ISA-B	0 [0]	60 [60]	60
6	ISA-B DRIVES ADDRESS, COMMAND, & DATA LINES FROM DACKx* ACTIVE	ISA-B	ISA-B	125 [120]		120
7	ADDRESS, COMMAND, & DATA LINES TRI-STATED FROM DACKx* INACTIVE	ISA-B	ISA-B		60 [60]	60
8	ADDRESS, COMMAND, & DATA LINES DRIVEN FROM DACKx* INACTIVE	PLAT	ISA-B	60 [60]		
9	DACKx* INACTIVE FROM DRQx INACTIVE	PLAT	ISA-B	250 [240]		300
10	MASTER* INACTIVE FROM COMMAND INACTIVE	ISA-B	ISA-B	60 [60]		
11	MASTER* INACTIVE FROM DRQx* INACTIVE	ISA-B	ISA-B		100 [100]	
12/B	AENx ACTIVE FROM MASTER* INACTIVE	PLAT	ADD-ON	71 [71]		
13/A	BALE ACTIVE FROM DACK* ACTIVE	PLAT	ADD-ON		125 [120]	

TABLE 9-1: ISA AND E-ISA ADD-ON BUS OWNER CARD ARBITRATION PROTOCOL

NOTE:
(1) No settling time is associated with tristate propagation on the bus.

ARBITRATION PROTOCOL FOR ISA OR E-ISA ADD-ON BUS OWNER CARDS ON ISA OR E-ISA COMPATIBLE PLATFORMS

The arbitration protocol consists of two parts: OBTAIN and RELEASE. Between the OBTAIN and RELEASE portions of the arbitration protocol, the ISA and E-ISA add-on bus owner cards execute standard, ready, or no-wait-state (E-ISA compatible platforms only) access cycles.

The OBTAIN portion of the cycle begins when the bus owner card activates a DRQx signal line and waits for an active DACKx* signal line. (See Figure 9-1.) In response to the active DACKx* request signal line, the add-on bus owner card activates the MASTER16* signal line. The platform circuitry responds to the active MASTER16* signal line by driving the AENx signal line inactive. Simultaneously, the DMA controller tri-states the ADDRESS, CONTROL and DATA signal lines. After the MASTER16* signal line goes active, the add-on bus owner card drives the ADDRESS, CONTROL, and DATA signal lines.

The RELEASE portion of the cycle begins when the add-on bus owner card drives the MASTER16* and DRQx signal lines inactive. (See Figure 9-1.) In response to the inactive DRQx signal line, the DMA controller drives the DACKx* signal line inactive. The inactive MASTER16* signal line causes platform circuitry to drive the AENx signal line inactive. An inactive DACKx* signal line causes the add-on bus owner card to tristate the ADDRESS, COMMAND, and DATA signal lines. Also, subsequent to an inactive DACKx* signal line, the DMA controller circuitry drives the ADDRESS, COMMAND, and DATA signal lines.

The arbitration protocol is defined as "voluntary" because the add-on bus owner card only releases the bus when it "wishes to"; there is no preemption protocol for ISA or E-ISA add-on bus owner cards.

ARBITRATION PROTOCOL FOR ISA OR E-ISA ADD-ON BUS OWNER CARDS ON EISA COMPATIBLE PLATFORMS

The arbitration protocol for ISA and E-ISA add-on bus owner cards on an EISA compatible platform is the same as on an E-ISA compatible platform (described above). As with ISA and E-ISA compatible platforms, the add-on bus owner card returns the bus in a "voluntary" fashion with no preemption protocol.

ARBITRATION PROTOCOL FOR EISA ADD-ON BUS OWNER CARDS ON EISA COMPATIBLE PLATFORMS

The arbitration protocol for EISA add-on bus owner cards is very different than for ISA and E-ISA add-on bus owner cards. First, the EISA add-on bus owner card uses MREQx* and MAKx* signal lines to arbitrate. Second, the arbiter is platform arbitration circuitry and not the DMA controller. Third, the add-on bus owner card can be preempted by the platform arbitration circuitry.

Table 9-2 summarizes the timing parameters for Figure 9-2. This table has several key pieces of information. First, the "#/DET" (parameter number / detail) column relates the parameter number of the table to Figure 9-2. Second, it provides detailed information on how the number was derived. The timing numbers are affected by the settling time on the bus. The table is based on the default values for eight slots as outlined in Chapter 10. The #/DET interpretations are shown below.

DETAIL	INTERPRETATION
#	A SETTLING TIME OF ONLY 5 NANOSECONDS IS USED BECAUSE OF THE POINT-TO-POINT NATURE OF THE SIGNAL LINES.

"DRIVEN BY" AND "MEASURED AT" INTERPRETATION

EISA-B	EISA COMPATIBLE ADD-ON CARD BUS OWNER
PLAT	PLATFORM CIRCUITRY

MIN. AND MAX. INTERPRETATION

ALL TIMES ARE IN NANOSECONDS WITH AN 8.00 MHZ BCLK.
THE NUMBER IN "[ ]" REFLECTS THE CALCULATED VALUE FOR AN 8.33 MHZ BCLK.

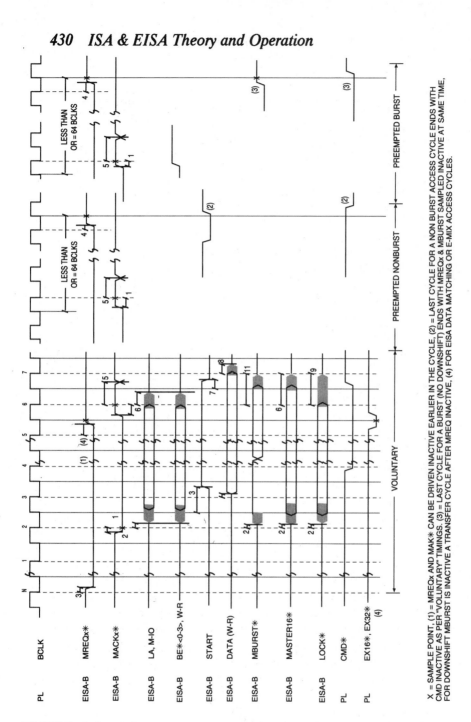

X = SAMPLE POINT, (1) = MREQx AND MAK* CAN BE DRIVEN INACTIVE EARLIER IN THE CYCLE, (2) = LAST CYCLE FOR A NON BURST ACCESS CYCLE ENDS WITH CMD INACTIVE AS PER "VOLUNTARY" TIMINGS. (3) = LAST CYCLE FOR A BURST (NO DOWNSHIFT) ENDS WITH MREQx & MBURST SAMPLED INACTIVE AT SAME TIME, FOR DOWNSHIFT MBURST IS INACTIVE A TRANSFER CYCLE AFTER MREQ INACTIVE, (4) FOR EISA DATA MATCHING OR E-MIX ACCESS CYCLES.

FIGURE 9-2   EISA ADD-ON BUS OWNER CARD ARBITRATION PROTOCOL

REF# /DET	DESCRIPTION OF EVENT	DRIVEN BY	MEASURED AT	MIN [8.33]	MAX	EISA
1	MAKx* VALID SETUP TO FALLING EDGE OF BCLK	PLAT	EISA-B	-12 [10]		10
2	LA, M-IO, BE*, W-R, MBURST*, DATA(WR) MASTER16*, & LOCK* DRIVEN FROM FALLING EDGE OF BCLK	EISA-B	EISA-B	0 [0]		0
3	MREQx* ACTIVE DELAY FRM FALLING EDGE OF BCLK	EISA-B	EISA-B		36 [34]	33
4	MREQx* INACTIVE DELAY FRM FALLING EDGE OF BCLK	EISA-B	EISA-B	2 [2]	36 [34]	2/30
5	MAKx* VALID HOLD FROM FALLING EDGE OF BCLK	PLAT	EISA-B	25 [25]		25
6	LA, M-IO, MASTER16*,BE*, MSBURST* TRISTATE FROM FALLING EDGE OF BCLK	EISA-B	EISA-B		125 [120]	120
7	START*, MASTER* TRISTATE FRM RISING EDGE OF BCLK	EISA-B	EISA-B		125 [120]	120
8	DATA (WR) TRISTATE FROM FALLING EDGE OF BCLK	EISA-B	EISA-B		125 [120]	120
9	LOCK* TRISTATE FROM FALLING EDGE OF BCLK	EISA-B	EISA-B		125 [120]	120
10	START* DRIVEN FROM RISING EDGE OF BCLK	EISA-B	EISA-B	0 [0]		0 [0]
11	MSBURST* TRI-STATED FROM RISING EDGE OF BCLK	EISA-B	EISA-B	35 [35]	125 [120]	NOT SPEC

TABLE 9-2: EISA ADD-ON BUS OWNER CARD ARBITRATION PROTOCOL

The arbitration protocol for an EISA compatible add-on bus owner card consists of both voluntary and preemption elements. First, consider the voluntary element (see Figure 9-2). The OBTAIN portion begins when the add-on bus owner card requests bus ownership by driving its respective MREQx* signal line active. When the associated MAKx* signal line is driven active, the appropriate signal lines have already been tri-stated by the previous bus master. The add-on bus owner card can immediately drive the LA, M-IO, BE*, W-R, MSBURST*, MASTER16*, and LOCK* signal lines. One half a BCLK signal line period later, the START* signal line can be driven. One BCLK signal line period later, the DATA (WR) signal lines can be driven for a write cycle.

When the add-on bus owner card releases the bus "voluntarily" (MAKx* signal line is active), the bus is relinquished as follows: The RELEASE portion begins with the add-on bus owner card driving the MREQx* signal line inactive. The platform arbitration circuitry will subsequently drive the appropriate MAKx* signal line inactive. The MREQx* and MAKx* signal lines can execute the above sequence long before the present cycle is complete. The LA, BE*, W-R, M-IO, MASTER16*, LOCK*, and MSBURST* signal lines in the voluntary element of Figure 9-2 are tri-stated relative to an active EXRDY* signal line sampled at the falling edge of the BCLK signal line. An active EXRDY signal line is sampled a minimum of 1/2 a BCLK signal line period. The START* signal line is tri-stated relative to the BCLK signal line when the CMD* signal line is driven inactive. Subsequently, the DATA signal lines (write) are tri-stated at the next falling edge of the BCLK signal line.

For an EISA data-matching or any E-MIX access cycle, the LA, BE*, W-R, M-IO, MASTER16*, LOCK*, and MSBURST* signal lines are tri-stated relative to the subsequent falling edge of the BCLK signal line after the EX16* or EX32* signal lines are sampled active. The START* signal line is tri-stated relative to the subsequent rising edge of the BCLK signal line after the EX16* or EX32* signal line is sampled active.

The preemption element of the arbitration protocol is similar to the voluntary element. For non-burst access cycles, the tri-stating of the signal lines are as outlined above. The only difference is that the MAKx* signal lines were driven inactive by the platform arbitration circuit to preempt the present EISA add-on bus owner card. The appropriate MREQx* signal line is not inactive at this time. The add-on bus owner card has a maximum of 64 BCLK signal line periods to drive the MREQx* signal line inactive and relinquish bus ownership (see Figure 9-2). The end of the 64th BCLK signal line period must coincide with an active START* signal line just prior to the CMD* signal line being driven active. The last cycle associated with the aforementioned signal line is allowed to complete and the signal lines are tri-stated like the above voluntary description.

If a burst access cycle is preempted, the end of the 64th BCLK signal line must coincide with the MSBURST* and MREQx* signal lines being sampled inactive. Like the burst access cycle protocol, this occurs just prior to the CMD* signal line being driven inactive. If the burst access cycle is executing a "downshift" version, the MREQx* signal line must still be sampled inactive at the end of the 64th BCLK signal line period provided the first 16 data bits have just been accessed. The platform arbitration circuitry will allow the subsequent 16 (or 8) data bits to be accessed to complete the downshift access cycle.

> *If the EISA add-on bus owner card does not follow the above protocol, the bus is "timed out". The time out will cause an NMI to be sent to the platform CPU, which will promptly reset the bus.*

> *According to the EISA Rev. 3.12 bus specification, the platform CPU is not bound by the preemption and can keep the bus as long as it wants; however, it is recommended that platforms enforce the 64 BCLK signal line protocol.*

> *Also according to the EISA Rev. 3.12 bus specification , the DMA controller will release the bus within 32 BCLK signal line cycles of the arbiter requesting preemption by driving the DACK* signal line inactive.*

> *The ISA or E-ISA bus master and some modes of the DMA controller cannot be preempted. See Chapter 7 for more information.*

For both voluntary and preemption elements, there is a minimum time before the signal lines can be driven by the next bus master. The minimum times are as follows:

- The LA, BE*, M-IO, W-R, LOCK*, and MSBURST*
  signal lines cannot be driven until 1/2 BCLK signal line
  period after the CMD* signal line is inactive.

- The START* signal line cannot be driven until one BCLK
  signal line period after the CMD* signal line is inactive.

- The DATA signal lines cannot be driven until 1 1/2 BCLK
  signal line periods after the CMD* signal line is inactive.

The above signal lines cannot be driven active for an additional BCLK signal line period to the above times (relative to the inactive CMD* signal line) if the last cycle of the previous bus owner was an EISA data-matching or any E-MIX access cycle. The EISA data-matching or E-MIX access cycle is identified by an active EX16* or EX32* signal line when the CMD* signal line goes inactive.

Finally, the EISA add-on bus owner card that was preempted cannot drive the MREQx* signal line active again until 1 1/2 BCLK signal line periods after the CMD* signal line is inactive. Additionally, the MREQx* signal line must remain inactive a minimum of two BCLK signal line periods.

SYSTEM ARBITRATION PRIORITIES

ISA or E-ISA COMPATIBLE PLATFORM

For ISA and E-ISA compatible platforms, bus ownership is very simple. The platform CPU normally owns the bus. When an ISA or E-ISA add-on bus owner card or DMA controller wants bus ownership, the DMA controller places the platform CPU in an inactive state. Similarly, the refresh controller can also place the platform CPU into an inactive state when it wants to own the bus. Some chip sets allow the platform CPU to execute out of cache, DRAM, and so forth, in parallel with the DMA or refresh controller owning the bus. The priority of bus ownership on an ISA or E-ISA compatible platform is as follows:

- The platform CPU is the default owner

- The refresh controller obtains immediate bus ownership unless the DMA controller presently owns the bus.

- Bus ownership priority by ISA or E-ISA add-on bus owner cards are based on whether the DMA controller is programmed in a "rotational" or "fixed" mode. See the EISA discussion for more information.

- Depending on the chip set and platform architecture, the platform CPU may operate in parallel with the DMA or refresh controller owning the bus.

EISA COMPATIBLE PLATFORM

The arbitration circuitry on an EISA compatible platform is more complex than the circuitry on an ISA or E-ISA compatible platform. As with the ISA and E-ISA compatible platforms, the platform CPU is the default bus owner and might have the capability to execute out of cache, DRAM, and so forth in parallel with the DMA or refresh controller owning the bus. The major difference between EISA and ISA or E-ISA compatible platforms in this case is the existence of CENTRAL ARBITRATION CIRCUITRY (CAC). The DMA and refresh controllers operate in the same fashion as on an ISA or E-ISA compatible platform. The ISA and E-ISA add-on bus owner cards still use the DMA controller to gain bus ownership (see Figure 9-3). The arbitration enhancements on EISA compatible platforms can be summarized as follows:

- The DMA and refresh controllers arbitrate with EISA add-on bus owner cards through the CAC. EISA add-on bus owner cards also arbitrate between each other through the CAC.

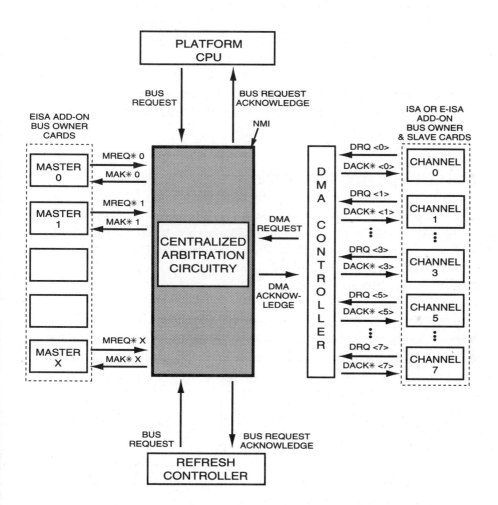

FIGURE   9-3   EISA COMPATIBLE PLATFORM ARBITRATION

- DMA block and demand mode operation of TYPE A, B, and C transfer cycles can be preempted for the refresh controller, EISA add-on bus owner cards, or the platform CPU.

- EISA add-on bus owner cards bus ownership can be preempted by the platform CPU, the DMA controller, the refresh controller, or by other EISA add-on bus owner cards.

The CAC operates with a rotating priority (see Figures 9-4 and 9-5). Bus ownership rotates among the three "groups" within the CAC. Every time a group receives bus ownership, a different member within the group obtains bus ownership. For the EISA Bus Master Group, the rotation is between the platform CPU and EISA add-on bus owner cards. There is a further rotation among the EISA add-on bus owner cards.

For the DMA Controller Group, bus ownership is awarded in two ways dependent upon software programming. One method establishes a fixed priority (Figure 9-4), and the other establishes a rotating priority among the DMA channels (Figure 9-5).

NMI has special priority; when it is active, bus ownership is immediately given to the platform CPU after preemption has occurred or refresh cycles are complete.

Some EISA compatible platforms implement different arbitration protocol than the one outlined above. It must be remembered that the order in which resources are granted bus ownership is NOT DEPENDENT upon the order of bus ownership requests.

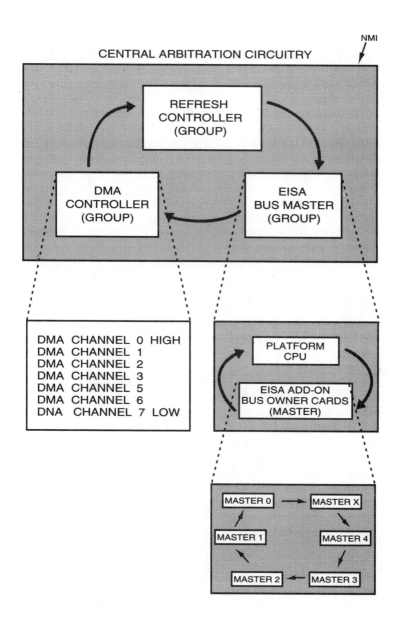

FIGURE 9-4 CAC OPERATION WITH FIXED DMA CHANNEL PRIORITY

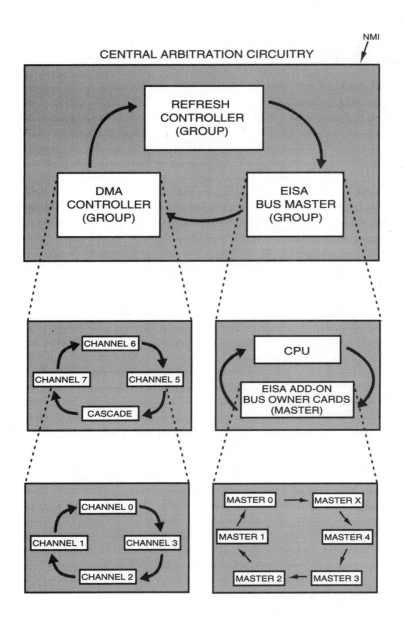

FIGURE   9-5   CAC OPERATION WITH ROTATING DMA CHANNEL PRIORITY

CHAPTER TEN

BUS INTEGRITY

INTRODUCTION

The use of a bus to interconnect add-on cards to platform resources generates a number of unique design requirements. These requirements are caused by effects that range from the transmission line nature of the bus traces to the effects of the bus on the input and output structures of the add-on boards.

The IBM technical reference manuals do not completely specify the backplane characteristics of trace separation, impedance, inductance, and so forth; consequently, bus backplanes developed by clone manufacturers have varied widely. Also, the IBM technical reference manuals simply state that the load of each slot should equal two low-power Schottky loads.

The EISA bus specification has attempted to more uniformly define the backplane. In addition, Intel has developed a high reliability AT compatible backplane which defines the backplane characteristics, DIN connector, and signal line placement on a EUROcard form factor. See Chapter 14 for more detailed information.

The diversity of the backplanes and add-on cards, the various interpretations of the bus, and the lack of engineering sophistication by some platform and board vendors requires a very conservative approach to the various topics in this chapter.

D.C. LOADING AND A.C. TIMING CONSIDERATIONS

Whenever the logic level of a signal line changes, there is a transition period before the signal line has settled to a new stable logic level at all the slot locations on the bus. The settling time is dependent on the length of the backplane, the total number of loaded slots, the load of each slot, the construction of the backplane, whether termination devices are used to minimize signal reflections, and so forth. In addition, the length of a signal line from the connector to the driver or receiver, and the types of drivers or receivers on the add-on cards and platforms vary greatly. The IEEE P996 committee, the EISA bus specification, and Intel have attempted to place "REASONABLE" parameters on slot interfaces to maximize compatibility and reliability. A summary of these parameters is contained in Table 10-1.

> *The EISA bus specification configuration space allows 15 logical slots in addition to the single (Slot 0) logical platform. However, all of the EISA timing specifications are based on seven add-on card slots in addition to the equivalent slot load of the platform.*

MAXIMUM LENGTH FROM DRIVER OR RECEIVER TO THE CONNECTOR	2.5 INCHES MAX. (3)
SPACING BETWEEN SLOT CONNECTORS	.8 INCHES MAX.
CAPACITIVE LOAD OF PLATFORM & PER SLOT	15 pF. (1)
V_{ih} AT PLATFORM OR SLOT V_{il} AT PLATFORM OR SLOT	2.0 VOLTS MIN. .8 VOLTS MAX.
V_{oh} AT PLATFORM OR SLOT V_{ol} AT PLATFORM OR SLOT	2.4 VOLTS MIN. .5 VOLTS MAX.
I_{ih} AT PLATFORM OR PER SLOT I_{il} AT PLATFORM OR PER SLOT	40 uA MAX. (2) -400 uA MAX. (2)
I_{oh} AT PLATFORM OR PER SLOT I_{ol} AT PLATFORM OR PER SLOT	SEE TABLES 10-2 & 10-3

TABLE 10-1: ISA, E-ISA, AND EISA PLATFORM AND SLOT INTERFACE

NOTES:
(1) E-ISA and EISA allows 20 pF per slot.
(2) For E-ISA and EISA compatible platforms, the current allowed is TWICE the stated current except for DRQx and IRQx (I_{il} = 20, I_{ih} = -20). The values in the table reflect the values from the original IBM technical reference manuals, which specify two LS loads per slot.
(3) E-ISA and EISA compatible platforms require a 7.5 inch maximum distance from a connector to the platform driver or receiver. It also requires a 2.5 inch maximum distance from a connector to the add-on card driver and receiver. The output drive characteristics of the platform and add-on cards have also been defined beyond the original IBM technical reference manuals.

SIGNAL LINE DRIVERS

On ISA, E-ISA, and EISA compatible platforms, there are several types of drivers. ISA and E-ISA platforms and add-on cards use low-power Schottky (LS) or advanced low-power Schottky (ALS) driver devices to limit the rise and fall times of the signal lines. This approach minimizes the settling time of the signals. The EISA bus specification does not state any such requirement.

The ISA, E-ISA, EISA busses require three types of drivers: tri-state (TS), totem pole (TP), and open collector (OC). The TS drivers are used on signal lines that are bi-directional or can be driven by different resources at different times. The TP drivers are used on signal lines that are only driven by one resource all the time. The OC drivers are used on signal lines that are driven by different resources at different times or several resources at the same time.

Each type of driver can have two minimum current requirements: version "1" and version "2". The existence of two versions of each driver is partly historical. The original IBM platforms had "line driver" quality drive devices for some signal lines, while other signal lines simply were outputs from "normal" TTL logic devices. The other reason for the existence of two versions is that some signal lines do not have to drive all of the slots.

On an ISA compatible platform, the DACKx*, IOCHK*, IOCHRDY, IOCS16*, MASTER16*, MEMCS16*, REFRESH*, TC, and SRDY* signal lines all are driven by "low power" drivers. The AC timings of these signal lines are not critical except for IOCHRDY, IOCS16*, MEMCS16*, and SRDY* signal lines. For these lines, the "low power" drivers as defined by the IBM technical reference manual is unacceptable. The 11 nanoseconds allocated in the timing tables in the book may not be sufficient for these signal lines in a fully loaded platform. The E-ISA and EISA platforms define a "high power" driver for the IOCHRDY, IOCS16*, MEMCS16*, and SRDY* signal lines that allows the 11 nanosecond settling time to be met. On EISA platforms, in addition to the above non-critical signal lines, some signal lines only drive one load (AENx, MREQX* etc.); consequently, these signal lines do not need a "high power" driver.

Table 10-2 is a summary of the output current requirements of the various drivers. TYPE 1 is "low power" and TYPE 2 is "high power".

DRIVER		I_{ol} MIN, mA		I_{oh} MIN, mA	
TYPE	VERSION	ISA	E-ISA EISA	ISA	E-ISA EISA
TP	1	2	5	-1	-.4
	2	24	24	-3	-3
TS	1	2	5	-1	-.4
	2	24	24	-3	-3
OC	1	8	5	-	-
	2	20	24	-	-

TABLE 10-2: OUTPUT CURRENT REQUIREMENTS

Table 10-3 is a summary of the drive devices' pull-up resistors for each signal line. The pull-up resistors reside only on the platform, not on the add-on cards.

LINE	DRIVER TYPE (1)	PULL-UP ISA	E-ISA EISA	LINE	DRIVER TYPE(1)	PULL-UP ISA	E-ISA EISA
AENx	TP2[TP1]	-	-	MEMR*	TS2[TS2]	4.7K	8.2K
BALE	TP2[TP2]	-	-	MEMW*	TS2[TS2]	4.7K	8.2K
DACKx*	TP1[TP1]	(5)	(5)	OSC	TP2[TP2]	-	-
DRQx	TP2[TS1]	(6)	(2,6)	REFRESH*	OC1[OC2]	4.7K	300
IOCHK*	OC1[OC2]	4.7K	4.7K	RESET	TP2[TP2]	-	-
IOCHRDY	OC1[OC2]	1.0K	1.0K	SA<0-19>	TS2[TS2]	(4)	(4)
IOCS16*	OC1[OC2]	300	300	SBHE*	TS2[TS2]	-	-
IOR*	TS2[TS2]	4.7K	8.2K	SD<0-7>	TS2[TS2]	(4)	8.2K
IOW*	TS2[TS2]	4.7K	8.2K	SD<8-15>	TS2[TS2]	(4)	8.2K
IRQx	TP2[OC1]	(3)	8.2K (6)	SMR/SMW*	TP2[TP2]	-	-
LA<17-23>	TS2[TS2]	(4)	(4)	BCLK	TP2[TP2]	-	-
MASTER16*	OC1[OC2]	300	300	TC	TP1[TS2]	-	-
MEMCS16*	OC1[OC2]	300	300	SRDY*	OC1[OC2]	300	300

TABLE 10-3-A: OUTPUT DRIVER TYPES FOR ISA, E-ISA, & EISA

LINE	DRIVER TYPE	PULL UP	LINE	DRIVER TYPE	PULL UP
BE*<0-3>	TS2	-	CMD*	TP2	-
EX16*	OC2	300	EX32*	OC2	300
EXRDY	OC2	300	LA*<24-31>	TS2	1K
LA<2-16>	TS2	(4)	LOCK*	TS2	1K
M-IO	TS2	-	MAKx*	TP1	-
MREQx*	TP1	8.2K	MSBURST*	TS2	8.2K
SLBURST*	OC2	300	START*	TS2	8.2K
W-R	TS2	-	SD<16-31>	TS2	8.2K
EMB66*(7)	OC2	300	EMB133*(7)	OC2	300

TABLE 10-3-B: OUTPUT DRIVER TYPES, EISA SPECIFIC

NOTES:
(1) The bracketed "[ ]" numbers are for E-ISA and EISA compatible platforms and add-on cards.
(2) Pull-down resistor of 5.6K.
(3) Older platforms may have a 2.2K pull-up resistor to support a shared-pulse IRQx signal line ... but this interrupt sharing method does not seem to work or to have been widely accepted.
(4) Some platforms have installed 10K pull-up resistors to prevent these signal lines from floating to unknown states. Sometimes these floating signal lines can oscillate at high frequencies, which can have secondary effects on the platform circuitry.
(5) A maximum of six slots can be attached to this signal line.
(6) Older designs may use a totem pole (TP) output driver. Thus, new designs should use a 47 ohm series resistor on this signal line to prevent driver damage due to TP, OC, and TS drivers on the same signal line. The resistor is not required if the driver can tolerate a buffer fight.
(7) These are defined for EISA Enhanced Master Burst (FAST EISA) platform.

NOTE: On EISA compatible platforms, the E14, F12, and F14 pins (See Chapter 14) are reserved and pulled high by individual 300 ohm resistors. E12 and E13 are Reserved on non-EISA-enhanced master burst platforms (Fast EISA); otherwise, they are used for EMB66* and EMB133* signal lines.

SETTLING TIME

A.C. timings are one of the most important considerations for reliable bus operations. Because IBM and other manufacturers have never published a comprehensive set of A.C. timing specifications, designers have had to "reverse engineer" from IBM platforms. The situation has now improved, with Intel (for the P2/aPC connector on Multibus II), IEEE (through the P996 technical committee), and COMPAQ (as part of the EISA consortium) providing A.C. timings for the bus.

In addition to the historical lack of timing specifications, problems are compounded further because many platforms and add-on cards have been developed without proper bus engineering. Trace spacing and width, layer location, and impedance have varied widely. The trace length from the connector to the drivers and receivers sometimes far exceeds 2.5 and 7.5 inches for add-on cards and platforms, respectively. Furthermore, the type and number of drivers and receivers have varied widely.

In order to resolve these problems while maintaining compatibility with existing platforms and add-on cards, the IEEE P996 committee, Intel, and this author have assumed an 11 nanosecond bus settling time including one nanosecond of clock skew. The EISA bus specification identified five nanoseconds of settling time with a table providing additional settling time dependent on the type of the driver. The board design is required to include these numbers. However, if the proper driver (as shown in Table 10-3-A & B) is chosen for a design, the 11 nanoseconds should be sufficient. As mentioned, boards designed like the original "AT" may have some problems with fully loaded backplanes.

The settling times, as well as the delay and setup times specified in this book are based on worst case conditions. The reason why even the original "AT" numbers work is because in the real world the timings generally are "typical" not "worst case".

The inclusion of 11 nanoseconds within the timing parameters will insure a very high degree of compatibility between past, present, and future platforms and boards. It assumes a fully loaded eight slot backplane (the platform is the ninth slot). For a low to high transition, the time is measured from .5 volts at the driver to 2.0 volts at the receiver. For a high to low transition, the time is measured from 2.4 volts at the driver to .8 volts at the receiver.

Another consideration is the distribution of the BCLK signal line. On an ISA compatible platform, the BCLK signal line is distributed in a "daisy chain fashion", that is, slot to slot starting at one end and progressing to the other end. The clock skew is at least 11 nanoseconds with such an arrangement. On an E-ISA or EISA compatible platform, the BCLK signal line is distributed in a "starburst" fashion. The starburst distribution is accomplished in two ways: One way is for a single driver to be the source for each individual line for each slot. Another way is to use a clock driver chip with an individual output line to each slot. The two methods, in conjunction with careful trace design and termination, allows the clock skew between slots to be about one nanosecond.

TIMING TABLE INTERPRETATION

The interpretation of the "#/DET" column in the A.C. timing tables of this book is as follows:

- #: The timing number with no Detail indicates that no bus settling time was included. An example is Parameter 5 of Table 6-1-A. A valid LA<17-23> signal line value is measured at the add-on card. A decoding of the address occurs on the add-on card and the MEMCS16* signal line is properly driven. Because both are measured at the add-on card, no bus settling time is included.

- **#/A:** These timing numbers include the skew between two signals driven by the same source and monitored by another. An example is parameter 4/A of Table 6-1-B. The platform CPU drives the LA<17-23> signal lines; subsequently, it drives the memory COMMAND signal line active. The platform CPU (for 16 bits) has a minimum of 120 nanoseconds between these two events. When measured at the add-on card, it is listed as 109 nanoseconds. This reflects the worst case assumption that the ADDRESS signal lines used the full 11 nanoseconds settling time while the COMMAND signal line has the absolute minimum settling time of 0 nanoseconds. This represents the theoretical worst case; the actual worst case for a reasonably designed or lightly loaded system is less.

- **#/B:** These timing numbers reflect bus settling in two directions. A "driving" resource drives a signal line to a "receiving" resource on the bus. The receiving resource responds by driving a signal back to the driving source. An example is parameter 5/B of Table 6-1-B. The platform CPU drives valid the LA<17-23> signal lines to the add-on card, and it takes 11 nanoseconds for the signal to settle at the add-on card. The add-on card decodes the ADDRESS signal lines and responds by driving the MEMCS16* signal line active. The platform CPU will not receive a stable MEMCS16* signal line until 11 nanoseconds after it was driven active by the add-on card. Thus, in addition to the 80 nanosecond decode time (see Parameter 5), there is an additional 22 nanoseconds of round trip settling time before the MEMCS16* signal line is valid relative to the LA<17-23> signal lines at the platform CPU.

- **#/C and #/D:** These parameters are similar to the #/B parameter in that a round trip settling time is involved. In the case of the #/B parameter, the round trip time was 11 + 11 = 22 nanoseconds. In the case of the #/C parameter, the signal line is "driven" active only by a 1K ohm pull-up resistor. Thus, the "round trip" is 11 + 78 = 89 nanoseconds for an ISA compatible platform. The extra capacitance on E-ISA and EISA compatible platforms results increases this to 115 nanoseconds. In the case of the #/D parameter, the signal line is "driven" active by a 300 ohm pull-up resistor. Thus, the "round trip" is 11 + 22 = 33 nanoseconds for an ISA compatible platform. The extra capacitance on E-ISA and EISA compatible platforms increases the time to 40 nanoseconds.

An example of the #/C parameter is 20/C of Table 6-1-B for the "OLD AT". The platform CPU will not receive a stable IOCHRDY signal line until 78 nanoseconds after the open collector driver of the add-on card has released it. Thus, in addition to the 301 nanoseconds (see parameter 20 for 8 data bits), there is an additional 89 nanoseconds of "round trip" settling time before the IOCHRDY signal line is valid relative to an active COMMAND signal line at the platform CPU.

An example of the #/D parameter is 5/D of Table 6-1-B. The platform CPU will not receive a stable MEMCS16* signal line until 22 nanoseconds after the open collector driver of the add-on card has released it. Thus, in addition to the 66 nanoseconds (see Parameter 5 for MEMCS16* signal line inactive), there is an additional 33 nanoseconds of "round trip" settling time before the MEMCS16* signal line is valid relative to valid LA<17-23> signal lines at the platform CPU.

- #/E: This parameter is the same as the #/A parameter, except that the theoretical worst case settling time is 0 nanoseconds. An example of this parameter is 6/E of Table 6-1-B. When the platform CPU drives the LA<17-23> signal lines invalid, there is a minimum hold time before the add-on card responds by driving the MEMCS16* signal line invalid. In this case, a pull-up resistor will drive the MEMCS16* signal line inactive. But from the view point of worst case hold time, 0 nanoseconds is used. The actual minimum hold time will be greater.

- **#/F**: This parameter simply reflects the delay due to a 300 ohm pull-up resistor in an EISA compatible platform. An example of this parameter is 10/F in Table 6-11-B. The EXRDY signal line is released by the open collector at the add-on card relative to the rising edge of the BCLK signal line. The EXRDY signal line must be valid 15 nanoseconds prior to the falling edge of the BCLK signal line at the EISA bus master. Given the minimum BCLK signal line high time of 55 nanoseconds (8.33 MHz BCLK), a rise time of 29 nanoseconds (due to the RC time constant), and the setup time of 15 nanoseconds, the maximum delay of the EXRDY signal line being released relative to the rising edge of the BCLK signal line is 11 nanoseconds.

-#/H This parameter is similar to Parameter #/F except the pull-up resistor value is 1K.

CHAPTER ELEVEN

PERFORMANCE

Tables 11-1 to 11-7 summarize the maximum bus performance for back to back access and transfer cycles. These tables are based on the BCLK signal being 8.00 MHz and 8.33 MHz. The access cycles assume the back to back timings specified in Tables 6-29 and 6-30. The ready access cycle assumes one wait state (one BCLK period). Also, the performance numbers assume no data-matching and no refresh cycles. The transfer cycles do not include any overhead for the time delay between active DRQx and DACKx* signal lines and assumes the maximum performance with demand or block modes without CONVERSION. The ready transfer cycles assume one wait state (one BCLK period). The COMPATIBLE transfer cycle has two BCLK signal line periods per wait state. I-MIX and E-MIX access cycles are not listed because of the diversity of possible implementations by various chip sets.

DATA SIZE (BITS)	8.00 MHZ AND [8.33 MHZ] MEGABYTES PER SECOND		
	NO WAIT	STANDARD	READY
8	2.66 [2.77] (1)	1.33 [1.39]	1.14 [1.19]
16	8.00 [8.33]	5.33 [5.55]	4.00 [4.165]

TABLE 11-1: ISA AND E-ISA PLATFORM CPU ACCESS TO ISA OR E-ISA SLAVE MEMORY PERFORMANCE

DATA SIZE (BITS)	8.00 MHZ AND [8.33 MHZ] MEGABYTES PER SECOND		
	NO WAIT	STANDARD	READY
8	2.00 [2.08] (4)	1.14 [1.19]	1.00 [1.04]
16	NA [NA]	4.00 [4.165]	3.20 [3.33]

TABLE 11-2: ISA AND E-ISA PLATFORM CPU ACCESS TO ISA OR E-ISA SLAVE I/O PERFORMANCE

DATA SIZE (BITS)	8.00 MHZ AND [8.33 MHZ] MEGABYTES PER SECOND		
	NO WAIT (2)	STANDARD	READY
8	2.66 [2.77] (1)	1.33 [1.39]	1.14 [1.19]
16	8.00 [8.33]	5.33 [5.55]	4.00 [4.165]

TABLE 11-3: ISA AND E-ISA ADD-ON BUS OWNER CARD ACCESS TO ISA OR E-ISA SLAVE MEMORY PERFORMANCE

DATA SIZE (BITS)	8.00 MHZ AND [8.33 MHZ] MEGABYTES PER SECOND		
	NO WAIT (2)	STANDARD	READY
8	2.00 [2.08] (4)	1.14 [1.19]	1.00 [1.04]
16	NA [NA]	4.00 [4.165]	3.20 [3.33]

TABLE 11-4: ISA AND E-ISA ADD-ON BUS OWNER CARD ACCESS TO ISA OR E-ISA SLAVE I/O PERFORMANCE

DATA SIZE (BITS)	8.00 MHZ AND [8.33 MHZ] MEGABYTES PER SECOND				
	STANDARD	READY	COMPRESSED	BURST	EMB66 (5)	EMB133 (5)
16	8.00 [8.33]	5.33 [5.55]	10.67 [11.11]	16.00 [16.66]	32.00 [33.32]	64.00 [66.64]
32	16.00 [16.66]	10.66 [11.10]	21.34 [22.22]	32.00 [32.32]	64.00 [66.64]	128.00 [133.28]

TABLE 11-5: EISA BUS MASTER ACCESS TO EISA MEMORY PERFORMANCE

DATA SIZE (BITS)	8.00 MHZ AND [8.33 MHZ] MEGABYTES PER SECOND		
	STANDARD	READY	COMPRESSED
16	8.00 [8.33]	5.33 [5.55]	10.67 [11.11]
32	16.00 [16.66]	10.66 [11.10]	21.34 [22.22]

TABLE 11-6: EISA BUS MASTER ACCESS TO EISA I/O PERFORMANCE

DATA SIZE (BITS)	8.00 MHZ AND [8.33 MHZ] MEGABYTES PER SECOND (6)	
	STANDARD	READY
8	1.00 [1.04]	.80 [.83]
16	2.00 [2.08]	1.60 [1.67]
32	4.00 [4.16]	3.20 [3.34]

TABLE 11-7: COMPATIBLE TRANSFER PERFORMANCE

DATA SIZE (BITS)	8.00 MHZ AND [8.33 MHZ] MEGABYTES PER SECOND (6)	
	STANDARD	READY
8	1.33 [1.39]	1.14 [1.19]
16	2.66 [2.78]	2.29 [2.38]
32	5.32 [5.56]	4.58 [4.76]

TABLE 11-8: TYPE A TRANSFER PERFORMANCE

DATA SIZE (BITS)	8.00 MHZ AND [8.33 MHZ] MEGABYTES PER SECOND (6)	
	STANDARD	READY
8	2.00 [2.08]	1.60 [1.67]
16	4.00 [4.17]	3.20 [3.33]
32	8.00 [8.34]	6.40 [6.66]

TABLE 11-9: TYPE B TRANSFER PERFORMANCE

DATA SIZE (BITS)	8.00 MHZ AND [8.33 MHZ] MEGABYTES PER SECOND (6) STANDARD	READY
8	8.00 [8.33]	4.00 [4.165]
16	16.00 [16.66]	8.00 [8.33]
32	32.00 [33.32]	16.00 [16.66]

TABLE 11-10: TYPE C TRANSFER PERFORMANCE

NOTES:
(1) The IBM AT only sampled the SRDY* signal line in the fourth BCLK period. E-ISA bus masters sample in the third BCLK signal line period. Thus, 2.66 [2.77 becomes 2.00 [2.08] for an AT platform.
(2) Only on an E-ISA or EISA compatible platform.
(3) EISA bus master access to 8 data bit EISA I/O resources.
(4) The IBM AT only sampled the SRDY* signal line in the fourth BCLK period. E-ISA bus masters sample in the third BCLK signal line period. Thus 2.00 [2.08] becomes 1.60 [1.67] for an AT platform.
(5) For EISA Enhanced Master Burst (Fast EISA) platforms.
(6) The times in the table assume continuous repetitive cycles. Initial BCLK signal line periods are not included. See page 360 for more information.

CHAPTER TWELVE

CONFIGURATION SPACE

INTRODUCTION

As mentioned in Chapter 2, there are specific I/O address locations assigned to each of the add-on card slots on the EISA bus. The AENx signal lines are specific to each slot. An access to an I/O address reserved for a specific slot results in the deactivation of the AENx signal line for that slot. The other AENx signal lines are activated to prevent the other add-on I/O slave cards from responding to the access cycle.

RESERVED REGISTERS

As outlined in Chapter 2, I/O addresses 0000H - 00FFH, 0400H - 04FFH, 0800H - 08FFH, and 0C00H - 0CFFH are reserved for the platform. I/O addresses 0000H - 00FFH are the traditional I/O peripherals, 0400H - 04FFH are reserved for present and future EISA platform peripherals, and 0800H - 08FFH and 0C00H - 0CFFH are reserved for manufacturer-specific I/O peripherals.

Within each set of the specific I/O address locations assigned to a specific slot there are five locations defined by the EISA bus specification. These registers are at addresses 0XC80H to 0XC84H. The value of X is the slot number with the value of X = 0 reserved for the platform.

These configuration registers may be supported on an E-ISA compatible platform, but are not supported on an ISA platform. The E-ISA or EISA compatible bus master will read an FFH from the 0XC80H location if the add-on card does not support this function or if no add-on card is present.

See the EISA Rev. 3.12 bus specification for further information concerning the use of these registers.

CHAPTER THIRTEEN

POWER AND INITIALIZATION

POWER TOLERANCE

The power to add-on cards is supplied only though the slot connectors, and must meet specific voltage and current requirements. Table 13-1 outlines these requirements.

VOLTAGE NOMINAL	VOLTAGE MIN	VOLTAGE MAX	CURRENT 8 MAX	CURRENT 8/16 MAX	VOLTAGE SENSE MIN	PEAK/PEAK NOISE MAX (5)
12	11.4	12.6	1.5 (1)	1.5 (1)	10.8	120 mV
-12	-10.8 (2)	-13.2 (2)	.3	.3	-10.2	120 mV
5	4.875 (3)	5.25	3.0	4.5	4.5	50 mV
-5	-4.5 (4)	-5.5 (4)	.2	.2	-4.3	50 mV

TABLE 13-1: POWER PER SLOT

NOTES:

(1) IEEE P996 specs 1.0
(2) IEEE P996 specs -11.4 and -12.6
(3) EISA specs 4.5
(4) IEEE P996 specs -4.75 and -5.25
(5) PEAK to PEAK noise voltage is defined by the IEEE P996

The above table represents the combination of the EISA and the IEEE P996 bus specifications. For the cases in which the IEEE P996 bus specification disagrees with the EISA bus

FIGURE 13-1: POWER ON SEQUENCE

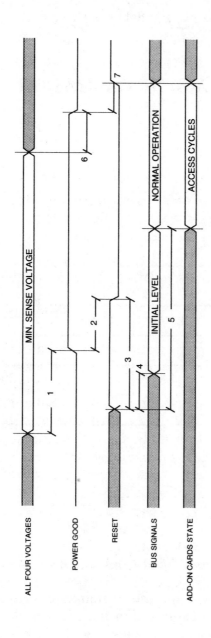

FIGURE   13-1:   POWER ON SEQUENCE

specification, the entry placed in the table for voltage is the one that was closest to the original IBM PC, XT and AT Technical Reference Manuals.

The minimum 5 volt signal of 4.875 is specified by the IEEE P996 and is higher than the 4.5 specified by the EISA bus specification and the IBM Technical Reference Manual. The higher voltage allows for the fact that some chips require a minimum of 4.5 volts.

INITIALIZATION

The VOLTAGE SENSE entries in Table 13-1 are from the original IBM PC and XT Technical Reference Manuals. The power supply in an IBM, ISA, E-ISA, or EISA system drives a power good signal to the reset control circuitry of the platform CPU. This signal remains inactive for a period between 100 and 500 milliseconds (#1) after the four voltages are above the minimum SENSE VOLTAGE. (See Figure 13-1.) The reset control circuitry on the platform drives the RESET signal line active during this period. The RESET signal is held active a minimum of 1 millisecond (#2) after the power good signal is active or until the RESET signal line is active for a minimum of nine BCLK signal line periods (TCLK), whichever is longer (#3). When the RESET signal line is driven active, the add-on cards have a maximum of 500 nanoseconds (#4) to drive the bus signal lines to their initial state. Also, there is a maximum of 1 millisecond (#5) from an active RESET signal line before the platform CPU can begin access cycles to the add-on cards.

Whenever any of the voltages drop below the SENSE VOLTAGE, the power good signal from the power supply will be driven inactive immediately (#6). (See Figure 13-1.) In response to an inactive power good signal, the RESET signal line is immediately driven active (#7).

The initial level of all signal lines is inactive except for the BCLK, OSC, IRQx, ADDRESS, and DATA signal lines. The BCLK and OSC signal lines are driven at their appropriate frequency. The ADDRESS and DATA signal lines are driven by the platform CPU but are invalid. The IRQ signal lines are active unless an add-on card has specifically driven individual lines inactive.

After normal operation, if the RESET signal line is driven active, all add-on cards should operate as if the platform was just powered up and initialized. All of the signal lines will follow the protocol outlined in the above paragraph.

Right after reset, the platform CPU is the first bus owner.

All of the above information concerning initialization is a combination of information from the IEEE P996 specification and various IBM technical reference manuals. It is sometimes unclear which platforms adhere to these specifications.

CHAPTER FOURTEEN

MECHANICAL NOTES

The following pages show some of the physical characteristics of the ISA and EISA busses. Three card configurations are shown, representing the 8 data bit (XT), 8/16 data bit (AT, ISA), or 8/16/32 data bit (EISA) cards.

The first four figures show the connector pin identification, board outline, and bracket position for the ISA bus. The connectors are readily available in either one- or two-piece construction. They are typically mounted on 0.8 inch centers on a platform CPU board or on a passive backplane.

The following figures show the same information for the EISA bus. Note that the EISA connector has a second level of contacts; the top level are the ISA contacts and the lower level are the EISA contacts. Physical stops (or "access keys") aligned with grooves in an EISA add-in card prevent ISA boards from reaching the EISA contacts.

Detailed mechanical drawings are beyond the scope of this book. For additional details, and for official bus specifications, please contact the following sources. In the case of connectors and brackets, other sources are available in addition to those listed.

ISA IEEE 996 Specification:

IEEE Standards Office
445 Hoes Lane
Piscataway, NJ 08854

ISA/EISA connectors and card-edge layout:

AMP, Inc.
PO Box 3608
Harrisburg, PA 17111

717-564-0100
717-986-7813 FAX

Card brackets:

Globe Manufacturing Sales Co.
1180 Globe Ave.
Mountainside, NJ 07092

908-232-7301

Signal	Pin	Pin	Signal
0V	B01	A01	IOCHK*
RESET	B02	A02	SD7
+5V	B03	A03	SD6
IRQ9	B04	A04	SD5
-5	B05	A05	SD4
DRQ2	B06	A06	SD3
-12V	B07	A07	SD2
SRDY*	B08	A08	SD1
+12V	B09	A09	SD0
0V	B10	A10	IOCHRDY
SMEMW*	B11	A11	AEN
SMEMR*	B12	A12	SA19
IOW*	B13	A13	SA18
IOR*	B14	A14	SA17
DACK 3*	B15	A15	SA16
DRQ3	B16	A16	SA15
DACK1*	B17	A17	SA14
DRQ1	B18	A18	SA13
REFRESH*	B19	A19	SA12
BLCK	B20	A20	SA11
IRQ7	B21	A21	SA10
IRQ6	B22	A22	SA9
IRQ5	B23	A23	SA8
IRQ4	B24	A24	SA7
IRQ3	B25	A25	SA6
DACK2*	B26	A26	SA5
TC	B27	A27	SA4
BALE	B28	A28	SA3
+5V	B29	A29	SA2
OSC	B30	A30	SA1
0V	B31	A31	SA0

P1

Bracket End ↑

← Add-in Board Component Side

Signal	Pin	Pin	Signal
MEMCS16*	D01	C01	SGHE*
IOCS16*	D02	C02	LA23
IRQ10	D03	C03	LS22
IRQ11	D04	C04	LA21
IRQ12	D05	C05	SA20
IRQ15	D06	C06	LA19
IRQ14	D07	C07	LA18
DACK0*	D08	C08	LA17
DRQ0	D09	C09	MEMR*
DACK5*	D10	C10	MEMW*
DRQ5	D11	C11	SD8
DACK6*	D12	C12	SD9
DRQ6	D13	C13	SD10
DACK7*	D14	C14	SD11
DRQ7	D15	C15	SD12
+5V	D16	C16	SD13
MASTER16*	D17	C17	SD14
0V	D18	C18	SD15

P2

FIGURE 14-1:   ISA BUS PIN IDENTIFICATION

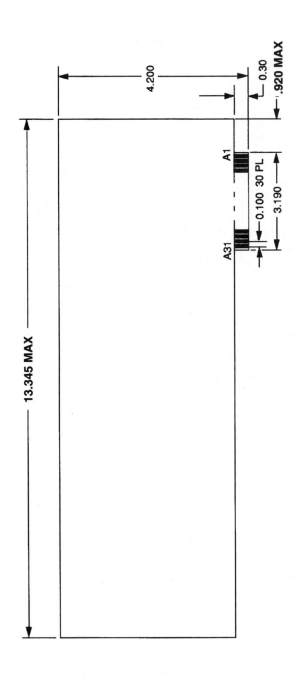

FIGURE 14-2:   ISA 8 BIT ADD-ON CARD CONFIGURATION

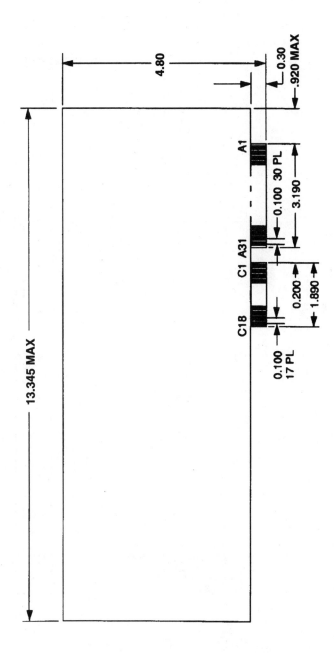

FIGURE 14-3:   ISA 8/16 BIT ADD-ON CARD CONFIGURATION

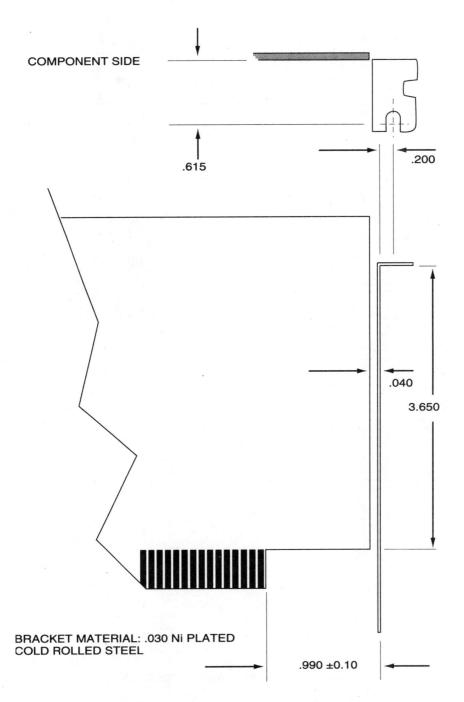

COMPONENT SIDE

.200

.615

.040

3.650

BRACKET MATERIAL: .030 Ni PLATED
COLD ROLLED STEEL

.990 ±0.10

FIGURE 14-4:   ISA AND EISA CARD BRACKET MOUNTING POSITION

ROW F	ROW B	PIN NO.	ROW E	ROW A
GND	GND	1	CMD*	IOCHK*
+5V	RESET	2	START*	SD<7>
+5V	+5V	3	EXRDY	SD<6>
XXXXX	IRQ<9>	4	EX32*	SD<5>
XXXXX	-5V	5	GND	SD<4>
KEY	DRQ<2>	6	KEY	SD<3>
XXXXX	-12V	7	EX16*	SD<2>
XXXXX	SRDY*	8	SLBURST*	SD<1>
+12V	+12V	9	MSBURST*	SD<0>
M-IO	GND	10	W-R	IOCHRDY
LOCK*	SMEMW*	11	GND	AENx
RESERVED	SMEMR*	12	EMB66*	SA<19>
GND	IOW*	13	EMB133*	SA<18>
RESERVED	IOR*	14	RESERVED	SA<17>
BE*<3>	DACK*<3>	15	GND	SA<16>
KEY	DRQ<3>	16	KEY	SA<15>
BE*<2>	DACK*<1>	17	BE*<1>	SA<14>
BE*<0>	DRQ<1>	18	LA*<31>	SA<13>
GND	REFRESH*	19	GND	SA<12>
+5V	BCLK	20	LA*<30>	SA<11>
LA*<29>	IRQ<7>	21	LA*<28>	SA<10>
GND	IRQ<6>	22	LA*<27>	SA<9>
LA*<26>	IRQ<5>	23	LA*<25>	SA<8>
LA*<24>	IRQ<4>	24	GND	SA<7>
KEY	IRQ<3>	25	KEY	SA<6>
LA<16>	DACK*<2>	26	LA<15>	SA<5>
LA<14>	TC	27	LA<13>	SA<4>
+5V	BALE	28	LA<12>	SA<3>
+5V	+5V	29	LA<11>	SA<2>
GND	OSC	30	GND	SA<1>
LA<10>	GND	31	LA<9>	SA<0>

ROW H	ROW D	PIN NO.	ROW G	ROW C
LA<8>	MEMCS16*	1	LA<7>	SBHE*
LA<6>	IOCS16*	2	GND	LA<23>
LA<5>	IRQ<10>	3	LA<4>	LA<22>
+5V	IRQ<11>	4	LA<3>	LA<21>
LA<2>	IRQ<12>	5	GND	LA<20>
KEY	IRQ<15>	6	KEY	LA<19>
SD<16>	IRQ<14>	7	SD<17>	LA<18>
SD<18>	DACK*<0>	8	SD<19>	LA<17>
GND	DRQ<0>	9	SD<20>	MEMR*
SD<21>	DACK*<5>	10	SD<22>	MEMW*
SD<23>	DRQ<5>	11	GND	SD<8>
SD<24>	DACK*<6>	12	SD<25>	SD<9>
GND	DRQ<6>	13	SD<26>	SD<10>
SD<27>	DACK*<7>	14	SD<28>	SD<11>
KEY	DRQ<7>	15	KEY	SD<12>
SD<29>	+5V	16	GND	SD<13>
+5V	MASTER16*	17	SD<30>	SD<14>
+5V	GND	18	SD<31>	SD<15>
MAKx*		19	MREQx*	

Order of reserved pin assignments: E14, F12, F14
XXXXX pins for manufacturer-specific use. Add-on cards must NOT CONNECT to these pins.

FIGURE 14-5:   EISA BUS PIN IDENTIFICATION

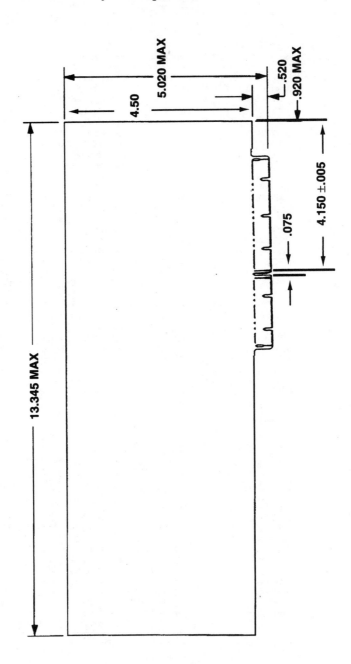

FIGURE 14-6:   EISA ADD-ON CARD CONFIGURATION

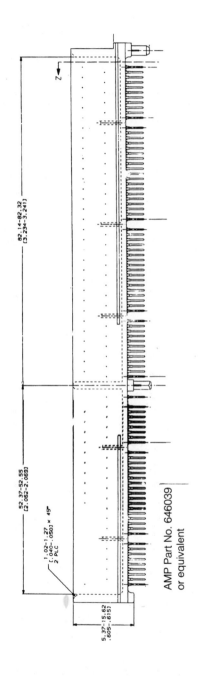

FIGURE 14-7: *EISA CONNECTOR DETAIL*

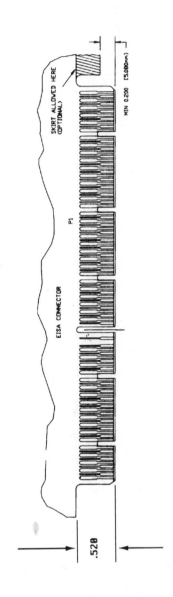

FIGURE 14-8:   EISA CARD EDGE DETAIL

APPENDIX A

EISA EMB (FAST EISA)

A consortium have expanded the EISA burst access cycle definition to provide increased performance. The name of this "evolved" EISA burst access cycle is the EISA Enhanced Master Burst (EISA EMB) access cycle. This cycle has also been called Fast EISA.

The method provides for the transfer of data through a 32 bit wide data path for a factor of two speed increase. That increased data width may also be coupled with a capability to transfer data at twice the rate, for an additional factor of two speed increase. These data rates are shown in Table 11.5, page 452.

The protocol makes use of two additional signal lines, EMB66* and EMB133*, which appear on Pins E12 and E13 of the EISA connector. The negotiation is initiated by the resource notifying the bus master of its data width and transfer speed abilities; the bus master responds with its capabilities and the resource confirms the arrangement.

The EISA EMB (Fast EISA) specification is explained and clarified by an Addendum to this book. The Fast EISA Addendum is available from Annabooks for $29.50. Annabooks' address and telephone numbers are listed at the end of this book.

Steve Robalino, Technical, or
Jim Habuda, Marketing
DPT
140 Candace Dr.
Maitland, FL 32751

407-830-5522

When available, the official specification will be available from:

BCPR Services, Inc.
1400 L St. NW
Washington, DC 20005

202-371-5921

APPENDIX B

PC/96 BUS

Intel has designed a version of the ISA bus that uses high-reliability connectors. This version is implemented on a EUROcard form factor, and uses a 96 pin DIN connector. The PC/96 bus improves the ground/signal line ratio, provides a larger card form factor, and has a more reliable connector for use in hostile environments. The connector has three rows of 32 pins each, and has the male part of the connector on the bus. This arrangement allows the optional use of a 128 pin connector on the card, leaving one row of pins available for user defined functions.

Figure B-1 shows the PC/96 bus pin identification, and Figure B-2 shows the backplane and stacking methods.

The connector used for the PC/96 bus is the DIN 41632. The EUROcard form factor is specified in the mechanical portion of ANSI/IEEE Std 1296-1987. This specification is an application of ANSI/IEEE Std 1101-1987.

See the IEEE P996 specification for additional information on the PC/96 bus. You may also obtain information from the Intel Multibus II group by asking about the P2/aPC bus.

Pin Number	Row A	Row B	Row C	Row D (Optional)
1	0V	IOR*	0V	UDP1
2	+5V	IOW*	+5V	UDP2
3	+12V	MEMR*	-12V	UDP3
4	BALE	MEMW*	SBHE*	UDP4
5	SA0	LACHn	SA1	UDP5
6	SA2	0V	SA3	UDP6
7	SA4	SA5	SA6	UDP7
8	SA7	SA8	SA9	UDP8
9	SA10	SA11	SA12	UDP9
10	SA13	SA14	SA15	UDP10
11	SA16	LA17	LA18	UDP11
12	LA19	LA20	LA21	UDP12
13	LA22	LA23	IRQ3	UDP13
14	IRQ4	IRQ5	IRQ6	UDP14
15	IRQ7	IRQ9	IRQ10	UDP15
16	IRQ11	IRQ12	IRQ14	UDP16
17	IRQ15	IOCHCK*	DRQ0	UDP17
18	DRQ1	DRQ2	DRQ3	UDP18
19	DRQ5	DRQ6	DRQ7	UDP19
20	DACK0*	0V	DACK1*	UDP20
21	DACK2*	DACK3*	DACK5*	UDP21
22	DACK6*	DACK7*	TC	UDP22
23	SD0	SD1	SD2	UDP23
24	SD3	+5V	SD4	UDP24
25	SD5	SD6	SD7	UDP25
26	SD8	SD9	SD10	UDP26
27	SD11	SD12	SD13	UDP27
28	SD14	SD15	IOCHRDY	UDP28
29	AEN	MEMCS16*	IOCS16*	UDP29
30	RESETDRV	ENDXFR*	MASTER*	UDP30
31	+5V	REFRESH*	+5V	UDP31
32	0V	SYSCLK	0V	UDP32

FIGURE B-1:   PC/96 PIN IDENTIFICATION

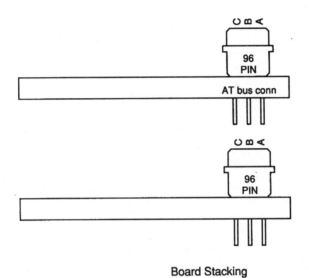

Board Stacking

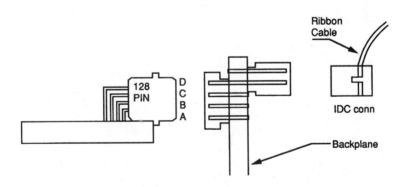

Through-Backplane Connections

FIGURE B-2:   *PC/96 BACKPLANE STACKING METHODS*

Notes

APPENDIX C

PC/104

The PC/104 Consortium was formed to provide ISA compatibility in a compact form factor more suited for use in embedded systems. The boards are 3.6 by 3.8 inches, and eliminate the need for a backplane by being stackable. The bus derives its name from the two connectors used: 64 pins on P1 and 40 pins on P2.

Figures on the following pages illustrate the mechanical features of the PC/104 bus. For additional information, including copies of the specification, please contact the following source:

PC/104 Consortium
990 Almanor Avenue
Sunnyvale, CA 94086

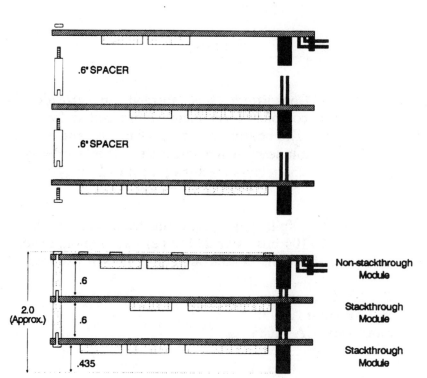

FIGURE C-1:   PC/104 TYPICAL MODULE STACK

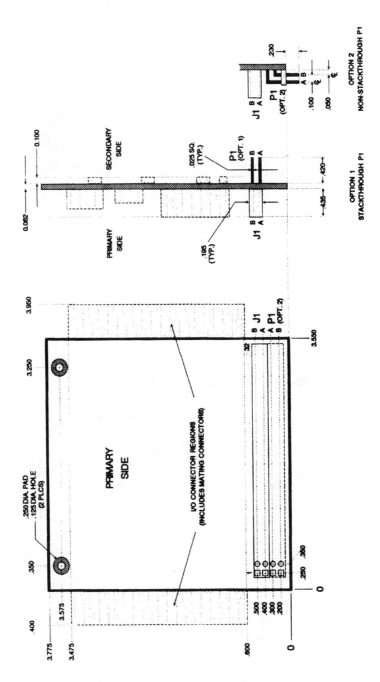

FIGURE C-2:   *PC/104 8 BIT MODULE DIMENSIONS*

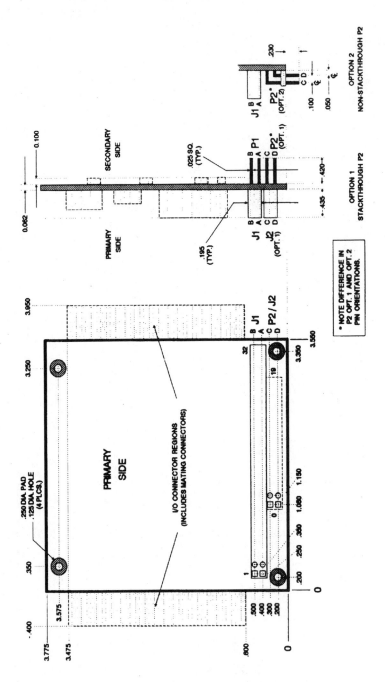

FIGURE C-3:   PC/104 16 BIT MODULE DIMENSIONS

Pin Number	J1/P1 Row A	J1/P1 Row B	J2/P2 Row C	J2/P2 Row D
0	--	--	0V	0V
1	IOCHCHK*	0V	SBHE*	MEMCS16*
2	SD7	RESETDRV	LA23	IOCS16*
3	SD6	+5V	LA22	IRQ10
4	SD5	IRQ9	LA21	IRQ11
5	SD4	-5V	LA20	IRQ12
6	SD3	DRQ2	LA19	IRQ15
7	SD2	-12V	LA18	IRQ14
8	SD1	ENDXFR*	LA17	DACK0*
9	SD0	+12V	MEMR*	DRQ0
10	IOCHRDY	(KEY)	MEMW*	DACK5*
11	AEN	SMEMW*	SD8	DRQ5
12	SA19	SMEMR*	SD9	DACK6*
13	SA18	IOW*	SD10	DRQ6
14	SA17	IOR*	SD11	DACK7*
15	SA16	DACK3*	SD12	DRQ7
16	SA15	DRQ3	SD13	+5V
17	SA14	DACK1*	SD14	MASTER*
18	SA13	DRQ1	SD15	0V
19	SA12	REFRESH*	(KEY)	0V
20	SA11	SYSCLK	--	--
21	SA10	IRQ7	--	--
22	SA9	IRQ6	--	--
23	SA8	IRQ5	--	--
24	SA7	IRQ4	--	--
25	SA6	IRQ3	--	--
26	SA5	DACK2*	--	--
27	SA4	TC	--	--
28	SA3	BALE	--	--
29	SA2	+5V	--	--
30	SA1	OSC	--	--
31	SA0	0V	--	--
32	0V	0V	--	--

NOTES:
1. Rows C and D are not used on 8-bit modules.
2. P2 has two connector options with differing physical pinout orientation.
3. B10 and C19 are key locations.
4. Signal timing and function are as specified in P996.
5. Signal source/sink current differ from P996 values.

FIGURE C-4: PC/104 BUS SIGNAL ASSIGNMENTS

Notes

APPENDIX D

PCXI EISA PASSIVE BACKPLANE

The PCXI Consortium was established in order to provide a uniform standard for a passive backplane for the EISA bus. It is intended to be used in conjunction with the EISA Rev. 3.12 specification, and in no way alters the EISA specification.

In order to implement a passive backplane version of the EISA bus, additional connectors are necessary. The PCXI specifies two additional connectors in addition to the EISA P1 and P2: P3 has 20 pins and P4 has 66 pins. Both of the new connectors are of the double-row configuration being used by EISA.

The connector scheme allows for two distinct types of extended edge-cards. One is for slot 0 (CPU) controller boards with special keying to fit only in slot 0 controller slots. There must be at least one Slot 0 board in the system. The other type is defined for P3 or P4 auxiliary boards (also called non-slot 0 boards) with a different keying method to fit only into auxiliary bus slots.

The figures in this Appendix show the connector configuration for Slot 0, Slot 0 pin assignments, and non-Slot 0 pin assignments. The keying methods are described in the specification, but are not shown in this book. Additional details are available from the following source:

Matthew Arksey
PCXI Consortium
433 North 34th St.
Seattle, WA 98103

FAX 206-548-0322

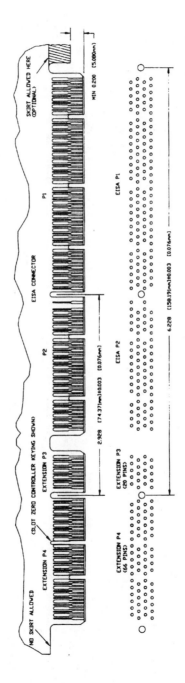

FIGURE D-1:   *SLOT 0 AND P3/P4 CARD-EDGE CONNECTOR*

ROW F	ROW B	PIN NO.	ROW E	ROW A
GND	GND	1	CMD*	IOCHK*
+5V	RESDRV	2	START*	SD<7>
+5V	+5V	3	EXRDY	SD<6>
XXXXX	IRQ<9>	4	EX32*	SD<5>
XXXXX	-5V	5	GND	SD<4>
ACCESS KEY	DRQ<2>	6	ACCESS KEY	SD<3>
XXXXX	-12V	7	EX16*	SD<2>
XXXXX	NOWS	8	SLBURST*	SD<1>
+12V	+12V	9	MSBURST*	SD<0>
M-IO	GND	10	W-R	IOCHRDY
LOCK*	SMWTC	11	GND	AENx
RESERVED	SMRDC	12	RESERVED	SA<19>
GND	IOWC	13	RESERVED	SA<18>
RESERVED	IORC	14	RESERVED	SA<17>
BE*<3>	DACK*<3>	15	GND	SA<16>
ACCESS KEY	DRQ<3>	16	ACCESS KEY	SA<15>
BE*<2>	DACK*<1>	17	BE*<1>	SA<14>
BE*<0>	DRQ<1>	18	LA*<31>	SA<13>
GND	REFRESH*	19	GND	SA<12>
+5V	BCLK	20	LA*<30>	SA<11>
LA*<29>	IRQ<7>	21	LA*<28>	SA<10>
GND	IRQ<6>	22	LA*<27>	SA<9>
LA*<26>	IRQ<5>	23	LA*<25>	SA<8>
LA*<24>	IRQ<4>	24	GND	SA<7>
ACCESS KEY	IRQ<3>	25	ACCESS KEY	SA<6>
LA<16>	DACK*<2>	26	LA<15>	SA<5>
LA<14>	TC	27	LA<13>	SA<4>
+5V	BALE	28	LA<12>	SA<3>
+5V	+5V	29	LA<11>	SA<2>
GND	OSC	30	GND	SA<1>
LA<10>	GND	31	LA<9>	SA<0>

ROW H	ROW D	PIN NO.	ROW G	ROW C
LA<8>	MEMCS16	1	LA<7>	SBHE*
LA<6>	IO16*	2	GND	LA<23>
LA<5>	IRQ<10>	3	LA<4>	LA<22>
+5V	IRQ<11>	4	LA<3>	LA<21>
LA<2>	IRQ<12>	5	GND	LA<20>
ACCESS KEY	IRQ<15>	6	ACCESS KEY	LA<19>
SD<16>	IRQ<14>	7	SD<17>	LA<18>
SD<18>	DACK*<0>	8	SD<19>	LA<17>
GND	DRQ<0>	9	SD<20>	MEMR*
SD<21>	DACK*<5>	10	SD<22>	MEMW*
SD<23>	DRQ<5>	11	GND	SD<8>
SD<24>	DACK*<6>	12	SD<25>	SD<9>
GND	DRQ<6>	13	SD<26>	SD<10>
SD<27>	DACK*<7>	14	SD<28>	SD<11>
ACCESS KEY	DRQ<7>	15	ACCESS KEY	SD<12>
SD<29>	+5V	16	GND	SD<13>
+5V	MASTER16*	17	SD<30>	SD<14>
+5V	GND	18	SD<31>	SD<15>
MAKx*		19	MREQx	

ROW J	ROW N	PIN NO.	ROW I	ROW M
RESERVED	RESERVED	1	RESERVED	RESERVED
RESERVED	RESERVED	2	RESERVED	RESERVED
RESERVED	RESERVED	3	RESERVED	RESERVED
RESERVED	RESERVED	4	RESERVED	RESERVED
RESERVED	RESERVED	5	RESERVED	RESERVED

ROW J	ROW N	PIN NO.	ROW I	ROW M
RESERVED	RESERVED	1	AENx2	AENx1
RESERVED	RESERVED	2	AENx4	AENx3
RESERVED	GND	3	AENx5	GND
RESET	+5V	4	AENx7	AENx6
SPKR	KBD LOCK	5	AENx9	AENx8
MOUSE CLK	MOUSE DATA	6	AENx11	AENx10
PWRGD	ACCESS KEY	7	AENx12	ACCESS KEY
KBD CLK	KBD DATA	8	AENx14	AENx13
GND	ISA AENx	9	GND	AENx15
MREQ1	MREQ0	10	MAK1	MAK0
MREQ3	MREQ2	11	MAK3	MAK2
MREQ4	ACCESS KEY	12	MAK4	ACCESS KEY
MREQ6	MREQ5	13	MAK6	MAK5
MREQ8	MREQ7	14	MAK8	MAK7
MREQ10	MREQ9	15	MAK10	MAK9
MREQ11	GND	16	MAK11	GND
MREQ13	MREQ12	17	MAK13	MAK12
	MREQ14	18		MAK14

FIGURE D-2:   SLOT 0 PINOUT

ROW F	ROW B	PIN NO.	ROW E	ROW A
GND	GND	1	CMD*	IOCHK*
+5V	RESDRV	2	START*	SD<7>
+5V	+5V	3	EXRDY	SD<6>
XXXXX	IRQ<9>	4	EX32*	SD<5>
XXXXX	-5V	5	GND	SD<4>
ACCESS KEY	DRQ<2>	6	ACCESS KEY	SD<3>
XXXXX	-12V	7	EX16*	SD<2>
XXXXX	NOWS	8	SLBURST*	SD<1>
+12V	+12V	9	MSBURST*	SD<0>
M-IO	GND	10	W-R	IOCHRDY
LOCK*	SMWTC	11	GND	AENx
RESERVED	SMRDC	12	RESERVED	SA<19>
GND	IOWC	13	RESERVED	SA<18>
RESERVED	IORC	14	RESERVED	SA<17>
BE*<3>	DACK*<3>	15	GND	SA<16>
ACCESS KEY	DRQ<3>	16	ACCESS KEY	SA<15>
BE*<2>	DACK*<1>	17	BE*<1>	SA<14>
BE*<0>	DRQ<1>	18	LA*<31>	SA<13>
GND	REFRESH*	19	GND	SA<12>
+5V	BCLK	20	LA*<30>	SA<11>
LA*<29>	IRQ<7>	21	LA*<28>	SA<10>
GND	IRQ<6>	22	LA*<27>	SA<9>
LA*<26>	IRQ<5>	23	LA*<25>	SA<8>
LA*<24>	IRQ<4>	24	GND	SA<7>
ACCESS KEY	IRQ<3>	25	ACCESS KEY	SA<6>
LA<16>	DACK*<2>	26	LA<15>	SA<5>
LA<14>	TC	27	LA<13>	SA<4>
+5V	BALE	28	LA<12>	SA<3>
+5V	+5V	29	LA<11>	SA<2>
GND	OSC	30	GND	SA<1>
LA<10>	GND	31	LA<9>	SA<0>

ROW H	ROW D	PIN NO.	ROW G	ROW C
LA<8>	MEMCS16	1	LA<7>	SBHE*
LA<6>	IO16*	2	GND	LA<23>
LA<5>	IRQ<10>	3	LA<4>	LA<22>
+5V	IRQ<11>	4	LA<3>	LA<21>
LA<2>	IRQ<12>	5	GND	LA<20>
ACCESS KEY	IRQ<15>	6	ACCESS KEY	LA<19>
SD<16>	IRQ<14>	7	SD<17>	LA<18>
SD<18>	DACK*<0>	8	SD<19>	LA<17>
GND	DRQ<0>	9	SD<20>	MEMR*
SD<21>	DACK*<5>	10	SD<22>	MEMW*
SD<23>	DRQ<5>	11	GND	SD<8>
SD<24>	DACK*<6>	12	SD<25>	SD<9>
GND	DRQ<6>	13	SD<26>	SD<10>
SD<27>	DACK*<7>	14	SD<28>	SD<11>
ACCESS KEY	DRQ<7>	15	ACCESS KEY	SD<12>
SD<29>	+5V	16	GND	SD<13>
+5V	MASTER16*	17	SD<30>	SD<14>
+5V	GND	18	SD<31>	SD<15>
MAKx*		19	MREQx	

P3

ROW J	ROW N	PIN NO.	ROW I	ROW M
RESERVED	RESERVED	1	RESERVED	RESERVED
RESERVED	RESERVED	2	RESERVED	RESERVED
RESERVED	RESERVED	3	RESERVED	RESERVED
RESERVED	RESERVED	4	RESERVED	RESERVED
RESERVED	RESERVED	5	RESERVED	RESERVED

P4

ROW J	ROW N	PIN NO.	ROW I	ROW M
USER-DEFINED	USER-DEFINED	1	USER-DEFINED	USER-DEFINED
USER-DEFINED	USER-DEFINED	2	USER-DEFINED	USER-DEFINED
USER-DEFINED	USER-DEFINED	3	USER-DEFINED	USER-DEFINED
USER-DEFINED	USER-DEFINED	4	USER-DEFINED	USER-DEFINED
USER-DEFINED	USER-DEFINED	5	USER-DEFINED	USER-DEFINED
USER-DEFINED	USER-DEFINED	6	USER-DEFINED	USER-DEFINED
USER-DEFINED	ACCESS KEY	7	USER-DEFINED	ACCESS KEY
USER-DEFINED	USER-DEFINED	8	USER-DEFINED	USER-DEFINED
USER-DEFINED	USER-DEFINED	9	USER-DEFINED	USER-DEFINED
USER-DEFINED	USER-DEFINED	10	USER-DEFINED	USER-DEFINED
USER-DEFINED	USER-DEFINED	11	USER-DEFINED	USER-DEFINED
USER-DEFINED	ACCESS KEY	12	USER-DEFINED	ACCESS KEY
USER-DEFINED	USER-DEFINED	13	USER-DEFINED	USER-DEFINED
USER-DEFINED	USER-DEFINED	14	USER-DEFINED	USER-DEFINED
USER-DEFINED	USER-DEFINED	15	USER-DEFINED	USER-DEFINED
USER-DEFINED	USER-DEFINED	16	USER-DEFINED	USER-DEFINED
USER-DEFINED	USER-DEFINED	17	USER-DEFINED	USER-DEFINED
	USER-DEFINED	18		USER-DEFINED

FIGURE D-3:   *NON-SLOT 0 PINOUT*

Notes

INDEX

Listing every occurrence of the bus signal line names would produce a very large and unwieldy index, whose value would ultimately be diminished. Therefore, for some terms, we have listed only the first occurrence in each chapter or section.

- Editor

You are welcome to send us comments or questions concerning this or other Annabooks products, or to request a catalog of our products and seminars.

Annabooks
11848 Bernardo Plaza Ct., Suite 110
San Diego, CA 92128
USA

619-673-0870

1-800-462-1042

619-673-1432 FAX